Fighting Irish
in the American Civil War
and the Invasion of Mexico

ALSO BY ARTHUR H. MITCHELL

*Understanding the Korean War: The Participants,
the Tactics, and the Course of Conflict* (McFarland, 2013)

*Hitler's Mountain: The Führer, Obersalzberg and the
American Occupation of Berchtesgaden* (McFarland, 2010 [2007])

Fighting Irish in the American Civil War and the Invasion of Mexico

Essays

Edited by
ARTHUR H. MITCHELL

McFarland & Company, Inc., Publishers
Jefferson, North Carolina

LIBRARY OF CONGRESS CATALOGUING-IN-PUBLICATION DATA

Names: Mitchell, Arthur, 1936– editor, author.
Title: Fighting Irish in the American Civil War and the invasion of Mexico : essays / edited by Arthur H. Mitchell.
Description: Jefferson, North Carolina : McFarland & Company, Inc., Publishers, 2017. | Includes bibliographical references and index.
Identifiers: LCCN 2017003947 | ISBN 9781476664804 (softcover : acid free paper) ∞
Subjects: LCSH: United States—History—Civil War, 1861–1865— Participation, Irish American. | Mexican War, 1846–1848—Participation, Irish American. | Irish American soldiers—History—19th century.
Classification: LCC E540.I6 F54 2017 | DDC 973.708916/2—dc23
LC record available at https://lccn.loc.gov/2017003947

BRITISH LIBRARY CATALOGUING DATA ARE AVAILABLE

ISBN (print) 978-1-4766-6480-4
ISBN (ebook) 978-1-4766-2726-7

© 2017 Arthur H. Mitchell. All rights reserved

No part of this book may be reproduced or transmitted in any form or by any means, electronic or mechanical, including photocopying or recording, or by any information storage and retrieval system, without permission in writing from the publisher.

Front cover: Five soldiers of the 63rd New York Infantry Regiment in uniform and one man in civilian dress with federal and state battle flags and rifle stack. This regiment was part of the Irish Brigade. (Library of Congress)

Printed in the United States of America

McFarland & Company, Inc., Publishers
 Box 611, Jefferson, North Carolina 28640
 www.mcfarlandpub.com

To Con Howard, diplomat extraordinaire,
impresario of conferences and enthusiast of Irish
involvement in the American Civil War,

And David N. Doyle, master chronicler
of the Irish American experience
and progenitor of this collection.

Table of Contents

Preface   1

Introduction   3

Part I: Mexican War

The Irish Soldiers of Mexico
    MICHAEL F. HOGAN   13

Irish Americans and the War with Mexico
    ARTHUR H. MITCHELL   24

Part II: American Civil War

The New York Irish Brigade Recruits and Their Families in the Era of the Civil War
    MARION TRUSLOW   37

Philadelphia Irish During the Civil War
    PHILLIP G. PATTEE   60

Preserving the Union: Shaping a New Image of Chicago's Irish Catholics and the Civil War
    LAWRENCE J. MCCAFFREY   78

The Boston Irish and the Civil War
    ARTHUR H. MITCHELL   96

What Made the "Fighting Irish" Fight
    D.R. O'CONNOR LYSAGHT   114

Irish Women in the Civil War
    EILEEN M. MCMAHON   121

Judge Charles Daly and the New York Irish in the Era of the Civil War
AIDAN O'HARA — 140

Irish and African Americans in the Civil War Era
ANDRE FLECHE — 156

Christopher Byrne, Civil War Soldier, Writes Home
RUTH-ANN HARRIS — 163

Bishop Patrick Lynch of Charleston and the Confederacy
DAVID HEISSER — 169

John Mitchel and the Confederacy
KELLY O'GRADY — 182

Patrick Cleburne, Irish Confederate General
MAURIEL P. JOSLYN — 193

Dick Dowling, Texas Irishman
ANN CARAWAY IVINS — 203

Mahan and Son: Master Purveyors of U.S. Policy for Over a Century
DESMOND TRAVERS — 215

Twice in the Gap of Danger
FRANK BOYLE — 225

The American Civil War, the Fenians and Ireland
OWEN MCGEE — 238

About the Contributors — 259

Index — 261

Preface

The who, what and why of war are the continuing concern and reality of modern living. Irish people are certainly aware of this fact, both in their homeland and abroad—and, in the latter case, in their deep involvement in the two major American wars of the mid–nineteenth century. Assembling and editing this collection of essays on that engrossing activity took a lot longer than I had anticipated, years longer, but I suppose that is typical of collaborative work. Now that it has at last been patched together, it is time to consider the course of the whole project.

I was initially stimulated by the recognition that my great-grandfather, Patrick Gallagher, had served in the Union Army at no less an engagement than Gettysburg. Then, in the late 1970s, I met Con Howard, Irish consul in Boston, who shared my strong interest in the role the Irish played in the American Civil War. Through Con I found out that David Doyle of University College Dublin had been doing substantial digging on the same subject, which led us to agree to assemble essays on unique aspects of this struggle, while also including some contributions on the American invasion of Mexico, which preceded the great regional explosion by roughly a dozen years.

We soon found out that there were several historians of varying interests and backgrounds on both sides of the Atlantic who were researching aspects of these conflicts. They sent along well-written and substantial articles. This actually presented a problem. After a tangled effort to get Irish Academic Press to proceed to publication, I contacted McFarland, which had previously published two of my books; McFarland was interested in the project but only wanted a relatively short work of about 120,000 words. This meant essays had to be kept to around 5,000 words each, involving substantial cutting and editing (largely provided by Dr. Doyle) of many of the essays while regretfully eliminating others.

Given the constraints of academic life, especially regarding teaching responsibilities, time marched on—and on. At length, due to declining health, David Doyle elected not to continue as coeditor. The loss of such an accomplished historian was a difficult burden to bear, but, sustained by what I saw as the high standard of scholarship and intrinsic interest in the full range of the essays, I was determined to guide the work through to final publication.

Over an inordinate length of time, it has been my pleasure to work with the other historians who did such fine work on this volume. Careful reading and observation of the text has been provided by a coterie of resolute friends and constructive critics, including Pádraig Ó Snodaigh, Chris Woods, Frank Darcy, Jim Watson, Tom Bingay, Jack Downey, Charley Callan, and, above all, Joe Siren, colleague and collaborator over decades. As always, many people at the Salkehatchie campus of the University of South Carolina were unwavering in moving along the process of manuscript preparation, including Daniel McDonald Johnson, Milton Harden, Gayle Walsh, Miranda Sutherland and Cheasta Scheller. *Go raibh míle maith agot!* (Gaelic—idiomatically, a thousand thanks!)

After being preoccupied for so long with the horrors and tragedies that are the inevitable accompaniment of war, it is with a sense of relief that I now hand over to readers for their consideration those aspects that we thought were important, or at least insightful, about these mighty events, in both military and political manifestations, that reddened the path of the United States' emergence as a world power. For the Irish, their substantial embroilment in these violent confrontations further solidified their organic meshing with their new country.

Introduction

From the action of the St. Patrick's Battalion in switching allegiances during the Mexican War to the exploits of the Irish Brigade and other Irish units in the Civil War, Irish soldiers and their supporters have long been a lively and significant element in U.S. history. In the mid–nineteenth century the United States plunged into two wars—one of aggression, the other a trial of strength between the two great regions of the country. In both tragic episodes Irish soldiers and civilians were swept up in the consuming violence. By this time there was a growing Irish population in the country, although initially most newcomers were part of a flood of refugees from the Irish famine of 1845–1847. The Irish role in these conflicts was not crucial to the outcome of either war, but it did reflect the dynamics and controversies of both. In addition, there were international dimensions to both conflicts. In the first of these, of course, the United States invaded and dominated its southern neighbor, with U.S. volunteer militias rampaging through Mexico. In the second episode, Ireland, a small European country then under British control, was caught up in the contest for support by both sides of the American divide.

Immigration from Ireland to the American colonies was an important, though often understated, factor in pre-revolutionary demographics. Both the so-called Scotch-Irish in the Appalachian backcountry and a stream of older-stock Irish arriving in growing urban centers gave substantial (and arguably vital) support to the cause of American independence. This participation was in part motivated by a powerful recollection of English exploitation of the Irish homeland. Another factor was a general Irish expectation that a new nation would provide them with a new beginning in freedom and equality, which it did. Indeed, a strong case can be made that Irish support for the revolutionary cause was a tipping point in its success. This assessment became dogma for successive portraitists of the history of the Irish in the new United States, although it was given scant recognition by mainstream historians embarking on a non-ethnic account of national development. There is also an Irish aspect to the War of 1812, with a contingent of Irishmen,

4 Introduction

responding to the British suppression of the 1798 rebellion in Ireland, joining in the U.S. attacks on Canada. Additionally, there were many Irish in the Canadian militia (see Taylor 2010, 354–362).

The continuing dismissal of the ethnic story of American history can be observed in most accounts of the Civil War, which contain hundreds of pages of text with almost no mention of immigrant reaction to and involvement in the conflict. A representative example of this propensity is found in Russell Weigley's 500-page treatment of the war in which the only inclusion of anything of an ethnic nature is a comment on the inept performance of a German American unit at Gettysburg (Weigley 2000, 242).

In the process of U.S. expansion to the Pacific coast in the 1840s, the country experienced a territorial problem—that whole area was part of Mexico, as the heir to the Spanish empire. The struggle over this territory led to the Mexican-American War of 1846–1848. Michael F. Hogan has provided an account of the Irish participation in this event, going back to the strong anti-Catholic and anti-Irish situation that proceeded the war. At this time there was a growing body of Irishmen in the U.S. Army—estimated as a quarter of the total—while Irish volunteer units from Boston down to Charleston, Savannah and New Orleans joined the campaign.

From an Irish point of view, one difficulty with the American expedition was that Mexico was predominantly Catholic. Arthur H. Mitchell gives attention to reports of deprivations committed by other volunteer units against the wholly Catholic Mexican people and their church institutions, as well as the conflicted feelings of the Irish regarding the conflict. Another problem was repeated assertions of Protestant Anglo officers mistreating immigrant soldiers.

Seeking to undermine the U.S. invaders, the Mexican government appealed to immigrant soldiers (mostly Irish) with offers of land and other inducements. A group of about one hundred artillerymen joined with diverse others in switching sides, forming the St. Patrick's Battalion, its name and regalia certainly stressing its Irish identity. It was led by the Irish-born (Galway) John Riley, a self-educated and articulate former British soldier. The unit members proved to be skilled artillerymen and have been honored in Mexican popular memory. Upon capture, most of the battalion's members were hanged, with Riley escaping this fate only because he had deserted the U.S. Army before the war began. What is not clear is whether their defection was mainly opportunistic or, at least in part, motivated by religious concerns or Irish identification with a smaller nation being oppressed by a powerful expansionist enemy, drawing a parallel with British domination of Ireland. It certainly was a daring and dangerous action. At their courts-martial only Riley proclaimed his support for Mexican independence. The foredoomed action of the San Patricios (as they were known) calls to mind the observation of Salvador de Madariaga that the Irish, like the Poles and Spanish, had the propensity to fight on even in a lost cause (see Madariaga 1967, 52).

This episode of defection provided evidence to their opponents that Irish Catholics were not worthy of American citizenship and constituted a dangerous growing element in the American population. Desertion certainly was a substantial problem among volunteers in the army, but Irishmen were no more prone to this action than any other group. Although the behavior of the San Patricios highlighted an undercurrent of intense dissatisfaction with their situation among many Irish soldiers, the great majority served honorably. In that regard, mention should be made of another proficient artilleryman, John Paul O'Brien, one of the few Irish American Catholics who had graduated from a military academy; during the Mexican War O'Brien commanded an artillery battery whose guns became known as "O'Brien's Bulldogs" and later were given an honored spot at West Point.

Concurrent with the Mexican conflict was the great Irish famine, which drove a million Irish people to the expanding cities of the United States, resulting in a greatly heightened awareness of this hugely expanded element in the population. The Irish flight from famine and death coincided with a large-scale influx of people from Germany and England. However, the latter group easily melded into the places where they settled, and the political impact of the German immigrants probably was not as great as that of the Irish. The majority of the Irish coming into the country were Catholics, with a historical commitment to that faith, whereas the Germans were divided between Catholics and Lutherans. Due to exposure to and involvement in political affairs under British rule, many Irish people were at least partly politicized (and remain so!). By contrast, the great majority of German immigrants had no experience in popular politics. There was also the language barrier, with few Germans being fluent in English, whereas most Irish people had at least a basic knowledge of that language. A further factor in German immigration was that the bulk of these newcomers arrived in an organized fashion complete with marketable skills, while most Irish poured into the country as a disorganized, destitute rabble fleeing from the famine.

Given the condition of most Irish immigrants, it is not surprising that their enormously expanded presence resulted in the growth of a nativist reaction in the mid–1850s. Although the impact of the "Know Nothing" agitation was soon muted when elements of it were subsumed into the new Republican Party, it undercut Irish civic participation and added to their existing grievances. It was certainly politically counterproductive for Republican aspirants to wage an anti-foreign campaign, particularly in the Midwest, as Abraham Lincoln realized, since it lumped the Germans in with the "Celtic gentlemen" (his expression), who uniformly supported the rival Democratic Party, which was seen as protective of immigrants. As a result, in both ensuing presidential elections Irish voters supported Lincoln's opponents. As president, he was well aware of the need to sustain Irish recruitment and was careful to avoid any negative comments about Irish involvements, most obviously seen in his silence after the great Irish-led draft riots of 1863.

With the nativist upheaval effectively quelled, Irish people on both sides of the slavery controversy joined in the widespread excitement about the crisis of the national identity. In northern cities, banned Irish marching organizations were revived, all supporting the defense of the Union, while in southern cities existing Irish volunteer units vigorously backed the new Confederacy. There was a general assumption that the emerging conflict would be short-lived, contributing to the widespread willingness of young men to get involved. In the case of the Irish, concentrated in northern cities, it was an opportunity to demonstrate their support of the Union, the dissolution of which threatened to fracture the political structure that most Irish people saw as providing them with the promise of economic and political opportunities in America.

In the early period of the Civil War Irishmen were generally willing to join the U.S. military, which was buttressed by federal, state and local bounties. State governments also proceeded to remove a variety of laws and practices that were objectionable to many Catholics. The federal government offered immediate citizenship to immigrants who joined the Union forces, which had the disadvantage of making them eligible for the draft. Meanwhile, across the Atlantic, federal agents scoured Ireland for recruits, holding out a variety of incentives, some of which were misleading or inaccurate. It surely was the case that Ireland was the most important country to augment the northern military. British authorities sought to stifle recruitment activities, but at that time conditions were bad for small farmers and laborers, particularly in the western Irish counties, which made enlistment an attractive option. Most of the print media and a significant number of Catholic clergy initially were dismayed by the violence on American soil, with some showing at least sympathy for the southern side.

The New York City area had by far the largest Irish population in the Civil War era, and Marion Truslow has delved into various aspects of their involvement of the great regional upheaval, probing the living conditions of the mass of Irish immigrants and their involvement in the "draft riots" of the summer of 1863. In the following chapter, Phillip G. Pattee begins with an account of a Philadelphia Irish regiment in the middle of the battle of Gettysburg but then reverts back to the ethnic violence in the city of twenty years before, going on to describe the convoluted political scene for the Philadelphian Irish residents during the war. Lawrence J. McCaffrey discusses how, as the major rail hub of the Midwest, Chicago became the destination of a mass of Irish immigrants, while others settled in Boston (as detailed by Arthur

H. Mitchell). While the Irish were not initially welcomed in either city, the outbreak of the Civil War prompted a dramatic shift in how the Irish were viewed.

In the South, one prominent Confederate advocate was the Irish-born Father John Bannon, who began his involvement while serving in a parish in St. Louis. After being released on parole following the Union capture of Vicksburg in 1863, with $1,500 in gold provided by the Confederate government, he returned to Ireland, where he campaigned against Irishmen leaving the country for the Union Army. Later he was reinforced by Bishop Patrick Lynch of Charleston, who, after a short tour of Ireland, traveled to Rome, where he produced an emphatic tome justifying slavery (not printed in English). As part of his biography of Lynch, David Heisser has provided a detailed account of the bishop's involvement in the southern cause. Confederate efforts to discourage Union enlistments included a barrage of pamphlets and posters, the parading of a badly wounded Irish soldier and a speaking tour of an Irish-born Confederate officer.

Joining the efforts of private Union enlistment agents were Bishop John Fitzpatrick of Boston, based in Brussels, and the redoubtable John Hughes, archbishop of New York (with his namesake, the archbishop of New Orleans, supporting the Confederacy). All the while, Confederate-sponsored publications in London and Paris kept careful watch on Union attempts to evade the British foreign enlistment act.

For the Irish, as well as others on both sides, the course of the war determined levels of support. With mounting casualties and extended warfare, initial enthusiasm soon was replaced by sober anticipation of more turmoil to follow, with the numbers of Irish volunteers correspondingly declining. American Catholic newspapers reported important Irish involvement in notable battles, but there emerged a widespread impression that Irish units were bearing a disproportionate burden of death and loss: in effect, Irish soldiers were being used as cannon fodder.

The burden of warfare on young men met with a major response by women, with their organizations on both sides being the principal means of addressing carnage. In her chapter, Eileen M. McMahon surveys the role of Catholic women congregations on the Union side. Additional civilian support for the Union forces is put into focus by Aidan O'Hara's chronicle of Charles Daly of New York, while Kelly O'Grady looks at John Mitchel's support for both slavery and the Confederacy. Ruth-Ann Harris surveys the experiences of a young Irishman in the Union Army's enlisted ranks. Two outstanding Confederate leaders are presented in Mauriel P. Joslyn's "Patrick Cleburne, Irish Confederate General," and Ann Caraway Ivins' account, "Dick Dowling, Texas Irishman." Frank Boyle has probed the crucial military involvements of a Philadelphia Irish unit (the 69th Pennsylvania Volunteer Infantry Regiment) in "Twice in the Gap of Danger," while Desmond Travers has provided an enlightening picture of the Mahans—father and son—in the field of naval strategy and development.

In the Union Army there were about twenty-two units, large and small, with unofficial Irish designations, the best known of these being the Irish Brigade, originally led by Thomas Frances Meagher; the Irish Legion of Michael Corcoran in New York; and, in Chicago, two Irish formations—the Western Irish Brigade, led by James Mulligan, and the Irish Legion, organized by Father James Dunne. On the Confederate side, in the Army of Northern Virginia alone there were dozens of Irish units at the company level. In her study of foreigners in the Civil War, Ella Lonn noted what she saw as the propensity of Irishmen to serve in their own units, which apparently held "a particular attraction for Irishmen; the green flag seemed to exert a magnetic control over the brawny sons of the Emerald Isle. Their fondness for their own companies is explicable: the Irishman fights better shoulder to shoulder with Irishmen as comrades" (1965, 92). However, a good proportion of the soldiers in these formations were not Irish, and most Irish participants served in mixed units, which undoubtedly helped to dissipate ethnic differences. There were about as many Germans as Irish in the Union Army, but German involvement does not get the same attention, possibly due to pronounced capacity of the Irish for self-celebration. James McPherson has declared that not only were immigrants under-represented as part of the military age group in the population but Irishmen were the "most under-represented" of these. He attributed this situation to strong Irish allegiance to the Democratic Party, which coincided with opposition to Republican war policies, including emancipation (McPherson 1988, 606–7).

A contrary view is that to the minimally estimated 144,000 Irish-born participants in the Union armed forces (including those in the navy) could be added some 90,000 of those who were born in America to Irish parents—culturally shaped products of Irish ghettos. Don H. Doyle has found that "the Irish and sons of Irish constituted almost 12 percent of the Union army forces and by this measure were its most numerous ethnic group." Although immigrant soldiers often were denigrated as mercenaries and soldiers of fortune by both Unionists and Confederates, Doyle cites Benjamin Gould, who was the first to examine the role of these people. Based on a massive collection of data about immigrant participants as well as other aspects, Gould concluded that many of these people believed the war was not just about America but also about the cause of freedom and democracy in their homeland and beyond. Their strong cultural connections across the Atlantic were clearly a factor in the Irish perception of the American maelstrom (see Doyle 2015, 176, 159–60, 348 ref. 4).

There were varying assessments regarding the effectiveness of Irish soldiers. One of these was provided by the Bostonian Robert Gould Shaw, noted for organizing a black infantry unit in Massachusetts, who believed that "Irishmen seem sometimes utterly unable to learn or understand anything." He contrasted them with the African American soldiers he was training in regard to proficiency in guard duty and camp service but did not mention Irish battlefield performance in the conflict. An essay in this collection by D.R. O'Connor Lysaught examines the matter.

Before the Civil War, free Irish workers often forced blacks out of a variety of menial jobs. The relationship between the two bottom dogs of American society carried over to the war itself. The decision to make ending slavery a primary objective of the Union war effort roused strong Irish opposition, though not enough to weaken Irish support in the North. D.R. O'Connor Lysaght and Andre Fleche both examine the subsequent development of Irish people as unintended liberators of enslaved African Americans.

Confederate forces included an estimated 20,000–30,000 Irish of various kinds, whose numbers, due to the U.S. Navy's effective blockade, did not increase. About 80–90 percent of young Irishmen in the South served in the Confederate forces, many of whom saw the cause of Confederate independence as similar to the effort to achieve Irish nationhood. As the war dragged on, in many cases desertion rates in Irish units exceeded those in other units, likely due to the fact that the Irish servicemen were not natives and few of them owned slaves. Moreover, there was a propensity of Irish people, notably in New Orleans, to consent to the Union occupation when that event occurred. The early Union capture of certain Irish population centers—New Orleans, Memphis and Nashville—further limited Irish involvement in the Confederate military (see Gleeson 2013, 89–92, 147–48; Doyle 2015, 159).

Well into the war came the decision of Abraham Lincoln to make the destruction of slavery a major objective of the Union cause, thus creating a crisis for many Irish people. (This was not a serious matter for most Germans, already established in trades and agriculture, who had opposed slavery from the beginning.) Earlier the issue of slavery for Irish people was clearly addressed by Daniel O'Connell in 1839 when he stoutly denounced the practice and disowned any Irish people who supported it. In the context of general Irish American rejection of this position, O'Connell was taken to task by southern Catholic leaders, principally Bishop John England of Charleston. At the same time, however, the Catholic Church voiced its opposition to the Atlantic slave trade, with the indirect assumption that if the slave trade was repugnant, so, too, was slavery. Initially, to the masses of Irish in America, struggling to gain a foothold in the country, the matter was of slight importance, but the sense of urgency increased when Lincoln, after the defensive success of Union forces at the battle of Antietam in September 1862, issued his Emancipation Proclamation, to take effect on New Year's Day of 1863.

Many Irish reacted to this development by protesting that they had supported the national government to defend the Union, not to end slavery. The situation was compounded by Lincoln's decision to recruit black soldiers, leading to the formation of the first all-black volunteer company in the army—the 54th Massachusetts Infantry Regiment. Many Irish people anticipated that black liberation would be followed by a flood of African Americans migrating north, posing a threat to Irish postwar economic prospects. Ironically, this was a period when Irish workers were already replacing African Americans in a variety of menial occupations. Andre Fleche examines this ambiguous and contentious relationship.

Other objectionable federal measures soon followed, the most important of which was the Conscription Act. One provision of this act was that young men could avoid forced military service by either hiring a substitute or paying $300. Due to outraged opposition, this escape route only lasted for a year, but it was long enough for several men who later rose to prominence and wealth to promptly take advantage of this opportunity—namely, Andrew Carnegie, J.P. Morgan, John D. Rockefeller, James Mellon and Grover Cleveland, as did the father of Theodore Roosevelt. This payment was utterly beyond the means of the overwhelming majority of Irishmen and others in similar circumstances. In many cases, however, local governments, political organizations, church groups and families provided the money for the commutation fee. In an effort to avoid forced military service, some foreign-born residents, despite having voted in a variety of elections, now claimed they were not citizens. This situation was so alarming to President Lincoln that he proposed that the false assertion of noncitizenship be made a criminal offense.

The efforts of federal marshals to enforce the conscription law ignited the most violent episode of its kind during the war—the New York City riots, in which Irish people were prominently involved. During four days of violence at least 119 people were killed and more than 300 injured. There were similar protests in several northern cities, but none matched the magnitude of the New York outbreak. In the end, there would be no repetition of this occurrence, as very few men were conscripted; attractive bounties proved to be adequate inducements to attract enlistments, with forced service the obvious alternative. The great irony of the New York episode is that it largely coincided with the decisive Union victory at Gettysburg, in which Irish soldiers played an important role, some of whom were later brought to New York to deal with the aftermath of the upheaval.

Due largely to the carnage of warfare, there had been a serious decline in Irish recruitment both in the Union North and in Ireland by the end of 1862, but this situation soon turned around. In Ireland some would-be immigrants sought exemptions from conscription, while others requested that American consuls provide paid passage to the United States, with both efforts failing. Nevertheless, volunteering for the Union forces in Ireland subsequently tripled, which can largely be explained by the continuing dire economic situation in the western counties, the prime venues of recruitment. Another factor may also have been the growing expectation that the Union cause was prevailing, with abundant evidence provided by the Union stranglehold imposed on the South. Thus, a relatively short spell in the military would result in American citizenship and subsequent employment in the booming American economy as well as the opportunity to take advantage of the "free land" provisions of the Homestead Act. If Irish adherence to the Union in the North varied over time, a similar situation prevailed among the estimated 20,000 or so Irishmen serving in the Confederate forces, with desertion rates being roughly the same as in non–Irish units.

In the later stages of the war there was an ongoing need to sustain Irish support for the war, leading to benevolent (if not encouraging) attitudes of northern authorities toward Irish political alignment in the Fenian movement, which was designed to use acquired military experience for the postwar purpose of freeing Ireland from British control. Owen McGee has spelled out the ramifications of the Fenian episode in both the United States and Ireland. An estimated 50,000 Union soldiers were listed as members of the Fenian Brotherhood. As far the U.S. government was concerned, what was necessary was a continuing stream of Irishmen who would fight for the Union; what happened afterward was another matter. In the end, most Irish survivors were content to return to their American abodes while providing financial and political support for the Fenian movement—nothing more. The ineffectual Fenian postwar actions—notably, the mini-intrusions along the Canadian border—reflected negatively on the political mentality of at least some Irish veterans of the Civil War. Another handicap was the continuing attachment of most Irish voters to the Democratic Party in an era of Republican domination, although this was the time when Irish political organizations began to take control of many city governments.

In no other country had there been such a large-scale flow of young men to the American war as from Ireland, and the corresponding deaths of multitudes of these volunteers were not compensated by bounty money for surviving families. A source of criticism was the federal $100 gratuity for burial expenses, which was only paid to family members resident in the United States. The great majority of soldiers from Ireland who survived the war did not return home, but many of them joined with Irish and sons of Irishmen who could celebrate their undoubted role in the survival of the American Union, an achievement that was honored for the rest of their lives and, after 1890, rewarded by modest government pensions for most veterans. On the losing side, Irish units had the consolation that they had earned public recognition for being steadfast in the cause of the Confederacy.

Due to these undeniable factors, and overlooking some contrary episodes, in their inimitable fashion, the Irish believed that they had arrived! What lay ahead, of course, was continued nativist hostility to the rise of the sons and daughters of old Erin and their offspring, fear and hostility to their religion, and the emerging tensions between rural and urban America, but all that largely was mitigated by recognition of Irish valor at Fredericksburg, Antietam, Gettysburg and other battles. The outcome of the conflict was seen by insightful foreign observers as determining the future balance of power in the Americas and abroad, and the Irish could legitimately claim to have made a singular contribution. Beyond that was the encouraging phenomenon of the Irish American example and concrete assistance to those who remained in the "old country."

Now we must move on to examine aspects of the role played by Irish people in the surge of U.S. expansion and then the great crisis of American identity, and its impact on Ireland, as presented in this wide-ranging collection. *Faugh a ballagh!* (Clear the way!)

BIBLIOGRAPHY

Doyle, Don H. *The Cause of All Nations: An International History of the American Civil War.* New York: Basic Books, 2015.
Gleeson, David T. *The Green and the Gray: The Irish in the Confederate States of America.* Chapel Hill: University of North Carolina Press, 2013.
Kenny, Kevin. "Abraham Lincoln and the American Irish." *American Journal of Irish Studies* 10 (2013).
Lonn, Ella. *Foreigners in the Confederacy.* Gloucester, MA: P. Smith, 1965.
Madariaga, Salvador de. *A Portrait of Europe.* Tuscaloosa: University of Alabama Press, 1967.
McPherson, James. *Battle Cry of Freedom.* New York: Oxford University Press, 1988.
Miller, Kerby. "Class, Culture, and Immigrant Group Identity in the United States: The Case of Irish American Ethnicity." In *Immigration Reconsidered: History, Sociology and Politics,* edited by Virginia Yans-McLaughlin, 96–129. New York: Oxford University Press, 1990.
Miller, Randall M. "Catholic Religion, Irish Ethnicity, and the Civil War." In *Religion and the American Civil War,* edited by Randall M. Miller, Harry S. Stout and Charles R. Wilson, 261–96. New York: Oxford University Press, 1998.
Taylor, Alan. *The Civil War of 1812: American Citizens, British Subjects, Irish Rebels, & Indian Allies.* New York: Alfred A. Knopf, 2010.
Weigley, Russell, *A Great Civil War: A Military and Political History, 1861–1865.* Bloomington: Indiana University Press, 2000.
Welch, Richard F. "America's Civil War: Why the Irish Fought for the Union." *Civil War Times Magazine* (October 2006).

PART I: MEXICAN WAR

The Irish Soldiers of Mexico
Michael F. Hogan

One of the least-known stories of the Irish people who came to America in the 1840s is that of the Irish-led battalion that fought on the Mexican side in the Mexican-American War of 1846–1848. These men came to Mexico and died—some gloriously in combat, others ignominiously on the gallows; united under a green banner, they participated in all the major battles of the war and were cited for bravery by General Antonio López de Santa Anna, the Mexican commander in chief and president. During the penultimate battle of the war, these Irishmen fought until their ammunition was exhausted, and even then they tore down the white flag raised by their Mexican comrades in arms, preferring to struggle on with bayonets until finally overwhelmed by the Yankees. Despite their brave resistance, eighty-five members of the Irish battalion were captured and sentenced to bizarre tortures and deaths at the hands of the Americans, resulting in what is even today considered the "largest hanging affair in North America."[1]

The War Begins

In the spring of 1846, the United States was poised to invade Mexico, its neighbor to the south. The ostensible rationale behind this action was collection on past due loans and indemnities. The real reason was to provide the United States with control of the ports of San Francisco and San Diego, the trade route through New Mexico Territory, and the rich mineral resources of the Nevada Territory—all of which at that time belonged to the Republic of Mexico. The United States had previously offered $5 million to purchase New Mexico Territory and $25 million for California, but Mexico had refused to sell.[2]

U.S. President James K. Polk ordered General Zachary Taylor to take a position south of the Nueces River in Texas with a force of 4,000 men. By January 1846 the general had built a fort in what was Mexican, or at least disputed, territory on the northern banks of the Rio Grande in an effort to put pressure on the Mexicans to agree to a settlement. As noted by the historian Bernard DeVoto, "Polk's intention was clear. This was a show of force intended to give the Mexicans a sense of reality in the settlement of various matters he intended to take up, among them the purchase of California."[3] On April 26, 1846, a Mexican cavalry troop crossed the Rio Grande upstream of Taylor's army. A patrol sent by Taylor to intercept them was attacked; during the skirmish, eleven Americans were killed and five wounded. When Polk received word of the attack, he delivered his war message, declaring that since the Mexicans had "shed American blood on American soil," a state of war existed between the United States and Mexico. Prior to the declaration of war by the United States, however, a group of Irish Catholics headed by a crack artilleryman named John Riley deserted from the American forces and joined the Mexicans.

Born near Clifden, County Galway, Riley was an expert on artillery, and it was widely believed that he had served in the British army as an officer or a non-com in Canada prior to enlisting in the American army. Riley's expertise would turn this new unit into an effective artillery arm of the Mexican defense. He is credited with changing the name of the group from the Legion of Foreigners and with designing their distinctive flag. Within a year, the unit's ranks would be swelled by Catholic foreign residents in Mexico City, as well as Irish and German Catholics who deserted the U.S. Army once the war broke out, coming to join a battalion known as *Los San Patricios*, or "Those of San Patrick." The unit varied in size from 200 to 500 members during the course of the war.[4]

The San Patricios fought under a green silk flag emblazoned with the Mexican coat of arms, an image of St. Patrick, and the words "Erin Go Braugh." The battalion was one of artillery, and it was observed in key positions during every major battle of the war. This aid was critical because the Mexicans possessed poor cannons with a range of 400 meters less than those of the Americans. In addition, Mexican cannoneers were inexperienced and poorly trained. The addition of veteran artillerymen to the Mexican side would result in at least two major battles being fought to a draw. At the Battle of Buena Vista, for example, the San Patricios held the high ground and enfiladed the Americans. At one point they even wrested cannons from the Yanks and led General Taylor's advisors to believe that the battle had been lost. Several Irishmen were awarded the Cross of Honor by the Mexican government for their bravery in that battle, and many received field promotions. At the Battle of Churubusco, holed up in a Catholic monastery and surrounded by a superior force of American cavalry, artillery and infantry, the San Patricios withstood three major assaults and inflicted heavy losses on the U.S. attackers. Eventually, however, a shell struck their stored gunpowder, the ammunition park blew up, and the Irishmen, after a gallant counter-offensive with bayonets, were overwhelmed by sheer numbers.[5] They were tried by a brutal court-martial that it is still remembered in Mexico today. In almost every Mexican account of the war, the San Patricios are considered heroes who fought for the noble ideals of religion and a just cause against the Protestant invader of a peaceful nation. In U.S. histories, however, they are often referred to as turncoats, traitors and malcontents who joined the other side for land or money.

Reasons for Defection

It seems odd that anyone would defect from a superior force sure of victory in order to join an obviously inferior one certain to be defeated, even if, as most U.S. accounts assert, there were offers of money or land from the Mexicans. After all, there was plenty of free land to the west, much easier to come by than risking one's life in combat against an American army. Simple desertion and seeking refuge in the rich valleys of California would have accomplished that purpose. To determine the true causes of the defection for these men, it is necessary to reflect on the temper of the times.

The potato blight that began in 1845 (roughly coinciding with the Mexican War and lasting for its duration) brought devastation more horrible than the Black Death. For the Irish it was the beginning of mass evictions, starvation, sickness and death. Of the many fortunate enough to afford the fare for an escape to the New World, tens of thousands would die en route as a result of the inhumane conditions aboard Great Britain's vessels.

Recipients of oppression in the Old World, the Irish immigrants were to experience it again in the New World. Confronted by enormous numbers of Irish Catholic immigrants in the 1840s, American nativism reared its ugly head. "All the world knows," wrote historian Thomas Gallagher, "that Yankee hates Paddy."[6] And so it seemed to those who had survived the perilous journey to America only to be labeled inferior by demagogic politicians and feared by Anglo-American workmen.

As victims of prejudice themselves, it is not strange that the Irish would shortly find themselves becoming sympathetic to the Mexicans. Here was another Catholic people being invaded by Protestant foreigners. According to a contemporary account, "On reaching Mexico they discovered they had been hired by heretics to slaughter brethren of their own church. On top of this they were confronted with the hatred of their fellow soldiers."[7] The intense prejudice of many of the American soldiers, especially the volunteers, has been commented upon by at least one careful historian. According to

K. Jack Bauer, author of *The Mexican War: 1846–48*, most American soldiers were products of a militantly Protestant culture that viewed Catholicism as a misdirected and misbegotten religion. This strengthened the tendency to ignore the rights and privileges of the church in a Catholic country as well as increasing the harassment of that church. Some of the volunteers' acts, like stabling horses in the Shrine of San Francisco in Monterrey, so upset the Mexicans that they are still mentioned in modern works.[8]

Origins of Anti-Catholicism in the United States

America was a nation founded by Calvinists, who, in rejecting the Church of England, had rejected the hierarchy both Anglican and Catholic institutions and, in discarding the spiritual hierarchy, had eliminated the temporal one as well. Free to elect their own ministers, they were equally free to elect their own governors. To most Anglo-Saxons living in the United States, this is what it meant to be an American: to be free of European authority, both that of the pope and that of the king. Those who still clung to a hierarchical model were considered regressive and unfit for self-government. The Catholic Church was, to the Calvinist way of thinking, connected politically to a repressive and antiquated system, even more so than the Anglican model. Catholics, it was widely believed, had not developed a habit of independent thought. They were still chained to a religion that accepted the pope, a foreign power, as their authority, rather than their individual consciences. It was believed that not only were Catholics unable to think for themselves in matters of faith or morals, but they were equally incapable of being part of a democratic system. Thus, by the early 1800s the Catholic religion was seen at best as retrograde, and at worst as inimical to a democratic republic.

As early as 1830 the American Bible Society urged the unity of Protestant sects to combat Rome's influence in the West and expressed the belief that "His Holiness the Pope, has, within his larger grasp, already fixed upon this fair portion of our Union and knows full well how to keep his fold."[9] While in the early republic there had been some tolerance of Catholic minorities, this situation would soon change with the increase in immigration of Irish Catholics during the 1830s and 1840s, reaching its peak during the years of the Irish famine as poor, rural Catholics flooded American towns and cities. Anti-Catholic riots broke out in Philadelphia in 1844; when they were over, the Irish ghetto lay in ruins, hundreds of homeless Irish roamed the streets, and two Catholic churches had been burned to the ground.[10]

Since solidarity in the face of commonly perceived oppression is a universal characteristic of any ethnic or religious group, it is hardly surprising that Irish Catholics would find solidarity together in the service. As the war progressed and they witnessed more depredations against their co-religionists in Mexico, some Irishmen naturally felt they had more in common with the Mexicans than the invading Americans. The destruction of Catholic churches in Mexico by some members of the invading U.S. Army and other depredations by Protestant volunteers was also well documented by both sides. And, just in case they needed a reminder of the connection between the American treatment of the Irish at home and the abuse of Mexicans abroad, Santa Anna's leaflets were widely distributed. They read in part:

> Can you fight by the side of those who put fire to your temples in Boston and Philadelphia? Did you witness such dreadful crimes and sacrileges without making a solemn vow to our Lord? If you are Catholic, the same as we, if you follow the doctrines of Our Savior, why are you murdering your brethren? Why are you antagonistic to those who defend their country and your own God?[11]

Why indeed? Many Irishmen would be quick to see that higher loyalties should prevail, leading them to join the Mexican side.

The Irish "Race"

The Protestants certainly saw similarities between the Mexicans and Irish, and they were quick to point them out. The Mexican, they asserted, like the Irishman, was unstable, ignorant, feckless, easily led, and incapable of participation in a republic. Using both the pseudo-science of phrenology and the more respectable science of physiology, contemporary American scientists determined that the short, full figures of the Irish indicated that they were "inactive, slothful and lazy." This was a stereotype also applied to the Mexicans. The coarse red hair of the Irish showed that they were "excitable and gushing." Their ruddy complexions likewise indicated that they were selfish, "with hearty animal passions." Irishmen of this period were variously described as having a "hanging bone gait ... the low brow denoting a serf of fifty descents ... dark eyes sunken beneath the compressed brows" with a look of "savage ferocity."[12] By the 1840s this legitimization of negative racial characteristics had reached its apex.

Manifest Destiny

Most of those who had settled in America in the eighteenth and early nineteenth centuries had no real sense of nationhood. Those in Virginia considered themselves Virginians, those in Texas as "Texans," and those from Maine were "Down Easters." Allegiances were territorial rather than nationalistic. When the triumphant American army finally entered Mexico City, the victors played three "national" anthems: "Hail Columbia," "Yankee Doodle" and "The Star-Spangled Banner." While there was no clear sense of nationhood, Americans were nevertheless engaged in the process of defining who they were. They did so essentially by stating quite clearly what an American was not—he was not a Negro, not a Mexican, not an Indian and certainly not Irish Catholic. Dale T. Knobel observes "the Irish would be seen increasingly as set apart by visible conduct and appearance. This development coincided with national self-satisfaction that accompanied the working out of the United States Manifest Destiny through geographical expansion."[13]

Manifest Destiny was another aspect of Calvinist belief. It held quite simply that the Anglo-American was predestined by God to inherit the entire American continent. Beginning with the "noble experiment" in New Jerusalem (i.e., Salem, Massachusetts), the "City on the Hill," this new breed would spread over the entire land mass of the Americas, displacing the indigenous people and buying out or running off French and Spanish land holders in their inevitable march of progress. The inheritors of Manifest Destiny, it must be remembered, were white, Anglo-Protestants, and they took steps to ensure that the distinctions between them and others, whether religious or racial or quasi-scientific, were constantly emphasized to prove that they were deserving of this gift. According to one newspaper editor, "We are believers in the superintendence of a directing Providence, and when we contemplate the rise and amazing progress of the United States, the nature of our government, the character of our people, and the occurrence of unforeseen events, all tending to one great accomplishment, we are impressed with a conviction that the decree is made, and in the process of execution, that this continent is to be but one nation."[14] Even the highly respected Ralph Waldo Emerson would write, "Men gladly hear of the power of blood or race. Everybody likes to know that his advantages cannot be attributed to air, soil, sea, or to local wealth, as mines or quarries, not to law and tradition nor to fortune, but to a superior brain, as it makes it more personal to him."[15]

The Scourgings, Brandings and Hangings

In September 1847, the Americans put the Irish soldiers captured at the Battle of Churubusco on trial. Forty-eight were sentenced to death by hanging. Those who had deserted prior to the declaration of war were sentenced to whipping at the stake, branding, and hard labor. Most American historians contend that these punishments were neither particularly brutal nor unusual given that there was no prescribed military code at the time. However, clear documentation exists that the codified Articles of War (1821) and Denis Hart's *Practice of Courts-Martial* (1847) governed military courts, which clearly stipulated the exact punishments these soldiers should have received. The Articles of War indicated that the penalty for desertion and/or defecting to the enemy during time of war was death by firing squad. Hanging was reserved only for spies (without uniform) and for "atrocities against civilians."[16] Nevertheless, forty-eight of the San Patricios were hanged: twenty-eight in San Angel, and a larger group of thirty in a place called Mixcoac.

Desertion prior to a declaration of war was punishable by *one* of the following punishments: branding on the hip in indelible ink, fifty lashes, or incarceration at hard labor. However, the surviving San Patricios received more than fifty lashes, "until their backs had the appearance of raw beef, the blood oozing from every stripe," according to one American witness. In addition, the punishment was administered by Mexican muleteers who were threatened with the same treatment if they did not "lay it on with a will."[17] The Irishmen were also branded with a "D" for deserter on the cheek by a red-hot branding iron, and they were sentenced to imprisonment at hard labor.

The sentence of the court, according to the Articles of War, should always be carried out promptly: "To prolong the punishment beyond the usual time would be highly improper, and subject the officer who authorized or caused such to be done, to charges."[18] In the case of the last of group of thirty San Patricios to be hanged, this article was cavalierly ignored.

The Hangings by Colonel Harney

General Winfield Scott chose an officer who had been twice disciplined for insubordination as his executioner of the last group of thirty San Patricios to be hanged. Colonel William Harney had been soldiering for almost thirty years and was notorious for his brutality. During the Indian wars he was charged with ravishing Indian girls at night and then hanging them the next morning after he had taken his pleasure. In St. Louis, Missouri, he had been indicted by a civilian court for the brutal beating of a female slave that resulted in her death.[19] The choice of Harney as executioner of the San Patricios seemed calculated by the American high command to inflict brutal reprisals on the Irish soldiers. Harney would not disappoint them.

At dawn on September 13, 1847, some days after the first group of twenty-eight had been executed, Harney ordered the remaining San Patricios to be brought to a hill in Mixcoac a few kilometers from Chapultepec Castle, where the final battle of the war was to be fought. Observing that only twenty-nine of the thirty prisoners were present, Harney asked about the missing man. The army surgeon informed him that the absent San Patricio had lost both his legs in battle. Harney, in a rage, replied, "Bring the damned son of a bitch out! My order was to hang thirty and by God I'll do it!"[20] After the guards dragged Francis O'Conner out and propped him up on his bloody stumps, nooses were placed around each man's neck and they were made to stand on wagons. Harney then pointed to Chapultepec Castle in the distance and told the prisoners that they would not be hanged until the American flag was raised over the castle, signifying that the Yankees had won the battle.

The prisoners yelled out in incredulity and protest. Some made jokes and sarcastic remarks, trying to goad the unstable colonel into giving an impulsive order. One prisoner asked Harney to take his pipe out of his pocket so that he might have one last smoke. Then, with a glint in his eye, he asked if the colonel would not mind lighting it with his "elegant hair."[21] The redheaded Harney did not appreciate the joke. He drew his sword and struck the bound prisoner in the mouth with the hilt, breaking several of the man's teeth. The prisoner was not intimidated, however. Spitting out blood and broken teeth, the irrepressible Irishman quipped, "Bad luck to ye! Ye have spoilt my smoking entirely! I shan't be able to have a pipe in my mouth as long as I live."[22] Meanwhile, the Battle of Chapultepec raged on. Finally, at 9:30 a.m., the Americans scaled the walls of the castle, tore down the Mexican flag, and raised the Stars and Stripes. With that, Harney drew his sword and, "with as much sang froid as a military martinet could put on," gave the order for execution.[23] The San Patricios, after four and a half hours of standing bound and noosed in the 90-degree heat, were finally "launched into eternity."[24]

Harney's violation of the Articles of War requiring prompt execution did not result in charges being brought against him. Rather, his behavior was rewarded. A month later Harney was promoted to brigadier general and accompanied Winfield Scott in a triumphal march in Mexico City. The punishments ordered for the San Patricios and the way in which they were carried out expressed more than the judgment of the court. They smacked of contempt and repulsion indicative of religious and racist reprisals. In spite of the fact that more than 5,000 U.S. soldiers deserted during the Mexican War, only the San Patricios were so punished, and only the San Patricios were hanged.

The Conquest of Mexico and Celtic-Americanism

Fueled by Manifest Destiny and its concomitant mixture of racial and religious animosity, the American government dictated terms to the Mexicans in the Treaty of Guadalupe Hidalgo in 1848. More than two-thirds of Mexican territory was taken (one-half if one includes Texas), and out of this land the United States would carve California, Nevada, New Mexico, Arizona, Utah, Wyoming and parts of Kansas and Colorado. It was a profitable American adventure, a conquest to put Napoleon to shame, and all done in the name of democracy and Manifest Destiny.

Among all the major wars fought by the United States, the Mexican War is the least discussed in the classroom, the least written about, and the least known by the general public. Yet it added more to the national treasury and to the land mass of the United States than all other wars combined.

After the war, so much new territory was opened up, and so many things had been accomplished, that a mood of self-congratulation and enthusiasm was felt in the United States. The deserters from the war were soon forgotten as they labored in the gold fields of California, homesteaded in the new U.S. territories, or, as the 1860s approached, put on the gray uniform of the Confederacy or the blue of the Union. Prejudice against the Irish lessened as the country was provided with a "pressure valve" to release many of its new immigrants westward. As Irish veterans returned from the Civil War and gained political power, they were increasingly seen as a branch of the white race (Celtic American) by the so-called scientific theorists who had previously denied them that privilege. Irish in the United States, anxious to be assimilated, gladly accepted the new designation. Ironically, the American Irish would be among the first to disassociate themselves from the San Patricios and promote the notion that it was not an Irish battalion at all!

Commemorations

Each year commemorations are held in San Angel in Mexico to honor the Irish who died in the war. A marble plaque in the town square reads, "In Memory of the Irish Soldiers of the Heroic Battalion of San Patrick Who Gave Their Lives for the Mexican Cause During the Unjust North American Invasion of 1847," followed by the names of 71 of the men. A color guard of Mexican troops marches forward with the Mexican and Irish colors to a flourish of drums and bugles. The "Himno National" is then played, followed by "The Soldiers Song." Students and dignitaries place floral tributes on the paving stones, and an honor roll of the fallen soldiers is called as the crowd collectively chants after each name, *Murio por la patria!* ("He died for the country!") In Clifden, Galway, the birthplace of John Riley, a similar ceremony is held on September 13.[25]

For most Mexicans, solidarity with the Irish is part of a long tradition. There is in both countries an emphasis on the spiritual center in the family and a nonmaterialistic viewpoint whereby a person's worth is determined not by what he owns but by the quality of his life. And if Paddy and Bridget, like Jose and Maria, were considered incapable of being assimilated into Anglo-Protestant society, their acceptance into Mexican society was seamless. In the words of John Riley, written in 1847 but equally true today, "A more hospitable and friendly people than the Mexican there exits not on the face of the earth … especially to an Irishman and a Catholic."[26] Riley sums up what cannot be clearly documented in any history: the basic, gut-level affinity the Irishman had then, and still has today, for Mexico and its people. The decisions of the men who joined the San Patricios were probably not well planned or thought out. They were impulsive and emotional, like many of Ireland's own rebellions—including the Easter Uprising of 1916. Nevertheless, the courage of the San Patricios, their loyalty to their new cause, and their unquestioned bravery forged an indelible seal of honor on their sacrifice.

Notes

1. National Archives, Record Group 84, Mexican War, Misc. Papers, Box 7. Language quoted is from a query letter to the adjutant general written at the turn of the century, in which he denied the existence of an Irish battalion in the Mexican War or that any soldiers were hanged en masse.
2. James K. Polk, *Diary*, May 8, 1846, p. 81.
3. Bernard DeVoto, *The Year of Decision: 1846* (Boston: Little, Brown, 1943), 14.
4. Executive Document No. 60, Polk's message to Congress, May 11, 1846.
5. Justin H. Smith, *War with Mexico*, Vol. I (New York: Macmillan, 1919), 391; Paul Foos, *A Short, Offhand Killing Affair: Soldiers and Social Conflict during the Mexican-American War* (Chapel Hill: University of North Carolina Press, 2002), 107.
6. Thomas Gallagher, *Paddy's Lament: Ireland 1846–47; Prelude to Hatred* (New York: Harcourt, Brace, 1982), 128.
7. *Ibid.*
8. William Jay, *A Review of the Causes and Consequences of the Mexican War* (Boston: Benjamin B. Mussey, 1849), 208.
9. K. Jack Bauer, *The Mexican War, 1846–48* (New York: Macmillan, 1974), 14.
10. Ray Allen Billington, *The Protestant Crusade* (New York: Rinehart & Co., 1952), 120.
11. *Ibid.*, 220–24.
12. Quoted in Gene M. Brack, *Mexico Views Manifest Destiny* (Albuquerque: University of New Mexico Press, 1975), 120.
13. Thomas Butler Gunn, *Physiology of the New York Boarding Houses*, quoted in Dale T. Knobel, *Paddy and the Republic: Ethnicity and Nationality in Antebellum America* (Middletown, CT: Wesleyan University Press, 1986), 92.
14. Knobel, *Paddy and the Republic*, 97–98.
15. William M. Swain, *Philadelphia Public Ledger*, October 15, 1847.
16. Emerson quoted by Knobel, *Paddy and the Republic*, 98.
17. William C. DeHart, *Observations on Military Law, and the Constitution and Practice of Courts Martial with a Summary of the Laws of Evidence as Applicable to Military Trials* (New York: Wiley and Putnam, 1846), 196.
18. Variously referred to as "well laid on" and "laid on with a will" in both orders signed by General Scott: Order 281 and Order 283, Headquarters of the Army in Mexico, 1847.
19. DeHart, *Observations on Military Law*, 246–47.
20. L.U. Reavis, *The Life and Military Service of William Selby Harney* (St. Louis: Bryan, Brand & Co., 1878), 8–12. See also Samuel Chamberlain, *My Confession* (New York: Harper, 1956), 227.
21. Chamberlain, *My Confession*, 227.
22. Dennis J. Wynn, *The San Patricio Soldiers: Mexico's Foreign Legion* (El Paso: Texas Western Press, 1984), 14–15.
23. James Reilly, "An Artilleryman's Story," *Journal of the Military Service Institution* 33 (1903): 443–44.
24. *Ibid.*, 444.
25. Mark R. Day, San Patricio Productions Newsletter, October 9, 1993, 2.
26. National Archives, Record Group 84, Mexican War, Misc. Papers, Box 7.

Bibliography

Bauer, K. Jack. *The Mexican War, 1846–48*. New York: Macmillan, 1974.
Billington, Ray Allen. *The Protestant Crusade*. New York: Rinehart & Co., 1952.
Brack, Gene M. *Mexico Views Manifest Destiny*. Albuquerque: University of New Mexico Press, 1975.
Chamberlain, Samuel. *My Confession*. New York: Harper, 1956.
DeHart, William C. *Observations on Military Law, and the Constitution and Practice of Courts Martial with a Summary of the Laws of Evidence as Applicable to Military Trials*. New York: Wiley and Putnam, 1846.
DeVoto, Bernard. *The Year of Decision: 1846*. Boston: Little, Brown, 1943.
Foos, Paul. *A Short, Offhand Killing Affair: Soldiers and Social Conflict during the Mexican-American War*. Chapel Hill, NC: University of North Carolina Press, 2002.
Gallagher, Thomas. *Paddy's Lament: Ireland 1846–47; Prelude to Hatred*. New York: Harcourt, Brace, 1982.
Jay, William. *A Review of the Causes and Consequences of the Mexican War*. Boston: Benjamin B. Mussey, 1849.
Knobel, Dale T. *Paddy and the Republic: Ethnicity and Nationality in Antebellum America*. Middletown, CT: Wesleyan University Press, 1986.
National Archives, Record Group 84, Mexican War, Washington, D.C.
Reavis, L.U. *The Life and Military Service of William Selby Harney*. St. Louis: Bryan, Brand & Co., 1878.
Reilly, James. "An Artilleryman's Story." *Journal of the Military Service Institution* 33 (1903).
Smith, Justin H. *War with Mexico*. Vol. I. New York: Macmillan, 1919.
Wynn, Dennis J. *The San Patricio Soldiers: Mexico's Foreign Legion*. El Paso: Texas Western Press, 1984.

Irish Americans and the War with Mexico

ARTHUR H. MITCHELL

The Mexican War of 1846–1848 presented Irish people in the United States with a challenge and an opportunity. The war itself had highly controversial origins. Despite the claims of President James K. Polk and other Democratic Party leaders that the conflict had been forced on them by Mexican provocation, many people viewed the event as both a war of territorial expansion and an extension of slavery (while a few saw the upheaval as an opportunity to spread Protestantism to their southern neighbor). It was the position of the U.S. government that "our soldiers are crossing the Rio Grande in their armed pursuit of a just and honorable peace with Mexico, which shall place our citizens and our soil in security from further invasion."[1]

Opposition to the war centered in the northeast, where many Irish people were living. This opposition was spearheaded by New England intellectuals. The most noted episode of objection was when Henry David Thoreau, protesting the war by refusing to pay his local poll tax, spent a night in the Concord town jail. Allegedly, when Ralph Waldo Emerson, the "Father of American Literature," visited him there, Emerson inquired, "Henry, what are you doing in there?" to which Thoreau replied, "Waldo, what are you doing out there?" Thoreau's action led to his famous essay on civil disobedience.[2]

Having lived with and keenly observed Irish squatters during his time in the woods near Walden pond, Thoreau had developed a considerable appreciation of these people, valuing their generosity, capacity for work and casual attitude toward life, money and property. In 1843 he wrote to Emerson, "The sturdy Irish arms that do the work are of more worth than oak or maple. Methinks I could look with equanimity upon a long street of Irish cabins and pigs and children reveling in the genial Concord dirt, and I shall still find my Walden wood and Fair Haven in their tanned and happy faces."[3] But his

Irish acquaintances did not stand with him on the question of the Mexican War.

Another leading intellectual, Orestes Brownson, a convert to Catholicism, had intimate knowledge of the teeming masses of Irish in Boston. He made the resounding prediction about these people: "out of these narrow lanes, dirty streets, damp cellars and suffocating garrets will come forth some of the noblest sons of our country, whom she will delight to own and to honor." He asserted, "There is no portion of our population superior to that in which there is a large infusion of the genuine Irish element."[4] Yet his characterization of the attack on Mexico as an "unjust war" found little echo among his Irish co-religionists.

This was not the first war in which many Irish people in New England found themselves opposing those of English colonial stock. Although there were not yet many of them in the region in the early nineteenth century, Irish people supported the War of 1812 as a means of striking a blow at England, while most of the other people in New England opposed the war because of its harmful effect on maritime trade.[5]

The Mexican War was a partisan issue. When Democrat and slave owner President James K. Polk declared that the cause of the war was a Mexican attack on Americans on American soil, Whig Abraham Lincoln, then serving a single term in Congress, demanded to know exactly on what spot this attack took place. No reply was forthcoming, and Lincoln's Democratic opponents in Illinois labeled him "Spotty" Lincoln and celebrated his apparent political demise. Fighting his last political battle, former president John Quincy Adams also took to the floor of the House of Representatives to denounce the war as a brazen southern effort to extend slavery.[6]

The war did not find favor among some members of the military. Captain Sam Grant told his wife that it was a war of aggression without justification. Writing his memoirs forty years later, the general and former president Ulysses S. Grant had not changed his view on the conflict: "It was one of the most unjust ever waged by a stronger against a weaker nation. It was an instance of a republic following the bad example of European monarchies, in not considering justice in their desire to acquire additional territory." (Incidentally, Grant valued his family's Irish heritage, which he declared upon his tour of Ireland in the 1880s.)[7]

As the largest and most prominent immigrant group in the country, Irish people were in a difficult position when the war broke out. Despite some upward mobility among long-present immigrants, most newcomers were largely poor and unskilled. Although they had a few newspapers, an increasing number of local societies and a rapidly expanding church, they had not secured a strong political position. There was no significant political leader who was their spokesman. Struggling to adapt to their new environment, Irish people generally were not concerned with the existence of slavery in the faraway southern states. Moreover, black people in the north were competitors with the Irish for jobs. The Irish generally supported the Democratic Party, which had provided them with aid and assistance when they came to America, unlike the Federalists and their successors, the Whigs.[8]

A more important factor was the vigorous nativist campaign carried out against the Irish, which argued that these people were an unwelcome foreign intrusion into the Republic who could not be expected to understand it or support the country in a war with a Catholic nation. The anti-foreign agitation boiled over in Philadelphia (which had the only overtly nativist congressman in the nation at the time) in May and July of 1844, when rioting resulted in at least 45 persons being killed and 145 injured, as well as two Catholic churches destroyed, a third vandalized and thirty houses burned. The threat of similar action loomed over other eastern cities. The combative Bishop John Hughes warned that "if a single Catholic Church was burned in New York, the city would become a second Moscow." William Lloyd Garrison, the abolitionist, believed that there was a direct connection between the failure of the American Irish to rally behind the fight to end slavery, as advocated by Daniel O'Connell, the great leader in Ireland, and the rising tide of nativism: "The Irish have disregarded the noble entreaties of their countrymen at home … and verily, they have had their reward." After the presidential election of 1844 there were repeated outcries from Whig politicians that the foreign-born vote (which could only mean the Irish), often fraudulently cast, had swung the election to the Democrats. In 1845—the year John L. O'Sullivan coined the term "Manifest Destiny"—a Native American national convention was held. This was the setting in which the Irish found themselves on the eve of the Mexican War.[9]

In no position to do otherwise, the Irish press accepted the president's justification of the war and, with a notable lack of enthusiasm, urged its readers to avoid any act of apparent disloyalty. However, there was muted sympathy for the Mexican people as they faced a determined army from the north. The leading Irish newspaper in the country, the Boston *Pilot*, reprinted a story that first appeared in the New Orleans *Picayune* in January 1847 about "The Maid of Monterrey" who rallied Mexican troops in the defense of that city, commenting, "It has remained for Mexico to produce a second Joan of Arc."[10]

Edited by the indomitable Patrick Donahoe, the Boston *Pilot* observed that many of the Yankee element who were antagonistic toward Catholics and Irish people were also opponents of the war: "Nearly all these anti–Popery folks are shirking from the support of the war." The weekly "Bible of the Irish" ruefully declared, "In times of peace we Irish are not fit to enjoy 'life, liberty and the pursuit of happiness,' but when the country needs our aid, we are capital, glorious fellows." It also recalled the assertion of nativist General Dearborn that "we will do our own voting and fight our own wars." Where was the general now? It was a good time for scoring points off their adversaries. The New York *Freeman's Journal*, probably the second leading Irish newspaper in the country, took the position that while it deplored the war, it was the patriotic duty of all to support the war effort.[11]

There was also the matter of the very large numbers of Irishmen already serving in the U.S. Army as well as those who joined volunteer units. In the regular army of only 6,500 on the eve of the war, 50 percent were foreign born, and 24 percent of Irish birth. Probably the Irish-born were not as well represented among the volunteers who joined for the war, as these disproportionately hailed from the pro-war south and west, and much less so from the northeast, where most new Irish had settled. Overall the German-born proportion was somewhat less than the Irish in each case. Although they did not beat the drum for recruitment, the Irish newspapers did chronicle the achievements of Irishmen in the war.[12]

Logically, then, distinctive Irish volunteer companies were formed in several southern cities with substantial Irish populations—in Charleston, Savannah, Mobile and New Orleans. The Irish Volunteers company of Charleston, dating to 1798, joined the conflict. The Irish Jasper Greens of Savannah got involved in a sectarian brawl with a volunteer company from the Georgia interior. Most newspaper accounts blamed the Jasper Greens for initiating the "riot on the Rio Grande."[13]

As mentioned previously, there was a groundswell of opposition to the war in New England, particularly in Massachusetts, with Theodore Parker, among others, opposing recruitment. Despite this opposition, several volunteers companies emerged, and in Boston a group of Irishmen formed the Irish Volunteers company. In the background to this event was the recollection that the Montgomery Guards, an Irish militia unit, had been disbanded a few years earlier as a result of nativist demands. Referring to this lost company, the *Pilot* thundered, "Where are the opponents now? It is much prettier and easier to play the soldier at home than to venture amongst the rude Mexicans." A correspondent declared that the formation of this new company was in the tradition of "patriotic exploits of Irish people in the American Revolution and the War of 1812."

Before it left for the war, the unit, commanded by Captain John Barry, attended Mass in the Boston cathedral and was addressed by Bishop John Fitzpatrick. After the fighting was over the *Pilot* declared, "From accounts from Mexico we hear that none are more universally beloved and make better soldiers than the Irish Volunteers from Boston." In his early history of the Irish in Boston, James B. Cullen estimated that two-fifths of the Massachusetts regiment was made up of Irish Americans.[14]

In Philadelphia several volunteer companies were formed, mostly comprising Irishmen. A victory rally in the city during December 1847 was told that "the natives of Ireland have rallied round the flag of the Republic and defended it with their blood, courageously and faithfully, as during the Revolution and the last war with England."[15]

An Irish hero soon emerged from the war. James Shields (1806–1879), a native of Altmore, County Tyrone, reportedly had the advantage of being tutored in Latin and Greek by an uncle who, besides having been a teacher in Charleston, South Carolina, also had served in the patriot forces during the American Revolution. Shields had arrived in the United States in 1827, and by the early 1840s he was elected Illinois state auditor. When the Mexican War began Shields became a brigadier general of the Illinois Volunteers and was severely wounded. Returning in triumph to Illinois, he was elected to the U.S. Senate in 1849. During the Civil War he also served as a general and afterward was elected to the U.S. Senate from two other states, a political record that still stands.[16]

Several other Irish and Irish American soldiers likewise achieved a measure of public acclaim. Andrew T. McReynolds, also born in Tyrone, left Ireland in 1808 and became a lawyer and state senator in Michigan; as a captain in the war, he led an infantry charge outside Mexico City and, like Shields, later served as brigadier general in the Civil War. American-born Captain John Paul Jones O'Brien first gained notoriety when, before the war, he refused to order Catholic soldiers to attend a Protestant church service. His leadership of his artillery unit at the battle of Buena Vista reportedly saved Zachary Taylor's army from disaster. He soon was confronted by another outstanding artillery captain, this one Irish-born, in a special unit of the Mexican army.[17]

The leaders of the Catholic Church in the United States decided to assume a low profile at the beginning of the war. Meeting in 1846, its bishops made no reference to the nativist onslaught of the previous few years and said nothing about the controversy surrounding the war. A delegation of three bishops, including John Hughes, met with President Polk, as a result of which two Jesuits from Georgetown College in Washington, D.C.—Irish-born Joseph McElroy and French-born Anthony Rey—were appointed unofficial Catholic chaplains to Zachary Taylor's invasion army, which led to objections by some nativists. McElroy and Rey received assistance from another priest, Bernard O'Reilly, who was in Mexico at that time. Considering that several thousand soldiers were Catholics, this was a very modest gesture of accommodation.

American church leaders also completely accepted Polk's reassurances that Mexican priests and property would not be violated (though this promise was ultimately not kept). Polk proposed that Hughes act as a mediator in the conflict with Mexico, but, due to an outcry from nativists, the archbishop reluctantly declined the invitation. After the fighting ended, in December

1847 Hughes was accorded the honor, the first given to a Catholic cleric, of addressing the House of Representatives; his subject was Christianity.[18]

Besides providing Catholic soldiers with religious services, the two Jesuits were active in opposing desertion, which they denounced as going not only against one's country but against God. In addition, McElroy took the opportunity to solicit $800 from Irish soldiers for the victims of the Great Famine in Ireland. Regrettably, Father Rey was murdered by Mexican irregulars and Father McElroy was forced by illness to withdraw after eleven months. Despite McElroy's estimate that a majority of the soldiers in the standing army were Catholics, no other priests replaced them, either in Taylor's army invading from the north or in Winfield Scott's force heading for Mexico City from the east coast at Vera Cruz.[19]

There were official U.S. disclaimers concerning sectarian purposes for the war; yet there were a variety of cross-currents. When some Polk supporters charged that a Father Mullen in New Orleans was discouraging the enlistment of members of his flock, the Boston *Pilot* rejected these reports as an example of the malicious falsehoods that were circulating about Catholics and their loyalty. With his army drained by desertion, General Taylor complained about evil priests in Mexico who were attempting to lure Catholic soldiers from the American ranks. Not all of them were Mexican—Irish-born Father Eugene Macnamara, after a stormy interlude in British Guiana and California, became involved with Mexican authorities in this activity. Shortly after the end of the war he disappeared from attention and reportedly died in 1848.[20]

Responding to the Mexican effort to win over Catholic soldiers, *The Union*, the Polk administration's mouthpiece in Washington, proposed that the property of the Catholic Church in Mexico be confiscated. This caused a roar of protest from American Catholics, and nothing further was heard of the matter.[21] Given the determined nativist, anti–Catholic agitation that preceded the war, it is not surprising that some Protestant zealots saw the invasion of Mexico as an opportunity to free the Mexican people from the thrall of a supposedly ignorant and superstitious religion and, of course, to substitute their new, improved model, with a flood of preachers descending on Mexico. Despite its declaration that it "deplored this war," the *Pilot* added that "we cannot but believe that many of its supporters are imbued with a spirit of Protestant propagandism at the point of a bayonet." When a Catholic altarpiece, obviously looted from Mexico, appeared for auction in New Orleans, the *Pilot* wondered about the U.S. government's assurances that there would be no disturbance of church property.[22]

This is as far as any Irish American newspaper went in criticizing the conduct of the war, although there was a range of people on the scene who observed systematic harassment of foreign-born soldiers, destruction of church property, and gross abuse, including murder, of Mexican civilians. When the war ended, the archbishop of Mexico City issued a statement charging that there had been wholesale attacks on Catholic churches and clergy. The most serious offenders were apparently volunteers in southern rural militia units (General Taylor spoke of "the wild volunteers") or some members of the Texas Rangers, with the latter being ordered out of Mexico. The Irish American press gave brief treatment to the archbishop's statement—the war was over, nothing could be done.[23]

There were many reports of substantial desertion among U.S. soldiers, with the total reaching more than 9,000, representing about 20 percent of the U.S. military forces sent to Mexico. Overall desertion rates were the highest of all America's wars. The Mexican government attempted to draw foreign-born soldiers—English and Irish, French, Germans, Poles and those from other nations—into its ranks with promises of citizenship, money and land. General Taylor declared, "Efforts are continually, being made to entice our men to desert, and, I regret to say, have met with considerable success." Although President Antonio López de Santa Anna had hoped to attract 3,000 deserters, only about 300 responded to his appeal. Santa Anna saw the attraction of forming them into a separate unit.

In November 1846 a company called the Irish Volunteers first appeared on the Mexican army payroll. By a decree of July 1, 1847, "a foreign legion" was established, and the men were organized into an effective artillery unit in the Mexican army. Called the St. Patrick's Battalion, only two-fifths of its members (about fifty) were Irish-born, with smaller numbers of Germans and a scattering of other Europeans and even a few American-born men. Its commander was John Riley, a Galway native who had first deserted from the British army in Canada and then from the U.S. Army along the Rio Grande *before* the war began (which would ultimately save him from the death sentence later). It was due to Riley that the unit was given its Irish identity.[24]

Following their very effective involvement in the battle of Churubusco, where they several times tore down with their own hands the white flags raised by Mexican troops, eighty-five of the San Patricios were captured in August 1847. The following month they were tried by courts-martial, with fifty of them receiving the death penalty, while most of the remainder were sentenced to be brutally whipped, branded and imprisoned while the army remained in Mexico. Upon orders from Scott that leaders of his units attend, the executions by hanging were conducted in three stages and locations, with sixteen of them hanged on 9 September and four more two days later. On 13 September the remaining thirty men were executed in a spectacular fashion. As staged by Colonel William Harney, the condemned men were placed on wagons with nooses around their necks. They were then forced to observe the American assault on Chapultepec Castle, the final Mexican defensive position before Mexico City. When the fortress was stormed, Harney gave the order for the wagons to depart, and the doomed men perished "in a fearful Dance of Death."[25]

It is probable that the executions would not have taken place if the peace negotiations following a truce in August had not broken down. Among the unacceptable Mexican demands were that slavery be excluded from formerly Mexican territory and that the San Patricio prisoners be returned. With the conflict resuming, General Winfield Scott, the commander of the American forces, saw the need to try to stop further defections, and it was he who appointed Harney to carry out the hangings.[26]

The capture, courts-martial and execution of members of the San Patricios, the first group of deserters to be hanged, received wide press coverage. Reporting in the New Orleans *Picayune* (which was the principal press source of the war), George Kendall declared, "To their credit be it spoken, the Irish in our army are loudest in denouncing the miserable wretches who fought and killed so many Americans," although he supposed the Patricios "will get off rather easily." In a book published in 1849, R.S. Ripley stated that the hangings "excited considerable attention, but no regret or distrust of its justice with Americans." However, he asserted, Mexicans "failed not to characterize it as barbarous and unjust in the extreme, as indeed it might have been expected they would, in their usual perversion of all things to the support of their own side of any question."[27]

The whole episode of the San Patricios caused understandable alarm among Irish Americans. Rumor quickly came to the rescue. The New York *Freeman's Journal*; the Mobile, Alabama, *Herald*; and then the Charleston, South Carolina, *Courier* reported that John Riley was really an Englishman named Ryder, who, among other things, had been a drill sergeant at West Point. The Boston *Pilot* took the position that the allegations that this "Riley" was Irish were just more attempts to slander patriotic Irish people. Moreover, "Riley is not an Irishman—we disown him." The matter was settled, as far as the newspaper was concerned.[28]

The attention given to the San Patricios affair led to charges from a variety of sources that Irish soldiers had shown a marked propensity to desert. To add to the embarrassment, the St. Patrick's Battalion continued in existence after the war ended. The *Pilot* and other Irish publications quickly pointed out that many soldiers in this unit were not Irish, but it was almost impossible to overcome the memory of Captain John Riley, the green flag, and the name of the battalion. The *National Police Gazette* compiled figures that demonstrated that the majority of deserters were American-born, with the natives of Ireland and Germany, in that order, following far behind. The *Pilot* made full use of these statistics. It pointed out that "there are five Yankees for every Irishman" on the lists. Referring to one of its Boston rivals, it asked, "Will the *Transcript* tell us what becomes of these native deserters? ... We hear none being hung but Irish deserters." A remnant of the unit made its way to the Pacific ports, while along the way the survivors were honored by the local people.[29]

It might be assumed that the fifty Irishmen who deserted the U.S. Army to form a unit on the other side were the first natives of Erin to take this fateful step. In fact, during the Revolutionary War desertions both ways were common, and Irishmen developed a considerable reputation for taking such action. In 1778 the British army in Philadelphia and New York City decided to take advantage of Irish defections from the patriot side. It formed a company of such Irish into the Volunteers of Ireland, commanded by an Irish nobleman, Lord Rawdon. This unit did not have a happy history. Shipped to Charleston, South Carolina, in 1780, it was dispatched to the Irish settlement of Waxhaw to gain recruits. Rather than adding to its numbers, however, it actually lost members who responded to the appeals of the Waxhaw Irish. Afterward, the unit was shipped to England and disbanded. Waxhaw is notable as the birthplace of Andrew Jackson, whose parents (and two of his brothers) were natives of Antrim. A teenaged participant in the Revolution, Jackson remained firm in both his antipathy to England and his pride in his Irish heritage.[30]

The onset of the Great Famine in Ireland diverted attention from the Mexican War. Generous contributions from a wide range of groups outside the orbit of the Irish and Catholics elicited statements of gratitude from the Irish American press.[31]

Both of the leading American generals in the Mexican War were to make use of Irish involvement in their subsequent political careers. Zachary Taylor, the successful presidential candidate in 1848, speaking from ten years of experience, was unstinting in his praise of Irish soldiers: "They deserve the honor of the country for the courage, zeal and fidelity with which they have defended her interest and honor." Winfield Scott, an unsuccessful presidential candidate four years later, during the War of 1812 had been instrumental in safeguarding Irish-born American soldiers who were captured by British forces. After the capture of the bulk of the surviving San Patricios, recognizing that few (if any) of them were U.S. citizens, Scott demonstrated great forbearance in reducing the death sentences imposed on several of them. In response to the services of all the other Irish soldiers in this conflict, Scott was outspoken in his words of respect and appreciation. Praise from such a source, declared the *Pilot*, "should silence forever the tongue of slander" and put an end "to the abuse and misrepresentation which too often disfigure the columns of some northern newspapers."[32]

During the course of the war the nativist press contained occasional complaints about Catholic influence and Irish desertions, but with more than nine thousand deserters, it was not possible to focus attention on the Irish or Catholic elements in their ranks. If this matter could have been built up into a major issue, it certainly would have been during the great anti-foreign Know Nothing movement that erupted in the early 1850s. Over time, even the episode of the San Patricios faded into obscurity.[33]

In the Mexican War thousands of Irishmen had served honorably, estimated at 24 percent of the regular army, but how many precisely of the 110,000–120,000 men who were mobilized overall is unclear. Only a handful of these had broken their oath of allegiance and joined the other side. The Irish in the United States again had demonstrated loyalty and support to their new country. To the Irish American community, this was the significance of the Mexican War. To many Mexicans, the formation of the St. Patrick's Battalion was a courageous example of a group of Irishmen (and others) who chose to join the cause of justice and freedom. For the past forty years the Mexican government has honored this action with a ceremony held on September 12.[34]

As the sounds of guns and drums from the Mexican War receded, there were rumblings of another American conflict on the horizon. In the coming struggle, as in that of 1846–1848, Irish people would be on both sides of the controversies and of the carnage.

NOTES

1. John H. Schroeder, *Mr. Polk's War: Opposition and Dissent, 1846–1848* (Madison: University of Wisconsin Press, 1973); *Pilot* (Boston), June 13, 1846.
2. Victor Alba, *A Concise History of Mexico* (London: Cessell, 1973), 93.
3. James P. Myers Jr., "'Till their ... bog-trotting feet get *talaria*': Henry D. Thoreau and the Immigrant Irish," in *The Creative Migrant* (*The Irish World Wide*), edited by Patrick O'Sullivan, volume 3 (Leicester and London: Leicester University Press, 1994), 44–56; Emerson to Thoreau, October 17, 1843, quoted *Ibid.*, 47.
4. Carl Wittke, *The Irish in America* (Baton Rouge: Louisiana State University Press, 1956), 294; Orestes Brownson, "Irish Immigrants and American Progress," *Brownson's Quarterly Review* (October 1855).
5. Ray A. Billington, *The Protestant Crusade, 1800–1860* (New York: Macmillan, 1938), 24.
6. Lincoln: *American National Biography*, vol. 13, 664–65; J.Q. Adams: Robert R. Miller, *Shamrock and Sword: The St. Patrick's Battalion in the U.S.-Mexican War* (Norman: University of Oklahoma Press, 1989), 23.
7. William S. McFeely, *Grant: A Biography* (New York: Norton, 1981), 30–31; Do Maol Blagaide (Padraig O Snodaigh), *Aut Ultach*, September 2014; David Clary, *Eagles and Empire: The United States, Mexico and the Struggle for a Continent* (New York: Bantam Dell, 2009), 250–51.
8. Robert F. Hueston, *The Catholic Press and Nativism, 1840–1860* (New York: Arno Press, 1976), 11–15.
9. Billington, *Protestant Crusade*, 220–21, 231; *New York Herald*, September 25, 1847; Hueston, *Catholic Press and Nativism*, 74–80, 105; *Liberator*, July 12, 1844, in Noel Ignatiev, *How the Irish Became White* (New York: Routledge, 1995), 224–25, n. 33; Thomas J. Curran, *Xenophobia and Immigration, 1820–1930* (Boston: Twayne, 1975), 42.
10. *Pilot* (Boston), January 6, 1847.
11. *Pilot* (Boston), June 13, 1846; George Potter, *To the Golden Door* (Boston: Little,

34   Part I: Mexican War

Brown, 1960), 477; Blanche M. McEniry, *American Catholics in the War with Mexico* (Washington, D.C.: Catholic University of America, 1937), 19.

12. McEniry, *American Catholics in the War with Mexico*, 77, 161; James M. McCaffrey, *The Army of Manifest Destiny: The American Soldiers in the Mexican War, 1846-1848* (New York: New York University Press, 1992), 195-96; William M. Sweeny, "The Irish Soldier in the War with Mexico," *Journal of American Irish Historical Society* 26 (1927): 255-59. The *New York Herald*, on August 26, 1847, reported 40,000 U.S. military in the war, presumably in Mexico only.

13. Arthur H. Mitchell, *History of the Hibernian Society of Charleston, South Carolina* (Charleston, SC, 1980), 53; Peter F. Stevens, *The Rogue's March: John Riley and the St. Patrick's Battalion* (Washington, D.C.: Brassey's, 1999), 144.

14. *Pilot* (Boston), December 12, 1846, and January 16 and September 25 and 18, 1847; James B. Cullen, *The Story of the Irish in Boston* (Boston: J.B. Cullen & Co., 1889), 103.

15. McEniry, *American Catholics*, 47; *Pilot* (Boston), December 23, 1947.

16. Timothy J. Moynihan, "James Shields," *Journal of the American Irish Historical Society* 23 (1924): 60-67; for Shields's grand national tour, see *Pilot* (Boston), January 5, 1848; *American National Biography*, vol. 19, 838-40.

17. *Journal of the American Irish Historical Society* 25 (1926), 207-10; Paul Foos, *A Short, Offhand Killing Affair: Soldiers and Social Conflict during the Mexican-American War* (Chapel Hill: University of North Carolina Press, 2002), 26; Stevens, *Rogue's March*, 37, 298; A.R. Ginsburgh, "O'Brien's Bulldogs," *Field Artillery Journal* (May-June 1937): 182-87.

18. McEniry, *American Catholics*, 13-14, 50, 54-55, 30-35, 43-46; Stevens, *Rogue's March*, 132-36; Billington, *Protestant Crusade*, 239, 257 n. 6.

19. Billington, *Protestant Crusade*, 175; McEniry, *American Catholics*, 161-66.

20. *Pilot* (Boston), June 13, 1846; John Fox, *Macnamara's Irish Colony and the United States Taking of California in 1846* (Jefferson, NC: McFarland, 2000), 15-20, 184-87.

21. McEniry, *American Catholics*, 16.

22. *Pilot* (Boston), April 22, 1848, and January 23, 1847; Clary, *Eagles and Empire*, 167.

23. Stevens, *Rogue's March*, 52-58, 66-67, 166-67, 170-73; Hueston, *Catholic Press and Nativism*, 118; Otis Singletary, *The Mexican War* (Chicago: University of Chicago Press, 1960), 144-46. The Rangers had a record of unspeakable atrocities, misconduct and desertion: see Thomas H. Kreneck, "Lone Star Volunteers: A History of Texas Participation in the Mexican War," MA thesis, University of Houston, 1971. For information on volunteer units from Arkansas and Missouri, see Clary, *Eagles and Empire*, 245, 268-69, 283, 375, 379.

24. Stevens, *Rogue's March*, 2-3, 162, 229-30, 302-3; Robert S. Henry, *The Story of the Mexican War* (New York: F. Ungar, 1950), 45; *New York Herald*, August 23, 1847; Clary, *Eagles and Empire*, 359-60.

25. Stevens, *Rogue's March*, 241-44, 265-76; Clary, *Eagles and Empire*, 367.

26. Singletary, *Mexican War*, 158; Thomas Barclay and Richard Coulter, *Volunteers: The Mexican War Journals of Private Richard Coulter and Sergeant Thomas Barclay*, edited by Allan Peskin (Kent, OH: Kent State University Press, 1991), 147, 158-59; R.S. Ripley, *The War with Mexico*, 2 vols. (New York: Harper & Brothers, 1849), 2:355-56; Henry, *Mexican War*, 368; Stevens, *Rogue's March*, 212.

27. George Kendall, *Dispatches from the Mexican War*, edited by Lawrence D. Cress (Norman: University of Oklahoma Press, 1999), 350 (see also 343, 378, 388, 413); *New York Herald*, September 16 and 17, 1847; Ripley, *War with Mexico*, 2:356.

28. *Pilot* (Boston), September 25 and October 16 and 23, 1847. Because they had deserted before the declaration of war, Riley and a dozen others could not be hung, but they were subjected to the following punishment: "Fifty lashes with a rawhide whip, well laid on the bare back of each ... with the addition, that each be branded on a cheek with the letter D, kept a close prisoner as long as this army remains in Mexico, and then be drummed out of the service." *American Star* (Mexico City), September 20 and 25, 1847.

29. *Pilot* (Boston), November 27 and December 4 and 11, 1847 (see also October 23 and November 27, 1847); Foos, *Short, Offhand Killing*, 11-112. The U.S. Army also employed deserters. The Mexican Spy Company, made up of Mexican defectors, was formed in May 1847 to combat Mexican guerrillas attacking supply lines and rear positions. Dennis J. Wynn,

The San Patricio Soldiers: Mexico's Foreign Legion (El Paso: Texas Western Press, 1984), 35–40; A. Brooke Caruso, The Mexican Spy Company: United States Covert Operations in Mexico, 1845–48 (Jefferson, NC: McFarland, 1991).

30. Oliver Snoddy, "Volunteers of Ireland," Irish Sword: Journal of Military History Society of Ireland 1 (Winter 1965–1966): 147–59; Arthur Mitchell, "Andrew Jackson," Encyclopedia of the Irish in America, 480–81.

31. Hueston, Catholic Press and Nativism, 118–20.

32. Taylor quoted in Pilot (Boston), November 13, 1848. Regarding Scott's actions during the War of 1812, what was at issue was the matter of allegiance by birth versus assumption of citizenship in another country. By means of hostage taking, Scott was instrumental in preventing the Irishmen from being tried for treason, and they were returned to the United States after the war. See Edward D. Mansfield, Life and Services of General Winfield Scott (New York: A.S. Barnes, 1852), 55–63. On the Mexican War, see Pilot (Boston), June 24, 1848; Sweeny, "The Irish Soldier in the War with Mexico"; Stevens, Rogue's March, 299–300; Wittke, Irish in America, 109. In his memoirs, published in 1864, Scott said nothing about the San Patricios. He was well aware of the balance of Irish service in the War of 1812, the Mexican War and the U.S. Civil War.

33. Billington, Protestant Crusade, 238–39; Ted C. Hickley, "American Anti-Catholicism during the Mexican War," Pacific Historical Review 31 (1962): 121–37. In The Rogue's March (282), Peter Stevens declares the matter of the St. Patrick's Battalion was employed in hundreds of nativist publications, but he only cites the 1856 Know-Nothing Almanac.

34. The September 2000 ceremony was attended by twenty members of the St. Brendan's Society of Ireland and was addressed by Art Agnew, ambassador to Mexico from the Republic of Ireland. Beginning in 1993 there has been an annual commemoration held on September 12 at Clifton, County Galway (Connemara.net website). In October 1999 the name of the San Patricio Battalion, inscribed in gold, was added to a list of national heroes on a plaque in the Mexican national assembly building (CNN World News, October 28, 1999). Scholars fully abreast of Mexican historiography and fluent in Spanish add a further element of understanding as to why Mexico so honors this group, untypical of most Irish in America but indicative of wider cultural and national issues: Christen I. Archer, "Discord, Disjunction and Reveries.... Mexico's First Decades of Independence, 1810–1853," Mexican Studies/Estudios Mexicanos 16 (2000): 189–210.

BIBLIOGRAPHY

Alba, Victor. A Concise History of Mexico. London: Cessell, 1973.
Archer, Christen I. "Discord, Disjunction and Reveries.... Mexico's First Decades of Independence, 1810–1853." Mexican Studies/Estudios Mexicanos 16 (2000): 189–210.
Barclay, Thomas, and Richard Coulter. Volunteers: The Mexican War Journals of Private Richard Coulter and Sergeant Thomas Barclay. Edited by Allan Peskin. Kent, OH: Kent State University Press, 1991.
Billington, Ray A. Protestant Crusade, 1800–1860. New York: Macmillan, 1938.
Caruso, A. Brooke. The Mexican Spy Company: United States Covert Operations in Mexico, 1845–48. Jefferson, NC: McFarland, 1991.
Clary, David. Eagles and Empire: The United States, Mexico and the Struggle for a Continent. New York: Bantam Dell, 2009.
Cullen, James B. The Story of the Irish in Boston. Boston: J.B. Cullen & Co., 1889.
Curran, Thomas J. Xenophobia and Immigration, 1820–1930. Boston: Twayne, 1975.
Foos, Paul. A Short, Offhand Killing Affair: Soldiers and Social Conflict during the Mexican-American War. Chapel Hill: University of North Carolina Press, 2002.
Fox, John. Macnamara's Irish Colony and the United States Taking of California in 1846. Jefferson, NC: McFarland, 2000.
Ginsburgh, A.R. "O'Brien's Bulldogs." Field Artillery Journal (May-June 1937).
Henry, Robert S. The Story of the Mexican War. New York: F. Ungar, 1950.
Hickley, Ted C. "American Anti-Catholicism during the Mexican War." Pacific Historical Review 31 (1962): 121–37.

Hueston, Robert F. *The Catholic Press and Nativism.* New York: Arno Press, 1976.
Ignatiev, Noel. *How the Irish Became White.* New York: Routledge, 1995.
Kendall, George. *Dispatches from the Mexican War.* Edited by Lawrence D. Cress. Norman: University of Oklahoma Press, 1999.
Kreneck, Thomas H. "Lone Star Volunteers: A History of Texas Participation in the Mexican War." MA thesis, University of Houston, 1971.
Mansfield, Edward D. *Life and Services of General Winfield Scott.* New York: A.S. Barnes, 1852.
McCaffrey, James M. *The Army of Manifest Destiny: The American Soldiers in the Mexican War, 1846–1848.* New York: New York University Press, 1992.
McEniry, Blanche. *American Catholics in the War with Mexico.* Washington, D.C.: Catholic University Press, 1937.
McFeely, William S. *Grant: A Biography.* New York: Norton, 1981.
Miller, Robert R. *Shamrock and Sword: The St. Patrick's Battalion in the U.S.-Mexican War.* Norman: University of Oklahoma Press, 1989.
Mitchell, Arthur H. *History of the Hibernian Society of Charleston, South Carolina.* Charleston, SC, 1980.
Moynihan, Timothy J. "James Shields." *Journal of the American Irish Historical Society* 23 (1924).
O'Sullivan, Patrick, ed. *The Creative Migrant (The Irish World Wide).* Vol. 3. Leicester and London: Leicester University Press, 1994.
Pilot (Boston), 1840–1848.
Potter, George. *To the Golden Door.* Boston: Little, Brown, 1960.
Ripley, R.S. *The War with Mexico.* 2 vols. New York: Harper & Brothers, 1849.
Schroeder, John H. *Mr. Polk's War: Opposition and Dissent, 1846–1848.* Madison: University of Wisconsin Press, 1973.
Singletary, Otis. *The Mexican War.* Chicago: University of Chicago Press, 1960.
Snoddy, Oliver. "Volunteers of Ireland." *Irish Sword: Journal of Military History Society of Ireland* 1 (Winter 1965–1966): 147–59.
Stevens, Peter F. *The Rogue's March: John Riley and the St. Patrick's Battalion.* Washington, D.C.: Brassey's, 1999.
Sweeny, William M. "The Irish Soldier in the War with Mexico." *Journal of American Irish Historical Society* 26 (1927).
Wittke, Carl. *The Irish in America.* Baton Rouge: Louisiana State University Press, 1956.
Wynn, Dennis J. *The San Patricio Soldiers: Mexico's Foreign Legion.* El Paso: Texas Western Press, 1984.

PART II: AMERICAN CIVIL WAR

The New York Irish Brigade Recruits and Their Families in the Era of the Civil War[1]

MARION TRUSLOW

> I have no trade—never had any—always been a laboring man. In the last eight or nine years I have put in coal or planted sod, or worked in gardens and did such other little jobs of work that I could get. I have had no steady work for the last ten years. During this time I have sometimes received one dollar a day, at other times perhaps not more than twenty-five cents. Never kept any account of my earnings, but can safely say that my earnings for the last eight or ten years have not averaged more than $2.50 or three dollars a week. When my son entered the army, I lived on 35th St. between 1st and 2nd Ave.—don't know the number. McMahon was the name of the landlord. Lived there about six or seven years. I paid at first four dollars a month rent and when I left there about 1868 paid him eight and a half ($8.50) dollars rent per month. My wife never earned fifty dollars altogether while she was in this country. As long as I was able to work I would not ask her aid.
>
> Signed,
X [Patrick Finn][2]

"For generations," wrote Dennis Clark, "New York above all American cities was America for the Irish." The Irish connection with New York is also obvious in Patrick Finn's opening statements from the pension file of his son Michael and suggests several lines of inquiry about New York Irish in the Civil War era. What can census results for mid-century show regarding the size, location, and other pertinent facts about the city's Irish population on the eve of the war? What was the city like economically? Did existing institutions help or hurt these new arrivals? The evidence suggests that while many New York City Irish from whom so many Union Army recruits were drawn were indeed poor, and the city was certainly harsh, dirty, dangerous, and alien to them, Irish traditions sustained them. Over time the Irish became attached to the city, the state, and the nation through the workplace, Tammany Hall's political activities, and Catholic Church parishes.[3] The War Department's Bureau of Pensions often ensured their final attachment. High Irish Brigade casualties consequent upon combat bravery created a sense of entitlement to be called Americans, regardless of what nativists said. Later grants of Civil War pensions meant that these Irish people had "no vicious habits" and were morally fit. Thus a long assimilation process was completed by the Pension Bureau as its red tape cemented the soldiers and their families in the social order. In the process, the Irish took a giant step toward becoming Americans by the end of the Civil War era.[4]

Census data from New York, with Brooklyn (then distinct), for the period just before the Civil War puts the total population at about one million people, of whom "on Manhattan Island alone, nearly forty-eight per cent, or 384,000 out of the 805,000 inhabitants were born outside the United States." Robert Ernst notes that more than 200,000 of these were natives of Ireland. Of the twenty-two wards in Manhattan, ranging from the first ward at the tip of the island to the 22nd at 59th Street ward near Central Park, the Irish had by 1853 reached 20 percent or more of the total population in seventeen wards. The Irish also constituted by far the largest overseas-born admissions to Bellevue Hospital, the lunatic asylum, the Alms House for Pauperism, and the city prison. No doubt the overall health of many of the famine-era immigrants was deplorable owing to their poor nutrition (and even partial starvation for some) before the voyage, due to the potato blight in Ireland (1845–1849), where at least one million had died, as well as British failure to feed promptly those in their care and the four to six weeks' travel between Ireland and New York, which obviously further debilitated these impoverished people.[5]

How prosperous, or not, was the city of New York in which these rural immigrants would settle? On the eve of the Civil War, "about 62% of the nation's commerce passed through the port of New York; in 1800 the figure had been 9%." Many federal forts with large garrisons were located in or near New York, so war stimulated the manufacturing of ships, clothing, and pharmaceuticals, with these industries employing many Irish workers. Additionally, the loss of the southern cotton trade was made up for by the now-customary inflow of agricultural goods from the Midwest via the Erie Canal, which had been dug by around 35,000 Irish before 1825. Other exports to Europe in 1862 included more than "6,880,000 gallons of oil, three times the volume from Philadelphia."

During the Civil War, the combined annual tonnage carried on the Erie Canal and on the New York Central railroad lines increased by about seventy percent. In general, transportation in the city itself was thriving. According to Miller's *New York As It Is*, an 1865 guide, it had twenty-nine omnibus lines "comprising 671 vehicles, which average about 10 down[town] and as many up[town] trips daily. Besides these stages there are five lines drawn by horses or mules along rails laid on the streets. The fare was only 5 cents."[6]

Where did the newly urban Irish peasants of the famine era fit in workwise in this thriving metropolis? Terrance Winch, winner of the American poetry prize for 1986, in "When New York Was Irish" sketched the situation of the 1870s–1880s poetically: "We dug all the subways, we ran the saloons/We built all the bridges, we played all the tunes/We put out the fires, we controlled city hall,/We started with nothing, wound up with it all." The work world and Irish identity were connected. Out of the pool of unskilled New York City male workers totaling 23,300, porters or laborers made up 21,800. The majority were Irish, 87 percent of all foreign-born Manhattan laborers in 1855. Aside from heavy laboring, transportation work as teamsters and carters occupied 3,000 immigrant workers (80 percent of them Irish-born). The 1855 New York State census also shows that Irish-born in Manhattan made up similar proportions of immigrant grooms (hostlers) and harbor boatmen. Of *skilled* workers, half in the building trades were born outside the United States, and more than half of these were Irish. Indeed, of the foreign-born workforce, Irish-born workers made up exactly three-quarters of the city's bricklayers, masons and plasterers and half of its carpenters, as well as precisely one-third of its painters, glaziers and shoemakers.[7]

Irish Brigade occupational data sampled from National Archives pension file data break down slightly differently, with more unskilled than skilled occupations represented. Out of more than 250 Irish Brigade veterans or soldiers surveyed who applied for a Civil War pension, from the 63rd, 88th and 69th regiments of the New York Infantry, almost 55 percent had held unskilled prewar occupations; the building trades accounted for a fifth of the occupations for skilled workers.[8] Of the few occupations known for their wives, most worked in employment related to housekeeping. These tasks included housekeeper, washer and ironer, laundress and washerwoman, servant, cleaning woman, and house worker; few actually labeled themselves as domestic. Out of 262 wives, then, we know that 38 of them had identified themselves in pension files. Only a few of these appeared to be skilled, including a maker of overalls, a seamstress and a milliner. That the occupations of the remaining 224 are unknown is perplexing; probably they were homemakers, but caution may have compelled the wives of pension-seeking veterans (often disabled) to suppress any source of income they brought to the family.[9]

What of the standard of living of the Irish immigrants? In 1853, the *New*

York Times estimated that skilled working men in New York City spent $600 a year: $550 went to food, clothing, rent, and household expenses; $13 was for other essential items.[10] One may gauge that unskilled workers earned $1.00 per day, and that they could count on 180 days of work per year. $240.00 was needed for a family of four, with yearly rent costing $60, clothing $60, and food $120. The wages increase of common laborers "from the decade following 1850 to the close of the century was approximately fifty percent."[11] In the depression of 1857–1858, wages had not kept up with expenses. Workers' income was sustained by means of military pay and enlistment bounties. Indeed, even after the war began in spring 1861, up through spring 1863, all wages witnessed an average increase of about 25 percent, or less than half the increase of prices. An "unprecedented surge of growth, construction and reorganization" in Manhattan at this time meant that "Manhattan property values appreciated more than fourfold ... [as] construction rates doubled, reaching two thousand new buildings per year in the frenzied markets." Yet, however difficult it was to survive in New York with the rise prices and tenement rents between 1855 and 1865, opportunities did exist, which were few enough in Ireland.[12]

Along with the benefits of being employed in urbanizing New York, the Roman Catholic Church provided continuity, education, and cultural cohesion to sustain these urban country people as they acculturated.[13] Archbishop John Hughes, the founder of both Fordham (then St. John's College) and Manhattan College, remarked of his fellow countrymen, "If he can be present at the holy sacrifice of Mass, [and] see the minister of his religion at the altar and hear the word of God and the language to which his ear was accustomed from childhood, he forgets he is among strangers in a strange country."[14] By ensuring their church attendance, Hughes tried to domesticate the Irish. Parish churches in New York City doubled from nineteen in 1850 to thirty-eight by 1868. At home, a "devotional revolution" was turning the Catholic Church of pre-famine Ireland, moribund in some areas, into a vital institution manifesting itself in "new buildings, increased devotions, and more responsible pastors."[15] In urban America, according to Oscar Handlin, the Irish saw religion "as the most important of all topics,"[16] whether they practiced it or not. Religious rituals in parish churches thus bonded the Irish to their neighborhoods and served as an agent of assimilation by turning nominal Catholics into practicing believers with frequent Masses available on Sundays.[17] The parish of the Transfiguration, home of many Irish Brigade families, offered a thirty-minute Mass at 7:00, another at 8:00, a solemn High Mass at 10.30 with a choir and organist, and vespers in the evening. At mid-century the bishops had legislated "that the ceremonies of baptism, marriage, confession and death must take place in the church."[18] Such ceremonies must have been welcome, as they allowed many Irish to forget the squalor of their daily living environments for a time.

Of the 262 marriages of the soldiers included in this study (detailed on their pension files), 51 were married in Ireland. But 109 couples were married in various Catholic churches in New York City and its environs, including ten in St. Stephen's, nine each in both St. Joseph's and St. Francis Xavier's, eight in the Church of the Nativity, six in the Church of the Transfiguration, and five in Old and New St. Patrick's. A further 102 partners were married in churches with uncertain geographic locations or outside the area of New York City. The locations of the known churches correspond closely with the Irish wards of New York City. Of the total sample of 262, there were about four Protestants, an insignificant figure considering the total number of families. Virtually every soldier's pension file included both a marriage certificate and a baptismal certificate. In a sworn deposition of January 1864, Fr. J.W. Cummings of St. Stephen's Church stated "that as such Pastor he has charge of the baptismal records of such church that by such records it appears that on the 13th day of June 1852 Matthew Sands the son of Mary and Michael Sands was baptized according to the rites and forms of the Catholic church, and that the sponsors of said child were Sarah and Michael Sands." The marriage of Mary and Michael Sands was likewise documented: "I hereby certify that Michael Sands was lawfully married to Mary Harper in the presence of John Byrne and Catherine O'Hare us appears from the marriage registry of the Roman Catholic parish of Donaghmore, Ireland, on the 8th day of May 1845."

That the church kept both marriage and birth certificates underscores its important role as record keeper. The church was a partner with the state and, as such, helped link the Irish to their new country. However, the related functions of the Catholic Church in bonding Irish immigrants together in their new cities was not as evident (at least initially) in education, since there were few parochial schools, and even the proportions of Irish in these schools actually fell with the new mass arrivals.

With Bishop John Hughes as a leader of community, the city became a parallel center of the parish schools movement (along with Philadelphia, whence Hughes had come in 1839).[19] Growth could not match the Irish influx. Their pupils numbered 5,000 in 1840, but only 16,000 by the end of the Civil War, whereas the city's Catholic population had increased between four and five times. Most Irish Brigade soldiers were thus not products of the educational system. However, in 1856, the Church of the Transfiguration built a schoolhouse that was run by the Sisters of Charity, while the next year the Christian Brothers took charge of 500 boys in exchange for some small tuition charge. By 1862 this institution was a free school with an enrollment of 1,200. In these schools the children were taught Catholicism from various catechisms. Many parents had used Butler's catechism in Ireland, and their American-born children now often learned from the same work.[20]

Reinforcing the solidarity of Catholicism in the immigrant church of New York was the *School Reader*, first published in the United States in 1837 to present "the facts of religion as the best refutation of its adversaries,"[21] rather than attacking other religions. Praising Irish culture, it painted a positive portrait of the Irish peasant as "shrewd," "hospitable," "heroic," "just" and "cheerful" while also instilling patriotic pride in America. Speeches by Patrick Henry, Daniel Webster and George Washington were included in the similar Christian Brothers' *Reader*. "History texts also reinforced this sense of national pride, and Catholic songbooks did not fail to include patriotic hymns in their repertoire."[22] Further, at Transfiguration Parish, where so many Irish recruits had married their wives and baptized their children, parents could watch their children perform in annual school shows in which Irish poetry was recited and "Yankee Doodle" sung. Still, they could not (and did not seek to) alter the social system of their new society, regardless of the hardships it brought with it.[23]

While the official position of the church was against any form of government intervention to help the Irish immigrant in need, the church did offer charitable parish organizations (the Society of St. Vincent de Paul, St. Vincent's Hospital, various protection agencies for children) that sought to help the poor in many ways.[24] Finally, when war came, the American flag flew from Catholic churches in New York, and Archbishop Hughes said, "Be patriotic, do for the country what the country needs, and the blessing of God will recompense those who discharge their duty."[25]

To understand the Irish, their adopted politics and their new patriotism, one must recall that, unlike Europeans, Americans were formed into a common nation by means of republican polity, agreed-upon laws, and shared rights, and that the benefits of citizens derived from these. No real nation existed before the independent confederation of 1776: "National identity was not a natural fact but an ideological structure."[26] Thus, according to Dale Knobel, "Citizenship was the basis for inclusion in the nation. Loyalty to nation meant loyalty to the Constitution." These conceptions made citizenship "contractual, volitional, and legal rather than natural and immutable."[27] Against this backdrop of citizenship one can view the political attitudes of the New York Irish prior to the Civil War.

Irish contributions to American life were many, including a proactive role in shaping the process politics of the Democratic Party, especially those of Tammany Hall, its Manhattan headquarters.[28] With all of its corruption, Tammany, the prototype of the big city political machine, ultimately failed New York City, but it helped many people, including Irish immigrants. These last, in turn, helped reshape city and, to a lesser degree, national politics. Irish newcomers became patriots through their participation in pre–Civil War Democratic Party politics in the city. Comprising 34 percent of all voters in

New York City in 1855, the Irish vote was critical. The party's machine offered ready help in various troubles to both recent Irish immigrants and seasoned Irish ward dwellers. Eventually these took over broadening sectors of the machine and, after 1871, ran it.

Police and fire companies were linked to this system. In 1855, a quarter of the city's police were Irish, and they supported Tammany Hall. Independent fire companies groomed future politicians, including Tammany's William Magear Tweed, helping wean him from an original anti–Irish bias. He had organized the Big Six Engine Company in 1849 and later controlled Tammany Hall itself. Success as a volunteer fireman led to status in the Irish community, though Tweed was not Irish. Only in 1865 did the New York legislature inaugurate a metropolitan fire department for the city.[29]

In their recent past the Irish had been subject to landlord exploitation at home, and where these doubled as a controlling magistracy, they had sought to bypass this problem through group mobilization in which they had the vote. Such prior experiences perhaps made it inevitable that they were open to working with political bosses in New York as a mark of their cohesion. The machine encouraged them to vote in a bloc, rewarding their polling behavior with free liquor, as had been long customary in other parts of America.

For the Irish, political activity, and the job referrals linked to it, came to center upon the saloon.[30] Immigrant saloon owners like John McSorley of 15 E. 7th Street in Manhattan were in key positions socially and politically. Thus his relative, William McSorley, who owned a publishing house on Barclay Street in lower Manhattan, released the first history of the Irish Brigade in 1867 by one its own war reporter, Captain David P. Conyngham: *The Irish Brigade and Its Campaigns, with, Some of the Corcoran Legion, and Sketches of the Principal Officers.* John McSorley himself was a cog in the Tammany machine. Brian Harrison's work on the importance of pubs in social change in Victorian England can be aptly applied to New York immigrant saloons. McSorley's saloon provided, like its Victorian counterparts, an oasis from the nagging wife, crying children, boredom and pain of day laboring. Social classes mixed in saloons that provided for male recreation and a public meeting place for working people. Regular Democratic votes were one outcome. Such mutuality also led to an agreed goal by the 1850s: opposing nativists and abolitionists nationally, and Great Britain in foreign policy.[31] As Carl Wittke said, "Nativist attacks retarded assimilation and welded the Irish into a solid unified group."[32] This bonding process was very important. According to Dale Knobel, "Paddy" became the negative ethnic stereotype of the Irishman. Once seen as malleable and reformable, his traits being the temporary result of poverty and injustice in Ireland, following the riots and then mass influxes of the 1840s, "Paddy's" character was increasingly seen by many in America as unchangeable, his traits racial in origin and thus fixed. It was now assumed neither education in republicanism nor improved economic conditions could improve this basic character. In the 1850s, Americans used pseudo-sciences to define "blood" as the criterion for nationality. "Paddy" was now thought by even conventional citizens to be "dirty," "ragged," and "unkempt" by nature. Even the supposed Irish physical appearance was now ascribed to such assumed hereditary formation.[33] The draft riots of the summer of 1863 suggested to many beyond those with hard-core prejudices that there might be something after all to these stereotypes, which more sober citizens had rejected. Collective loyalty to the "machine" and its party catchwords offered both a method to bypass and rhetoric to refute such repressive stereotypes.[34]

How exactly did the riots start? The prelude and precondition was Lincoln's Emancipation Proclamation, announced in September 1862, which came into effect on January 1, 1863. An associated stimulus was an initial draft law by Congress in July 1862, as well as the full legislation of conscription in March 1863. Unlike the first law, the second extended its scope to immigrants. Lincoln's proclamation effectuating the second law notified such aliens that they had sixty-five days' grace to leave the country if they did not wish to come under its provisions. Irish America had cogently criticized any conscription of aliens during debate on the first law.[35] Now, with the hypothetical turned real, the *Irish American* and the *Freeman's Journal* of May 16 were both incensed. The *New York Tribune* (Horace Greeley's Republican paper) covered the speech of New York's Democratic governor, Horatio Seymour, on July 4 at the Academy of Music, "in which he said the draft was unconstitutional and thus a violation of our rights." He pleaded with the Republicans to rescind it, lest "the bloody and treasonable and revolutionary doctrine of public necessity can be proclaimed by a mob as (well as by a government)." Lee's invasion of Pennsylvania meant that twenty-three regiments from the city, Brooklyn and its environs had been drawn elsewhere, leaving it open to disorder, as even the *New York Times* later noted. Nine days later, around 10:30 a.m., on Monday, July 13, 1863, a large crowd had gathered at the corner of 677 Third Avenue and 46th Street for the public reading of names for service in the Union Army. Names had already been drawn on July 11 elsewhere in the city without incident. Suddenly, members of a volunteer fire company charged the public building, overpowering soldiers and police on duty. Thus began one of the worst episodes of civil disorder in U.S. history. Six thousand soldiers brought in from Pennsylvania, Maryland and Washington on the following Thursday joined 2,200 police already on hand to disperse many rioters with shot. Contrary to legend, only a few were actual combatants fresh from Gettysburg, although they had mobilized against Lee's movements. On Friday, July 17, 1863, after a plea from Archbishop Hughes to the quiet Irish majority, the remaining mobs broke up and scattered. But perhaps the major factor in stopping the riots occurred earlier, on Wednesday, when the City

Council had passed an ordinance appropriating $2.5 million to pay the fee of $300 for any poor New Yorker who was drafted and wished to avoid service through making the required payment. If the drafted man did agree to serve, the money would be paid to him as a bounty.

The facts need to be stated at the outset because of great discrepancies in data. The riots cost New York County $1,516,424. More than 50 buildings were burned. Between 105 and 120 known people died, and 128 were seriously wounded in the rioting, both rioters and victims. Thirty-five soldiers and thirty-two policemen were seriously wounded. Three hundred fifty-two people can be identified as rioters, though names are available for only 92 of them. Two hundred and forty-one were male and nineteen were female. People at the bottom of society thus dominated this mob of the industrial age— a fair cross-section of New York's younger male working class with no prior arrests. Out of 184 whose country of birth can be determined, 117 were born in Ireland, and forty in the United States. Irish Catholics serving in the metropolitan police and in the various military units performed well. Sixty-seven out of 81 rioters who went to trial were convicted, but the stiffest sentence most convicted rioters received was six months in the city penitentiary. Only one of those who attacked Negroes during the riot got a heavy sentence of 10 years in the state prison. Why so few were punished was the result of several factors: lack of evidence, poor work by prosecutors, and judges giving the lightest possible sentence in many cases. "Yet the principal significance of the New York City draft riots is that most—probably 99 percent—of the city's 800,000 citizens ... did not participate."[36] As one-quarter of New York City residents were Irish-born, and many more the offspring of such parents, this meant that only a small minority of Irish New Yorkers of any class were involved.[37] And both they and the city maintained strong support of the Union's war efforts afterward, albeit with more reservations.

Recent scholarship has maintained that the slogan "rich man's war but poor man's fight" was misleading. James McPherson has declared that unskilled workers and Irish Americans were proportionately underrepresented in the Union Army, but for his own purposes he conflated the two categories.[38] Based on the massive records assembled by Benjamin Gould in the immediate postwar period, Don H. Doyle has concluded that when the soldier sons of Irish participants are included, the Irish ethnic group was the largest, representing almost 12 percent of the Union Army.[39] In regard to the looming draft, insurance societies and appropriations by city councils or political machines to pay the commutation fee of any drafted man who did not want to go enabled poor men to buy their way out of the draft almost as readily as wealthy men.

Perhaps as a patriotic gesture, the high reenlistment rate in the face of significant casualties speaks very well of the largely unskilled and artisan

New York regiments of the Irish Brigade. But the heavy casualties they and others suffered during 1862–1863, and the interplay of emancipation, conscription, the draft riots, family poverty, renewed nativism and disparagement of their contributions, all diminished (but did not erase) the patriotic stimulus for further service. Monetary incentives were obviously a secondary and growing reason for reenlistment by Irish Brigade soldiers, if probably a primary consideration for others. For example, the *New York Times* carried the following advertisement as 1864 started:

> NEW YORK COUNTY VOLUNTEER COMMITTEE
> 30,000 VOLUNTEERS NEEDED.
> The following are the pecuniary inducements offered:
> County Bounty, cash down $300
> State Bounty $75
> United States Bounty to new recruits $302
> United States Bounty additional to veteran soldiers $100–$477
> TOTAL $777
> Applications to be made personally at the office of the committee Signed
> George Opdyke, Mayor, William Marcy Tweed, Supervisor, County Committee[40]

How did the better-off Brigade recruits and their families respond to the bounties? In a letter from the pension file of Private John Gorman, 63rd Regiment, New York Infantry, of January 11, 1862, in the National Archives, we have a clue. In his letter to the dead soldier's wife, Lieutenant Laurence Daidy wrote from brigade headquarters near Falmouth, Virginia, that Mary Gorman should "sell" the bounty. This letter not only shows the cohesiveness of the unit and the officer's concern for Gorman's family but also serves as evidence for a "modern" outlook—a monetary one. The Irish were being attached to the state: they were dealing with red tape.[41] According to Lieutenant Daidy's letter to Mary Gorman, the lieutenant had already notified E.B. French in the Department of the Treasury that the late Private John Gorman "was paid up to the 30th of June ... the government owes you about $57 dollars and some cents besides $100 dollars bounty." Obviously aware of the many hardships that some New York Irish endured, Daidy suggested that Mrs. Gorman "sell this claim at a little discount" because Washington's inefficient bureaucracy would take months to pay her. In a final, if grim, effort to console her, Daidy added that her husband "was well cared for [and] was buried with a coffin and I have not known another private having been buried in one from our regiment but him."[42]

"Pecuniary considerations" obviously helped prompt reenlistments. "The soldiers were justified in expecting liberal bounties, and it was the duty of the government to offer them," reported the *New York Times*. Such bounties were not seen as unpatriotic. Various levels of the government raised these monies to support the soldiers' families while they served their country. But the later systems of conscription substitutes and bounties produced three-quarters of a million new men who did little to help win the war. This task fell mainly to the pre-bounty veterans of 1861 and 1862, who looked with contempt on the substitutes and bounty men of 1864, even when they themselves received reenlistment bounties.[43]

Can the patriotism of the Irish Brigade recruits be indicated from pension file data? About 260 Union Army privates have been analyzed in terms of their service, using lists identifying their enlistment history, battle participation, and occupations. When did these soldiers enlist? Did most do so in 1861–1863, before the time of high bounties, purchase of substitutes, and commutation? Of 250 relevant privates, 177 enlisted in the 1861–1862 period, or 71 percent, and one in 1863. Fifty-seven, by contrast, enrolled in the 1864–1865 period (23 percent). Such a high initial percentage (71 percent) indicates an early rush on the part of these Irish-born New York soldiers to defend the Union. As James McPherson points out, it was the soldiers who joined in 1861 and 1862 who won the war for the Union. (The average volunteer signed up to serve for 2.5 years.)

Of the sample of 260, just 41 were killed in action. In theory, 214–216 "effectives" were eligible to reenlist. But 86 of these (40 percent) had been wounded and could not or would not do so. Sixty-nine ostensibly healthy soldiers also chose not to reenlist and made up 32 percent of those available, although some were probably traumatized, a condition then unrecognized. Fifty-eight of the remainder did join up again, or 27 percent of the "effectives." They represented 45 percent of those who were uninjured. As for bounty jumpers or deserters, I found only four deserters, and one soldier, James Burke, who committed fraud.

Were both unskilled workers and Irish Americans proportionately underrepresented in the Union Army, as McPherson claims? Out of the soldiers sampled from the Irish Brigade, I found occupational categories in the pension files for 214 men. More than half were unskilled workers: 60 soldiers described themselves as "laborers." Most of the other self-descriptions are relatively unskilled, with 55 labeling themselves as painters, porters, hawkers, street cleaners, or fruit vendors. Skilled workers included shoemakers, blacksmiths, bakers, a bookbinder, a tinsmith and so forth. McPherson's assumption that *Irish* and *unskilled* were interchangeable terms does not hold up for the Irish Brigade. Nor were its skilled members the American-born Irish. Indeed, 98 percent of the original sample were Irish-born who were also married to Irish Catholics.

What connection, if any, exists between the time our soldiers came to America and patriotic commitment? Of the 100 for whom we know the year of immigration, 71 came before 1859 and 29 arrived in 1860 or later. Thus less than one-third arrived when war seemed likely or had already begun. Only the latter may have hoped to find employment in the army. There is no way of knowing if these soldiers were impressed into the service. Many Irish-born did join the regiments of Dan Sickles' Excelsior Brigade. While one Tammany regiment supported the Irish Brigade's recruiting efforts, pension file data do not indicate whether Tammany played anything but a patriotic role in encouraging Irish Brigade volunteering.[44]

How many of our soldiers had arrived during the 1845–1848 famine migration? Only about a fifth, or 20 percent. Another fifty had come in the 1850s. Thus the bulk of the Irish Brigade recruits arrived during 1850–1865. While the aftershocks and smaller bouts of famine persisted until 1853–1854, and family reconstitution overseas continued to affect migration through those years, the real impetus for immigration shifted to the jobs boom in American capitalist expansion, which drew myriads of foreign workers from Britain and Germany as well as Ireland.[45] However, the recession of 1857–1859 halved the inflow from Ireland in 1858. In 1857, the Democratic Congress had passed the lowest tariff since 1790. Northern bankers and manufacturers blamed this development for the panic and low prices that followed. Yet "traders" in migration still hyped the country's opportunities and rarely spoke of the hard work facing such people. Soldiering offered more social status as the war for the Union expanded, thus becoming a preferred occupation over street paving or dock work.

After patriotism, one can rank other secondary motives for enlisting in the Irish Brigade. Foremost was the desire for political and social inclusion. Immigrants could earn admission into U.S. society through bravery in combat and honorable service. Even if, as in case of the Irish, such might be diminished as the acts of a "Celtic primitive warrior," such bravery and service were still assets. Second were a variety of material motives, including inducements offered to all Union soldiers, such as military pay and bounties. Of the sample of 250 Irish Brigade recruits providing exact years of enlistment, 23 percent enrolled in 1864–1865; some of these might have been "bounty hunters" (although there is no evidence to suggest this). All Union soldiers were eligible to receive 160 acres of public land under the 1862 Homestead Act if they would undertake to cultivate it. Third, Irish nationalism (that is, hostility toward England and its perceived ally, the South) was a motive. That the speeches of Brigade recruiters and leaders successfully pitched this last motive for enlisting underlines the effectiveness of shrewdly tapping into volunteers' feelings for their homeland.[46]

What was the impact of Civil War pensions on the New York Irish? Between 1861 and 1899, Congress passed 6,791 Civil War pensions acts. Although most were rate modifications, some were fundamental. The Grand Army of the Republic, the nationwide Union veterans' body, lobbied for these, aided by claims agents and pension lawyers and supported by their congressmen.

Claimants needed help for themselves and their dependents. The acts also covered deceased soldiers' widows and children (from 1861), as well as their dependent mothers and minor siblings (from 1862). Theda Skocpol has established the pensions' central role in the origin of modem federal social provision and the significance of pensions as a means of both honoring veterans and their families and embodying their pro-Union values in postwar policy. In an age when ordinary welfare entitlement was unknown, even unthinkable, these soldiers and their families were seen as fully deserving of not only belonging in civil society but also living honorably and decently, free from severe want. Such pensions certified as fully American even those who could not achieve normal living standards themselves, and who otherwise would have had lowly places in the social structures of the north and west.[47] Precisely which Brigade veterans and their dependents received these monies throws light on how much their service to America was rated.

The changing scope of these many pension acts showed increasing generosity of benefits and eligibility: "more money for more veterans over time." Around 2.4 million Union veterans survived the war, and 520,000 were classified as pensionable invalids by 1890 under general law and disability law criteria, apart from widows and others. Costs rose more than fourfold from 1870 to 1900, with Civil War pensions constituting more than 90 percent of these. The acts also exemplify the early effect of interest group mobilization on party platforms and congressional procedures. Precedents were strong: military pensions went back to the Revolutionary War, were federalized in 1789, and placed under a Bureau of Pensions after 1849. Now rapid economic growth eased their acceptance. Competition between political parties quickened improvements. General law provisions from 1862 required a degree of disability (or death) during actual service, pensioning only such men or their survivors. Rates and criteria for the awarding of such pensions changed between the 1860s and 1890. Disability was very broadly understood, but higher pension rates were reserved for severe and permanent incapacity.[48]

The first wartime act of July 22, 1861, granted any volunteer and regular soldier a pension if he was "wounded or disabled while in the service," awarding only a lump sum of $100 and any arrears of service monies to his widow in the event of his death. The second act, dated July 14, 1862, extended the pension entitlement to all who served in the Union forces, as well as to soldiers who suffered disease while in service. In a crucial precedent, it provided that a soldier's actual pension would be transferred to his immediate next of kin in the case of his death, although upon remarriage his widow would lose this benefit, as would his children upon reaching the age of sixteen. Other dependents, such as a mother or orphaned sisters, might claim such a pension, though with similar cut-off conditions. The basic award was made from the date of discharge, if the soldier filed for it within one year, or from the date of his death, if his eligible kin filed for it within that year. If the application were made after such deadlines, and then allowed, such pensions dated from the time at which the papers were filed.

Many subsequent acts amplified these decisions. A Pension Arrears Act of 1879 added a lump sum for date of discharge or death, the latter bringing welcome amounts to families. The most radical extension came in 1890, when Congress passed the Disability Pension Act.[49] This established the new principle of the "service pension": veterans could now receive pensions for disabilities that were not war related, and these could also be transferred to widows and other dependents. But the rates were markedly lower—one-half to one-third the sums for equivalent war-service disabilities. Still, the pensions committee of the Grand Army of the Republic (GAR) rightly held that the new act would give pensions to "all of the survivors of the war whose conditions of health are not practically perfect."[50] As one scholar has noted, the 1890 act passed because "it was the high bid for the political support of the 450,000 G.A.R. men and other ex-soldiers, with both the Republican and the Democratic parties bidding."[51] The Republican Congress of 1890 thus won the GAR vote with very generous legislation, and this helped to ensure the era of Republican congressional dominance from the early 1890s until 1912, partly as it cushioned many against the effects of the Depression of 1893–1897. By 1890, one in every seventy-seven people in the country received such a pension.[52]

Did the receipt of a pension help the New York City Irish gain security and respectability in America? Even if recipients were elderly and in poor health when they started receiving one, their children would often inherit what was left of the pension, and thereby enjoy a head start, as well as some respectable social status. Given Kerby Miller's darker view of the situation for many poorer industrial Irish in this time of their wider advancement, such a benefit was not insignificant, although the very details of applicants' circumstances may confirm part of his picture.[53] But survivability was also at stake. The later nineteenth-century income yardstick for a passable standard of living for un-pensioned workers in New York was $240 yearly. This was set against the type and amount of pension received by Irish Brigade veterans' or dependents' families calculated over the years of their receipt. Before the 1890 liberalization law, recipients had to be attested as neither criminal nor alcoholic. Witnesses had to verify how long, and in what circumstances, they had known the applicant, and then swear that the claimant was of sound moral character.[54] This process, when joined with service records, created a solid base of evidence linking those with Irish Brigade connections to the federal government, and especially to the Pensions' Bureau in Washington. It also linked these citizens directly to the Union, where most of their previous public links had been local, municipal and state-centered.

We can now benchmark fairly accurately the costs and living standards of the Irish (and of New Yorkers generally) between 1860 and 1900. Did such pensions enable these soldiers' families to achieve a standard equivalent to that of the annual $240 (living wage) baseline income required, often in the absence of permanent employment by some or all members of the household? Were the soldiers' families able to achieve this standard of living with the help of pensions? Of 260 pension applications from all three New York Irish Brigade regiments, 200 were awarded. Fifty pensions were awarded, and then completed, before 1890, presumably due to the death or remarriage of recipients. Ninety-three pensions were awarded before 1890 and continued thereafter. Fifty-four pensions were awarded after 1890. In all, pensions were granted to three-quarters of original applicants.[55]

Virtually all the pension recipients were respectable (or thus made so). Irish Brigade service proved to be worth a great deal in postwar terms. But only half of the recipients had gained assured "'living wage" standards. And one does not know if the 25 percent to whom grants were not made were left impoverished or simply did not really need them (perhaps a mix of these is true). For privates and their families, the average total income from pensions over the years was $2,462, and the soldiers received this money from age 38, on average. This would be striking enough in today's terms. Of those pensioned before 1890, their households divided roughly in half between those twenty families who were carried above the line of $240 by pensions and twenty-three families who fell below the line and were in the range that Lee Soltow labeled as poor, having a total estate of less than $100. Still, although the criteria of eligibility never included income status, the evidence suggests that the Irish (and human) tendency to furnish sob stories to solidify their claim was ever present, and it may have distorted the picture of aggregate family income downward, especially, for example, if the wife or widow took in lodgers or washing, or if older offspring contributed to the household.[56]

Of the 98 who received a pension before 1890 that continued thereafter, less than half, or 44 of them, exceeded the $240 per year figure, whereas half (54) did not and were poor. Of those pensioned only after 1890, 32 families had incomes of $240 per year or more, and 22 families had incomes approaching Soltow's baseline $100 poverty level. Had there been no Civil War safety net, many families in the Soltow poverty range would have perished in anonymity. Every family from all three groups obviously was drawn into purview of the federal pensions bureaucracy and, to that extent, was further assimilated. Most of these Irish Brigade recruits and their families had achieved their part of the social contract whereby to serve the country's army meant winning full citizenship, with various modes of empowerment. Sometimes the United States failed them, but their own grasp of its traditions, and of their own, did not. Witness the history of the Finn family.

Michael Finn was born on December 20, 1841, in Kings County (now Offaly), Ireland. With his family, he came to America in 1846 and later enlisted as a private in Company A, 88th New York Infantry Regiment. He was wounded at Antietam on September 17, 1862, and died three weeks later. His father, Patrick, and his mother, Catherine, had married on November 23, 1841, in Kings County, just in time for Michael's birth a month later. Another child named Julia was born, who became an invalid from age 10 onward. The family lived in perhaps half a dozen rented places in the 1860s and 1870s, always in lower midtown, on the east side. This was then the emergent Irish and German area above their older concentrations in lower Manhattan, the parishes being St. Gabriel and St. Stephen. It coincided with the 21st ward and was consistently populated by more than a quarter Irish-born from 1855 to 1875.[57] Patrick Finn lived with a friend in same ward after 1877, his wife having died on February 24, 1867.

Michael Finn's death had been both an economic and an emotional blow, for he had supported his family prior to his death. The father was "unable to earn sufficiently to support the family without the son's assistance," and Michael's enlistment left them hard pressed, "the father being only able to work on odd jobs whenever he could get one."[58] Other neighbors remembered Michael buying food with his mother at Mrs. Healy's store: "She would buy groceries and he would pay for them; the father did not earn over one hundred and fifty dollars a year previous to and since 1862; after the son went away to the army the family appeared to be very poor and were often in want of the necessities of life, the father being unable to support them."[59] The father was tired and old, and he lacked a skill with which to earn a living, but he was not intemperate. By his own recollection, Patrick said, "I have always been temperate. I might have gone on a little spree but only once in a great while."[60] The last $100 of the son's bounty policy paid for his mother's funeral expenses. As a common laborer with asthma, Patrick was willing to accept work but often could not find it. When he did, it was usually for "the usual laborer's wages of one dollar a day."[61] In an examination on September 6, 1876, the surgeon noted that "the right eye has been emptied of its contents. He is aged beyond his years—is poorly nourished. Disability is total, $8.00 a month."[62]

The Civil War and its aftereffects had firmly established the New York Irish Brigade recruits and their families as Americans. The *Irish American* had told Irishmen in its issue of November 11, 1851, to "thoroughly integrate as American citizens." The important prewar contexts for this long process of assimilation were the slums, laboring, parish life, church and Tammany assistance, and, perhaps most commonly, the general hustle to survive in the city. Discrimination experienced at Anglo-American hands sometimes created additional troubles for the Irish. But by volunteering in the federal war, they could make a major claim on full acceptance afterward. Recruitment posters made this situation explicit:

> YOUNG AMERICA AND OLD IRELAND
> ONE AND INSEPARABLE
> The COTTON-LORDS and TRAITOR-ALLIES of ENGLAND
> Must Be Put Down!
> ONCE AND FOR ALL—ONCE AND FOR EVER!
> IRISHMEN, TO THE FIELD !
> Irishmen up, Arm and Strike Victoriously for
> DEMOCRACY AND LIBERTY!
> The Rights and Power of the People.

With such emotive slogans, recruits were sought for New York regiments. The placard quoted above went on invoke the famous 69th Regiment, though it directed young Irishmen to another unit altogether. Orators like Charles P. Daly and Thomas F. Meagher used such themes to fill up Irish Brigade ranks, and Abraham Lincoln and Jefferson Davis made the same appeal for manpower at similar patriotic levels (and with a similar high moral tone). Only as such motives weakened after Antietam and Fredericksburg did stronger economic incentives come fully into play.

Thus nativism was now portrayed as contrary to the spirit of Irish American gallantry, as is evident in broadsides from the New York Historical Society. In "No Irish Need Apply," one John F. Poole skillfully wove these themes: "Though fools may flout and bigots rave, and fanatics may cry, Yet when they want good fighting men, the Irish may apply, And when for freedom and the right they raise the battle-cry, Then the Rebel ranks begin to think: no Irish need apply." And in "The Gallant 69th Regiment," another writer held forth:

> When rebels first attempted desolation,
> And swore they our land would deform,
> The "69th," our brave Army's foundation,
> Swore our Country should ride the foul storm.[63]

With the system of Civil War pensions, the federal government showed its gratitude to its soldiers, as it had after 1812–1815 and 1846–1848, but more generously than before. Most Irish Brigade families who applied for a pension were granted one. About half of those who received pensions were, at the very least, drawn up to the minimum standard of living for a family of four in New York City during those years. Even for those who still fell below the baseline figure, their receipt of a pension allowed them to stay in the lower class rather than falling into the underclass.

Other conclusions are revealed by analysis of these pension files regarding Irish Brigade family resilience and, by implication, their traditions. A comparison of privates and sergeants suggests that the average family size of privates was just over four members; their own life expectancy was 54 years, while that of their wives was 56 years. The privates had typically married at just over thirty (their wives just under thirty), and they were married for an average of 21 years (logically so, given their relatively late marriages and early deaths). Sergeants did marginally better in every category. Their family size averaged four and a half, and while they, too, married at 30, their wives, at 25, were younger. Sergeants lived until 60, and their wives until 73. Their marriages were thus longer, on average 27 years. Privates received, at 39 years of age, a gross total award of about $2,462 spread over fifteen years, while sergeants got $3,208, when aged 43 years, spread over 18 years. Clearly sergeants had better peacetime and wartime incomes (those of higher artisans), since they could choose younger brides long before receiving a pension. Privates had to wait and marry their contemporaries from home.[64]

Most recruits had volunteered for the Irish Brigade in the first three years of the war, before recruiting became big business, and, as recent immigrants, they were prone to extreme patriotism, perhaps as a unconscious technique of assimilation. Probably the pension culture, as much as the GAR that won it, gave the recruits grounds to continue this style long beyond the actual commitments of the 1860s.

NOTES

1. This chapter is a summary and revision of Marion Archer Truslow, "Peasants into Patriots: The New York Irish Brigade Recruits and Their Families in the Civil War Era, 1850–1890," unpublished Ph.D. diss., New York University, 1994, hereafter cited as Truslow, "Peasants into Patriots."

2. The pension file of Michael Finn, 1877, National Archives, Washington, D.C.

3. Dennis Clark, *Hibernia America: The Irish and Regional Cultures* (Westport, CT: Greenwood Press, 1986), 68. The fullest account is Ronald H. Bayor and Timothy J. Meagher, eds., *The New York Irish* (Baltimore: Johns Hopkins University Press, 1996).

4. Truslow, "Peasants into Patriots," tables, chapter IV, which sort and tabulate pension data for soldiers and families. The original pension case files in the National Archives are listed by their name and Irish Brigade regiment, on the microfilm index reel T-289, main microfilm room, National Archives, fifth floor.

5. Patrick J. Blessing, "The Irish in America," in *The Encyclopedia of the Irish in America*, edited by Michael Glazier (Notre Dame, IN: University of Notre Dame Press, 1999), 460–62. See also Robert Ernst, *Immigrant Life in New York City, 1825–1863* (Syracuse, NY: Syracuse University Press, 1994), 20, and Appendices I–IX, 185–231, for the 1855 New York State Census, which is more detailed since the U.S. Census for 1860. For an online version of the U.S. Census, see Campbell J. Gibson and Emily Lennon, "Historical Census Statistics on the Foreign-born Population of the United States: 1850–1990," in *Population Division Work Paper No. 29* (Washington, D.C.: Population Division, U.S. Bureau of the Census, February 1999), 1–18, available at http://www.census.gov/population/www/documentation/twps0029/twps0029.html.

6. Jeffrey A. Kroessler, *New York Year by Year: A Chronology of the Great Metropolis* (New York: New York University Press, 2002), 106; Edward K. Spann, *Gotham at War: New York City, 1860–1865* (Wilmington, DE: Scholarly Resources, 2002), 32–33 and 138–141; James Miller, *Miller's New York as It Is; or the Stranger's Guide-Book to the Cities of New York, Brooklyn, and Adjacent Places* (New York, 1865), 99.

7. Winch is quoted in William H.A. Williams, "Irish Song in America," in *The Encyclopedia of the Irish in America*, edited by Michael Glazier (Notre Dame, IN: University of Notre Dame Press, 1999), 477; Clark, *Hibernia America*, 1–33; Ernst, *Immigrant Life in New York City*, 69.

8. Pension files in the National Archives for the 88th, 69th, and 63rd Regiments of New York Infantry; and Truslow, "Peasants into Patriots," tables, 205-99.

9. Hasia Diner, *Erin's Daughters in America: Irish Immigrant Women in the Nineteenth Century* (Baltimore: Johns Hopkins University Press, 1983), 27. Interestingly, Irish women had few noneconomic activities. They were fully occupied running a household and raising children, as the pension case files demonstrate.

10. Ernst, *Immigrant Life in New York City*, 83; Carol Groneman, "The Bloody Ould Sixth: A Social Analysis of a New York City Working-Class Community in the Mid-19th Century," unpublished Ph.D. diss., University of Rochester, 1973; Edith Abbott, "Wages of Unskilled Labor in the United States, 1850-1900," *Journal of Political Economy* 8 (1905): 321-67; Edgar W. Martin, *The Standard of Living in 1860* (Chicago: University of Chicago Press, 1942), 393, 409, 422 (see 428 for the four-room tenement rent of $50 in 1860); Lee Soltow, *Men and Wealth in the United States, 1850-1970* (New Haven, CT: Yale University Press, 1975).

11. Abbott, "The Wages of Unskilled Labor," 359-60; E.D. Fite, *Social and Industrial Conditions in the North during the Civil War* (New York: F. Ungar, 1910), 184-85.

12. David Scobey, *Empire City: The Making and Meaning of the New York City Landscape* (Philadelphia: Temple University Press, 2002).

13. See Jay P. Dolan, *The Immigrant Church: New York's Irish and German Catholics, 1815-1865* (Notre Dame, IN: Notre Dame University Press, 1983), on which this section is based; John A. Hassard, *Life of Most Reverend John Hughes, D.D.* (New York: D. Appleton, 1866), 212; Emmet Larkin, "The Devotional Revolution in Ireland, 1850-1875," *American Historical Review* 77 (June 1972): 625-52; R.J. Purcell, "John Hughes," in *Dictionary of National Biography*, edited by Dumas Malone, vol. 9 (New York, 1943), 352-55.

14. Oscar Handlin, *Boston's Immigrants*, 2nd ed. (Cambridge, MA: Belknap Press of Harvard University Press, 1959), 128.

15. Dolan, *The Immigrant Church*, 46ff.

16. Handlin, *Boston's Immigrants*, 128.

17. John Miller, *The End of Religious Controversy* (New York, n.d.), 243 and 122; Robert Gorman, *Catholic Apologetical Literature in the United States, 1784-1858* (Washington, D.C.: Catholic University of America Press, 1939), 53ff.; Dolan, *The Immigrant Church*, 55-56.

18. Dolan, *The Immigrant Church*, 62. The quotations in the following paragraphs are from the pension file of Michael Sands in the National Archives.

19. James A. Burns, *The Growth and Development of the Catholic School in the United States* (New York: Benziger, 1912), 124; Dolan, *The Immigrant Church*, 105; Ernst, *Immigrant Life in York City*, 140-41.

20. Ernst, *Immigrant Life in York City*, 115-16.

21. Christian Brothers, *The Third Book of Reading Lessons* (Montreal, 1860), 4; Christian Brothers, *The Literary Class-Book or Fourth Series of Select Reading Lessons in Prose and Rhyme* (New York, 1855), 248-50.

22. The Rev. Dr. J. Cummings, *Songs for Catholic Schools and the Catechism in Rhyme* (New York, 1862), 35-37; Dolan, *The Immigrant Church*, 118.

23. Orestes Brownson, "The Church and the Republic," *Brownson's Quarterly Review* (July 1856): 303.

24. Dolan, *The Immigrant Church*, 137.

25. *Ibid.*, 162.

26. Yehoshua Arieli, *Individualism and Nationalism in American Ideology* (Cambridge, MA: Harvard University Press, 1964), 297.

27. Dale T. Knobel, *Paddy and the Republic* (Middletown, CT: Wesleyan University Press, 1986), 40; James H. Kettner, *The Development of American Citizenship, 1608-1870* (Chapel Hill: University of North Carolina Press, 1978), 128.

28. Clark, *Hibernia America*, introduction and 54-55.

29. Florence Gibson, *The Attitudes of the New York Irish toward State and National Affairs, 1848-1892* (New York: Columbia University Press, 1951), 18; Sidney D. Brummer, *Political History of New York State during the Period of the Civil War* (New York: Longmans,

Green, & Co., 1911); Ernest A. McKay, *The Civil War and New York City* (Syracuse, NY: Syracuse University Press, 1990), 13; Ernst, *Immigrant Life in New York*, ch. 14.

30. Adrian Cook, *Armies of the Streets* (Lexington: University Press of Kentucky, 1974), 189; Ernst, *Immigrant Life in New York*, 103; Eugene Weber, *Peasants into Frenchmen* (Stanford, CA: Stanford University Press, 1976), 255; Carl Wittke, *The Irish in America* (reprint, New York: Russell & Russell, 1970), 104. On pubs, see Brian Harrison, "Pubs," in *The Victorian City: Images and Realities*, 2 vols., edited by H.J. Dyos and Michael Wolff (London: Routledge & Kegan Paul, 1973), 1:171–82.

31. Ernst, *Immigrant Life in New York*, 163–66.

32. Wittke, *The Irish in America*, 122.

33. Knobel, *Paddy and the Republic*, 65–82.

34. This account stems from Cook, *The Armies of the Streets*, 158–209.

35. Susannah Ural Bruce, *The Harp and the Eagle* (New York: New York University Press, 2006), 147–48.

36. James F. MacManus III, Phoenix, to James M. McPherson, February 6, 1999, courtesy of the sender.

37. Bruce, *The Harp and the Eagle*, 13, table 1.1, "Irish-born Populations in Major U.S. Cities, 1860." The data is the same as that which underpins the point in note 38 below.

38. James McPherson, "Civil War," *New York Review of Books* 37 (September 13, 1990), 33–34; James McPherson, *Battle Cry of Freedom* (New York: Oxford University Press, 1985), 606–10.

39. Don H. Doyle, *The Cause of All Nations: An International History of the American Civil War* (New York: Basic Books, 2015), 176.

40. New York State overall provides the best alternative model. The city itself, including Brooklyn, provided just under 43 percent of the state's manpower and of its casualties; yet it made up only 28 percent of the state population. By contrast, the Irish-born of New York and Brooklyn in 1860 constituted 24.6 percent of the combined population of the two cities and, even apart from the American-born Irish, logically provided much of these cities' disproportionate state service. "A Statistical Analysis of the Immigrant Hypothesis," section VII, p. 9, in James F. MacManus III to James McPherson, February 2, 1998.

41. The *New York Times* of January 14, 1864, hyped such reenlistment at 66 percent to encourage it. Contrast the original tradition with recent skepticism: David P. Conyngham, *The Irish Brigade and Its Campaigns* (New York: W. McSorley & Co., 1867), 424–44; Bruce, *The Harp and the Eagle*, 82, 102–10, 119–21, 132–35, 136, 151–59, 171–78, 188–89, 190–95. Bruce should be read in the light of J.F. MacManus's data (see note 36).

42. From the pension file of Private John Gorman, 63rd Regiment of New York Infantry, National Archives.

43. See McPherson, *Battle Cry of Freedom*, 322–30, 430, 485, 491–93, 592, 606–9, for that author's various views; Eugene C. Murdock, *Patriotism Limited* (Kent, OH: Kent State University Press, 1967), and *One Million Men: The Civil War Draft in the North* (Madison: State Historical Society of Wisconsin, 1971), 3–177; Peter Levine, "Draft Evasion in the North during the Civil Wet 1862–1865," *Journal of American History* 67 (March 1981): 816–34.

44. See Truslow, "Peasants into Patriots," 130–42, for Irish Brigade recruiting.

45. Thomas Brinley, *Migration and Economic Growth* (Cambridge: Cambridge University Press, 1973); W.F. Adams, *Ireland and Irish Emigration to the New World* (New Haven, CT: Yale University Press, 1932); George Potter, *To the Golden Door* (Boston: Little, Brown, 1960); Terry Coleman, *Passage to America* (London: Hutchinson, 1972).

46. See Grady McWhiney and Perry P. Jamieson, *Attack and Die: Civil War Military Tactics and the Southern Heritage* (Tuscaloosa: University of Alabama Press, 1982), for an imagined warrior tradition and its supposed impact on the South in the Civil War. Critiques show that such were not in fact the Confederacy's battle tactics: see R.E. Beringer et al., *Why the South Lost the Civil War* (Athens: University of Georgia Press, 1986), 458–81; Herman Hattaway and Archer Jones, *How the North Won* (Urbana: University of Illinois Press, 1983), 721–32.

47. William Henry Glasson, *History of Military Pension Legislation in the United States* (New York: Columbia University Press, 1900), 122, and his expanded and updated *Federal*

Military Pensions in the United States (New York: Oxford University Press, 1918); John William Oliver, *History of Civil War Military Pensions, 1861-1885* (Madison, WI, 1917); Theda Skocpol, *Protecting Soldiers and Mothers: The Political Origin of Social Policy in the United States* (Cambridge, MA: Belknap Press of Harvard University Press, 1992).

48. Claudia Linares, *The Civil War Pension Law: Working Paper 2001-2* (Chicago: Center for Population Economics, University of Chicago, 2001), 2-3, 4-5, 8-15.

49. See Glasson, *Federal Military Pensions*, 234ff., on which this summary is based, and Oliver, *History of the Civil War Military Pensions*, 6-70.

50. Glasson, *Federal Military Pensions*, citing the *Journal of the 24th National Encampment, G.A.R. 1890*, 169.

51. Glasson, *Federal Military Pensions*, 238.

52. *Ibid.*, 250-95.

53. Kerby Miller, *Emigrants and Exiles: Ireland and the Irish Exodus to North America* (New York: Oxford University Press, 1985), 499-505.

54. The pension file of Private Michael Daly, 63rd Regiment New York Infantry, National Archives, includes the list of just under a dozen documents required of all soldiers (or heirs) who applied for Civil War pensions. These included, where relevant, a marriage license, proof of divorce, various depositions and death certificate.

55. Groneman, "The Bloody Ould Sixth," 92; Abbott, "Wages of Unskilled Labor," 321-367; Martin, *The Standard of Living in 1860*, 378, 393, 409, 422, 425, 428; Marion Casey, "The Irish Middle Class in New York City, 1850-1870," MA thesis, New York University, 1986 (which put the percentage of the Irish-born male population with some wealth at 42); Wittke, *Irish in America*, 217; Ernst, *Immigrant Life in New York*, 73-79; W. Lloyd Warner, *Social Class in America* (New York: Harper, 1960); Report of National Bureau of Economic Research, *Trends in American Economy in the Nineteenth Century* (Princeton, NJ: Princeton University Press, 1960), 141-90, 449-99; James D. Smith, ed., *Studies in Income and Wealth* (New York: Columbia University Press, 1975), 233.

56. Pension file of Michael Finn, National Archives. This account is derived from documents in that file (see below).

57. Bayor and Meagher, *The New York Irish*, 553. The known addresses were 311B 35th Street from 1861 to 1869; 46th Street and 2nd Avenue from 1869 to 1874; and 46th Street between 2nd and 3rd Avenues from 1875 to 1876.

58. Michael Finn pension file, deposition of Catherine Corrigan, October 17, 1876.

59. *Ibid.*, deposition of Julia Fay, n.d.

60. *Ibid.*, deposition of Patrick Finn, May 21, 1877.

61. *Ibid.*, deposition of Martin Carregan, May 13, 1877.

62. *Ibid.*, surgeon's deposition, September 6, 1870. The joint savings account book found in his pension file upon her death showed a yearly balance between $115 and $55.

63. William D. Griffin, *A Portrait of the Irish in America* (Dublin: Academy Press, 1981), illus. 198.

64. Truslow, "Peasants into Patriots," tables, chapters IV and V.

BIBLIOGRAPHY

Abbott, Edith. "Wages of Unskilled Labor in the United States, 1850-1900." *Journal of Political Economy* 8 (1905): 321-67.
Adams, W.F. *Ireland and Irish Emigration to the New World*. New Haven, CT: Yale University Press, 1932.
Bayor, Ronald H., and Timothy J. Meagher, eds. *The New York Irish*. Baltimore: Johns Hopkins University Press, 1996.
Blessing, Patrick J. "The Irish in America." In *The Encyclopedia of the Irish in America*, edited by Michael Glazier. Notre Dame, IN: Notre Dame University Press, 1999.
Brinley, Thomas. *Migration and Economic Growth*. Cambridge: Cambridge University Press, 1973.
Brownson, Orestes. "The Church and the Republic." *Brownson's Quarterly Review* (July 1856).

———. "Irish Immigrants and American Progress." *Brownson's Quarterly Review* (October 1855).
Bruce, Susannah Ural. *The Harp and the Eagle*. New York: New York University Press, 2006.
Brummer, Sidney D. *Political History of New York State during the Period of the Civil War*. New York: Longmans, Green, & Co., 1911.
Casey, Marion. "The Irish Middle Class in New York City, 1850–1870." M.A. thesis, New York University, 1986.
Clark, Dennis. *Hibernia America: The Irish and Regional Cultures*. Westport, CT: Greenwood Press, 1986.
Coleman, Terry. *Passage to America*. London: Hutchinson, 1972.
Conyngham, David P. *The Irish Brigade and Its Campaigns*. New York: W. McSorley & Co., 1867.
Cook, Adrian. *The Armies of the Streets*. Lexington: University Press of Kentucky, 1974.
Diner, Hasia. *Erin's Daughters in America: Irish Immigrant Women in the Nineteenth Century*. Baltimore: Johns Hopkins University Press, 1983.
Dolan, Jay P. *The Immigrant Church: New York's Irish and German Catholics, 1815–1865*. Notre Dame, IN: Notre Dame University Press, 1983.
Doyle, Don H. *The Cause of All Nations: An International History of the American Civil War*. New York: Basic Books, 2015.
Ernst, Robert. *Immigrant Life in New York City, 1825–1863*. Syracuse, NY: Syracuse University Press, 1994.
Fite, E.D. *Social and Industrial Conditions in the North during the Civil War*. New York: F. Ungar, 1910.
Gibson, Florence. *The Attitudes of the New York Irish toward State and National Affairs, 1848–1892*. New York: Columbia University Press, 1951.
Glasson, William H. *Federal Military Pensions in the United States*. New York: Oxford University Press, 1918.
———. *History of Military Pension Legislation in the United States*. New York: Columbia University Press, 1900.
Gorman, Robert. *Catholic Apologetical Literature in the United States, 1784–1858*. Washington, D.C.: Catholic University of America Press, 1939.
Griffin, William D. *A Portrait of the Irish in America*. Dublin: Academy Press, 1981.
Groneman, Carol. "The Bloody Ould Sixth: A Social Analysis of a New York City Working-Class Community in the Mid-19th Century." Unpublished Ph.D. dissertation, University of Rochester, 1973.
Handlin, Oscar. *Boston's Immigrants*. 2nd ed. Cambridge, MA: Belknap Press of Harvard University Press, 1959.
Kettner, James H. *The Development of American Citizenship, 1608–1870*. Chapel Hill: University of North Carolina Press, 1978.
Knobel, Dale T. *Paddy and the Republic*. Middletown, CT: Wesleyan University Press, 1986.
Kroessler, Jeffrey A. *New York Year by Year: A Chronology of the Great Metropolis*. New York: New York University Press, 2002.
Larkin, Emmet. "The Devotional Revolution in Ireland, 1850–1875." *American Historical Review* 77 (June 1972): 625–52.
Levine, Peter. "Draft Evasion in the North during the Civil Wet 1862–1865." *Journal of American History* 67 (March 1981): 816–34.
Linares, Claudia. *The Civil War Pension Law: Working Paper 2001-2*. Chicago: Center for Population Economics, University of Chicago, 2001.
Martin, Edgar W. *The Standard of Living in 1860*. Chicago: University of Chicago Press, 1942.
McKay, Ernest A. *The Civil War and New York City*. Syracuse, NY: Syracuse University Press, 1990.
McPherson, James. *Battle Cry of Freedom: The Civil War Era*. New York: Oxford University Press, 1985.
McWhiney, Grady, and Perry P. Jamieson. *Attack and Die: Civil War Military Tactics and the Southern Heritage*. Tuscaloosa: University of Alabama Press, 1982.
Miller, James. *Miller's New York as It Is; or Stranger's Guide-Book to the Cities of New York, Brooklyn, and Adjacent Places*. New York, 1865.

Miller, John. *The End of Religious Controversy.* New York, n.d.
Miller, Kerby. *Emigrants and Exiles: Ireland and the Irish Exodus to North America.* New York: Oxford University Press, 1985.
Murdock, Eugene C. *One Million Men: The Civil War Draft in the North.* Madison: State Historical Society of Wisconsin, 1971.
———. *Patriotism Limited.* Kent, OH: Kent State University Press, 1967.
National Archives, Civil War pension files, Washington, D.C.
Oliver, John William. *History of Civil War Military Pensions, 1861–1885.* Madison, WI, 1917.
Potter, George. *To the Golden Door.* Boston: Little, Brown, 1960.
Purcell, R.J. "John Hughes." In *Dictionary of National Biography*, edited by Dumas Malone, volume 9. New York, 1943.
Report of National Bureau of Economic Research. *Trends in American Economy in the Nineteenth Century.* Princeton, NJ: Princeton University Press, 1960.
Scobey, David. *Empire City: The Making and Meaning of the New York City Landscape.* Philadelphia: Temple University Press, 2002.
Skocpol, Theda. *Protecting Soldiers and Mothers: The Political Origin of Social Policy in the United States.* Cambridge, MA: Belknap Press of Harvard University Press, 1992.
Smith, James D., ed. *Studies in Income and Wealth.* New York: Columbia University Press, 1975.
Soltow, Lee. *Men and Wealth in the United States, 1850–1970.* New Haven, CT: Yale University Press, 1975.
Spann, Edward K. *Gotham at War: New York City, 1860–1865.* Wilmington, DE: Scholarly Resources, 2002.
Truslow, Marion A. "Peasants into Patriots: The New York Irish Brigade Recruits and Their Families in the Civil War Era, 1850–1890." Ph.D. dissertation, New York University, 1994.
Warner, W. Lloyd. *Social Class in America.* New York: Harper, 1960.
Weber, Eugene. *Peasants into Frenchmen.* Stanford, CA: Stanford University Press, 1976.
Wittke, Carl. *The Irish in America.* Reprint, New York: Russell & Russell, 1970.

Philadelphia Irish During the Civil War

PHILLIP G. PATTEE

Deployed in front of a copse of trees along Cemetery Ridge just south of the little town of Gettysburg, Pennsylvania, on July 3, 1863, was the 69th Pennsylvania Volunteer Infantry Regiment. The 69th Pennsylvania, along with the 71st, 72nd, and 106th Pennsylvania, was part of the Philadelphia Brigade, so called because each of these regiments was recruited from the Philadelphia area, the city of brotherly love.[1] The 69th Pennsylvania was one of the Union Army's Irish regiments, recruited from the Irish Catholic population in Philadelphia, while the 72nd Pennsylvania, or Fire Zouaves, was made up of recruits from Philadelphia's fire companies. The soldiers in the other regiments were drawn from the population at large.[2] Although the men of the 69th had seen some hard fighting the previous day, beating back a Confederate attack made by Wilcox's Brigade, they were still deployed along the front line at their brigade's left, with the 71st Pennsylvania on the right and the 106th Pennsylvania in the center and slightly behind. The 72nd Pennsylvania was the brigade reserve even though it had been the least engaged during the second day of fighting at Gettysburg.[3]

Major General George G. Meade, the commander of the Army of the Potomac, had expected the Confederates to attack again and that the attack would come in the center of his formation, where the Philadelphia Brigade was deployed. After an opening artillery barrage, the likes of which had not been seen previously in battle—and that lasted nearly two hours—the men of the 69th Pennsylvania saw the Confederates line up to commence their attack, confirming Meade's expectations about where the attack would come. Colonel Dennis O'Kane attempted to reassure his men with patriotic words, reminding reminded them that they were fighting on the soil of their own state, but, as Frank Boyle pointed out in *A Party of Mad Fellows*, these words did not ring true with the actual Irish Catholic experience during the war.[4] The irony of fighting in their own state was not lost on them. What stake did the Irish have in Pennsylvania? Many of the men within the ranks of the Irish regiments were immigrants; others were the sons of immigrants. The Irish potato famine had caused starvation, and Ireland felt the continued impact of the social, political, and economic forces that had been transforming the island since the Napoleonic wars. As a result, millions of Irish migrated to America.[5]

For the Irish, the concern was twofold: they sought political and economic status.[6] Gains in these two areas would solve most of the problems that confronted many of them on a daily basis. For those born in Ireland, the journey to Philadelphia had not changed their basic concerns or improved their political and economic situation. If things could not get better for those born in Ireland, how and when could it improve for their sons and daughters? Perhaps fighting in the war to preserve the Union would make Pennsylvania their state, but on July 3, 1863, it was not.

Nearly twenty years before the three-day battle at Gettysburg, the Irish and their fellow Philadelphians fought each other in a period of violent rioting. The fighting in 1844 was between local Native Americans and Irish Catholics. As the time, the term "Native Americans" did not refer to the indigenous tribes that originally inhabited North America, as it does now. During the 1800s, Native Americans were generally white Protestants, born in America, who were staunchly anti-immigration and, as a consequence, anti-immigrant. Their aggression and frustration over competition for jobs was directed at the largest group of immigrants in Philadelphia: the Irish Catholics.

One Native American rally to protest immigration was located in the center of an Irish Catholic neighborhood, apparently with the intention of offending the residents, and was broken up by heckling Irish Catholics throwing rocks and garbage. The Native Americans responded with another rally three days later, which provoked further fighting. This time the Irish used weapons to break up the rally, killing one Protestant man, George Shiffler. In the following days Native American groups attacked an Irish fire company; then they set fire to Irish homes and burned both St. Michael's and St. Augustine's churches. This violence was finally stopped when the governor placed Philadelphia under martial law. On July 4, 1844, another Native American rally paraded to Independence Hall, involving some 5,000 marchers and a crowd nearly double that size cheering from the sidewalks.[7]

The backlash from the riots prompted the mayor, who was of the Native American Party, and the city government to incorporate the city with the outlying areas and professionalize the Philadelphia police force.[8] Because the Native Americans had political power, an all-white, native police force of 900 men was appointed. This group had little credibility among the Irish Catholic community, and the police were often fearful of venturing into Irish neighborhoods.[9]

When Democratic leaders Lewis Cassidy and William McMullen helped get Richard Vaux elected mayor in 1856, Vaux appointed some Irish to the police force.[10] In one early example of patronage, William McMullen was offered an appointment as a lieutenant of the force. Although McMullen did not accept, he did get six members of the Moyamensing Hose Company appointed to the force.[11] The addition of Irish Catholics among the police lent stability to Philadelphia, but Native American sentiments toward the Irish did not disappear.[12] There was a significant political resurgence of nativism in the mid–1850s when the Native American Party reappeared as the Know Nothing Party.[13] The Native American Party had split over expansion of slavery into new territories and lost its political power. This did not mean that concerns over immigrants had ceased to be an issue; it merely became politically less important than the question of what to do about slavery. The benefits for the Irish Catholic population in Philadelphia was that this spelled an end to organized political opposition to them as a group.[14]

The benefit derived from the splintering of organized political opposition to Irish Catholic immigrants, however, did not translate into increased opportunities or improved public opinion. A 20 percent sample of Philadelphia's fourth ward in the 1860 census showed that 44 percent of Irish immigrant men worked as laboring men, while another 9 percent held jobs as watermen, or men who did odd jobs for hire on the waterfront. Eleven percent were mariners or seamen, and 26 percent operated or worked in some small business, such as a store operator, a clerk, or something like a blacksmith that required more skill. Only 8 percent held jobs in the new industrialized trades. There were a total of 58 different job types listed for Irish immigrant men in this sample.[15]

In a similar sample of Irish immigrant women, 74 percent had no employment listed, while 16 percent worked as domestic servants of some type. Seven percent worked as seamstresses and 2 percent were tailoresses. Of twelve types of jobs listed, the remaining five made up only 1 percent of the sample.[16]

Classified advertisements from the *Public Ledger*, a leading Philadelphia newspaper, in 1849 show something of what sentiment toward immigrants was like when Native Americans held power in the city, thus providing a type of benchmark for public feeling toward Irish immigrants. While the *Public Ledger* did not represent the opinions of the entire population of Philadelphia, it did have the widest circulation of any newspaper in the city and presented itself as independent of political affiliation. (That claim notwithstanding, the *Public Ledger* actually supported James Buchanan, the Democratic candidate, for the presidency in 1856.[17]) The *Public Ledger* from November 12, 1849, has several jobs listed for domestic help. Many of these advertisements called for "an American Protestant woman to do light cooking," "a white American girl as child nurse," or a "white Protestant girl," indicating that a German girl might have been acceptable for employment, but not an Irish Catholic. Other advertisements that called for dressmakers and "thirty women to do plain sewing" did not specify Protestant or American in the text, perhaps indicating that Irish Catholics could be hired as long as they were not allowed in the employer's home.[18] Classified advertisements from the *Public Ledger* in early 1860 showed the same open discrimination against Irish Catholic women. Postings asking for servants, chambermaids, and cooks called for a "Protestant girl," a "White American girl," or a "Protestant child nurse," for example. Once again, advertisements for seamstresses did not specify white, Protestant, or American. Such advertisements, and the editor's willingness to publish them in a paper with at least a mildly Democratic stance, is one indicator that underlying social attitudes toward Irish Catholic immigrants had not changed due to the collapse of the Native American Party.

In contrast, advertisements soliciting male employees did not specify "white, Protestant, or American."[19] A possible explanation for this discrepancy is that the supply of jobs for seamstresses or laborers exceeded the demand. For immigrant men, this argument may have merit, because less than 1 percent of the Irish immigrant men in the above census sample had nothing listed for employment.[20] But this does not explain the discrimination toward Irish Catholic women. Apparently the lower wages and demand for labor was enough for Irishmen to routinely find work, but when it came to accepting a girl into one's home as a servant, the discrimination remained consistent throughout the Civil War, when there was glut of women working as seamstresses.[21] The number of girls available for work exceeded demand, so employers and unscrupulous contractors diminished wages. But the advertisements in the *Public Ledger* only openly discriminate against Irish Catholics for the jobs that would place them in a household. Discrimination against Irish Catholic men was more subtle; they were accepted a low-wage laborers, but few could get work where they would learn skills and earn higher wages. This social environment kept most Irish Catholics firmly in support of the Democratic Party.[22]

When the Civil War erupted, however, many Irishmen supported the Union cause even though the Democratic Party platform was sympathetic to southern states' concerns. William McMullen and many of his cohort in the Killers (an Irish street gang associated with the Moyamensing Hose Company) joined the Union Army under a three-month enlistment. A local group of Irishmen met at McDonough's on Sixth Street on April 22, 1861, with the idea of forming their own company. Their activity included electing officers. William McMullen was elected captain and Folyarnd E. Degan first lieutenant, with John Beam and James T. Hamer elected as second lieutenants.[23] This appears to have been a precaution taken to avoid the experiences that McMullen and other Irish volunteers had during the Mexican-American War, when they originally had officers placed in charge of their company who were members of the Know Nothings. McMullen and his fellow soldiers had refused to serve under those appointed officers.[24]

By April 23, 1861, the newspapers were calling for the formation of several companies under the leadership of Colonel Pleasanton.[25] McMullen's company was incorporated into the newly formed 24th Pennsylvania Volunteer Infantry, served for three months and disbanded. Later, when recruiting began for three-year terms, the 24th was reformed into the 69th Pennsylvania Volunteer Infantry, which was styled after the 69th New York Volunteer Infantry, an Irish regiment.[26]

Rachel Filene Seidman cites articles from newspapers at this time urging women to assume a role of self-sacrifice to support the war. She argues that the editors of these articles believed that the women's proper political role was in the home.[27] However, there are other publications that called for the women to make uniforms and other items for the army. In response, the women turned out in droves at the Girard House (and other less well-known places) to make the uniforms, haversacks, and other implements that the men would need for war.

One article called on women to do all manner of activities to support the war:

> In this supplying our soldiers with clothing, in making cartridges, in forming societies to attend to families of those wounded or killed, and in various other ways, our women may make themselves helpmeets of the brave men who are marching to the battlefield, and we are very sure that nothing falling within their province will be left undone.[28]

Another advertisement also showed the ladies where they could make material contribution to the war effort:

> Attn Ladies! Ladies wishing to volunteer for the Union cause will find an opportunity at Girard House. 10,000 Suits of Clothing needed without delay. ... All able to manage a sewing machine or handle a needle may find something to do and be paid for their services if they wish.[29]

But by April 25, 1861, only a few days later, at least one reporter recognized the impact that volunteering would have on the poor women who had been dependent on husbands or only themselves for income. In an article titled "The Poor Sewing Women," the reporter states,

> It may be very patriotic in ladies of wealth to offer their gratuitous service to the govt. to assist in the manufacture of clothing for the soldiers, but it seems to be also a want of charity on their part to occupy places desired by so many industrious poor status women whom the Government are willing and able to pay.[30]

As the war went on, even those women working for wages continued to suffer at the hands of unscrupulous contractors. Wages declined while contractors' profits increased, and inflation made even modest wage increases insubstantial.[31] As a point of comparison, the piece rate for lined blouses decreased from $0.45 at the Schuylkill Arsenal in 1861 to $0.40 in 1864. The rate paid to sewing women by contractors was much lower, nominally $0.20 paid per lined blouse in 1864.[32] Yet, in a contract awarded in late May 1864, the federal government paid contractors $3.54 for each lined blouse.[33]

Despite the profits made by contractors, the government took pains to protect them by delaying the publication of contracts for several days. Apparently, if contracts were announced before contractors had an opportunity to purchase the necessary raw materials, dealers in fabrics would raise prices and make an unreasonable profit. Contractors were notified of the awards, but the government would not release the information for several days to allow contractors to purchase raw materials at fair prices.[34] These same contractors were generally unwilling to pass this consideration on to their employees. Over several years, rates paid to women declined to the point that some earned as little as $1.50 a week.[35] Another example is of two women, who worked together and were paid only $0.25 per haversack. It took both of them working a fourteen-hour day to turn out five haversacks.[36]

The situation had gotten so bad that some newspapers urged the women to organize and strike or, as argued in the *Public Ledger*, to swallow their foolish pride and find employment in higher-paying domestic servant jobs. Rachel Seidman points out that many thousands of women first entered the work force as seamstresses at this time.[37] This claim is supported by the newspaper calls for women to turn out 10,000 uniforms immediately.[38] The women elected not to organize into unions initially and instead directly petitioned the government to intervene on their behalf for higher wages. As weeks went by, the ladies became split over the appropriate action to take. While some eventually formed a union, it was not supported by a sufficient number of women, did not strike, and was formed so late in the war that it did not prove effective in raising the wages of the sewing women.[39] Rachel Seidman's evidence from Philadelphia's "Register of Prostitutes" shows that many women—deprived of financial support from husband and relatives who were in the Union Army, and not regularly paid, or who had been killed—were forced to turn to prostitution as a means of economic survival.[40]

All sewing women were affected by the low wages for seamstresses, but Irish Catholic women were particularly dependent upon these jobs. Through 1863, and even as late as April 1864, advertisements for domestic servants still called for "Protestant, American girls."[41] Because of discrimination, Irish Catholic women had fewer opportunities to find better employment than their Protestant, American-born counterparts.

Nevertheless, there were those sensitive to Irish women's plight. The *Public Ledger* ran a notice calling for information on women who felt that they were underpaid, whatever their occupation, making it clear that the organization helped all women, not just sewing women. The solicitation for information was strategically placed in the classified section so that any woman looking for work would find it and perhaps respond.[42]

At least one business had started to assist widows and relatives in collecting back pay and bounties that women felt were owed to them for their husbands' and relatives' military service.[43] As the war progressed and casualties mounted, even the sporadic pay sent home by individual soldiers often stopped. Widows could then turn to collectors, who would help them get bounty money and back pay owed. Bounties were significant as an inducement to get men to enlist. Recruits would receive $302 from the federal government; veterans would be paid $402. To this sum, Philadelphia would add $250, and the ward another $25. This bounty was sufficient to help Philadelphia repeatedly fill its quota for soldiers and avoid the necessity of filling the ranks through the draft.[44] However, not all of the bounty money was paid to an enlisting soldier up front. Most of it was withheld as a hedge against desertion, so often widows and relatives would have to seek help to get money owed for a man who had served honorably and died in the line of duty. Obviously this was a considerable sum to a woman earning about $1.50 per week and important to collect even if a significant amount would be lost in compensating a bounty collector.

With things this bad on the home front throughout 1861 and 1862, they were not much better for those serving in the Union Army. The Confederates had won battle after battle, many times inflicting terrible losses on their Union foes. The back-to-back Union losses at Fredericksburg and Chancellorsville were particularly unsettling. The Irish Brigade, including the 116th Pennsylvania Volunteer Infantry, another Irish regiment from Philadelphia, suffered severely in successive charges at Marye's Heights in the Battle of Fredericksburg.[45] With hard economic times, and a dismal war record for the Union Army, Peace Democrats in Philadelphia argued that the war was unwinnable. They pushed for a negotiated peace with the Confederacy, claiming that it was in the best interests of the nation so that the economy could return to a normal state.[46]

Regarding the heavy Irish losses at Fredericksburg, Craig A. Warren argues that despite the subsequent heroic accounts of this battle written by Father William Corby, these losses demoralized the Irish in America.[47] Warren also quotes the *Irish American* as portraying the Irish troops on and off the battlefield as the target of unjust discrimination and abuse by nativist leaders.[48] The formation of exclusive Irish regiments, such as those in the

Irish Brigade and the 69th Pennsylvania in the Philadelphia Brigade, which were ostensibly designed to protect Irishmen from the depredations of nativist officers, might have instead facilitated the abuse of the Irish by brigade and division commanders. After the Battle of Fredericksburg, Brigadier General Thomas Francis Meagher had asked for relief for the Irish Brigade for rest and recruiting. Other brigades had been given such relief, particularly black regiments from Maine, Massachusetts, and Connecticut, but Meagher's request was denied.[49]

After the Union disaster in the next major battle at Chancellorsville, the 116th Pennsylvania was assigned as the rearguard to protect the retreating Union Army from Confederate pursuit.[50] Major St. Clair Mulholland was credited with leading the 116th Pennsylvania in a brilliant fight, for which he was eventually awarded the Congressional Medal of Honor.[51] It is difficult to discern whether the Irish regiments were used excessively because of anti-immigrant sentiments or whether commanders relied upon them because they had a reputation as hard fighters. The truth is probably some of both. Some commanders disparaged the Irish while others thought highly of them.

By the second day of fighting at Gettysburg, the entire Irish Brigade—which included the 116th Pennsylvania and four other Irish regiments—had only 530 men.[52] This is the equivalent of five full-strength companies. They were called on to reinforce General Daniel E. Sickles' Third Corps and given a position on his extreme left. At one point the brigade paused during its march to support Sickles, whereupon Father William Corby, the brigade chaplain, gave them a general absolution. Although this practice was common in Catholic countries of Europe, it was new in America, and Corby had never done this for the brigade before. The men of the 140th Pennsylvania, in Samuel K. Zook's brigade, marching directly behind the Irishmen in column, were Presbyterian almost to a man. Private Robert Laird Stewart, a witness to the event, remarked later,

> At a given signal every man of the command fell on his knees and with head bowed low received from [Father Corby] the sacrament of extreme unction. Instinctively every man of our regiment took of his cap and no doubt many a prayer from men of Protestant faith, who could conscientiously not bow the knee in a service of that nature, went up to God in the impressive and awe inspiring moment.[53]

In a moment it was over and they were off once again to reinforce Sickles.

As the 116th Pennsylvania advanced to the right of Sickles' line, there remained a large gap between the Third Corps and General Hancock's Second Corps. It was in this area that the Confederate soldiers of Ambrose Wright's brigade attacked the flank of the 116th Pennsylvania and the Confederates of Cadmus Wilcox's brigade attacked the flank of the 69th Pennsylvania. After some desperate fighting, Wright and Wilcox were compelled to give up their gains because there were not supported by subsequent Confederate troops.[54]

That evening, Major General George G. Meade's war council concluded that if General Robert E. Lee attacked again on the third day, his attack would be in the center of the Union line. Meade and his generals presumed that Lee would attack there because he had come closer to breaching the Union position near the center earlier that day, while his attempts on the flanks of the Union position at Culp's Hill and Little Round Top had failed. The center of the Union line was where Brigadier General John Gibbon, commanding the Second Division of Second Corps, was placed. Where Gibbon's division held its position in the Union line, Brigadier General Alexander Webb's 2nd Brigade (the Philadelphia Brigade) held the center at a copse of trees near what is known as the Angle atop Cemetery Ridge.[55]

Webb placed the 69th Pennsylvania in front of the copse of trees, even though they had also been engaged in hard fighting the day before, and placed the better-rested troops of the 72nd Pennsylvania behind the trees as a reserve. Why Webb deployed his troops in that manner when he expected to be attacked the next day is a matter of speculation. Webb was new in command of the Philadelphia Brigade. Perhaps his view of the 69th commander, Colonel Dennis O'Kane, was tainted due to the events leading to the relief of the brigade's former commander, Brigadier General Joshua T. Owen. One afternoon, when O'Kane's wife had come to visit him, the two were enjoying a carriage ride. Brigadier General Owen, obviously drunk, rode up to the carriage on his horse and began to menace the O'Kanes. Owen insulted O'Kane, referring to him as "an Irish son of a bitch," and invited O'Kane's wife to spend the night with him in his tent. O'Kane forcefully pulled Owen from his horse and threw him down, at which time his head hit the ground with an audible crack. O'Kane was court-martialed for the incident, but Major General Winfield S. Hancock, commanding the Second Corps, saw the event for what it was and acquitted him. At best Webb seemed indifferent to the officers of the 69th; possibly he thought O'Kane hot tempered and unfit to command. Nevertheless, the men of the 69th accepted their fate and prepared for the expected assault.[56]

After the previous day's fighting, the men of the 69th took care of their wounded, as well as the wounded prisoners from Wright's brigade. Once this was accomplished, the men collected the guns and ammunition of the dead, extracting the buckshot from the common three-buckshot-and-a-ball load and reloaded their own guns with twelve shots of buck. They then placed the spare muskets against the stone wall that was near their position in the Union line. Every man in the regiment had two to five muskets available, which they later used to great effect when the Confederates approached within fifty feet of the stone wall.[57]

On July 3, 1863, General Lee preceded his attack with a preparatory artillery barrage, which began at 1:00 p.m. and lasted a full hour and forty-five minutes. The Confederates lined up in two ranks, each two files deep, and proceeded toward the Union line. When the Confederates got near the wall, the 69th was standing with muskets leveled. With less than 250 men available to fight and 300 yards of front to hold, the 69th had put every man into its line. The "word to fire was given and a solid sheet of flame blazed out and the Virginians were halted in their tracks." The Irishmen reached for the muskets they had loaded the evening before and used them in a desperate duel with Brigadier General James L. Kemper's brigade at a range of about 50 yards.[58] Then two companies of the 71st Pennsylvania broke under the Confederate attack and fled their positions, leaving a gap to the right of the 69th Pennsylvania. Kemper's brigade and Brigadier General Richard B. Garnett's brigade had led the attack but began to falter when the two commanders fell dead from the return fire delivered by the Union line. It was into this gap that Brigadier General Lewis A. Armistead urged the men in the second. The 69th Pennsylvania soldiers fought without giving any ground, adjusting their position to attack the Confederates pouring through the Union line. The brigade's officers had trouble getting the 72nd Pennsylvania to move up to fill the gap. By some accounts, the 72nd never moved forward despite the personal efforts of Brigadier General Webb,[59] so there were several moments when the situation was desperate. Later, in trial testimony, Captain William Hall of the 19th Massachusetts recalled, "The 69th appeared to be fighting on their own hook. They did not yield one inch and the enemy swarmed right over them." Fortunately, General Hancock sent reinforcements. The 19th Massachusetts Infantry and the 42nd New York Infantry from First Brigade responded to the emergency. When General Armistead fell, mortally wounded, the fighting slowed, then stopped.

The furious fighting of the 69th Pennsylvania during this time rescued the Union position. Saving the position at the Angle was also the key to winning the battle on the third day. General Lee withdrew the following day. This was the last time the Confederate army ever took the offensive.

General Webb was subdued in his official report submitted on July 12, 1863: "The Sixty-ninth Pennsylvania Volunteers lost all its field officers, but held its ground. The cover in its front was not well built, and it lost many men lying on the ground; still, I saw none retire from the fence." Here, Webb merely states what happened. In contrast, when discussing the 106th Pennsylvania Volunteer Infantry, Webb lamented, "I lost gallant officers and men." Even though others described the incredible performance of the 69th Pennsylvania at the Battle of Gettysburg on July 3, 1863, Webb singled no one out for conspicuous bravery as he did for Lieutenant Joseph S. Milne, Battery B, 1st Rhode Island Artillery, and his assistant adjutant-general, Captain C.H. Banes. Surprisingly, even though all of the 69th's field officers were killed in the battle, and the remaining line officers and noncommissioned officers directed a superb fight, he did not recommend anyone in the regiment for promotion. Webb's lack of enthusiasm for the regiment's performance and miscarriage of due reward stemmed from his perceptions of the Irish.

Additional evidence of Webb's discrimination against the Irish regiments is seen in his letter to Pennsylvania Governor Andrew G. Curtin after the battle. Part of the letter states, "I would especially call the attention of your Excellency to the fact that it is impossible to govern the 'Irish Regiments,' when the officers do not belong to a more intelligent class than that of which Murdoch Campbell, Lieut. McAnally, and Lieut. Fitzpatrick 69th P.V. are typical. I shall do all in my power to get rid of these disorganizing stumbling blocks."[60] This was Webb's reward to the Irish for valor in battle. If the Irish could not shake perception of being ill disciplined, difficult to govern, and of lower intelligence in spite of performing with bravery and honor in the army, how would public perception about them at home change?

The Union victory at Gettysburg, coupled with the fall of Vicksburg to General Ulysses S. Grant, made it apparent to many that the Union would eventually prevail in the war. Over the next year, Union progress made the Peace Democrats' arguments increasingly specious, which in turn marginalized their power within the Philadelphia community. Power in the local Democratic Party shifted to the War Democrats, headed at that time by the Irish Catholic Lewis Cassidy.[61] The Keystone Club, where William McMullen had held the presidency in 1850,[62] once again became Philadelphia's principal social setting for local Democrats. The Central Democratic Club, home of the Peace Democrats, faded into the twilight of insignificance.[63]

Although ward bosses like William McMullen would have to contend with a Republican majority in the city, they did use their new political clout to establish themselves and find positions for their constituency within the forming Republican political machine.[64] Noel Ignatiev points out that McMullen was both a supporter and a fishing buddy of James McManes and William R. Leeds, two of Philadelphia's prominent Republican bosses. McMullen used his influence as the boss of the fourth ward to garner votes for whoever would produce the most patronage for his constituency. Thus he and his ward sometimes supported Republican candidates.[65] McMullen timed his political moves such that he always obtained a new position in advance of events that could have pushed him out of political office. For example, prior to the city abolishing the position of alderman in 1873, McMullen won election to the Common Council. When a vacancy opened up on the Select Council, McMullen was likewise elected to fill that position. McMullen had traded his support to Republicans to get elected to the Common Council and from there to the Select Council, where he had uninterrupted tenure from 1874 until his death in 1901.[66]

Although McMullen was nominally a Democrat, from his position on the Select Council he could participate actively in the nominally Republican party political machine, operated by career politicians.[67] For these men, pragmatic solutions mattered more than principled party affiliation. The Select Council and James McManes ran Philadelphia's infamous Gas Ring, a citadel of bossism, with the help of McManes' chief lieutenant William R. Leeds. William S. Stokley nominally controlled the Building Ring, sometimes from a position on the Select Council and sometimes as the mayor. Because there was no clear and permanent Republican boss, McMullen and Lewis Cassidy could direct their support to whoever would give them something in return.[68] As a practical matter, the Republicans used their power to erode Irish solidarity to and within the Democratic Party, which manifested as differing alliances in other cities. For instance, James Aloysius from Grassy Point, New York, visited his father at Verplanck's Point, only a few miles away. He could not understand why the Irish living there were Republicans. The reason was that local politicians helped members of the Irish Catholic community obtain jobs in the local brickyard in return for their enrollment in the Republican Party. In Boston, the Irish were solidly Democrats because that party was dominant in Boston politics. Republicans dominated in Philadelphia, so, in the interests of self-advancement, the Irish sought the protective coloration of the dominant party.[69]

Ignatiev indicates that what McMullen got in return for his support was jobs and services for his constituents. Jobs went to Irishmen inside the custom house, on federal construction projects, and at the Eastern State Penitentiary and the Navy Yard. McMullen also had influence with some private employers, including the Baldwin Locomotive Works.[70]

Moreover, Philadelphia experienced a constant influx of Irish immigrants replacing those killed in the Civil War.[71] Throughout the nineteenth century Irish Catholics remained Philadelphia's most significant ethnic population.[72] A 20 percent sample of the 1870 census in Philadelphia's fourth ward showed new diversity in jobs for Irish immigrants. The number of separate types of jobs for Irishmen increased from 58 in 1869 to 89 in 1870. A relatively flat 45 percent still were employed as laborers, while 7 percent made livings as mariners or seamen. Small businessmen were up slightly to 28 percent from 26 percent in 1860. The waterman position had seemingly completely disappeared (perhaps this job was reclassified as laborer). Twenty percent of the Irish immigrants gained employment in trades, compared to only 8 percent in 1860. Among the new jobs listed were policemen, machinists, molders, locomotive builders, telegraph operators, brakemen, and coachmen.[73]

The story remained grim, however, for Irish Catholic women. Nearly all the women in the 1870 census listed something as an occupation, which was a difference from the 1860 census, where the space for occupation was typically left blank. That said, two-thirds of the Irish women indicated their employment as keeping house, housekeeping, or housekeeper. Nine percent listed "at home" as an occupation, and 3 percent still had nothing listed at all. Thus nearly 80 percent had no income. Those employed as any of the various types of domestic servants actually decreased from 16 percent in 1860 to 10 percent in 1870. A mere 4 percent worked as seamstresses when thousands had been employed during the Civil War six years earlier.[74]

Irish women remained the subject of discrimination for employment as domestic servants. Advertisements in the *Public Ledger* throughout 1865 and early 1866 still reflected the social prejudices inherent in Philadelphia society twenty years earlier when "Native American" politics ruled the city. The advertisement from one household stated, "Wanted—a Protestant Cook (NOT IRISH)"; another requested a "Protestant chamber maid."[75] The pattern was consistent and continued.[76]

One bright spot regarding Irish women's occupation was that the types of jobs they held had expanded from 12 in 1860 to 21 by 1870. Some were nurses; others ran small businesses or worked in hotels, or even as an innkeeper. The most significant new occupation was in sales, known at the time as a huckster.[77]

Men's occupations diversified as the economy expanded. They joined trades that were closed to them before the war. By 1870, there were few unemployed Irishmen and a flat percentage remained in labor. Irishmen working as policemen, locomotive builders, molders, and machinists were not evident in the 1860 census, as they were in 1870.[78] Dennis Clark and other historians argue that improved public opinion was responsible for much of the change, pointing out that St. Clair Mulholland returned to Philadelphia as a hero and became the first Irish Catholic chief of police in 1868.[79] Yet Philadelphia had many heroes during the Civil War and dozens of winners of the Congressional Medal of Honor.[80] St. Clair Mulholland actually received his Medal of Honor in 1895, thirty years after the end of the Civil War, so this did not set him apart from other returning veterans at the time of his appointment as chief of police. Before the war he had worked as a printer and a painter of window shades (some biographies list him as an artist)—hardly a qualification for chief of police when there were at this time professional policemen on a force that had been operating efficiently for nearly twenty years. And, in fact, the chief of police was not an elected position, so it was not greatly influenced by public opinion. The mayor appointed the chief of police, subject to approval by the Select Council; hence the holder of the office was determined by Philadelphia's political machine.[81] When William S. Stokley was elected mayor in 1871, he had won in part because the public expected him to overhaul the police department. The public remained dissatisfied with the management of the department while the Democrat Daniel Fox was mayor.[82]

The Irish Catholics of Philadelphia did see improvement in their social mobility after the Civil War, but they only experienced a modest improvement in terms of reduced religious and ethnic discrimination. Irish Catholic men's participation in the war as soldiers played a key role in improving their social mobility after the war, along with their increased political power within Philadelphia's Democratic Party. As soldiers they were significant in turning the tide of the conflict. The reputation of Irish regiments in the Army of the Potomac did contribute to more favorable public opinion, but more important was the political clout that Irish Catholics gained. The key victory at Gettysburg finally discredited prominent Peace Democrats in Philadelphia who had argued that the war could not be won. When the public perceived that the war would be won by the Union, the War Democrats seized control of the party in Philadelphia. The War Democrats had made common cause with Republicans during the war, so they were in a position to gain concessions. Heavily Irish Catholic, the War Democrats used their power to obtain better jobs in growing industries. The power in the Democratic Party consisted mainly of voting in large blocs for particular candidates (some of them Republicans) in return for jobs and other favors granted to Irish Catholics. This patronage system helped move significant numbers of Irish working men into better-paying jobs in railroads, the gas company, the shipyard, the police force, and other areas. There were sectors where industry in Philadelphia grew considerably during and after the Civil War. In contrast, the textile industry reduced employment, predominantly that of women, after losing lucrative government contracts.[83] Thus the patronage system benefited Irish Catholic men much more than it benefited women.

Unfortunately, Irish Catholics still experienced ethnic and religious discrimination after the Civil War. This persisted long enough so that even in 1895, thirty years later, they were driven to form organizations such as the Knights of Equity and Daughters of Erin, organizations whose purpose was to advance Irish Catholics spiritually, intellectually, and socially for promotion of their material interest and well-being.[84] The Irish fought for their place in Philadelphia society. The men who fought bravely in the Civil War helped turn the tide of the war and also turned the political tide in Philadelphia. Union victory gave the Irish soldiers' patrons on the home front political clout, which was parlayed into improved economic status. Many of the stigmas, however, that the greater Philadelphia Protestant communities had attached to the Irish Catholics remained. Additional employment opportunities seem a small gain for such large sacrifices. The sacrifices of Irish women were no less important; yet their economic improvement was much less significant. Women's suffrage and improved political clout would have to wait for the end of World War I to become reality. There was much more for the Irish to do to make Philadelphia their own, but their participation in the war was a significant start.

74   Part II: American Civil War

NOTES

1. Frank Boyle, *A Party of Mad Fellows: The Story of the Irish Regiments in the Army of the Potomac* (Dayton, OH: Morningside, 1996), 76.
2. Helen More, "The Philadelphia Brigade: 69th Pennsylvania Infantry," http://ourworld.compuserve.com/hompages/HMore/69th_pennsylvania_infantry.htm (accessed November 27, 2001).
3. Jack Kelly, "The 69th Pennsylvania," http://www.gdg.org/Research/OOB/Union/July1-3/kellytour.htm (accessed November 27, 2001).
4. Boyle, *Party of Mad Fellows*, 283–85.
5. Ann Orlov, Stephan Thernstrom, and Oscar Handlin, eds., *Harvard Encyclopedia of American Ethnic Groups* (Cambridge, MA: Belknap Press of Harvard University Press, 1980), 529.
6. Bob Considine, *It's the Irish* (Garden City, NY: Doubleday, 1961), 9.
7. Noel Ignatiev, *How the Irish Became White* (New York: Routledge, 1995), 151–52.
8. Ignatiev, *Irish Became White*, 156–57; Russell F. Weigley, Nicholas B. Wainwright, and Edwin Wolf, eds., *Philadelphia: A 300-Year History* (New York, London: W.W. Norton, 1982), 368.
9. Ignatiev, *Irish Became White*, 159–60; Weigley et al., *Philadelphia*, 369.
10. Weigley et al., *Philadelphia*, 371.
11. Peter McCaffery, *When Bosses Ruled Philadelphia: The Emergence of the Republican Machine, 1867-1933* (University Park: Pennsylvania State University Press, 1993), 15.
12. Weigley et al., *Philadelphia*, 369–71.
13. *Ibid.*, 350.
14. *Ibid.*, 385.
15. United States Census Bureau, *1860 U.S. Federal Census* (Washington, DC: U.S. Census Bureau, 1860).
16. *Ibid.*
17. Weigley et al., *Philadelphia*, 388.
18. *Public Ledger*, November 12, 1849.
19. *Ibid.*
20. *1860 U.S. Census.*
21. Rachel Filene Seidman, "Beyond Sacrifice: Women and Politics on the Pennsylvania Homefront during the Civil War," Ph.D. diss., Yale University, 1995, 129.
22. Dennis Clark, *The Irish in Philadelphia: Ten Generations of Urban Experience* (Philadelphia: Temple University Press, 1973), 171; Ignatiev, *Irish Became White*, 75–76.
23. *Philadelphia Inquirer*, April 23, 1861.
24. Ignatiev, *Irish Became White*, 161.
25. *Philadelphia Inquirer*, April 23, 1861.
26. Boyle, *Party of Mad Fellows*, 33.
27. Seidman, "Beyond Sacrifice," 20.
28. *Philadelphia Inquirer*, April 23, 1861.
29. *Ibid.*
30. *Ibid.*
31. James Matthew Gallman, *Mastering Wartime: A Social History of Philadelphia during the Civil War* (Cambridge, New York: Cambridge University Press, 1990), 243–44; Seidman, "Beyond Sacrifice," 129–30.
32. Gallman, *Mastering Wartime*, 244.
33. *Philadelphia Inquirer*, June 1, 1864.
34. *Public Ledger*, June 1, 1864.
35. Seidman, "Beyond Sacrifice," 150–57.
36. Gallman, *Mastering Wartime*, 243–44.
37. *Ibid.*
38. *Public Ledger*, April 23, 1861.
39. Seidman, "Beyond Sacrifice," 150–57.
40. *Ibid.*, 127.

41. *Public Ledger*, various January 1863–April 1864.
42. *Ibid.*, April 29, 1864.
43. *Ibid.*, April 1, 1864.
44. *Philadelphia Inquirer*, June 2, 1864.
45. Boyle, *Party of Mad Fellows*, 222; Craig A. Warren, "'Oh, God, What a Pity!' The Irish Brigade at Fredericksburg and the Creation of Myth," *Civil War History* 47, no. 3 (2001): 194–95.
46. Weigley et al., *Philadelphia*, 413.
47. Warren, "Irish Brigade at Fredericksburg," 197–99.
48. *Ibid.*, 194.
49. Boyle, *Party of Mad Fellows*, 234–35.
50. St. Clair A. Mulholland, *The Story of the 116th Regiment, Pennsylvania Volunteers in the War of the Rebellion: The Record of a Gallant Command* (Philadelphia: F. McManus, Jr. & Co., 1903), 103–7.
51. "Irish Medal of Honor Recipients," http://irishvolunteers.tripod.com/medal_honor.htm (accessed January 15, 2015); "Medal of Honor Recipients, Civil War M-R: Mulholland, St. Clair A.," http://www.history.army.mil/html/moh/civilwar_mr.html#MULHOLLAND (accessed January 15, 2015).
52. Boyle, *Party of Mad Fellows*, 270.
53. *Ibid.*, 265–67.
54. Winfield S. Hancock, "Report of Maj. Gen. Winfield S. Hancock, U.S. Army, Commanding Second Army Corps, Gettysburg Campaign," http://irishvolunteers.tripod.com/hancock_gettysburg_report (accessed January 15, 2015); Armistead L. Long, *Memoirs of Robert E. Lee*, ed. Stanley Schindler (New York: Crescent Books, 1994), 110; Jay Luvaas and Harold W. Nelson, eds., *Guide to the Battle of Gettysburg*, U.S. Army War College Guides to Civil War Battles (Lawrence: University Press of Kansas, 1994), 126–28; St. Clair A. Mulholland, "Report of Maj. St. Clair A. Mulholland, One Hundred and Sixteenth Pennsylvania Infantry, Gettysburg Campaign," http://irishvolunteers.tripod.com/mulholland_report.htm (accessed January 15, 2015); Alexander S. Webb, "Report of Brig. Gen. Alexander S. Webb, U.S. Army, Commanding Second Brigade, Gettysburg Campaign," http://www.civilwarhome.com/webbgettysburg.html (accessed January 15, 2015).
55. Boyle, *Party of Mad Fellows*, 287.
56. Arthur C. Devereaux, "Letter of Colonel Arthur C. Devereaux, 19th Massachusetts Infantry, to Colonel John B. Bachelder, July 22, 1989," in *The Bachelder Papers*, trans., ed., and annotated by David L. Ladd and Audrey J. Ladd (Dayton, OH: Morningside, 1994), 1609–10, http://www.gdg.org/Research/OOB/Union/July1-3/kellytour.htm (accessed January 15, 2015); Anthony W. McDermott, "Letter of Anthony W. McDermott to Colonel John B. Bachelder, September 17, 1889," in *The Bachelder Papers*, trans., ed., and annotated by David L. Ladd and Audrey J. Ladd (Dayton, OH: Morningside, 1994), 1627–29, http://www.gdg.org/Research/OOB/Union/July1-3/kellytour.htm (accessed January 15, 2015).
57. Boyle, *Party of Mad Fellows*, 286–92.
58. *Ibid.*, 292.
59. Webb, "Report of Brig. Gen. Webb."
60. Boyle, *Party of Mad Fellows*, 296–97.
61. Ignatiev, *Irish Became White*, 166; Weigley et al., *Philadelphia*, 412.
62. McCaffery, *When Bosses Ruled Philadelphia*, 14.
63. Ignatiev, *Irish Became White*, 166; Weigley et al., *Philadelphia*, 412.
64. Ignatiev, *Irish Became White*, 167; McCaffery, *When Bosses Ruled Philadelphia*, 15.
65. Ignatiev, *Irish Became White*, 172; McCaffery, *When Bosses Ruled Philadelphia*, 15.
66. Ignatiev, *Irish Became White*, 175; McCaffery, *When Bosses Ruled Philadelphia*, 15.
67. Ignatiev, *Irish Became White*, 172–75; McCaffery, *When Bosses Ruled Philadelphia*,
68. 4–15.
68. McCaffery, *When Bosses Ruled Philadelphia*, 33; John St. George Joyce, ed., *Story of Philadelphia* (New York: Harry B. Joseph, 1919), 281.
69. Considine, *It's the Irish*, 123–24.
70. Ignatiev, *Irish Became White*, 175.

71. United States Census Bureau, *1870 U.S. Federal Census* (Washington, DC: U.S. Census Bureau, 1870).
72. McCaffery, *When Bosses Ruled Philadelphia*, 116.
73. *1870 U.S. Census*.
74. Ibid.
75. *Public Ledger*, April 13, 1865.
76. Ibid., various January 1, 1865–February 28, 1866.
77. *1870 U.S. Census*.
78. *1860 U.S. Census; 1870 U.S. Census*.
79. Clark, *Irish in Philadelphia*, 123.
80. "PA Civil War Medal of Honor Recipients, Philadelphia County, PA," *Pennsylvania Volunteers of the Civil War*, http://www.pacivilwar.com/medalofhonor/philadelphia.html (accessed January 15, 2015).
81. McCaffery, *When Bosses Ruled Philadelphia*, 40.
82. Joyce, *Story of Philadelphia*, 274.
83. Gallman, *Mastering Wartime*, 257–64.
84. Knights of Equity: An Irish-Catholic Fellowship, http://www.knightsofequity.com (accessed January 15, 2015).

Bibliography

The Bachelder Papers. Translated, edited, and annotated by David L. Ladd and Audrey J. Ladd. Dayton, OH: Morningside, 1994. http://www.gdg.org/Research/OOB/Union/July1-3/kellytour.htm.
Boyle, Frank. *A Party of Mad Fellows: The Story of the Irish Regiments in the Army of the Potomac*. Dayton, OH: Morningside, 1996.
Clark, Dennis. *The Irish in Philadelphia: Ten Generations of Urban Experience*. Philadelphia: Temple University Press, 1973.
Considine, Bob. *It's the Irish*. Garden City, NY: Doubleday, 1961.
Fox, Walter. "Dennis O'Kane and the 69th Pennsylvania Volunteers: Against Lee's Best Troops They Stood Their Ground." https://walterfox.wordpress.com/dennis-okane-and-the-69th-pennsylvania-volunteers-2/.
Gallman, James Matthew. *Mastering Wartime: A Social History of Philadelphia during the Civil War*. New York, Cambridge: Cambridge University Press, 1990.
Hancock, Winfield S. "Report of Maj. Gen. Winfield S. Hancock, U.S. Army, Commanding Second Army Corps, Gettysburg Campaign." http://irishvolunteers.tripod.com/hancock_gettysburg_report.
Ignatiev, Noel. *How the Irish Became White*. New York: Routledge, 1995.
"Irish Medal of Honor Recipients." http://irishvolunteers.tripod.com/medal_honor.htm.
Joyce, John St. George, ed. *Story of Philadelphia*. New York: Harry B. Joseph, 1919.
Kelly, Jack. "The 69th Pennsylvania." http://www.gdg.org/Research/OOB/Union/July1–3/kellytour.htm.
Knights of Equity: An Irish-Catholic Fellowship. http://www.knightsofequity.com.
Long, Armistead L. *Memoirs of Robert E. Lee*. Edited by Stanley Schindler. New York: Crescent Books, 1994.
Luvaas, Jay, and Harold W. Nelson, eds. *Guide to the Battle of Gettysburg*. U.S. Army War College Guides to Civil War Battles. Lawrence: University Press of Kansas, 1994.
McCaffery, Peter. *When Bosses Ruled Philadelphia: The Emergence of the Republican Machine, 1867–1933*. University Park: Pennsylvania State University Press, 1993.
"Medal of Honor Recipients, Civil War M–R: Mulholland, St. Clair A." http://www.history.army.mil/html/moh/civilwar_mr.html#MULHOLLAND.
More, Helen. "The Philadelphia Brigade: 69th Pennsylvania Infantry." http://ourworld.compuserve.com/homepages/HMore/69th_pennsylvania_infantry.htm.
Mulholland, St. Clair A. "Report of Maj. St. Clair A. Mulholland, One Hundred and Sixteenth Pennsylvania Infantry, Gettysburg Campaign." http://irishvolunteers.tripod.com/mulholland_report.htm.

_____. *The Story of the 116th Regiment, Pennsylvania Volunteers in the War of the Rebellion: The Record of a Gallant Command.* Philadelphia: F. McManus, Jr. & Co., 1903.
Orlov, Ann, Stephan Thernstrom, and Oscar Handlin, eds. *Harvard Encyclopedia of American Ethnic Groups.* Cambridge, MA: Belknap Press of Harvard University Press, 1980.
"PA Civil War Medal of Honor Recipients, Philadelphia County, PA." *Pennsylvania Volunteers of the Civil War.* http://www.pacivilwar.com/medalofhonor/philadelphia.html.
Philadelphia Inquirer. Microfilm.
Public Ledger. Microfilm.
Samuel L. Paley Library, Temple University, Philadelphia, Pennsylvania.
Seidman, Rachel. "Beyond Sacrifice: Women and Politics on the Pennsylvania Homefront During the Civil War." Ph.D. dissertation, Yale University, 1995.
United States Census Bureau. *Records of the U.S. Federal Census.* Washington, D.C.: U.S. Census Bureau.
Warren, Craig A. "'Oh, God, What a Pity!' The Irish Brigade at Fredericksburg and the Creation of Myth." *Civil War History* 47, no. 3 (2001): 193–221.
Webb, Alexander S. "Report of Brig. Gen. Alexander S. Webb, U.S. Army, Commanding Second Brigade, Gettysburg Campaign." http://www.civilwarhome.com/webbgettysburg.html.
Weigley, Russell F., Nicholas B. Wainwright, and Edwin Wolf, eds. *Philadelphia: A 300-Year History.* New York, London: W.W. Norton, 1982.

Preserving the Union: Shaping a New Image of Chicago's Irish Catholics and the Civil War

LAWRENCE J. MCCAFFREY

On August 1 and 2, 1864, Chicago wakened and buried James Adelbert Mulligan, colonel of the 23rd Illinois Infantry Regiment (the Western Irish Brigade). After waiting in long lines for hours outside Bryan Hall, thousands passed the bier supporting his coffin. Union flags "entwined with black and white crepe" hung above the main entrance. Inside, mourners could read Mulligan's dying words ("Lay me down and save the flag"), as well as his defiant reply when Confederate General Sterling Price had asked for his surrender at Lexington, Missouri, in July 1861: "If you want us, come and take us."[1]

On the morning of the funeral, men, women, and children jammed suburban trains and city railway cars to view the event. And, according to the *Chicago Tribune*, "buggies, carriages, wagons and vehicles of every description were pressed into service by their eager owners, while multitudes swelled the throng by arriving on foot from every point in the compass." Chicago's mayor, entire city council, judges, and army and naval officers joined pallbearers and members of the funeral arrangement committee and marched in a body from the Tremont Hotel to Bryan Hall, where various military and Catholic parish societies in ceremonial dress met them. After the Light Guard Band played a dirge, Mulligan's body was placed in a funeral car drawn by "six fine black horses furnished by the United States Express Company."

Members of the Fenian Brotherhood were conspicuously absent from the ceremonies. According to Civil War historian William L. Burton, Colonel Mulligan "had cleverly managed to convince the clergy that he was not a Fenian while giving ardent support to the Fenian cause." Chicago's Catholic bishop James Duggan, a native of County Kilkenny, following the lead of the Irish hierarchy, had condemned the Brotherhood. His pronouncement caused a stir on both sides of the Atlantic. When the Fenians discovered that funeral arrangements placed them last in the procession, behind all other civic and religious organizations, they withdrew from the cortege. In a letter to the *Tribune*, Major Michael Scanlan, a Fenian leader, paid tribute to the brigade colonel and nationalist comrade, praising his courage and virtue, but (implying the machinations of Duggan and other Catholic clerics), complained that the Fenians' designated position in the funeral insulted revolutionary Irish republicanism.[2]

When the funeral procession arrived at Saint Mary's Cathedral at Madison and Wabash streets, the assembled clergy chanted the office for the dead and the Rev. Thaddeus Butler, chaplain of the Western Irish Brigade, sang the High Mass. According to the *Tribune*, a unique feature of the funeral ceremony was the Light Guard Band's performance of "Mulligan's Requiem," arranged from the Oratorio of Elijah. In his eloquent, stirring eulogy, the Rev. John J. McMullen, D.D., president of Saint Mary of the Lake University (and later the first bishop of Davenport, Iowa), praised his long-time friend as an American patriot and devout Catholic, whose "profession and practice of religion were pleasures to him, rather than a duty."

Following the Mass, Chicago's most prominent citizens, as well as religious and secular organizations and ordinary citizens, walked behind the carriage carrying the casket. From Saint Mary's, they headed north along Michigan Avenue to Lake Street, west to Wells Street, and then north to the railroad depot at Kinzie Street, where a train waited to transport Mulligan's body to Evanston for burial in Calvary Cemetery. As the funeral retinue moved slowly along its route, the bells of City Hall and various churches tolled a solemn requiem. Considering the contempt and hatred heaped on his people by Anglo-Protestant nativists in Chicago and throughout the United States, it is ironic that the city's first and most beloved Civil War hero was an Irish Catholic.

Mulligan's Western Irish Brigade

Utica, New York, was the 1830 birthplace of James A. Mulligan, the son of Irish immigrants. Six years later, he and his widowed mother moved to Chicago. When they arrived, the once small frontier town on the southwest shore of Lake Michigan was on its way to becoming the fastest-growing, most economically dynamic city in the United States. In the early 1830s, Irish laborers who had worked on the Erie Canal arrived in Chicago to dig the Illinois and Michigan Canal, thus linking the city with commerce on the Mississippi, Missouri, and Ohio rivers. Then, in the 1850s, through the efforts of Senator Stephen A. Douglas (a Chicago native), the Illinois Central Railroad connected the city with Mobile, Alabama, and other places in the South. By means of Great Lakes shipping, canal and riverboats and barges, and railway cars, Chicago supplied much of the nation with grain, meat, and lumber. An expanding economy radically increased the population from 29,963 in 1850 to 109,260 in 1860. Many newcomers were German or Irish-born.[3]

Although Irish Catholic immigrants found a wide range of job opportunities in Chicago, from digging the Illinois and Michigan Canal to paving streets, laying railroad tracks, working in packinghouses, and serving in the homes of upper- and middle-class Protestants, they also represented a serious social problem. Indeed, wretched famine immigrants in the late 1840s and early 1850s canceled out much of the progress that earlier settlers had made on the road to economic and social prosperity.

As in other American centers, many of Chicago's Irish immigrants arrived technologically unskilled and frequently ignorant and illiterate. Having previously been agricultural laborers or small tenant farmers in Ireland, they had to make difficult adjustments to commercial and industrial cities in the United States. Traumatized by a drastic environmental change and released from the restraining mores of a homogeneous, rural society, Irish immigrants often exhibited antisocial behavior such as drunkenness, disorderly conduct, petty crime, and family violence. This uncivil deportment irritated Anglo-American Protestant sensibilities. But nativists found the religion of the Irish even more obnoxious than their lifestyle. Rooted in British anti-popery, American nativism viewed Catholicism as an alien, subversive creed, the breeder, enabler, and nourisher of ignorance, superstition, and authoritarianism threatening American culture and institutions.[4]

The *Chicago Tribune*, the local press voice of the Republican Party, was a particularly vicious voice of anti–Catholicism, especially in its Hibernian manifestation. Editorials constantly heaped criticism on the Irish, their conduct, their turbulent impact on politics, and, most of all, their alien, essentially anti–American religion. "Who does not know," thundered the *Tribune* on February 26, 1855, "that the most depraved, debased, worthless and irredeemable drunkards and sots which curse the community, are Irish Catholic? Who does not know that five-eighths of the cases brought up every day before the Mayor for drunkenness and consequent crime are Irish Catholics?" That same year anti–Catholicism figured in the election of a member of the American (Know Nothing) Party, Levi Boone (nephew of the famous Daniel), as mayor and a nativist majority city council. A year later the anti-saloon policies of the administration forged a German-Irish alliance that reversed the previous election results.[5]

James Mulligan, a handsome man, was an exceptionally articulate writer and speaker, a devout Catholic, an influential Douglas Democrat, and a committed Fenian, dedicated to an independent Irish Republic, to be achieved through a revolution supported by the American Diaspora. In 1850, he was the first graduate of the University of St. Mary of the Lake. Founded by Bishop William Quarter, it was Chicago's first institution of higher learning, embodying the hopes and dreams of ambitious and idealistic Catholic immigrants. Stricken with gold fever while reading law in the offices of Judge Isaac N. Arnold, Mulligan struck out for California but became ill in Panama, where his funds ran out. After regaining his health, he assisted explorer John Lloyd Stephens in mapping out a railroad route across the isthmus. When Stephens died in 1852, Mulligan returned home to resume his legal studies and to edit the *Western Tablet*, Chicago's first Catholic newspaper. In 1855, he joined the Illinois bar, and two years later he served briefly in Washington, D.C., as a clerk in the Department of the Interior's Bureau of Indian Affairs.[6]

On April 15, 1861, the day after Fort Sumter in Charleston Harbor surrendered to secessionist South Carolina, President Abraham Lincoln asked for volunteers to save the Union, an appeal repeated frequently over the next four years. Realistically, Irish Catholics had little motivation to respond. They were fervent Douglas Democrats and despised Lincoln's Republican Party, which had absorbed anti–Catholic, anti-immigrant Know Nothings and Whigs. And they were unsympathetic to the anti-slavery moral dimension of the Union cause.

During the repeal agitation of 1843, Daniel O'Connell, the founding father of modern Irish nationalism, linked Irish and black freedoms and urged Irish Americans to support the abolition of slavery in the United States and the elevation of its victims to first-class citizenship. They rejected his advice. Their racial prejudice expressed ignorance, fear of competition in the unskilled labor market, anger that some employers used blacks as scab strike breakers, and an inferiority complex that encouraged them to persecute another despised minority.[7]

Despite resentment against abolitionists, nativists, and Republicans, as well as pro–Confederate opinion in nationalist Ireland, a large number of Irishmen enlisted in the Union Army.[8] Somewhere over 140,000 men born in Ireland fought on the northern side (and 40,000 on the southern side) during the Civil War. An 1869 United States Sanitary Commission report placed the Irish-born Union figures at 144,221, about five thousand more than might have been expected in proportion to the total Irish American population. Of this number, 51,206 came from New York, 17,418 from Pennsylvania, 12,041 from Illinois, 10,007 from Massachusetts, 8,129 from Ohio, 4,362 from Missouri, and 3,621 from Wisconsin.[9] It is reasonable to assume that second and third generations would have at least doubled the Irish contribution to the war effort.

For a variety of reasons, the Irish chose military service. For some, money was the incentive. Enlistment bounties or payments to substitute for Anglo-American Protestants appealed to those who were unskilled (and often unemployed). The army also offered an alternative to many jobless, recently arrived immigrants. In Ireland, many youths, escaping the boredom and destitution of rural life and searching for adventure, frequently joined the British army or navy; similar inducements motivated many Irish Americans to fight for the Union or Confederacy. In 1861, Senator Douglas also influenced northern Irish American opinion when he reminded a Chicago audience that there were "only patriots—or traitors." Irish Catholic admirers, who the year before had voted for him in the presidential election, enthusiastically applauded.[10]

Fenianism also was a factor in the Irish presence in both armies, especially in the North. Contradicting pro-southern nationalist sympathies in Ireland, revolutionary republicans in America wanted a strong United States to eventually aid Ireland in a future conflict with Britain. Fenian leaders encouraged army enlistments, not only to prevent a divided United States but also as a training ground for the coming great battle with the ancient Sassenach enemy.[11]

Like a great number of insecure Irish American Catholics in Illinois and throughout the country, Mulligan viewed the Civil War as a great test and challenge, an opportunity to prove their love of their new country. Altogether, the Union Army contained forty largely Irish regiments. New York's Irish Brigade, including the "Fighting 69th," was the most famous, but Irish Catholics from all over the nation played a role in preserving the Union, including two from Chicago: the Western Irish Brigade and the Irish Legion, the 23rd and 90th Illinois Infantry Regiments.

Responding to President Lincoln's call for volunteers, in April 1861, Chicago's Irish Catholics organized their own brigade dedicated to the "Honor of the Old Land ... and the Defense of the New." Core membership came from three local militia companies—the Montgomery Guards, the Fenian-supported Emmets, and the Shields' Guards. Brigade members elected Mulligan, captain of the Shields' Guards, as their colonel. The Western Irish Brigade also included the Jackson Guards from Detroit, Michigan, and other northern Illinois militia groups from Earlsville, Morris, Ottawa, and LaSalle County. The last mentioned also had close Fenian ties.[12]

Chicago gave quick and enthusiastic support to the Western Irish Brigade. The city presented Mulligan with a personal sword, and his wife, Marian Nugent Mulligan, took the lead in raising money for the brigade's American flag. The *Chicago Tribune* applauded this symbolic act, calling on all Chicagoans to assist "these warm-hearted patriotic ladies" and praising their efforts to "preserve the honor and integrity of the flag of our beloved country."[13]

Although more than a thousand men enlisted in the Brigade, state officials initially rejected their services because Illinois had already filled its recruitment quota. Undeterred, Mulligan visited the dying Senator Douglas in the Tremont Hotel and secured a letter from him on behalf of the brigade that he personally delivered to President Lincoln in Washington. Coupled with Mulligan's persistence, Douglas' recommendation resulted in the War Department's May 17, 1861, acceptance of the Irish Brigade as the 23rd Illinois Infantry, the state's first independent regiment.

Over nine hundred strong, the Irish Brigade left Chicago on July 14, 1861, for Quincy, Illinois, and then proceeded to St. Louis. By the time it reached Jefferson City, Missouri, Mulligan's force had expanded to 1,135 infantry, 138 cavalry, and 76 artillerymen. Three weeks later, the War Department dispatched the brigade to defend Lexington on the south branch of the Missouri River, about forty miles from Kansas City. As senior officer, Mulligan also commanded the 13th Missouri Infantry and the 1st Illinois Cavalry. Vastly outnumbered, inadequately equipped, and enduring food and water shortages, Mulligan's troops bravely resisted General Sterling Price's Confederate army for nine days, suffering the loss of twenty-four dead and eighty-one wounded. As a tribute to his courage, Price refused to accept Mulligan's sword of surrender. In turn, the colonel rejected parole. With his wife, Marian, who had traveled to Lexington to be with her husband, Mulligan remained a prisoner until October 30, 1861, when he was exchanged for Confederate General D.M. Frost.

Not only did Marian Nugent Mulligan raise funds for her husband's brigade and follow him into a dangerous combat situation, but, largely through her efforts, in September 1861 Mother Francis Monholland sent twenty Irish-born Sisters of Mercy to nurse wounded members of the 23rd Illinois Infantry. When Confederate forces prevented the nuns from reaching Lexington, they established a field hospital in Jefferson City. As a student at Saint Xavier's Academy, Marian Nugent had established ties with the Sisters of Mercy, Chicago's "walking nuns." These indomitable women, known throughout the city for their educational, social, and hospital work, soon earned another complimentary title: "angels of the battlefield."

Despite his defeat and surrender at Lexington, the Chicago area gave Mulligan a glorious welcome home on his release from Confederate captivity. On November 8, 1861, the St. Louis, Alton, and Chicago Railroad sent a special train to meet the Mulligan family in Joliet, where thousands waited along the platform. According to the *Chicago Evening Journal*, "The roofs of the cars, of the depot, and other adjacent buildings were thronged with male and female spectators, the female population of Joliet exhibiting an astonishing agility in climbing." After a brief speech, the hero of Lexington boarded the train for Chicago. Along the way bonfires burned brightly and crowds cheered. Despite the late hour, thousands of Chicagoans of all ages greeted the Mulligans with a torchlight procession that "turned night into day." Even the Irish Catholic–disparaging *Tribune* conceded, "Probably no man ever received such a spontaneous and triumphant welcome to this city or was ever greeted by such a vast assemblage.... His gallantry upon the field of battle, and his well-directed and indomitable efforts in the cause of Freedom merited the respect and honors, if not the worship, which were showered upon him."[14]

Prominent members of the Irish Catholic community such as William J. Onahan and Philip Conley wanted to honor Mulligan with a public banquet, but he declined, preferring to devote his energies to reassembling the Irish Brigade. This effort involved another journey to Washington. After securing official permission to continue recruiting, Mulligan and his wife visited New York, where he reviewed the "Fighting Irish" 69th Infantry. On December 17, 1861, Gotham's mayor approved a resolution extending "the hospitalities of the city of New York" to Colonel Mulligan, "the gallant defender of the Stars and Stripes at Lexington." The *New York Times* described his Cooper's Union speech as "a thrilling description" of the nine-day siege at Lexington, one that "abounded in passages of eloquence, of humor, and of patriotism, rarely equaled." Mulligan donated his lecture fee to victims of hunger and poverty in Ireland.[15]

Back in Chicago, Mulligan received a new assignment as the commander of Camp Douglas on the city's South Side. Named after the deceased senator and close to his grave, it had opened in September 1861 as a training ground for Union soldiers. Eleven months later, after General Ulysses S. Grant took Fort Donelson in the Tennessee campaign, Camp Douglas began to host captured Confederates. It was a notorious example of Civil War prison camps. More than three thousand of its residents are buried in Chicago cemeteries, victims of disease, malnutrition, and general mistreatment. Historian Harold Smith has observed that "Mulligan did all he could to improve conditions, giving particular attention to medical care and food." While not particularly cruel or insensitive for the time and situation, the colonel certainly deserves some blame for the wretched conditions on his watch. He was an exemplary soldier in the field but an inadequate and rather indifferent prison camp administrator. However, in defense of Mulligan and other Camp Douglas commanders, it must also be mentioned that at large number of Confederate soldiers arrived already ill, undernourished, and inadequately outfitted.[16]

After brief duty at Camp Douglas, the Western Irish Brigade returned to the ravages of war. On June 14, 1862, it left for Harper's Ferry. During almost three years of action in Virginia, the brigade waged "guerrilla warfare at its worst, raids, ambushes, and night fighting against some of the most skilled partisan irregulars of the Confederacy." Soldiers of the 23rd Illinois Infantry served with General Philip Sheridan in the Shenandoah Valley and with Grant when he forced the surrender of General Robert E. Lee at Appomattox Court House. In July 1865, the much-depleted brigade was mustered out in Richmond, Virginia. Deaths from bullets and disease, serious wounds, and other physical impairments had reduced the brigade to one-third its original size.[17]

Of the brigade's personnel losses, Mulligan's was the most difficult to bear. On July 23, 1864, during the second battle of Kernstown in the Shenandoah, Confederate fire mortally wounded the colonel. When his men started to carry him from the field, Mulligan shouted, "Lay me down and save the flag." They obeyed his order, and two days later he died in enemy hands. Marian Nugent Mulligan and her three daughters were in nearby Cumberland, Maryland, when she heard that her husband had been wounded. She rushed to the battle scene only to discover that he had died a Confederate captive. She also confronted the bad news that her brother, Lieutenant James Nugent, had sacrificed his life attempting to save his colonel.

Mrs. Mulligan recovered her husband's body from a courteous foe. On July 31, 1864, she brought it back to Chicago for the grieve-the-death-but-celebrate-the-life funeral that Irish Catholics have given their chieftains from the time of Daniel O'Connell in 1847 to that of John F. and Robert Kennedy in the 1960s.[18]

The Irish Legion

It was especially fitting that on August 2, 1864, the Rev. Denis Dunne, D.D., rather than Bishop Duggan, gave the final absolution and benediction at Mulligan's funeral. He was one of the most imposing, popular, powerful, and productive priests in Chicago. Not only was he vicar general of the diocese (the most important member of the bishop's council), but since 1854 Dunne had also been pastor of St. Patrick's, the mother church of the city's Irish. In addition to supervising the construction of a new church in 1857, he had established Chicago's first chapter of the Saint Vincent de Paul Society to relieve the suffering of the poor.

Born February 10, 1824, in Stradbally, Queens (now Laois) County, Ireland, Dunne, his parents, and other family members had immigrated to Canada. His ship carpenter father and uncles found well-paying employment in the Chatham, New Brunswick, shipyards. After completing elementary school, Dunne became a classical studies student at Saint Andrew's College, Charlottetown, Prince Edward Island—the only Catholic school in the Maritime Provinces. Around 1845, William J. Quarter, Chicago's first Catholic bishop, toured the eastern United States and Canada, searching for clerical candidates to man the increasing number of parishes under his supervision. Intrigued by the bishop's description of his diocese, young Dunne decided to enter the Quebec City seminary to prepare for ordination and a clerical career in Chicago. Around this time, his father died and the family suffered a financial calamity when the Cunard shipyards went bankrupt.

By 1845, Dunne's brothers were working as ship carpenters in Chicago, and they brought the rest of the family from New Brunswick to the city. According to Len Hilts, the Dunnes constructed a boat that would navigate the Welland Canal and set out for Quebec in the spring of 1848 to witness Denis's ordination. He met them with the news that Bishop Quarter had died and that his entry into the priesthood would take place in Detroit, Michigan—a journey through fifty-three more locks.

Denis Dunne began his Chicago priesthood as a faculty member at Saint Mary of the Lake University, situated close to the present-day Holy Name Cathedral. His next assignment was in the lead-mining town of Galena. From there he moved to Ottawa, at the western end of the Illinois and Michigan Canal. In the autumn of 1854, Dunne returned to Chicago as the pastor of St. Patrick's, succeeding the Rev. Patrick McLaughlin, who had perished in a cholera epidemic. His relatives moved into the parish, purchasing homes on Adams Street, directly across from the church. Dunne then became the patriarch of an important Chicago family, distinguished in its religious and secular life. One of his nephews, Patrick Riordan, became an esteemed archbishop of San Francisco; another, Finley Peter Dunne, in his Mr. Dooley essays, created, as Charles Fanning has said, the first genuine ethnic community in American literature.[19]

Like so many Irish Catholic immigrants, Father Dunne was a fervent American. He encouraged his parishioners and other Irishmen throughout the city to demonstrate their devotion to the United States by enlisting to preserve its existence. Although Illinois had met its quotas without resorting to a draft, Dunne believed that many Irish were reluctant to serve because many regiments lacked Catholic chaplains. To rectify this situation, he decided to form a legion from his own parish.[20]

On August 8, 1862, Dunne presided over a meeting at St. Patrick's school, including such prominent laymen as Aldermen Redmond Sheridan and James Conlan. Those present endorsed plans for an Irish Legion and passed a resolution viewing "with contempt, abhorrence and detestation those unfortunate Irishmen who have sought, or who are now seeking, the protection of the blood-stained flag of Great Britain, to escape their duty to the United States; and that such men deserve, if not hanging, at least to be put out of the country." Unanimously, the meeting chose Father Dunne as pro-tem colonel of the Irish Legion.[21]

In reporting on the meeting, the *Chicago Times* lauded the bravery and patriotism of Irish immigrants and noted that thousands of Irish Catholics had rushed to rescue their adopted country, leaving "peaceful avocations" to bring "terror and dismay" to Confederate foes. However, in its organization stage and early combat experience, the Legion experienced some turmoil. Father Dunne successfully lobbied for the appointment of Timothy O'Meara, a New Yorker, as colonel over William Snowhook, a Mexican War veteran with strong backing from Chicago Republicans. In battle, heavy-drinking O'Meara was brave, but he frequently quarreled with other officers.[22]

On September 22, 1862, the War Department mustered in the Irish Legion as the 90th Illinois Infantry Regiment and assigned it to guard Confederate prisoners at Camp Douglas. A week later, however, Legionnaires headed south to serve under General Grant during the Mississippi campaign, participating in many battles, including the siege of Vicksburg. The legion also marched with General William Tecumseh Sherman through Georgia and the Carolinas. Casualties were high, particularly on November 25, 1863, at Missionary Ridge, where the 90th Illinois suffered 143 killed, wounded, and missing. In this contest, O'Meara lost his life and Lieutenant Colonel Owen Stuart suffered severe injury. (Stuart eventually recovered to take command of the Irish Legion.)

During its military service, the 90th Illinois experienced some three hundred combat casualties. Considering the primitive conditions of medicine and health care in the 1860s, wounds constituted a much greater threat than they would in subsequent wars. Numerous members of the legion succumbed to such diseases as diphtheria, cholera, smallpox, dysentery (often the result of contaminated food), and the old Irish nemesis of tuberculosis. Sickness could be more frightening than combat. In a May 1863 letter to his wife from "hot as hell" Lafayette, Tennessee, Captain Peter Casey expressed fear of hospitalization. He worried that he might become sick before too long, and "if a man gets into the (hospital there) is a poor chance for him." If he did fall ill, Casey instructed his wife to come to headquarters, where five ladies, all "the wives of officers," were staying.[23]

When President Lincoln signed the Emancipation Proclamation in January 1863, in an effort to both please the abolitionist wing of his party and keep Britain and France neutral, he dampened lower-class urban and rural as well as Irish Catholic enthusiasm for the war effort. Abolition did not sit well with many Irish and other Union soldiers, who did not consider the liberation of black slaves the main purpose of their efforts. In a letter to his wife, poorly schooled Peter Casey wrote, "I was officer of the day yesterday and I have to be in the saddle nearly twenty-four hours. And I am sick sore and downhearted.... I wish every dam abolitionist in Chicago felt as I do this morning they would be careful how they have rushed the country into war."[24]

The most obvious indication of negative reaction to the proclamation was the July 1863 New York City draft riot. A largely Irish mob (much of it fueled by liquor), protesting a law that would permit the rich to buy their way out of military service, killed eleven African Americans (and an Indian they mistook for one), burned an orphanage housing black children, and destroyed millions of dollars' worth of property. Although Germans and Anglo-Americans also participated in anti-conscription demonstrations in Boston, Massachusetts; Pottsville, Pennsylvania; Troy, New York; Milwaukee, Wisconsin; and Dubuque, Iowa, newspapers emphasized the heavy Irish Catholic involvement. The press also reported physical and verbal harassment of African Americans in Chicago and many rural parts of the North.[25]

On August 1, 1863, the *Chicago Tribune* singled out Irish Catholics who "resist the draft, mob or murder conscription officers, get up bloody riots, vote en masse for the worst Copperheads and rebel sympathizers." The writer warned, "The conduct of the Irish toward this beneficent country in the hour of its direst peril is not only ungrateful and wicked but absolutely suicidal to the Irish if they succeed in overthrowing it." To bolster its complaint against the anti-abolitionist Irish, the *Tribune* reprinted Daniel O'Connell's statement of 1843 when he appealed to Irish Americans to oppose slavery and to remember their own victimization by British colonialism.

When War Department officials announced a September 1864 draft, Alderman John Comiskey led the opposition in the Chicago City Council. Although the Comiskey name is associated with the White Sox baseball team that his son, Charles, founded, "Honest John" was an ardent patriot who had assisted in launching both Mulligan's Irish Brigade and Father Dunne's Irish Legion. Comiskey denounced the draft lottery as a capitalist plot to make money while poor working-class lads risked, and often lost, their lives on battlefields. He argued that the lottery permitted the rich to avoid combat by purchasing substitutes and insisted that if the poor had to do the fighting, the government should reward them with substantial bonuses.[26]

Unfavorable reactions to the Emancipation Proclamation not only multiplied abuse of African Americans in Chicago and elsewhere but also fueled Copperhead efforts to end the war on favorable terms for the South. Newspapers dwelled on Irish participation in "treasonous" activities, such as Charles Walsh's failed November 1864 plot to free Camp Douglas prisoners. Antiwar agitation and draft evasion infuriated the writers of *Chicago Tribune* editorials. One on July 2, 1863, denounced Irish Catholics as disloyal ingrates but rejected the notion that their behavior was the result of "inherent cowardice or hatred of freedom ... for they are a fighting, pugnacious race, and passionately fond of the enjoyment of the largest liberty compatible with public safety." Predicting that it would take years for Irish Catholics to live down the stigma of disloyalty, the *Tribune* called on "every intelligent Irishman to use his influence with his more illiterate countrymen to open their eyes and instruct them in the obligations of patriotism and good citizenship."

When the Democratic Party held its August 1864 national convention in a hastily constructed auditorium on Chicago's Michigan Avenue, delegates selected General George McClellan as their candidate. Early in the campaign it seemed as though a war-weary electorate might make the contest close, but after Sherman took Atlanta and Sheridan cleared the Shenandoah of rebel forces, Lincoln's political fortunes soared. However, though he easily won in November, Lincoln lost the Irish Catholic urban vote by a wide margin.[27]

At Appomattox, on April 9, 1865, General Robert E. Lee surrendered to Grant and the manpower and economic superiority of the North. Five days later, the actor John Wilkes Booth assassinated Lincoln. During the public mourning period, life was uncomfortable for Irish Catholics and other Democrats who had opposed the martyred president's war policies and his liberation of black slaves. Nevertheless, there was only praise for all returning veterans. Chicago welcomed them back "bronzed and battle-torn, begrimed with the smoke of a hundred conflicts—toughened by thousand miles of marching." On June 12, 1865, at the door of St. Patrick's rectory, Father Dunne received three cheers from Irish Legion survivors. Still, it was a sad as well as happy occasion for the priest and his parishioners: of the 980 Legionnaires who had left Chicago for Mississippi in late September 1862, only 221 had returned for discharge. And forty-one of those were too crippled to carry a rifle.[28]

The next day, Chicagoans feted the Irish Legionnaires as they marched through the city carrying their regimental colors, "one of which was literally torn to shreds." When they reached the Board of Trade, Governor Richard Yates paid tribute to the memory of Colonel James Mulligan as well as to the "thousands of humble men, now sleeping in nameless graves far down in Chattanooga." The *Tribune* reminded readers that the "gallant old 90th regiment—the Irish Legion—(was) one of the oldest regiments in the field, having entered Sherman's army at Vicksburg."[29]

On December 23, 1868, three years and six months after receiving and acknowledging the plaudits of the men he sent off to save the Union, Father Dunne, disgraced and impoverished, died of heart failure in the West Adams street home of his brother, in clear sight of St. Patrick's church. Earlier that year, Bishop Duggan had returned from Rome, where he had successfully defended his administration of the Chicago diocese. Back in the city he retaliated against Dunne, Revered John McMullen, and two of his St. Mary of the Lake University faculty colleagues, Fathers James McGovern and Joseph P. Roles, who had requested his removal. They justly complained about the bishop's frequent absences from the diocese and his erratic, arbitrary, and irresponsible administration. Duggan stripped Dunne of the vicar generalship and ordered him and his colleagues to leave the diocese.[30]

Despite his quarrel with Duggan, Dunne retained the loyalty of most priests and the overwhelming majority of the laity. This was evident at his funeral and burial. St. Patrick's hosted the requiem Mass on Saturday, December 26, but the funeral procession and interment were delayed for a day so that the city could pay proper tribute to one of its most notable and respected citizens. Thousands of people passed by Father Dunne's coffin in St. Patrick's. Many organizations, Western Irish Brigade and Irish Legion veterans, the mayor and members of the city council, and other prominent citizens participated in the funeral procession through Chicago streets crowded with a multitude of viewers. Flags along the way were at half-mast. Three trains with twenty-one cars apiece left the northwestern station at Kinzie and Canal, carrying Father Dunne's body and more than two thousand mourners to Calvary cemetery. After a graveside service, the founding father of the Irish Legion was laid to rest a few yards from the remains of James A. Mulligan, colonel of the Irish Brigade.[31]

Post–Civil War Chicago Irish

Impressive records of courage and sacrifice by Irish Brigade and Irish Legion members challenged conventional wisdom concerning the Americanism of Irish Catholics. But only three years after Chicago welcomed them home, the shrill voice of nativism reappeared in a September 9, 1868, *Evening Post* editorial. The writer complained of the large numbers of Irish in jails, reform schools, hospitals, and charitable institutions: "Scratch a convict or a pauper and the chances are that you tickle the skin of an Irish Catholic, an Irish Catholic made a criminal or a pauper by the priest and politician who have deceived him and kept him in ignorance, in a word, a savage as he was born."

Despite this kind of venom, Irish Catholic Civil War blood sacrifices were not an entire waste. A substantial number of other Americans, especially those who served with them in combat, appreciated their valor and patriotism and admired the contributions of priest chaplains and nun nurses. Like World Wars I and II, the Civil War united Americans in common cause and, for quite a few (if not a majority), diminished prejudices. But post–Civil War employment needs, a higher quality of immigrants and the more sedate and civilized conduct of Irish America had more to do with Irish progress than battlefield bravery.

During the war years Chicago clearly surpassed rivals St. Louis and Cincinnati as the Midwest's commercial and transportation hub. Railroads entering and leaving Chicago carried soldiers, military equipment, and a variety of products throughout the country. Engine and locomotive construction fostered a rapidly growing industry, eventually including a steel empire. Chicago continued and increased its role as collector and distributor of agricultural goods and lumber. By the time peace arrived, it was the world's largest meatpacking center. A vital economy brought massive numbers of people to the city, tripling its population during the 1860s. Jobs were abundant for incoming Irish and those already in Chicago. Newer immigrants from eastern and southern Europe and free blacks from the South also came to feast on good times. They started on the bottom rung, thereby pushing the Irish up the economic and social ladder.[32]

As the nineteenth century progressed, the public image and private personality of Irish America changed for the better. In Ireland, a post-famine gradual rise in the standard of living, plus an effective national education system, British government reforms (efforts to sabotage nationalism with kindness), and a "Devotional Revolution" in Irish Catholicism, resulted in better-qualified immigrants. In the United States, an increasingly powerful Catholic Church and its parochial schools significantly elevated the conduct and culture of Irish America. By the end of the nineteenth century most Irish Chicagoans were psychologically, morally, and educationally equipped to take advantage of American opportunities without relying on the reluctant tolerance of Anglo-Protestants.[33]

NOTES

1. The following information on Mulligan's wake and funeral is from the *Chicago Tribune*, August 2, 1864; *Chicago Times*, August 2 and 3, 1864; and *Chicago Evening Journal*, August 2, 1864.

2. William L. Burton, *Melting Pot Soldiers: The Union's Ethnic Regiments* (Ames: Iowa State University Press, 1988), 33; March 26 letter from William West to Secretary of State William Seward, quoted in William D'Arcy, *The Fenian Movement in the United States, 1858–1886* (New York: Russell & Russell, 1971), 62; Michael Scanlan's letter, "The Fenian Brotherhood—An Explanation," *Chicago Tribune*, August 4, 1864.

3. For a discussion of Chicago's economy, population, and atmosphere on the eve of the Civil War, see Theodore J. Karamanski, *Rally 'Round the Flag: Chicago and the Civil War* (Chicago: Nelson-Hall, 1993), xi–xiv. Studies of the Chicago Irish include Lawrence J. McCaffrey, Ellen Skerrett, Michael F. Funchion, and Charles Fanning, *The Irish in Chicago* (Urbana and Chicago: Illinois University Press, 1987); Ellen Skerrett, "The Development of Catholic Identity among Irish Americans in Chicago, 1880 to 1920," in *From Paddy to Studs: Irish American Communities in the Turn of the Century Era, 1880 to 1920*, edited by Timothy J. Meagher (New York and Westport, CT: Greenwood Press, 1986), 117–38; Charles Fanning, Ellen Skerrett, and John Corrigan, *Nineteenth Century Chicago Irish: A Social and Political Portrait* (Chicago: Center for Urban Policy, Loyola University of Chicago, 1980); Paul Michael Green, "Irish Chicago: The Multi-ethnic Road to Machine Success," in *Ethnic Chicago: A Multicultural Portrait*, edited by Peter Jones and Melvin G. Holli (Grand Rapids, MI: William B. Eerdmans, 1981), 212–59; and Michael F. Funchion, "Irish Chicago: Church, Homeland, Politics, and Class—The Shaping of an Ethnic Group," in *Ethnic Chicago*, edited by Jones and Holli, 57–92.

4. For examinations of early nineteenth-century anti–Irish Catholicism, see Ray Allen Billington, *The Protestant Crusade, 1800–1860* (Chicago: Quadrangle Books, 1964), and Dale T. Knobel, *Paddy and the Republic: Ethnicity and Nationality in Antebellum America* (Middleton, CT: Wesleyan University Press, 1986). Knobel argues that anti–Irish prejudices were more ethnic than religious. Considering that the nativists did not focus on Irish Protestants or Scots-Irish Presbyterians, his thesis is questionable.

5. Anti-Catholic nativism in 1850s Chicago is discussed in Thomas M. Keefe, "Chicago's Flirtation with Political Nativism," *Records of the American Catholic Historical Society of Philadelphia* 82 (September 1971): 131–58, and "The Catholic Issue in the *Chicago Tribune* Before the Civil War," *Mid-America* 57 (October 1975): 227–45; and Michael Funchion, "Political and Nationalist Dimension," in *The Irish in Chicago*, 62.

6. *Chicago Tribune*, July 30, 1864. Fourteen years after his death, on December 17, 1878, the Rev. John McMullen presented a paper on Mulligan to the Chicago Historical Society: see James A. Mulligan Papers, Chicago Historical Society.

7. For Daniel O'Connell's views on the slavery issue, see Lawrence J. McCaffrey, *Daniel O'Connell and the Repeal Year* (Lexington: University of Kentucky Press, 1966), 73–74, 205 n.54. Carl Wittke's *The Irish in America* (reprint, New York: Russell & Russell, 1970), 123–34, contains valuable information on black-Irish conflict in the period under discussion. Other studies that emphasize Irish and African American rivalries are Robert Ernst, *Immigrant Life in New York City, 1825–1863* (New York: Kings Crown Press, 1949); Florence E. Gibson, *The Attitudes of the New York Irish toward State and National Affairs, 1848–1892* (New York: Columbia University Press, 1951); and Phyllis F. Field, *The Politics of Race in New York: The Struggle for Black Suffrage in the Civil War Era* (Ithaca, NY: Cornell University Press, 1982). Noel Ignatiev, in *How the Irish Became White* (New York: Routledge, 1995), argues that the downtrodden, insecure Irish adopted racism as a route to white status in the United States. While it reveals much, the academically fashionable whiteness theory also distorts the truth. Legally and in self-perception, the Irish were white. In *The Irish in New Orleans, 1800–1860* (New York: Arno Press, 1976), 51–54, Earl F. Niehaus describes Irish versus African American conflicts in that important southern city preceding the Civil War. But Graham Hodges, "'Desirable Companions and Lovers': Irish and African Americans in the Sixth Ward, 1830–1870," in *The New York Irish*, edited by Ronald H. Bayor and Timothy J. Meagher (Baltimore: Johns Hopkins University Press, 1996), 107–24, presents a different story in one part of the city where tolerance existed in community and workplace and African-American men and Irish women mated and often married.

8. Joseph M. Hernon, *Celts, Catholics, and Copperheads: Ireland Views the American Civil War* (Columbus: Ohio University Press, 1968), and Toby Joyce, "The American Civil War and Irish Nationalism," *History Ireland* 4 (Summer 1996): 36–41, analyze the various reason for pro-Confederate sentiments among the Irish in Ireland. Since Irish nationalists wanted to dissolve the union that tied Ireland to Britain, it was only natural that they would sympathize with the intention of the American South to go its own way. The Catholic laity and clergy also reacted to the heavy Irish mortality rate in the Civil War and suspected that people were encouraged to immigrate for jobs in the United States that really ended in military service. Certainly the Irish Republican Brotherhood in Ireland had less sympathy for the Union cause than American Fenians.

9. According to Hernon, *Celts, Catholics, and Copperheads*, "In the Union armies there were at least 150,000 soldiers of Irish birth. Young Irelander John Mitchel claimed there were 40,000 Irish born Confederate soldiers" (11). Wittke, in *The Irish in America*, writes, "The number of Irish in the Union army has been estimated from 150,000 to 170,000" (134–35). In these pages, he also gives the 1869 United States Sanitary Commission numbers.

10. After the 1860 election, Douglas, though quite ill, with his last ounce of energy, attempted to save the Union through compromise. When that failed, he traveled through the North preaching solidarity behind Lincoln and the war. Douglas died on June 3, 1861. Bishop Duggan led the funeral procession to the gravesite, near Lake Michigan on the South Side. Karamanski's valuable *Rally 'Round the Flag* (60–65), describes Douglas's patriotic effort. His book was an important source in the writing of this chapter.

11. See notes 1 and 8.

12. Information on Mulligan and the Irish Brigade comes from the following sources: T. Andreas, *History of Chicago*, vol. 2 (reprint, New York: Arno Press, 1975), 190–95; Harold F. Smith, "Mulligan and the Irish Brigade," *Journal of the Illinois State Historical Society* 56 (Summer 1973): 164–76; T.M. Heady, *The Patriotism of Illinois*, vol. 2 (Chicago: Clark and Company, 1866), 567–79; Burton, *Melting Pot Soldiers*, 11–13, 43, 136–38, and "Ethnic Regiments in the Civil War: The Illinois Experience," *History Symposium, Illinois State Historical*

Society, Selected Papers, (Springfield: Illinois State Historical Society, 1980), 31–39; Victor Hickin, foreword to *Illinois in the Civil War*, by E.D. Long (Urbana and Chicago: University of Illinois Press, 1991), 7, 18–19, 333; and *Chicago Tribune*, July 30, 1864.

13. "In the Hour of Need," *Chicago Tribune*, April 24, 1861.

14. "Reception of Colonel Mulligan: Chicago Welcomes the Hero of Lexington," *Chicago Evening Journal*, November 9, 1861; "Reception of Colonel Mulligan: Honors to the Defender of Lexington," *Chicago Tribune*, November 9, 1861.

15. Letter of James A. Mulligan, November 12, 1861, and "Proclamation from the City of New York," December 17, 1861: Mulligan Papers, Chicago Historical Society. For accounts of Mulligan's activities in New York, see *New York Times*, December 21, 1861.

16. Smith, "Mulligan and the Irish Brigade," 173. For a more critical view of Mulligan's administration of Camp Douglas, see Karamanski, *Rally 'Round the Flag*, 83–85. According to Ed Gleason's *Rebel Sons of Erin: A Civil War History of the Tenth Tennessee Infantry Regiment (Irish) Confederate States Volunteers* (Indianapolis: Guild Press of Indiana, 1993), 40–41, Colonel Mulligan and Tennessee Camp Douglas Irish prisoners shared a mutual respect.

17. Frederick H. Dyer, *A Compendium of the War of Rebellion*, vol. 1 (New York: Yoseloff, 1959), 40, lists the Irish Brigade's fatalities as four officers and fifty enlisted men killed or mortally wounded, as well as two officers and ninety-three enlisted men dead of diseases.

18. In September 1861 Lincoln offered Mulligan the rank of brigadier general. He rejected the promotion to remain with his men, expecting that his regiment would expand into a large Western Irish Brigade. Later Mulligan unsuccessfully lobbied for a star on his shoulder, blaming his failure on anti-Irish bigotry in Washington. Immediately following his death, the government brevetted him as brigadier general. Twenty years later, an Illinois state legislature grant and local donations financed an impressive monument crowned with a Celtic cross close to the western entrance of Calvary Cemetery in Evanston, next to Mulligan's grave. The formal dedication took place on May 30, 1885. In 1899, Chicago began construction of the James A. Mulligan School at 1800 N. Sheffield Avenue in what is now the Lincoln Park neighborhood. The school building still exists but is without students.

19. Biographical information on Denis Dunne and his family is based on Len Hilts, "The Dunnes of New Brunswick and Chicago," unpublished manuscript. Articles on Denis Dunne's life and funeral were published in the *Chicago Times*, December 24, 27, and 28, 1868. For additional information on Father Dunne, see James P. Gaffey, *Citizen of No Mean City: Archbishop Patrick Riordan of San Francisco, 1841–1914* (Wilmington, NC: Consortium Books, 1976), 6–8; and Ellen Skerrett, "The Irish in Chicago: The Catholic Dimension," in *Catholicism, Chicago Style*, by Ellen Skerrett, Edward R. Kantowicz, and Steven M. Avella (Chicago: Loyola University Press, 1993), 35–38. Charles Fanning's *Finley Peter Dunne and Mr. Dooley: The Chicago Years* (Lexington: University of Kentucky Press, 1978) is a masterful study of Father Dunne's nephew.

20. The following information on the Irish Legion was gathered from *Chicago Tribune* and *Chicago Times* news reports; Andreas, *History of Chicago*, vol. 2, 249–52; and Burton, *Melting Pot Soldiers*, 139–40. According to D'Arcy, *The Fenian Movement in the United States*, 43, in 1864 the Irish Legion donated $507 to the Fenian Brotherhood.

21. *Chicago Tribune*, August 10, 1862.

22. For information on conflicts in the Irish Legion between Dunne and Snowhook partisans and between O'Meara and fellow officers, see Burton, "Ethnic Regiments," 33–34, 38. The Ryan Guards company of Galena, Illinois, was included in the new regiment. For a full treatment of the legion, see James B. Swan, *Chicago's Irish Legion: The 90th Illinois Volunteers in the Civil War* (Carbondale: Southern Illinois University Press, 2009), 13.

23. Bruce Catton, in *Reflections on the Civil War*, edited by John Leely (New York: Berkeley, 1994), 41–42, 69–69, 161, 177–78, 232, mentions food problems and the toll that disease took on the troops. See also letter from Peter Casey to his wife from Irish Legion 90th Regiment Illinois Headquarters, May 13, 1863, in the Mulligan Papers, Chicago Historical Society.

24. May 11, 1863: Mulligan Papers, Chicago Historical Society.

25. Iver Bernstein, *The New York City Draft Riots: Their Significance for American Society and Politics in the Age of the Civil War* (New York: Oxford University Press, 1990).

26. Karamanski, *Rally 'Round the Flag*, 213–14. Earlier in his book, on pages 179–80, Karamanski describes Chicago Irish hostility to blacks and the Emancipation Proclamation.

27. *Ibid.*, 223. In Chicago, Lincoln's margin over McClellan was less than two thousand votes: 14,388 to 12,691.

28. Karamanski, *Rally 'Round the Flag*, 238–39; *Chicago Tribune*, June 13, 1865.

29. *Chicago Tribune*, June 15, 1865; *Chicago Times*, June 14, 1865.

30. After Duggan was institutionalized in St. Louis for a mental breakdown, his successor in Chicago, Bishop Thomas Foley, restored Dunne's allies to good standing. McMullen became vicar general of the diocese and rector of Holy Name Cathedral before moving to Davenport, Iowa, as its first bishop. McGovern became pastor of Holy Trinity, Bloomington, Illinois, and roles pastor of Saint Mary's, Rock Island, Illinois. When Duggan died, he was buried in Calvary Cemetery in Evanston, Illinois. In the spring of 2001, his remains were transferred to the bishop's mausoleum in Holy Sepulcher Cemetery in Chicago's western suburbs.

31. Dunne's funeral was reported in the *Chicago Times*, December 25, 27, 28, and 29, 1868, and *Chicago Tribune*, December 27, 1868.

32. For descriptions of Chicago's economic development, see Karamanski, *Rally 'Round the Flag*, and William Cronon, *Nature's Metropolis: Chicago and the Great West* (New York: W.W. Norton, 1991).

33. For a study of the "Devotional Revolution," see Emmet Larkin, *The Historical Dimensions of Irish Catholicism* (Washington, D.C.: Catholic University of America Press, 1997), 57–89. For surveys of the Irish American experience, see Dennis Clark, *Hibernia America: The Irish and Regional Cultures* (Westport, CT: Greenwood Press, 1986); Maureen Dezell, *Irish America, Coming into Clover: The Evolution of a People and a Culture* (New York: Doubleday, 2001); Marjorie Fallows, *Irish American Identity and Assimilation* (Englewood Cliffs, NJ: Prentice Hall, 1977); Kevin Kenny, *The American Irish: A History* (New York: Longman, 2000); Lawrence J. McCaffrey, *The Irish Catholic Diaspora in America* (Washington, D.C.: Catholic University of America Press, 1997) and *Textures of Irish America* (Syracuse, NY: Syracuse University Press, 1998); and Kerby Miller, *Emigrants and Exiles: Ireland and the Irish Exodus to North America* (New York: Oxford University Press, 1985).

BIBLIOGRAPHY

Andreas, T. *History of Chicago*. Vol. 2. Reprint, New York: Arno Press, 1975.
Bernstein, Iver. *The New York City Draft Riots: Their Significance for American Society and Politics in the Age of the Civil War*. New York: Oxford University Press, 1990.
Billington, Ray Allen. *The Protestant Crusade, 1800–1860*. Chicago: Quadrangle Books, 1964.
Burton, William L. "Ethnic Regiments in the Civil War: The Illinois Experience." *History Symposium, Illinois State Historical Society, Selected Papers*.
_____. *Melting Pot Soldiers: The Union's Ethnic Regiments*. Ames: Iowa State University Press, 1988.
Catton, Bruce. *Reflections on the Civil War*. Edited by John Leely. New York: Berkeley, 1994.
Chicago Evening Journal, 1860–1865.
Chicago Times, 1856–1867.
Chicago Tribune, 1860–1866.
D'Arcy, William. *The Fenian Movement in the United States, 1858–1886*. New York: Russell & Russell, 1971.
Dyer, Frederick H. *A Compendium of the War of Rebellion*. Vol. 1. New York: Yoseloff, 1959.
Fanning, Charles. *Finley Peter Dunne and Mr. Dooley: The Chicago Years*. Lexington: University of Kentucky Press, 1978.
Fanning, Charles, Ellen Skerrett, and John Corrigan. *Nineteenth Century Chicago Irish: A Social and Political Portrait*. Chicago: Center for Urban Policy, Loyola University of Chicago Press, 1980.
Funchion, Michael F. "Irish Chicago: Church, Homeland, Politics and Class—The Shaping of an Ethnic Group." In *Ethnic Chicago: A Multicultural Portrait*, edited by Peter Jones and Melvin G. Holli, 57–92. Grand Rapids, MI: William B. Eerdmans, 1981.

Gaffey, James P. *Citizen of No Mean City: Archbishop Patrick Riordan of San Francisco, 1841-1914*. Wilmington, NC: Consortium Books, 1976.
Green, Paul Michael. "Irish Chicago: The Multi-ethnic Road to Machine Success." In *Ethnic Chicago: A Multicultural Portrait*, edited by Peter Jones and Melvin G. Holli, 212-59. Grand Rapids, MI: William B. Eerdmans, 1981.
Heady, T.M. *The Patriotism of Illinois*. Vol. 2. Chicago: Clark and Company, 1866.
Hernon, Joseph M. *Celts, Catholics, and Copperheads: Ireland Views the American Civil War*. Columbus: Ohio University Press, 1968.
Hilts, Len. "The Dunnes of New Brunswick and Chicago." Unpublished manuscript.
James A. Mulligan Papers, Chicago Historical Society.
Karamanski, Theodore. *Rally 'Round the Flag: Chicago and the Civil War*. Chicago: Nelson-Hall, 1993.
Keefe, Thomas M. "The Catholic Issue in the *Chicago Tribune* Before the Civil War." *Mid-America* 57 (October 1975): 227-45.
_____. "Chicago's Flirtation with Political Nativism." *Records of the American Catholic Historical Society of Philadelphia* 82 (September 1971): 131-58.
Knobel, Dale T. *Paddy and the Republic: Ethnicity and Nationality in Antebellum America*. Middletown, CT: Wesleyan University Press, 1986.
Long, E.D. *Illinois in the Civil War*. Urbana and Chicago: University of Illinois Press, 1991.
McCaffrey, Lawrence J. *Daniel O'Connell and the Repeal Year*. Lexington: University of Kentucky Press, 1966.
_____. *The Irish Catholic Diaspora in America*. Washington, D.C.: Catholic University of America Press, 1997.
McCaffrey, Lawrence J., Ellen Skerrett, Michael F. Funchion, and Charles Fanning. *The Irish in Chicago*. Urbana and Chicago: University of Illinois Press, 1987.
Skerrett, Ellen. "The Development of Catholic Identity among Irish Americans in Chicago, 1880 to 1920." In *From Paddy to Studs: Irish American Communities in the Turn of the Century Era, 1880-1929*, edited by Timothy J. Meagher. New York and Westport, CT: Greenwood Press, 1986.
_____. "The Irish in Chicago: The Catholic Dimension." In *Catholicism, Chicago Style*, by Ellen Skerrett, Edward R. Kantowicz, and Steven M. Avella. Chicago: Loyola University Press, 1993.
Smith, Harold F. "Mulligan and the Irish Brigade." *Journal of the Illinois State Historical Society* 56 (Summer 1973): 164-76.
Wittke, Carl. *The Irish in America*. Reprint, New York: Russell & Russell, 1970.

The Boston Irish and the Civil War

ARTHUR H. MITCHELL

The year of 1860 set the stage for traumatic events in the nation; it also marked a change in the relationship between natives and newcomers in Massachusetts, as elsewhere in the country. After decades of hostility and rejection, Irish people emerged as an important component in political ebbs and flows as the disunion of the American community emerged as a reality. What would be their position regarding this development? Would they stand aloof from the pleas of the antagonists who for so long had scorned them?

In Massachusetts an important factor in the gradual and limited reconciliation of Yankees and Irishmen was the 1860 election of John Andrew as governor. A Republican, to be sure, but he totally rejected the coy, indirect party linkage with nativism. Gone from the state leadership were Nathaniel Banks and his coterie of ex-Know Nothings. Both Massachusetts and the nation would shortly have desperate need of the services of thousands of young Irishmen, and securing these services would, at a minimum, require the creation of an atmosphere of good will and appreciation.

A question inevitably arises: Was Andrew's election fortuitous or was it a calculated gesture? No previous governor had shown understanding and sympathy to people from Ireland. The Protestant clergymen who had made careers of denouncing popery in all its manifestations turned to other subjects; the voices of ranting nativist politicians were stilled. Now all was changed. Did it occur to some of these people that the disruptive, bedraggled Paddies now could be turned to a useful purpose—as candidates for cannon fodder?[1]

In the presidential election Irish voters in Massachusetts, as in other northern states, provided strong support for Democrat Stephen A. Douglas. Throughout the campaign Patrick Donahoe's *Pilot* and other organs of Irish opinion warned of the dangers of disunity if Abraham Lincoln were to be elected. Although he gained only a minority (39.8 percent) of the national vote in a four-way contest, Lincoln carried Massachusetts by 60 percent, as did Andrew. In Boston Douglas received strong support in the two Irish wards (one and seven), while Lincoln won large majorities in the other ten wards.[2]

Like many people in the country, the Boston Irish and their mouthpiece, the *Pilot*, for a time seemed confused about what position to take as South Carolina led the way in southern secession little more than a month after the election. Recalling the blatantly bigoted actions of the Know Nothing movement a few years before, John C. Tucker (not an Irish name), the leading Irish politician in Boston, declared that "Irishmen could not be expected to risk lives for those who did this." The *Pilot* observed that every member of the Irish militia companies that had been disbanded following their 1855 participation in leading a runaway slave back into bondage "has shown a disposition to throw the remembrances of the affront to the winds."[3]

At least one Irish organization in Boston clearly took its stand at this time. Having been told by President Hugh O'Brien, later the first Irish-born mayor of the city, of the need for affirmation, the Charitable Irish Society in December 1860 resolved to stand by the nation: "We invoke our brethren and fellow-citizens throughout the Union, by the memories of our past united career, to lay aside all sectional or partisan animosities, and devote themselves to the cause of our endangered common country." On St. Patrick's Day in 1862, the society saluted its members who were serving in "the war to fight for the restoration of the glorious Constitution and Union of the States," such service having "rebounded to the honor of their nationality."[4]

With the bombardment of Fort Sumter in Charleston Harbor in April 1861, the *Pilot* assumed an unequivocal position. In an editorial dated April 27, it stated that the South had long been tortured by rabid abolitionists and opportunistic northern politicians, but this did not justify the destruction of the Union. Speaking in the name of all of its constituency, it declared, "The Irish will stand up for the Union, and surround it like a wall of fire." With dramatic flourish, it went on to say, "We have hoisted the American Stars and Stripes over *The Pilot* Establishment and there they shall wave till the 'star of peace' returns."[5]

This declaration of loyalty to the Union undoubtedly reflected the views of the Irish people of Boston, Massachusetts, and New England—indeed, of Irish people throughout the North. This affirmation, followed by initial large-scale Irish enlistment in Union regiments, was an important ingredient in solidifying Unionist support, and it did not go unnoticed by the neighbors of the Boston Irish.

Harvard University quite unexpectedly decided to honor the Catholic bishop of Boston and in July 1861 awarded John Fitzpatrick an honorary doctorate of divinity. This honor was followed by others. At the beginning of

1862, the American Academy of Arts and Sciences, upon the nomination of five Harvard professors, voted to recognize Fitzpatrick as a scholar of eminence and inducted him into its membership. At the same time, a Yankee state senator proposed that Fitzpatrick should be elected to the Harvard Board of Overseers, a power not granted to the state legislature. The sudden esteem was acknowledged without irony.[6]

By the spring of 1861, the Irish generally decided to rally to the cause of the Union. Despite some initial concern, it was also clear that many young Irishmen and Irish Americans were prepared to volunteer for military service. The Civil War gave many of them the opportunity to demonstrate with word and deed their deep-held attachment to this country. About 150,000 Irish-born persons served in the Union forces, while those of Irish parentage probably supplied a similar number. This response more than refuted the long campaign of contumely heaped on the heads of Irish and Catholic people by the Know Nothings and other nativists, who until then had so often condemned these people as inassimilable foreigners, drunkards, troublemakers and religious subversives. From the point of view of at least some Irish people, the naysayers, begrudgers and bigots had received their comeuppance. Referring to its Know Nothing opponents, a writer in the *Pilot* asserted that "when the base thing crawled to light ... the first lie it uttered was that Irish Catholics couldn't be depended on in their oath of naturalization," but the Irish response to the national crisis clearly refuted their detractors: "The Irish have won many victories," but "the squelching of 'Nativism' is the best in their American annals."[7]

With a mass of Irishmen now available for enlistment in the U.S. Army, a new, benevolent atmosphere pervaded the Yankee Protestant Republican political establishment. It was with obvious pleasure that Governor John Andrew wrote to the new secretary of war about forming volunteer units: "Will you authorize the enlistment here ... of Irish, Germans and other tough men...? We have men of such description, eager to be employed, sufficient to make three regiments." Bishop Fitzpatrick apparently wrote to President Lincoln on the same subject. He was also credited with anticipating that the war would be long and bitter, reportedly declaring, "We will be lucky to see it ended in five years."[8]

In September 1861, Thomas Francis Meagher came to Boston to promote the proposed Irish Legion, to be led by Michael Corcoran (both Meagher and Corcoran were participants in the 1848 rebellion in Ireland). "Meagher of the Sword" was a hero to many Irish Americans. At a huge meeting presided over by Governor Andrew, he referred to the Irish militia companies that had been disbanded under nativist pressure in the 1840s: "Here at this hour I proclaim it in the center of that city where this insult was offered to the Irish soldier—Know-Nothingism is dead. This war, if it brought no other excellent and salutary fruits, brought with it this result, that the Irish soldier will henceforth take his stand proudly by the side of the native-born, and will not fear to look him straight and sternly in the face, and tell him that he has been equal to him in his allegiance to the Constitution." He clearly overstated the case when he claimed that all Irishmen in the North were pro–Union, but, he added, "If there is one who is not, let him take the next Galway steamer and go home."[9]

The Ninth Massachusetts Regiment was the first Irish unit formed. Its core of recruits came from the old Columbian Artillery, the militia company that had been disbanded in 1855 after escorting a fugitive slave back to bondage. All was now forgiven. Colonel Thomas Cass, a native of County Laois and a successful businessman in Boston as well as the former leader of the militia unit, was appointed commander of the new regiment. It was composed of ten companies—six from Boston (with Bernard Treanor as captain in one of them) and one each from Marlboro, Milford, Salem and Stoughton. Special permission was quickly granted to allow the unit to march under the green flag of Erin as well as the Stars and Stripes.

The organization of the unit had its difficulties. After visiting its training camp on Long Island in Boston Harbor, George Welles, Governor Andrew's investigator, declared that both officers and enlisted men were totally incompetent misfits who loomed as a disgrace to Massachusetts. Treanor, editor of the *Irish Patriot*, who had been active in promoting such a regiment, echoed Welles' assessment. However, Andrew decided to overlook these problems, and the regiment was given an enthusiastic send-off in Boston upon its departure "for the front" in June 1861.[10]

Colonel Cass had been determined to impose strict discipline on both officers and enlisted men in the regiment. In July 1862 he was mortally wounded in the battle of Malvern Hill in the Peninsula Campaign and was succeeded by Patrick R. Guiney, a native of County Tipperary who became a Boston lawyer and elected official before the war. As his letters to his wife show, Guiney was not only an effective and brave military leader but also a man who had to deal with dissension and plotting by his fellow Irishmen in the regiment. When it required replacements in August 1862, a regimental advertisement stated its case as follows: "Let the ranks of the glorious Ninth be at once manned by heroes, worthy successors of those who have fallen, and fit companions of the veterans still eager for the fight. That regiment is yours. Its history—its glorious past—it future is yours, and sheds a luster not on you only, but on the Irish race." The participation of the "Fighting Ninth" at Graines's Mills was noted by the *New York Herald*: before the Confederate line "waved the stars and stripes and the green flag of Erin, and with loud huzzas they rushed upon the rebels, driving up-hill." During the war, the regiment, which left service in July 1864, suffered 250 dead and 613 wounded.

Upon its expiration of service, accompanied by faltering enlistments, the unit was given a grand reception when it returned to Boston.[11]

A second Irish regiment—the Twenty-eighth Massachusetts, or "Faugh-a-Ballaughs" (Gaelic for "clear the way")—was called into federal service in December 1862 and became part of the Irish Brigade. Bernard Treanor, critic of the first Irish regiment, sought an appointment as quartermaster in this one, while noted Catholic writer Orestes Brownson begged for an appointment for his son. The regiment's first commander was William Monteith, who was soon removed for incompetence. Pressured by a variety of people about Monteith's successor, Governor Andrew wisely reached into the officer corps of the regular army and appointed Richard Byrnes, a native of County Cavan who had risen through the ranks and was commissioned a lieutenant at the beginning of the war. Byrnes killed in the battle of Cold Harbor in 1864. As part of the illustrious Irish Brigade in November 1862, the Twenty-eighth was torn to shreds at the battle of Fredericksburg a month later. A Confederate officer observed the brigade in action: "In the foremost line we distinguished the green flag with the golden harp of old Ireland, and we knew it to be Meagher's Irish Brigade." Peter Welsh, an Irish-born carpenter, was proud to be regiment's bearer of its green battle flag: "I will carry it as God gives me the strength for I know that he can as easily protect me there as if I was in the strongest tower ever built by the hands of man." He knew the importance of the cause he was serving: "This is the first test of a modern free government in the act of sustaining itself against internal enemies.... America is Ireland's refuge, Ireland's last hope; destroy [this] nation and her hopes are blasted." Welsh was killed at Spotsylvania. At the battle of Gettysburg the regiment lost one hundred and one men killed, wounded or missing. At the end of the war it stood seventh on the list of 2,000 regiments in numbers of fatalities.[12]

There also were a substantial number of Irishmen in the 19th Massachusetts Regiment, recruited in the Worcester area, including the members of Andrew Mahoney's Guards (19th Massachusetts Regiment), who fought in battles during the Peninsula Campaign and at Antietam and Fredericksburg. At Gettysburg the regiment lost more than half its soldiers, either killed or wounded in the mighty effort to defeat Pickett's Charge.[13]

Many of the ten thousand Irishmen from Massachusetts served in other units. For example, Private Patrick Gallagher of Boston, a native of Ballyfarne, County Galway, who immigrated in 1858, joined the mixed 43rd Massachusetts Infantry Regiment in 1862 for a nine-month enlistment and was present at the decisive battle of Gettysburg.[14]

Eventually at least thirty-eight Irish regiments, all boasting green flags, were formed in the Union Army. The presence of the Irish units was noted by Confederate soldiers. In the face of the repeated charges of Meagher's Irish Brigade at the battle of Fredericksburg in 1863, General A.P. Hill responded,

"There are those damn green flags again!" The bravery of the Irish troops on this occasion gained the admiration of the likes of George Pickett, James Longstreet and Robert E. Lee. John Devoy recalled that after that battle, John Cashel Hoey presented a poem that later became a feature of covert Fenian meetings in Dublin.[15]

About 40,000 Irishmen served in the Confederate military, with all-Irish units being formed in eight states. John Boyle O'Reilly was later to write a poem, "At Fredericksburg—December 13, 1862," inspired by the encounter when Cobb's Georgia Brigade, with many Irish members, poured fire on the Irish Brigade in its near-suicidal assault of Maye's Hill.[16]

As could be expected, there were difficulties when Yankees and Irishmen soldiered side by side in the Union Army, but care was taken to prevent these incidents from getting out of hand. Permission was freely granted for Catholic priests to accompany concentrations of Irish troops.[17]

In sharp contrast to past attitudes, Massachusetts officials almost invariably adopted a friendly and cooperative stance in regard to matters of Irish concern. For many years Catholic priests had not been allowed to enter public institutions to minister to the many Irish people there. In 1861 all was changed: the doors were flung open. The controversy concerning Bible reading in public schools was smothered by conciliatory legislation passed the following year. The two-year waiting period for voting was removed from the state constitution. In 1864 the state attorney general ruled that aliens who served in the military could become voters upon discharge (with a year's residence) even if they had not made a declaration of intent to become citizens. Of greater importance was a federal law, passed in June 1862, that granted immediate citizenship to foreign-born soldiers.[18]

Then there was the matter of the establishment of a Catholic college in the city. In 1861 the Jesuit Order constructed a church and school building on Harrison Avenue in Boston's South End. It was with some anxiety that Father John McElroy, S.J., approached the state legislature for a charter for the college. To his surprise, he received a friendly reception, and the charter bill promptly secured passage in March 1863. Governor Andrew also took the opportunity to deal with the unpleasant matter of a charter for Holy Cross College. Established at Worcester in 1843, this Jesuit institution had been refused a charter in 1849, ostensibly because the college would only be for Catholic students. In 1865 that little difficulty was overlooked, and Holy Cross at last got its charter. That same year the legislature approved a charter for the first Irish-controlled bank—the Union Institution for Savings. The new spirit of toleration was a sight to behold. Oscar Handlin has commented, "The war had produced an issue on which the Irish did not menace, indeed supported, the existing social order and its ideals"; the sectional conflict "created an appearance of harmony within the city."[19]

In March 1862—while civil war raged—Bishop John Fitzpatrick left Boston for a European sojourn. The stated purpose of this visit, which was to last two years, was to provide the leisure for his health to be restored. After traveling through Italy and France, he settled in Brussels, Belgium, which was not noted as a health resort. There he quickly became involved in the affairs of the U.S. legation. Although his health probably was a factor, the actual purpose of Fitzpatrick's European presence was mustering support for the Union cause. Irish-born Bishop John Hughes of New York also was in Europe for this purpose. The Confederate government had among its official representatives in Europe the Rev. Patrick Lynch, bishop of Charleston, South Carolina, slave owner and native of Clones, County Monaghan. As part of his campaign on behalf of the Confederacy, Lynch published (in Italian and French, but not in English) a lengthy pamphlet defending "domestic" slavery. Another Catholic priest who was active in the Confederate cause in Ireland was Father John Bannon, a native of County Roscommon who originally had served in the diocese of St. Louis.[20]

Ireland became a battleground in the fight for international public opinion. Union recruiters worked to secure volunteers, while Confederate agents attempted to prevent this from happening. Irishmen could not go to join the Confederate forces because of the Union naval blockade of the South, but the sea lanes to the North were open and welcoming. Fitzpatrick apparently did not get directly involved with the struggle in Ireland, but Hughes and Lynch certainly did.[21]

Some Union agents in Ireland attracted young men with glowing inducements concerning employment in American war industries. The movement of young men out of Ireland for military and industrial purposes caused a diplomatic flurry between the United States and the United Kingdom. It was a matter of law versus law: the U.S. contract labor law provided that immigrants could be brought in under employment contracts, while the British Foreign Enlistment Act made recruitment of its subjects by foreign governments illegal.[22]

A notable episode occurred at the beginning of 1864. An Irishman working as an American employment agent signed up one hundred Irishmen who were shipped to Portland, Maine. Then problems arose. Upon receiving inducements, seven of the immigrants promptly enlisted in the Twentieth Maine Infantry; one of them later claimed that "they were imprisoned on trumped-up charges and refused freedom unless they enlisted." Eighty-six others proceeded to Boston, where they were informed that the promised employment did not exist. They were then urged to join the Massachusetts Twenty-eighth, which many of them did.[23]

Some people in the Boston Irish community saw the whole operation as a form of exploitation. A relief committee was organized and a protest meeting held, at which the chairman declared that "the original intent of the parties who brought the men over was to make them part of the quota of Massachusetts." As the incident gathered momentum, the British foreign secretary charged that the men had been illegally recruited. In response, Secretary of State William H. Seward ordered that the men, already serving in Virginia, be returned to Portland for an inquiry. There were reports that in transit the men were treated as convicts, but the inquiry was inconclusive. Noting that the bounties for enlistment could be as high as $825 per person, the British consul in Boston informed his government that "the poor Irish are generally made drunk and given at the outside 25 dollars, the sharks who prey on them collect the balance, and thus a cargo of 120, as instance, would net a very large profit to the speculators."

The concern of the British government about Union recruitment in Ireland came at the very time when that government was allowing Confederate warships to be constructed in British shipyards (though armed in French ports). These frictions would cause problems in Anglo-American relations after the war, in which Irishmen happily participated.[24]

An important incentive to Irishmen to join and continue to serve in the U.S. Army was found in the emergence of the Fenian Brotherhood. Based in both Ireland and America, this movement was a revolutionary organization dedicated to the violent liberation of Ireland. Its agents were to be found wherever there were concentrations of Irish troops. Military service by Irishmen was seen as preparation for the postwar campaign to be conducted in Ireland. U.S. military authorities did nothing to discourage or suppress Fenian activity. As far as they were concerned, Fenian discussions and meetings did not impede military discipline or effectiveness. There was a war to be won and soldiers were needed; what they planned to do after it was over was their own business.[25]

In the wake of Lincoln issuing the preliminary Emancipation Proclamation in September 1862, and undoubtedly sharing the views of most Irish people in Boston and the nation, the *Pilot* launched a campaign against the looming abolition of slavery. Its pages were thrown open to correspondents who condemned Lincoln, Republicans, abolitionists and particularly black people. An often-cited argument was that the recruitment of black soldiers would have a disastrous effect on white (specifically Irish) volunteers. They resisted the momentous changes that the war had wrought. An Irish journalist attending the funeral of an Irish soldier in Indiana in November 1864 grasped what was happening: "Mars has abolished slavery."[26]

The appeals to patriotism and offers of substantial bounties began to be less effective by the beginning of 1863. As the war surged ahead and casualties mounted, the need for soldiers increased. At that time the federal government produced a draft law that makes the Vietnam War system look like a model of fairness and equity. Among its amazing features were provisions to gain exemption from military service upon payment of $300 or by hiring a substitute (John D. Rockefeller, Andrew Carnegie and J.P. Morgan chose the former option, while Grover Cleveland used the latter). There was no distinction made between men who had dependents and those who were single. To many poor working men, including immigrants, this was an elitist measure of the most brazen variety; a phrase was coined—"$300 or your life!" When the name of the son of New York mayor George Opdyke was drawn for the draft, the commutation fee was immediately paid; the next man called was Timothy O'Hara, who "could not afford $300 for exemption, and he quickly ended up in the army." Coming in the wake of the Emancipation Proclamation, the draft was particularly objectionable to many Irish people, but often the $300 fee was paid by political, union or church organizations.[27]

As conscription went into operation during the summer of 1863, draft riots swept the cities of the North. By far the greatest of these was the three-day uprising in New York City. A significant percentage of the rioters were Irish, and more than one hundred persons were killed and/or injured. Troops from the Irish Brigade had to be brought from Gettysburg, where the 69th Pennsylvania Volunteers, an all-Irish regiment from Philadelphia, had been at the head of the forces that broke Pickett's Charge, to quell the disturbance.[28]

Boston had a much smaller-scale outburst. Father James Healy, the diocesan chancellor, noted that several priests had spoken out against the draft law, and he anticipated trouble in Boston. A day after the beginning of the New York conflict, two provost marshals delivering conscription notices were attacked in the North End. A mob quickly gathered, and the police were forced to barricade themselves in the neighborhood station. The crowd then attempted to storm the nearby Cooper Street armory. Three militia companies and available regular soldiers were called into the city. Six persons were killed during the one-day riot. Healy ordered that every parish should urge its members not to continue such activity and priests took to the streets to urge calm and restraint. The *Pilot* likewise concluded that the draft law should be peacefully observed. There were no further incidents of violent opposition to conscription in New York, Boston or anywhere else. In fact, of the more than two million soldiers in the Union Army, many participated under the pressure of conscription and the lure of bounties; only 42,000 men were drafted. For Boston residents, 26,119 men served in the military, but probably only 713 were drafted.[29]

But some people fled from the draft. One of these was an Irishman from Boston who was later found dying from hunger on a street in Montreal. Another Massachusetts Irishman was a reluctant recruit: "He said he didn't know how it was at all, but they got him to enlist and if he got back to Lowell he didn't think they'd 'git him again.'"[30]

The Irish Brigade had such devastating losses that a major recruitment effort was launched at the beginning of 1864. Richard Byrnes, commander of the 28th Regiment, led a successful recruitment effort in Massachusetts for almost three months. The campaign received strong support from Patrick Donahoe and Martin Griffin. When Byrnes was about leave Boston to return to the war, he responded to the gift of a new green flag with unusual eloquence:

> [O]n behalf of my fellow-soldiers I thank you, and, through you, the kind friends who have presented us this beautiful flag. It will be dearly cherished; and, in their name, *I* promise it shall be gallantly defended. I can promise no more, sir, than to assure you that it will be a fresh incentive to the brave men who are periling their lives in defense of that flag which typifies union and liberty, and beneath which the shamrock has ever bloomed. In a few days, sir, that flag will throw its emerald folds to the breeze, and the smoke of battle will encircle it; its freshness and beauty may be tarnished, but while there is an Irish arm to strike in its defense, its honor shall never be sullied nor impaired.... Again, sir, I thank you for the flag, and trust that one day we shall return it to the care of Massachusetts, crowned with the laurel of victory of union and liberty forever.[31]

The service and sacrifice of nearly 150,000 Irish soldiers in the Union cause won the respect of the American public and filled Irish people with pride and a sense of self-esteem. Whether Irish-born or of Irish blood, they were loyal and accomplished American citizens. They had their own war heroes: Philip Sheridan, George Meade, Meagher of the Sword, James Shields, Philip Kearney and others. Those from Boston included Thomas Cass, Patrick Guiney and Patrick Hanley.[32]

Born in Tipperary in 1835, Guiney came to this country as a child; he rose to be a lawyer and helped to organize the Ninth Massachusetts Regiment at the start of the war. He took command of the unit after the death of Colonel Thomas Cass and lost on eye in the battle of the Wilderness in May 1864. At the same time he had to contend with opposition within the regiment and growing desertions. He ended the war as a brigadier general and became an assistant district attorney in 1866. He was at the beginning of a promising political career when he was elected (as a Republican) registrar of probate for Suffolk County in 1868. Disease caused by his head wound brought about his premature death in 1877; he was forty-two.[33]

When Guiney was wounded, he was succeeded by Lt. Colonel Patrick T. Hanley, a native of County Roscommon who, following his arrival in Boston in 1848, became a member of the Columbian Artillery militia company. Leading the regiment in the last desperate battles of the war, he rose to the rank of brigadier general. Having married in 1864, after the war he had thirteen children and became a prominent brewer.[34]

In a continuing feature, "Records of Irish American Patriotism," the *Pilot* celebrated the contributions of Irish soldiers in the conflict. This commitment largely silenced hostile commentary in Boston papers such as the *Atlas* and the *Bee*, with at least the daily *Post* recognizing Irish involvement, while *Harper's Magazine* continued its scornful and derogatory comments on Irish people, without observing any positive participation in the struggle.[35]

Boston was also the base of operations for the remarkable Patrick Sarsfield Gilmore (1829–1892), bandmaster extraordinaire. Born in County Dublin, he became a musician in the British army and traveled with his unit to Canada. In 1850 he moved to Boston and formed his own band. It was during the Civil War that he gained fame as a music man. As chief bandmaster in the Union Department of Louisiana, he staged his first "monster band concert" in 1864. It was also during this time that he wrote his popular song "When Johnny Comes Marching Home," based on an Irish song. Returning to Boston after the war, he staged two gigantic concerts—the "National Peace Jubilee" in 1869 and the "World Peace Jubilee" in 1872, with the latter consisting of 2,000 musicians and a chorus of 20,000 along with a "battery of cannon, electrically fired, and a half a dozen church bells, with members of the Boston Fire Department in full uniform beating out the 'Anvil Chorus' on fifty anvils." He continued his flamboyant career in New York and the Midwest, introducing a form of classical music to the masses. He also was a strong supporter of Irish nationalism and often staged concerts for Irish causes.[36]

As far as most Irish voters in Boston were concerned, allegiance to the Union did not mean support for Abraham Lincoln and the Republican Party. As it had done four years before, during the 1864 election the *Pilot* was outspoken in its opposition to Lincoln, while it lauded his opponent, General George McClellan, who was very popular with Union soldiers (though ultimately not as popular as Lincoln himself). As in 1860, the two Irish wards voted Democratic, while the rest of the city and almost all of the state voted Republican.[37]

In the immediate postwar period, the *Pilot* saw a new world for its community. In an editorial on March 21, 1866, it declared, "There is a large … and increasing number of Americans who welcome Irish American citizens to an equal share in the prizes of business and political life, and who are proud to associate with them upon the same social plane." However, the atmosphere of good will and common endeavor soon dissipated. Irish bodies were no longer required. It was back to prewar sectarian rivalry. But the Irish ranks were growing, and the Civil War experience, both for those who had been in the military and for those who had remained at home, was a galvanizing one, socially as well as politically.

Despite the growth of the Irish community, the number of Irish Americans elected to public office in Boston grew only gradually in the immediate postwar period. This modest political presence was in sharp contrast to the influence of Irish voting bloc in national politics. During the late 1860s and early 1870s the national Republican Party made a singular but largely unsuccessful effort to win Irish support.[38]

With the ending of the war, the focus of attention for many Irish people was the Fenian movement. During the conflict there was considerable Fenian activity among the Union forces. In addition, Fenianism increased in Irish areas in northern cities. In Boston, a twenty-year-old upholstery shop foreman, Patrick A. Collins, a native of Fermoy, County Cork, joined the Fenian Brotherhood in 1864 and soon rose to be its chief organizer. The same year Hugh O'Brien, then thirty-seven and born in County Dublin, also was involved in the movement. A weekly paper, *Fenian Spirit*, was published in the city at this time. When the war ended the Fenians hoped to use their trained supporters to overthrow British rule in Ireland. Fenian spokesman P.S. Sinnott of Boston argued that "if Irishmen fought and died for the preservation of the Union and the freedom of four and a half millions of African blacks, would not Irish Americans fight for the freedom of four and a half millions of Irish whites and the establishment of an Irish republic?"[39]

Public rallies for the Fenians in the immediate wake of the war drew large crowds and substantial support. Following a speech by Collins at North Attleborough, Massachusetts, in June 1865, it was said that many joined the organization, including "a dashing young fellow of three years experience in the tented field." The *Irish People* of Dublin reported great support for the revolutionary movement in the northeast of the United States: "You will find the Fenians in every town and hamlet up and doing. They catch at *every* opportunity to impress the 'yearnings' with the practical ring of their creed quaintly denominated by our Chicago friends as the 'fighting gospel' of Irish Nationality." Regarding charges that the Fenians constituted a secret society, which was condemned by the Catholic Church, Collins had a ready reply: "I am inclined to accept the lamented Mulligan dictum—'As a soldiers I obey my general, as a Catholic I obey my bishop. But I will not obey religious commands from the general nor military or political orders from the bishop.'"[40]

In 1866, the Boston Circle of the Fenian Brotherhood voted not to participate in the St. Patrick's Day parade in order to save money for the cause. Then a split erupted within the organization. While James Stephens, leader of the Fenian movement in Ireland, was making a widely hailed speaking tour of New England that August, P.A. Sinnott, a supporter of a rival Fenian group, had him arrested on a "groundless claim." This action was heatedly denounced by the New York *Irish American*, which declared that Sinnott was "one whose loud-mouthed professions of patriotism have served but to cover the plottings and damnable designs of a brazen political adventurer, the servile tool of a wretched cabal of political pirates."[41]

Also in 1866, the New York *Irish People* declared that "the blood of Corcoran and his comrades bore a bountiful crop of Fenian soldiers," and about

150 Union Army veterans went to Ireland to join forces with the Fenian organization there. Attempts to stage a rebellion focused on disorganization and mass arrests. After failing to set off a revolt in Ireland, the American Fenians turned their attention to Canada. Arms were purchased from the federal arsenals and Fenian units were mobilized. Due to British actions during the war, many supporters believed the U.S. government would not impede Fenian actions directed at Canada. With Buffalo as the center of activity, in 1866 the organization mounted three brief incursions across the border. Due to informers and open mobilization, their efforts were repulsed. For the small number of Irish Americans who were involved, this was the end of their affiliation with armed rebellion against Britain. Four years later, with young John Boyle O'Reilly along as a reporter for the *Pilot*, an even more feeble Fenian effort was made against Canada at St. Albans, Vermont, the site of a Confederate raid in 1864. There remained a base of support for a campaign of violence to attain Irish freedom within the Irish American community, but the majority of those who were interested in the cause of Irish nationality turned to peaceful, democratic organization.[42]

Patrick Collins, for example, soon plunged into domestic politics, winning election to the Massachusetts legislature in 1868 and eventually rising to be mayor of Boston. As a strong supporter of Charles Stewart Parnell and the Irish home-rule movement, he was president of the American Land League in 1881–1882.[43]

The participation of large numbers of their men in the Union Army gave the Irish community a greatly elevated status, not least in its own eyes, and prepared the way for political and social advancement and recognition in postwar Boston, Massachusetts, and the nation. On that solid basis, it was all uphill from there.[44]

Speaking at the banquet honoring the fiftieth anniversary of the establishment of the Ninth Regiment in 1911, Boston mayor John F. Fitzgerald viewed the significance of the past half-century:

> Looking back calmly on the events of these days, we can afford to smile at the failure of the New Englanders of the older stock to appreciate the sterling worth of the new comers, whose numbers were sufficient to excite grave apprehension among some of their leaders.... Happily those days have long vanished and the Irish race in Boston, by the exhibition of those very qualities which were displayed by the men of the Ninth Regiment, have advanced to a position from which they cannot be dislodged by narrow hatred or sectarian envy.... It has been my belief for a long time that the cause of Ireland is merely a local and particular phase of the cause of democracy and of humanity in general.[45]

NOTES

1. Dale Baum, "The Political Realignment of the 1850s: Know-Nothingism and the Republican Majority in Massachusetts," *Journal of American History* 64 (1978): 976–77.

2. George Potter, *To the Golden Door* (Boston: Little, Brown, 1960), 620–21; Francis R. Walsh, "The Boston *Pilot* Reports the Civil War," *Historical Journal of Massachusetts* 9 (July 1981): 6–7; Philip S. Klein, *President James Buchanan* (Newtown, CT: American Political Biography Press, 1995), 351–52; Baum, "Political Realignment," 977; Thomas O'Connor, *Fitzpatrick's Boston, 1846–1866: John Bernard Fitzpatrick, Third Bishop of Boston* (Boston: Northeastern University Press, 1984), 186–87; Dale Baum, "The 'Irish Vote' and Party Politics in Massachusetts, 1860–1876," *Civil War History* 26 (1980): 119–20.

3. Potter, *To the Golden Door*, 592, 623.

4. James B. Cullen, *The Story of the Irish in Boston* (Boston: J.B. Cullen & Co., 1889), 42–43; Melvin Holli and Peter Jones, eds., *Biographical Dictionary of American Mayors, 1820–1980: Big City Mayors* (Westport, CT: Greenwood Press, 1981), 271.

5. It also declared that the Irish, adopted citizens or not, would fight to protect the Union. Walsh, "Boston *Pilot* Reports," 7; *Pilot*, April 27, 1861. On Irish affirmation, see William Joyce, *Editors and Ethnicity: A History of the Irish American Press, 1848–1883* (New York: Arno Press, 1976).

6. O'Connor, *Fitzpatrick's Boston*, 197–99.

7. Walsh, "Boston *Pilot* Reports," 8.

8. Oscar Handlin, *Boston's Immigrants, 1790–1865: A Study in Acculturation* (Cambridge, MA: Harvard University Press, 1941), 207–8; O'Connor, *Fitzpatrick's Boston*, 195, 269 n. 18; Cullen, *Irish in Boston*, 139.

9. Paul Jones, *The Irish Brigade* (Washington, D.C.: Robert B. Luce, 1969), 73.

10. Handlin, *Boston's Immigrants*, 209–10; Cullen, *Irish in Boston*, 104–18, 441–43; John L. Garland, "Some Notes on the Irish during the First Month of the American Civil War," *Irish Sword: Journal of Military History Society of Ireland* (Summer 1961): 23–28, 31–34.

11. Frank Boyle, *A Party of Mad Fellows: The Story of the Irish Regiments in the Army of the Potomac* (Dayton, OH: Morningside, 1996), 37. A statue of Cass was erected on the Boston Common. See Marty Carlock, *A Guide to Public Art in Greater Boston* (Cambridge, MA: Harvard Common Press, 1988); Christian G. Samito, ed., *Commanding Boston's Irish Ninth: The Civil War Letters of Colonel Patrick R. Guiney, Ninth Massachusetts Volunteer Infantry* (New York: Fordham University Press, 1998); William L. Burton, "Irish Regiments in the Union Army: The Massachusetts Experience," *Historical Journal of Massachusetts* (June 1983): 107–8; *Irish American* (New York), August 2, 1862, in Ella Lonn, *Foreigners in the Union Army and Navy* (Baton Rouge: Louisiana State University Press, 1952), 73–74. The regiment's chaplain, Father Thomas Scully, who had been accused of disorderly conduct at the Long Island training camp, was twice censured and, after contracting a disease, discharged in 1863: Frank Farley, *The Fighting Ninth for Fifty Years* (Boston, 1911), 92–93, in Stephen Griffin Collection, National Library of Ireland. See also Christian G. Samito, *Becoming American Under Fire: Irish Americans, African Americans and the Politics of Citizenship during the Civil War Era* (Ithaca, NY: Cornell University Press, 2009), 174.

12. Burton, "Irish Regiments," 112–13; Kevin O'Brien, "Sprig of Green: The Union Irish Brigade," in *The History of the Irish Brigade*, edited by P.S. Seagrave (Fredericksburg, VA: Sergeant Kirkland's Museum and Historical Society, 1997), 94, 98; Barry Spink, "Colonel Richard Byrnes, Irish Brigade Leader," in *The History of the Irish Brigade*, edited by P.S. Seagrave, 119–76; Cullen, *Irish in Boston*, 106–19; Laurence Kohl and Margaret Richard, eds., *Irish Green and Union Blue: The Civil War Letters of Peter Welsh* (New York: Fordham University Press, 1986), 65–66, 82–83; William L. Burton, *Melting Pot Soldiers: The Union's Ethnic Regiments* (Ames: Iowa State University Press, 1988), 129.

13. William F. Hanna, "The Boston Draft Riot," *Civil War History* 36, no. 3 (September 1990): 263; Lonn, *Foreigners in the Union Army and Navy*, 118. The two Worcester Irish militia units in the war were the Jackson and Emmet Guards: see Richard O'Flynn journals, Box 3, College of Holy Cross Archives. See also Vincent Powers, "Invisible Immigrants: the Pre-Famine Irish Community in Worcester, Massachusetts from 1826 to 1860," Ph.D. thesis, Clark University, 1967, 439–44.

14. From Massachusetts there came 10,007, the fourth largest contingent in the Union Army, along with 51,206 from New York, 17,418 from Pennsylvania, 12,041 from Illinois, 8,129 from Ohio, 3,621 from Wisconsin and 4,362 from Missouri. See Carl Wittke, *Irish in America*

(Baton Rouge: Louisiana State University Press, 1956), 136. Patrick Gallagher was the great-grandfather of this writer. Gallagher returned to Boston and had his son read him newspapers (thereby gaining knowledge of sundry affairs that surely impressed Patrick's other, apparently illiterate colleagues in the city's road repair department), and he also belonged to the Grand Army of the Republic. With the federal government now freely granting pensions to aging veterans, in 1895 he complained of a stiff elbow, which he attributed to wartime service (as opposed to rubbing it on the bars of Boston, as at least one relative alleged), and received a pension of twelve dollars a month until his death in 1909. Gallagher/Mitchell family records; Family Archive database, National Library of Ireland. By the 1880s a majority of surviving Union veterans were receiving pensions. See Larry Logue, *To Appomattox and Beyond? The Civil War Soldier in War and Peace* (Chicago: I.R. Dee, 1996), 99–101.

15. Joseph M. Hernon, *Celts, Catholics, and Copperheads: Ireland Views the American Civil War* (Columbus: Ohio University Press, 1968), 18, 11–12, 38fn; John Devoy, *Recollections of an Irish Rebel* (New York: Young, 1929), 34. The recitation or poem, attributed to "J.F. Cork," probably first appeared in printed form in the *Irishman* on November 29, 1862. What seems to be the earliest mention of the Hill comment in a book is found in George W. Pepper, *Under Three Flags* (Cincinnati, OH: Curts & Jennings, 1899), 333.

16. Ella Lonn, *Foreigners in the Confederacy* (Chapel Hill: University of North Carolina Press, 1940), 218; "At Fredericksburg—December 13, 1862," *Songs, Legends and Ballads* (Boston, 1878), 109–15; O'Brien, "Sprig of Green," 65; William McCarter, *My Life in the Irish Brigade*, edited by Kevin O'Brien (Campbell, CA: Savas, 1996), 253, n. 16.

17. Burton, "Irish Regiments," 107–8; Robert Lord, John Sexton and Edward Harrington, *History of Archdiocese of Boston, 1604 to 1943* (New York: Sheed & Ward, 1944), ii, 715; O'Connor, *Fitzpatrick's Boston*, 199–202.

18. Lord et al., II, 626–27; Samito, *Commanding Boston's Irish Ninth*, 143; Samito, *Becoming American Under Fire*, 106–7; Thomas O'Connor, *Civil War Boston: Home Front and Battlefield* (Boston: Northeastern University Press, 1997), 102–4, 199; Baum, "Political Realignment," 976; Joyce, *Editors and Ethnicity*, 152.

19. O'Connor, *Civil War Boston*, 118–21; Lord et al., II, 606–7; Handlin, *Boston's Immigrants*, 211.

20. O'Connor, *Fitzpatrick's Boston*, 203–6; David Heisser, ed. and trans., "A Few Words on the Domestic Slavery in the Confederate States of America by Bishop Patrick N. Lynch," *Avery Review* 2, no. 1 (Spring 1999); Hernon, *Celts, Catholics, and Copperheads*, 13–14.

21. Charles P. Connor, "Archbishop Hughes and the Question of Ireland, 1829–1862," American Catholic Historical Society of Philadelphia, *Records and Studies*, no. 45 (March–December 1984): 15–26. See also David Heisser chapter on Patrick Lynch in this book.

22. Charles P. Cullop, *Confederate Propaganda in Europe, 1861–1865* (Coral Gables, FL: University of Miami Press, 1969), 100–113.

23. Hernon, *Celts, Catholics, and Copperheads*, 31–32.

24. Ibid., 32–33.

25. William D'Arcy, *The Fenian Movement in the United States: 1858–1886* (New York: Russell & Russell, 1947), 40–44, 68–69, 409; Arthur Mitchell, "Fenian Movement in America," *Eire-Ireland* 11, no. 4 (Winter 1967): 6–8.

26. Walsh, "Boston *Pilot* Reports," 9–12; B. O'Lynn, *Irish People* (Dublin), December 31, 1864.

27. The exemption provision was removed the next year. See Wittke, *Irish in America*, 143; Ernest McKay, *The Civil War and New York City* (Syracuse, NY: Syracuse University Press, 1990), 214; James W. Geary, *We Need Men: The Union Draft in the Civil War* (DeKalb: Northern Illinois University Press, 1991).

28. Wittke, *Irish in America*, 143–47; Michael H. Kane, "The Irish Lineage of the 69th Pennsylvania Volunteers," *Irish Sword: Journal of Military History Society of Ireland* 18, no. 72 (Winter 1991): 184. See also Phillip Pattee's and Frank Boyle's chapters in this volume.

29. Lord et al., II, 708–9; O'Connor, *Fitzpatrick's Boston*, 209–13; James M. Bugbee, "Boston under the Mayors," in *Memorial History of Boston*, vol. 3, edited by Justin Winsor (Boston: Ticknor and Company, 1881), 271; James W. Davidson et al., *Nation of Nations: A Narrative History of the American Republic* (New York: McGraw-Hill, 1990).

30. *Fenian Spirit* (Boston), August 22, 1864; Charles Dickson, "John Mitchel and the South," *Irish Sword: Journal of Military History Society of Ireland* 3, no. 13 (Winter 1958): 282. See also Kelly O'Grady, "John Mitchel and the Confederacy," in this volume.
31. Spink, "Colonel Richard Byrnes," 160–63.
32. For the effect of the Civil War on Irish status, see Dale T. Knobel, *Paddy and the Republic: Ethnicity and Nationality in Antebellum America* (Middletown, CT: Wesleyan University Press, 1986), 171–79.
33. Joyce, *Editors and Ethnicity*, 138; Cullen, *Irish in Boston*, 248–49.
34. Cullen, *Irish in Boston*, 105, 118, 364.
35. Walsh, "Boston *Pilot* Reports," 9, 15 n.17.
36. Cullen, *Irish in Boston*, 219–21; *Dictionary of American Biography*, vol. IV, 312–13; Wittke, *Irish in America*, 237.
37. Thomas O'Connor, *The Boston Irish: A Political History* (Boston: Northeastern University Press, 1995), 90–91; Baum, "The 'Irish Vote,'" 122–26.
38. Brian Jenkins, *Fenians and Anglo-American Relations during Reconstruction* (Ithaca, NY: Cornell University Press, 1969), 178–201, 211, 313–17, 322, 325–26. Patrick Guiney, a strong supporter of Ulysses S. Grant, was elected Suffolk County (Boston) registrar of probate in 1871, the first Irishman to win a county office in Boston. See Samito, *Commanding Boston's Irish Ninth*, 255, 256. Patrick Collins became one of the few Irishmen in the Massachusetts legislature when he was elected from South Boston to the House of Representatives in 1866, and two years later he became the first of his kind to be elected to the state senate. In 1870 Christopher Connor was the first Irish American elected to the Boston Board of Aldermen. See Potter, *To the Golden Door*, 281.
39. M.P. Curran, *Life of Patrick A. Collins* (Norwood, MA: Norwood Press, 1906), 18; *Fenian Spirit*, August 20, 1864; *Irish People* (Dublin), September 9, 1865.
40. *Irish American* (New York), June 29, 1865; *Irish People* (Dublin), May 6, 1865. On June 17, 1865, *Irish People* reprinted a report from the *Philadelphia Universe*, which stated that in the northern part of Pennsylvania Irishmen were joining the Fenian organization "with the rapidity of a contagious disease." For Collins' response, see Curran, *Life of Patrick A. Collins*, 21.
41. *Irish People* (New York), March 24, 1866; *Irish American*, August 18, 1866.
42. *Irish People* (New York), August 18, 1866; D'Arcy, *Fenian Movement*, 156–67, 355–58.
43. Vincent Lapomarda, "Twelve Irish American Mayors of Boston," in *Encyclopedia of the Irish in America*, edited by M. Glazier (Notre Dame, IN: University of Notre Dame Press, 1999), 63; Curran, *Life of Patrick A. Collins*, 59–62.
44. O'Connor, *Boston Irish*, 91.
45. Farley, *The Fighting Ninth for Fifty Years*, 82–83.

BIBLIOGRAPHY

Baum, Dale. "The 'Irish Vote' and Party Politics in Massachusetts, 1860–1876." *Civil War History* 26 (1980).
_____. "The Political Realignment of the 1850s: Know-Nothingism and the Republican Majority in Massachusetts." *Journal of American History* 64 (1978): 959–86.
Boyle, Frank. *A Party of Mad Fellows: The Story of the Irish Regiments in the Army of the Potomac*. Dayton, OH: Morningside, 1996.
Bugbee, James M. "Boston under the Mayors." In *Memorial History of Boston*, vol. 3, edited by Justin Winsor. Boston: Ticknor and Company, 1881.
Burton, William L. "Irish Regiments in the Union Army: The Massachusetts Experience." *Historical Journal of Massachusetts* (June 1983).
_____. *Melting Pot Soldiers: The Union's Ethnic Regiments*. Ames: Iowa State University Press, 1988.
Connor, Charles P. "Archbishop Hughes and the Question of Ireland, 1829–1862." *American Catholic Historical Society of Philadelphia, Records and Studies*, no. 45 (March–December 1984): 15–26.
Cullen, James B. *The Story of the Irish in Boston*. Boston: J.B. Cullen & Co., 1889.

Cullop, Charles P. *Confederate Propaganda in Europe, 1861–1865.* Coral Gables, FL: University of Miami Press, 1969.
Curran, M.P. *Life of Patrick A. Collins.* Norwood, MA: Norwood Press, 1906.
D'Arcy, William. *The Fenian Movement in the United States: 1858–1886.* New York: Russell & Russell, 1947.
Davidson, James W., et al. *Nation of Nations: A Narrative History of the American Republic.* New York: McGraw-Hill, 1990.
Devoy, John. *Recollections of an Irish Rebel.* New York: Young, 1929.
Dickson, Charles. "John Mitchel and the South." *Irish Sword: Journal of Military History Society of Ireland* 3, no. 13 (Winter 1958).
Farley, Frank. *The Fighting Ninth for Fifty Years.* Boston, 1911. Stephen Griffin Collection, National Library of Ireland.
Garland, John L. "Some Notes on the Irish during the First Month of the American Civil War." *Irish Sword: Journal of Military History Society of Ireland* (Summer 1961).
Handlin, Oscar. *Boston's Immigrants, 1790–1865: A Study in Acculturation.* Cambridge, MA: Harvard University Press, 1941.
Hanna, William F. "The Boston Draft Riot." *Civil War History* 36, no. 3 (September 1990).
Heisser, David, ed. and trans. "A Few Words on the Domestic Slavery in the Confederate States of America by Bishop Patrick N. Lynch." *Avery Review* 2, no. 1 (Spring 1999).
Hernon, Joseph M. *Celts, Catholics, and Copperheads: Ireland Views the American Civil War.* Columbus: Ohio University Press, 1968.
Holli, Melvin, and Peter Jones, eds. *Biographical Dictionary of American Mayors, 1820–1980: Big City Mayors.* Westport, CT: Greenwood Press, 1981.
Irish American (New York), 1860–1866.
Irish People (Dublin), 1860–1867.
Irish People (New York), 1866.
Jenkins, Brian. *Fenians and Anglo-American Relations during Reconstruction.* Ithaca, NY: Cornell University Press, 1969.
Jones, Paul. *The Irish Brigade.* Washington, D.C.: Robert B. Luce, 1969.
Joyce, William. *Editors and Ethnicity: A History of the Irish American Press, 1848–1883.* New York: Arno Press, 1976.
Kane, Michael H. "The Irish Lineage of the 69th Pennsylvania Volunteers." *Irish Sword: Journal of Military History Society of Ireland* 18, no. 72 (Winter 1991).
Kohl, Laurence, and Margaret Richard, eds. *Irish Green and Union Blue: The Civil War Letters of Peter Welsh.* New York: Fordham University Press, 1986.
Lapomarda, Vincent. "Twelve Irish American Mayors of Boston." In *Encyclopedia of the Irish in America*, edited by M. Glazier. Notre Dame, IN: University of Notre Dame Press, 1999.
Lonn, Ella. *Foreigners in the Confederacy.* Chapel Hill: University of North Carolina Press, 1940.
———. *Foreigners in the Union Army and Navy.* Baton Rouge: Louisiana State University Press, 1952.
McCarter, William. *My Life in the Irish Brigade.* Edited by Kevin O'Brien. Campbell, CA: Savas, 1996.
Mitchell, Arthur. "Fenian Movement in America." *Eire-Ireland* 11, no. 4 (Winter 1967).
O'Connor, Thomas. *The Boston Irish: A Political History.* Boston: Northeastern University Press, 1995.
———. *Civil War Boston: Home Front and Battlefield.* Boston: Northeastern University Press, 1997.
———. *Fitzpatrick's Boston, 1846–1866: John Bernard Fitzpatrick, Third Bishop of Boston.* Boston: Northeastern University Press, 1984.
Pilot (Boston), 1850–1868.
Potter, George. *To the Golden Door.* Boston: Little, Brown, 1960.
Samito, Christopher G. *Becoming American Under Fire: Irish Americans, African Americans and the Politics of Citizenship during the Civil War Era.* Ithaca, NY: Cornell University Press, 2009.

_____, ed. *Commanding Boston's Irish Ninth: The Civil War Letters of Colonel Patrick R. Guiney, Ninth Massachusetts Volunteer Infantry*. New York: Fordham University Press, 1998.
Seagrave, P.S., ed. *The History of the Irish Brigade*. Fredericksburg, VA: Sergeant Kirkland's Museum and Historical Society, 1997.
Walsh, Francis R. "The Boston *Pilot* Reports the Civil War." *Historical Journal of Massachusetts* 9 (July 1981): 6–7.
Wittke, Carl. *The Irish in America*. Baton Rouge: Louisiana State University Press, 1956.

What Made the "Fighting Irish" Fight

D.R. O'Connor Lysaght

The role played by the United States' Irish immigrants in their adopted country's wars has been neglected in the published studies of their community. Hopefully, this volume will help fill the gap. This contribution can only begin to summarize the causes for immigrants' military activities by relying on the findings of those better informed than the author. They combine to produce a coherent general picture of the pressures that made the Irish Americans the most dependable source of cannon fodder for the United States in its nineteenth-century wars.

Those pressures arose from the Irish immigrant experience. For nearly two centuries before the 1880s, Ireland was the major source of North American settlers. In the eighteenth century, these had come mainly from Ulster Protestant stock, ancestors of those whom nineteenth-century nativism would coerce into reinventing their forebears as "Scots Irish." From those forebears came an estimated one-third to one-half of the American Continental Army in the War of Independence.[1]

Like the Irish arrivals in the next century, these earlier immigrants were seen as being the bottom of the white social pile. An immigrant serving girl wrote of her condition, "Many negroes are better used."[2] Nonetheless, such people had an advantage unpossessed by most of the immigrants in the 1800s: unlike the later arrivals, their Protestantism helped them integrate into mainstream society. The bulk of those who came after were mistrusted as followers of reactionary popes and suspected of conspiring against republican institutions.

Despite this discouragement, Irish Catholics crossed the Atlantic—one million between 1815 and 1845, and a million and an half during the famine decade from the latter year.[3] They established themselves in two main ways.

In civil life they took the menial jobs that had been traditionally left to the free Negroes. Banned from organizing[4] and dependent on the convention that no white would compete with them, blacks were unable to stop the white Irish from undercutting them and establishing their own unions to monopolize their usurped callings.[5]

Unfortunately, their higher social position could not quell the fear of Irish immigrants, particularly those in the southern states, that abolishing slavery would create a free black workforce strong enough to reverse their gains. This was a real, albeit meager, justification for upholding the pre–Civil War status quo.[6] Starting in 1828, this fear was expressed politically through Irish American membership in the Democratic Party, which combined urban Populism with an Agrarianism that appealed to both slavers and free settlers.

This situation also created an ideological context in which immigrants joined the U.S. armed forces. Recruitment involved no challenges from even free blacks.[7] In addition, there were other factors at work. It was believed that the average immigrant lifespan was no more than six years,[8] which meant the risks of military life did not deter prospective soldiers. Furthermore, soldiering was a legal and socially approved way for immigrants to work out their resentments, even if not on those who most deserved to receive the backlash.

For the Irish, this last point was less instinctive and more strategic. The American army gave them training and the potential means to prepare for a military showdown on more equal terms than before with the old enemy whose rulers had driven them across the Atlantic: Britain.[9] In the U.S. forces there was no danger of the penalties that might be experienced in the British forces. What was more, after a span of one hundred years that included the wars of 1776 and 1812, it seemed likely that a new conflict would provide Ireland's opportunity to strike back.[10]

In the Mexican War of 1846–1848, most attention has been fixed, and deservedly so, on the heroic Irish of the San Patricio Battalion who fought against the stream and against the United States. More significant is the fact that nearly a quarter of the army that they opposed consisted of their fellow Irish immigrants.[11]

Partly because of the American victory in that war, the two rural groups that maintained the hegemony of the Democratic Party grew increasingly separate over the question whether the western territories should be open to slavery or reserved for small-farming settler capitalists. Having little capital or inclination to leave the cities, the Irish remained loyal to the Democratic Party, which continued to represent the slavery interest. The Democrats had organized them in the cities against the anti–Irish nativists, many of whom turned to the Republican Party, which the industrial and finance capitalists of the eastern seaboard used as the instrument of their alliance with the actual and potential free homesteaders.

Though hostile to abolition, the majority of Irish Americans do not seem to have been positively pro-slavery. In the absence of opinion polls, it is only possible to judge the general opinion from the community's most prominent and articulate figures. It did not produce any abolitionist of equal stature to the pro-slavery racist John Mitchel, but Mitchel was an extremist even in the Irish community in the northern states; he moved swiftly to the more congenial south.[12] His most prominent contemporaries tended to consign the problem to the inevitability of gradualness. John Hughes, archbishop of New York, opposed both abolition and the slave trade.[13] Thomas Meagher disliked slavery passively.[14] A future celebrity, the young Philip Sheridan, was not interested.[15] Even the future Confederate general Patrick Cleburne owned no slaves[16] and was to be criticized by Mitchel and others for demanding that slaves be freed if they would fight for their cause.[17]

In 1860, the Irish American community divided. Few voted for Abraham Lincoln; those in the south voted for the ardent slavery supporter, John C. Breckenridge, and the northerners backed the more ambivalent Democrat, Stephen Douglas.

Lincoln was elected by a minority of votes in the face of a divided opposition. The slavers might have used this fact to gain time to negotiate—if not to gain a better settlement, then to show their fellow countrymen, including the northern Irish, that they were reasonable, thus neutralizing more of them when war came. This was not to be. The slave owners' fears for their property and capital had caused them to split the Democratic Party. Now their leaders prepared openly to secede from the Union. Thomas Keneally describes how this affected the South's main trading partner and most sympathetic northern city, New York, where a quarter of the population had been born in Ireland: "By the close of January [1861] six states had seceded, and Southern clients began to refuse to pay their bills to the Sterling Iron Works and New York–based railroads until payment could be made in Confederate currency."[18] Two months later, only a month after Lincoln had been inaugurated, South Carolina troops fired on Fort Sumter.

The Irish tended to participate enthusiastically on whichever side they found themselves. In the Confederacy, Mitchel boasted 40,000 Irish-born soldiers,[19] though, as the total Irish-born population there totaled only 84,763,[20] it would seem that even the more realistic figure of 30,000 is too high. In the states loyal to the Union, Irish recruitment was less dramatic but still impressive. The Irish-born soldiers numbered 144,000[21] out of a community of 1,611,304.[22] Meagher's 69th Irish Militia, which became the Fighting 69th Brigade, attracted an initial 3,000 recruits, nearly three times the number it could handle.[23] How many were loyal to the Union and how many looked to a future war with Britain is impossible to say. Certainly, on September 1, 1862, the eve of the brigade's greatest victory at Antietam, its soldiers were singing "John Brown's Body," commemorating one whose execution most of them would have accepted at the time and some might well have approved.[24]

Five days after Antietam, Lincoln issued the Emancipation Proclamation. The following December, the 69th Brigade was decimated at Fredericksburg. In May 1863, Meagher resigned his command.[25] On top of these events came the plan to draft men into the Union Army, while allowing the rich to buy exemption from military service. This burden was borne particularly by the poorest members of society, and disproportionately by the Irish. The subsequent draft riots in New York and Boston would endanger the reputation the Irish community had gained at Antietam. Yet the riots involved only the industrial workers[26] and, in their anti-black aspects, only the labourers.[27] Indeed, in New York, the black dead totaled only 10 out of 100 fatalities (a disproportionate percentage of its share of the total population, but not one that stamps the riots as predominantly racist).[28] According to Bernstein, the Fighting 69th helped restore order once the riots had ended.[29]

Where the desire to exploit England's difficulty seems to have been more of a motive can be seen in the fact that the armed forces' immigrant ranks were swelled by recruitment of those just off the boat from Ireland. Between 1861 and 1864, Irish-born arrivals tripled in number.[30] The British authorities worried about U.S. recruiting officers in their colony, though no definite evidence of such activity has been found.[31] The one example of prospective recruitment within Irish waters was the *Kearsage* case, which involved the prosecution of six men who stowed away on the so-named Union ship. They claimed that they did so to enlist and that they knew of 150–300 others with similar plans. This does not mean that such men were dedicated to fighting slavery (after all, the Union blockade of the Confederacy prevented easy access to the latter combatant[32]), nor does it mean that they were Fenians (Union Army wages promised better living than was obtainable for many in their homeland).

Those who did hope to fight Britain after the Civil War would ultimately be disappointed. The only action was the Fenian invasion of Canada, an adventure even more peripheral than the San Patricios' action had been. Instead, there followed a period of coexistence between the North Atlantic powers. Britain even paid indemnification for having released a Confederate battleship to attack Union shipping. There would be no more strife between the two powers during the nineteenth and twentieth centuries.

Even before Canada, the majority of Irish Civil War partisans had found new commitments. Mitchel did return to his native land, but as a civilian (his sons had fought for the Confederacy), and too compromised by his pro-slavery past to have many prospects in his adopted country. Far more of his fellow immigrants went west rather than east. Meagher died beginning a new career in organizing Montana. Philip Sheridan was the outstanding figure among those who fought to clear the land of Indians with even less compassion than they had bestowed on black slavery.[33]

By 1890, the Irish position as the major immigrant community in the United States was challenged by waves of oppressed people from Central and Eastern Europe. The newcomers found that large sections of Ireland's former "huddled masses" had advanced in the New World. The lace curtain Irish were distinguished from their WASP neighbors only by their religion, and often the resulting education, while being united with them, in contrast to the new arrivals, through their ability to speak English.[34]

In times of war there would still be the old murmurings. There was considerable Irish American opposition to the Spanish-American War of 1898[35] and to American entry in the First World War while Ireland was resurgent. Though Joseph Kennedy had little real sympathy for Irish aspirations, his doubts about Britain's prospects in the Second World War reflected a deeper Irish American hostility.

At the same time, Irish American serving men continued to uphold the Stars and Stripes without the nineteenth-century distractions that had concerned their forebears. However, by the 1960s, a century after the Civil War, they found themselves superseded as America's cutting edge by the descendants of the Negroes whose cause they had supported tardily, and mainly for other reasons.

Unlike the privileged Wild Geese of the seventeenth and eighteenth centuries, Irish America had been integrated into its host society. Insofar as it supported the national aspirations of its ancestral homeland, it did so as a pressure group for political change (albeit often revolutionary) but not transatlantic war.[36] Ironically, its original desire for such a war had helped it pay the blood price of integration.

Notes

1. Ann Kathleen Bradley, *History of the Irish in America* (Secaucus, NJ: Chartwell Books, 1986), 32.

2. Ibid.

3. Lawrence J. McCaffrey, *The Irish Catholic Diaspora in America* (Washington, D.C.: Catholic University of America Press, 1997), 64–65.

4. Philadelphia went as far as to ban a black fire brigade company; see Noel Ignatiev, *How the Irish Became White* (New York: Routledge, 1998), 143.

5. James D. Gannon, *Irish Rebels, Confederate Tigers* (Campbell, CA: Savas, 1998), 397: The Irish "immigrants ignored local taboos about 'nigger work' and smashed Into free black monopolies everywhere, from day laboring to barbering." See also Ignatiev, *How the Irish Became White*, 87–88, 100–101, 109, 111.

6. By 1861, scabbery against white strikers was "almost the only employment open to negroes." Ignatiev, *How the Irish Became White*, 111. See also Iver Bernstein, *The New York City Draft Riots: Their Significance for American Society and Politics in the Age of the Civil War* (New York: Oxford University Press, 1990), 5, 27, 289.

7. Since 1792, the state militias had been restricted to white males; see Ignatiev, *How the Irish Became White*, 142.

8. See the immigrant's letter quoted in Kerby Miller and Paul Wagner, *Out of Ireland: The Story of Irish Emigration to America* (London: Aurum Press, 1994), 40.

9. After Irish revolutionaries failed to employ the United States as a military base, the General Council of the International Workingmen's Association (First International) noted disapprovingly, "Driven off their native soil by sheep and cattle, the Irish find a new home in the United States, where they represent a considerable and growing proportion of the population. Their sole idea, their sole passion is hatred of the English. The English government and the American government—that is to say the classes which they represent—feed these sentiments in order to perpetuate the international antagonisms which prevent any serious and sincere alliance between the working classes of the two countries, and, consequently, their common emancipation" (statement of January 16, 1870). This may seem to contradict the International's support for the Irish struggle for independence. In fact, an oppressed nation's struggle against its oppressor is intended to liberate the workers of both nations: those of the oppressor (from their illusions) as well as those of the oppressed. The war desired by the American Fenians between sovereign states could only reinforce nationalist illusions.

10. Ignatiev, in *How the Irish Became White*, 75, ascribes the victory of the Democrats in the 1844 presidential election to the Irish vote. This was after their opponents had defused a potential conflict with Britain over the Canadian boundary. He also remarks that Daniel O'Connell's much-praised stand for abolition owed a great deal to his need to maintain his alliance with the traditionally pro-abolitionist British Whigs. *Ibid.*, 24–26.

11. *Ibid.*, 161.

12. Thomas Keneally, *The Great Shame* (London: Chatto & Windus, 1998), 272–73. Mitchel's biographer quotes his subject's definitive view: "I consider negro slavery the best state of existence for the negro, and the best for his master; and if negro slavery in itself be good, then the taking of negroes out of their brutal slavery in Africa and promoting them to a humane and reasonable slavery here is also good" (letter to Mary Thompson, 1858). See William Dillon, *Life of John Mitchel*, vol. 2 (London: K. Paul, Trench & Co., 1888), 107.

13. Hughes declared slavery "a *crime* to reduce men naturally free to a condition of servitudes and bondage as slaves." Quoted in John R.G. Hassard, *Life of the Most Reverend John Hughes, D.D.: First Archbishop of New York* (New York: D. Appleton, 1866), 436. Nonetheless, he opposed the outright abolition of the South's "peculiar institution" (*Ibid.*, 436–37, 440).

14. In the *New York Times*, August 27, 1856, Meagher stated, "It would be well if America could get rid of slavery. But we can't, in our time, and should therefore confine our efforts to alleviate the evils that accompany it." Keneally, *The Great Shame*, 299.

15. Philip Sheridan, *Personal Memoirs of P.H. Sheridan*, vol. 1 (London, 1888), 123. In 1861, "Settled as I had been through the years spent in the wilderness, my patriotism was untainted by politics, nor had it been disturbed by any questions out of which the war grew."

16. Ella Lonn, *Foreigners in the Confederacy* (Gloucester, MA: P. Smith, 1965), 53.

17. Joseph M. Hernon, *Celts, Catholics, and Copperheads* (Columbus: Ohio University Press, 1968), 39 (Endnote 6).

18. Keneally, *The Great Shame*, 317. The percentage of Irish-born New Yorkers is from Steve Garner, *Racism in the Irish Experience* (London: Pluto Press, 2003), 94.

19. Lonn, *Foreigners in the Confederacy*, 218.

20. *Ibid.*, 31.

21. Carl Wittke, *The Irish in America* (Baton Rouge: Louisiana State University Press, 1956), 135.

22. Hernon, *Celts, Catholics, and Copperheads*, 38 (Endnote 1).

23. Keneally, *The Great Shame*, 320–21.

24. William McCarter, *My Life in the Irish Brigade*, edited by Kevin O'Brien (Campbell, CA: Savas, 1996), 2.

25. Keneally, *The Great Shame*, 382–83.

26. Bernstein, *The New York City Draft Riots*, 41.

27. *Ibid.*, 35.

28. Letter in *History Ireland* (Spring 2004).

29. Bernstein, *The New York City Draft Riots*, 113. This exploit of the company is not

mentioned in the collection of its histories; see P.S. Seagrave, ed., *History of the Irish Brigade* (Fredericksburg, VA: Sergeant Kirkland's Museum and Historical Society, 1997).

    30. Kerby Miller, *Emigrants and Exiles: Ireland and the Irish Exodus to North America* (New York: Oxford University Press, 1985), 359.

    31. Hernon, *Celts, Catholics, and Copperheads*, 23–30.

    32. *Ibid.*, 30–31.

    33. Garner, *Racism in the Irish Experience*, 104–5.

    34. Bradley, *History of the Irish in America*, 98.

    35. Garner, *Racism in the Irish Experience*, 109–10.

    36. Though less formally revolutionary, this perspective was closer to that of the First International than those of the International's contemporaries. See note 9.

BIBLIOGRAPHY

Bernstein, Iver. *The New York City Draft Riots: Their Significance for American Society and Politics in the Age of the Civil War.* New York: Oxford University Press, 1990.

Bradley, Ann Kathleen. *History of the Irish in America.* Secaucus, NJ: Chartwell Books, 1986.

Dillon, William. *Life of John Mitchel.* Vol. 2. London: K. Paul, Trench & Co., 1888.

Gannon, James D. *Irish Rebels, Confederate Tigers.* Campbell, CA: Savas, 1998.

Garner, Steve. *Racism in the Irish Experience.* London: Pluto Press, 2003.

Hassard, John R.G. *Life of the Most Reverend John Hughes, D.D.: First Archbishop of New York.* New York: D. Appleton, 1866.

Hernon, Joseph M. *Celts, Catholics, and Copperheads.* Columbus: Ohio University Press, 1968.

Ignatiev, Noel. *How the Irish Became White.* New York: Routledge, 1998.

Keneally, Thomas. *The Great Shame.* London: Chatto & Windus, 1998.

Lonn, Ella. *Foreigners in the Confederacy.* Gloucester, MA: P. Smith, 1965.

McCaffrey, Lawrence. *The Irish Catholic Diaspora in America.* Washington, D.C.: Catholic University of America Press, 1997.

McCarter, William. *My Life in the Irish Brigade.* Edited by Kevin O'Brien. Campbell, CA: Savas, 1996.

Miller, Kerby. *Emigrants and Exiles: Ireland and the Irish Exodus to North America.* New York: Oxford University Press, 1985.

Miller, Kerby, and Paul Wagner. *Out of Ireland: The Story of Irish Emigration to America.* London: Aurum Press, 1994.

Seagrave, P.S., ed. *History of the Irish Brigade.* Fredericksburg, VA: Sergeant Kirkland's Museum and Historical Society, 1997.

Sheridan, Philip. *Personal Memoirs of P.H. Sheridan.* Vol. 1. London, 1888.

Wittke, Carl. *The Irish in America.* Baton Rouge: Louisiana State University Press, 1956.

Irish Women in the Civil War

EILEEN M. MCMAHON

> "They comforted the dying, nursed the wounded, carried hope to the imprisoned, gave in His name a drink of water to the thirsty."
> —Civil War Nurses Memorial, Washington, D.C., 1924

The monument dedicated to nurses of the Civil War on Connecticut Street in the nation's capital includes a bas-relief sculpture that portrays Roman Catholic sisters dressed in the religious habits of their respective orders. It was commissioned by Congress at the request of the Ancient Order of Hibernians and has become known as the "Nuns of the Battlefield." It is one of the few memorials to any women who shared in the war effort. Nineteenth-century American society chose to forget the role that women played in the Civil War because war was not a proper place for females. The fact that the monument honors Catholic women in particular reflects the living memory of a few in the Catholic and Irish American community who realized the singular importance of the sisters' efforts during the war and the role they played in Protestant America's grudging acceptance of Catholics in this country.

In the antebellum period Irish women, like Irishmen, were considered outsiders in America society. They were immigrants, generally poor and working class, and predominantly Catholic in an Anglo-Protestant culture. Irish women also entered a gendered world in which womanhood was idealized by the cult of domesticity as middle class and in the home. Protestant ladies did not work outside their homes, but they influenced the external world through nurturing their families with their moral superiority. Irish women, by contrast, faced more daunting challenges of survival and did not have the luxury of indulging in these refined ideals. They viewed themselves as independent agents taking whatever opportunities came their way. However, their lives were often constrained by this ideology, and Protestant America used it as another weapon of condemnation. The Nuns on the Battlefield proved worthy of memorializing years later, as they embodied the gentle, caring spirit of Catholic sisters as well as an expanded notion of true womanhood. Other Irish women who asserted themselves as military laundresses, soldiers, street political demonstrators, or factory laborers were exceptions best forgotten.[1]

Modern warfare breaks down gendered norms, and the American Civil War revealed some of the social limitations placed on all women during this period.[2] As casualties mounted and the war lengthened, women's labor became a necessity. By the end of the war, Irish women had challenged prevailing notions of a woman's proper place. Irish Catholic sisters served as nurses on the battlefields in both the North and the South. Many Irish women washed clothes for the troops. Some served in disguise as soldiers in their own right. One notable Irish American woman spied for the South. Irish women also engaged in street politics to resist the draft in places such as Boston, New York, and Chicago, as it threatened to take their loved ones to the carnage of the battlefield. They participated in bread riots in the South that exposed weaknesses in the Confederate war effort. Some sewed uniforms for their respective armies, and many grieved their losses in obscurity.

Since the days of the Revolution, Americans had loathed the idea of a permanent standing army, preferring to rely on locally recruited militias led by professionally trained officers from military academies, such as West Point. When the Civil War began, a portion of that professional army stayed in the South. The remaining Union Army was not only short on trained soldiers but also in need of a professional staff of commissaries to provide the logistics for supplies, as well as a support staff of cooks, laundresses, and, most especially, medical personnel.

When the conflict began with the assault on Fort Sumter, many women eagerly sought ways to play a part in the war effort. Both the North and the South experienced the spontaneous growth of female aid societies. In the North, those efforts became formalized through an act of Congress on June 18, 1861, with the formation of the U.S. Sanitary Commission (modeled on the British Sanitary Commission founded during the Crimean War seven years before). Although run by men, women became the commission's foot soldiers, and by the war's end they had managed to raise $15 million through door-to-door solicitations and fairs. Their efforts provided much-needed food, clothing, medical supplies, and ready cash for local suppliers. Many of these women were middle-class Protestants who stayed on the home front. At times their role expanded to looking after working-class and poor women left without a provider.[3]

When the war began, many women wanted to nurse, but few had ever done so in a professional way. Modern professional nursing had just begun in 1854, when Florence Nightingale organized specially trained women to tend British soldiers during the Crimean War. While Americans voiced admiration for her, they did nothing to found nursing schools during the prewar years. Propriety dictated that a gentle lady have no bodily contact with men not related to her. Nursing strange men suffering from horrendous wounds was inconceivable, and conditions in field hospitals were considered too makeshift and primitive for proper middle-class women. Commanders on both sides of the conflict were adamant that military life—let alone the battlefield—was no place for a woman. On top of that, no one expected the war to last long.

When Fort Sumter was attacked in April 1861, Catholic sisters were already operating twenty-eight hospitals in addition to orphanages and other charitable institutions. Catholic ascetic tradition formed the basis of this sisterhood of independent female organizations dedicated to serving others. In 1861, however, Secretary of War Simon Cameron appointed Dorothea Dix superintendent of nursing for the army due to her prior experience in reforming institutions for the mentally ill.[4] At this time, most Protestant American women had just begun exploring a public version of the cult of domesticity, so they entered the conflict without real nursing experience or organizational leadership (though this did not stop them from flooding the war office with applications to nurse).[5]

As the war slogged on and the army searched for well-trained medical hands, they came to prefer Roman Catholic sisters. By the end of the war in both the North and the South, an estimated six hundred Roman Catholic sisters from twelve different religious orders served the sick. Of these, 320 were Irish born or of Irish descent. Most were affiliated with the Sisters of Mercy, founded by Mother Catherine McAuley in Dublin. Some of the sisters in America expanded their public presence when they served local communities during cholera epidemics.[6]

The nursing skills of Catholic sisters were very basic and their knowledge of medicine primitive by today's standards. They changed dressings and bed linens, fed and cleaned patients, administered medicine, assisted doctors treating patients, and eventually assisted in surgeries. They also ran laundries and kitchens, supervised other nurses or orderlies, and provided spiritual comfort. While unsophisticated, these women were the only ones who had experience with the sick and dying on a large scale. This organizational experience and the training manuals they had written proved invaluable in the field.[7]

Anti-Catholic and anti-immigrant sentiment initially made military doctors reluctant to recruit nuns, and Roman Catholic sisters did not immediately volunteer. In 1834 anti-Catholic mobs burned an Ursuline convent in Charlestown. This taught Catholics to keep a low profile, and most sisters served in immigrant neighborhoods. However, when the Sanitary Commission and Dorothea Dix were overwhelmed by enthusiastic but inexperienced volunteers, military, political, and medical authorities (including the new secretary of war, Edwin Stanton) reconsidered their opinion of the sisters. They came to appreciate that the nuns knew how to function as a cohesive unit and to cope with physical and material hardship without complaint. Their vows of celibacy removed issues of sexuality, and their spirituality made them nonpartisan in the care they gave to both Union and Confederate men.[8]

In the early months of the war, as men from the countryside reported to recruiting stations and training camps, many soldiers died from communicable diseases due to lack of modern immunizations or earlier exposure to childhood diseases. This was actually the leading cause of death during the Civil War, and it was one of the first reasons Catholic nuns were called to service. In May 1861 new enlistees at the Ohio military recruitment and training ground of Camp Dennison just outside of Cincinnati suffered an outbreak of the measles. Local leaders appealed to the Sisters of Charity to help take care of the men. Sister Anthony O'Connell recalled that

> the most Rev. Archbishop [John] Purcell and Mayor [George] Hatch called upon me at the desire of Governor [William] Dennison, and requested that a colony of the Sisters be sent to Camp Dennison to attend the sick soldiers, the worst form of measles had broken out among them and they needed immediate attention.[9]

In Chicago, in anticipation of casualties, Colonel James A. Mulligan, commander of the 23rd Illinois Infantry Regiment—or the Illinois Irish Brigade—asked the city's Sisters of Mercy to join him on his campaign to the Missouri River town of Lexington in July 1861. By September 12 Mulligan's forces were cornered for a nine-day siege, which lasted until they surrendered. Casualties were low, only numbering in the hundreds for both sides. While the captured soldiers were immediately paroled, the sisters had been sent to Jefferson City when their ship, the *Sioux City*, was fired on by Confederate forces. The U.S. Sanitary Commission, impressed with their work, asked Sister Mary Francis Monholland to take charge of the Jefferson City Hospital until it was closed in April of the following year.[10]

In April 1862 the bloodiest engagement to that date in U.S. history unfolded on the Shiloh battlefield. Any prejudice toward Catholics or women in a war zone was quickly put to rest when the army had no choice but to call on civilians for help. Beginning in February 1862, Major General Ulysses Grant and the Army of the Tennessee, composed of units from the Old Northwest, began its aggressive movement into southern territory with the battles of Fort Henry and Fort Donelson on the Tennessee River. Their success there brought the army to Pittsburgh Landing by April 6, where for the next two days Union and Confederate soldiers fought until 1,754 Union men lay dead and 8,408 were wounded; Confederate casualties numbered 10,699. While a clear victory for the Union, these figures stunned the country and overwhelmed the medical staff as men lay on the battlefield unattended for days.

The North's Sanitary Commission moved to meet the needs of the fallen, but their efforts were not enough to handle the volume of men needing care.[11] In Cincinnati, Mayor Hatch, aware of the work of the Sisters of Charity at Camp Dennison, asked Archbishop Purcell for sisters to tend to Ohio soldiers. They responded to the call, as did the Sisters of the Poor of St. Francis and the Sisters of Mercy. Two of the Mercy sisters had worked in Ireland during an epidemic, and they had met fellow Mercy sisters who had served in the Crimean War. The sisters shared in the logistics of evacuating the wounded and assisted in transporting the men to field hospitals or back home by boat. Transport boats also had their challenges and hazards. Women shared cramped quarters with their patients, with little privacy or rest, uncertain of when they might arrive at their destination. When one transport boat carrying seven hundred men ran aground off Louisville en route to Cincinnati, the Union officer in command told the sisters they were not obliged to stay but could return home by other means. Sister O'Connell replied, "None would think of doing so." Inspired by their bravery, one doctor declared, "Since you weak women display such courage, I, too, will remain."[12]

In July 1862, Secretary Stanton sent his aide, Brigadier General John G. Foster, to the New York Diocese's vicar general to ask the Sisters of Mercy to assist the army of General Ambrose Burnside at the conclusion of his North Carolina campaign. Foster successfully reported to Stanton that, "at the request of Major General Burnside, nine Sisters of Mercy have arrived from New York to take charge of the hospital at Beaufort [North Carolina] and under their kind and educated care I hope for a rapid improvement in the health of patients."[13] In November 1862, Secretary Stanton again sought the help of Pittsburgh's Bishop Michael Domenec from the Sisters of Mercy who had operated Mercy Hospital since 1847. Eventually West Penn Hospital in Pittsburgh overflowed into a "City of Tents." One sister claimed that it provided shelter for thousands of wounded soldiers and prisoners.[14]

One reason the military medical staff came to prefer Catholic sisters to lay women was that religious life made them accustomed to hierarchy, leadership roles, and taking order—a critical necessity for military life. In addition, Catholic nuns were mobile. As field hospitals moved to the next battleground, they could move as well, unencumbered by family protests or concerns. Doctors also thought that since they were not looking for husbands, the nuns gave equal care to all soldiers, regardless of their appearance or injury, and soldiers appreciated this as well.[15]

This preference for Catholic sisters, however, rankled Dorothea Dix. She had a reputation for being controlling and dictatorial and engaging in frequent power struggles with her own staff and surgeons, which explains some of the military's preference for Catholic sisters. Regrettably, Dix's anti-Catholicism made it impossible for her to work with the nuns. When Dix send Sister Anthony O'Connell an order to leave a hospital in Nashville, the sister appealed to Archbishop Purcell, saying, "I hardly thought you would be willing to leave us to Miss Dix's whims." The conflict reached the newspapers, and the public rallied to the sisters' cause. Dix was never given authority over Catholic women, and she resented it.[16]

In the Confederacy, Catholic sisters took up nursing when the Union Navy laid siege to southern ports and northern armies penetrated the Confederacy in an effort to cripple its war effort. Nursing in the South, however, was even more challenging because the gradually tightening Union naval blockade of southern ports eventually strangled supply lines. Southern armies also usually lacked commissaries and medical staffs. States' rights ideology further hampered the Confederate government's ability to respond to these challenges, and it never authorized a Sanitary Commission. Southern women were even more constrained by gender roles than their northern counterparts, as slavery created a very hierarchical and patriarchal order that mandated white female helplessness and dependence. Roman Catholic sisters stood apart from some of these constraints.[17]

Unlike their counterparts in the North, Irish women who nursed soldiers in grey were often in the lines of fire as federal forces advanced on strategic sites in the South. In 1861 Union shells descended on the hospital of the Sisters of Mercy near Pensacola Bay, Florida. After evacuating the wounded and dying into a nearby shed, the sisters bravely walked back and forth in front of the hospital all day to let the enemy know who they were. When no attack came, the sisters moved the men back into the main building. "We were merely settled," wrote one sister, "when too [sic] our astonishment they opened fire on the hospital without the least warning."[18]

In the western theater from May 18 until July 4, 1863, General Grant's Army of the Tennessee laid siege to the Mississippi city of Vicksburg. It was the last Confederate stronghold on the Mississippi River and key to Grant's strategy of dividing the South through control of the waterway. Casualties for the North totaled 4,835; for the Confederacy, the number of casualties reached 3,202. The lengthy dramatic battle and shelling of the city led to food and water shortages for even the civilian population, who fled to the bluffs overlooking the Mississippi, where they lived in caves or dugouts.

The local Sisters of Mercy were teachers—not nurses. However, when their students fled with their families, they became nurses. The sisters stayed with the Confederate army to nurse the wounded as they retreated from the

Union advance. Their travels with Confederate forces eventually took them Jackson, Mississippi, and later into Alabama.[19]

The Arkansas Sisters of Mercy also went from teaching to starting a new hospital in Little Rock when Confederate army hospitals could not handle any more wounded. When the city was captured in September 1863, Union officers vented their anger at the sisters for their kindness to Confederates with violent, insulting language. However, like their counterparts in the North, the sisters served both Union and Confederate soldiers with impartiality. Their focus on their corporal and spiritual mission impressed many men, who came to believe there was "some virtue in the rolls of lint that came from the convent" that gave it special healing properties.[20]

Many of these women religious on both sides died as a result of their service, as they were often subject to the elements, isolated from creature comforts, and exposed to contagious diseases ranging from typhoid fever, smallpox, and measles to pneumonia, scurvy, and dysentery. Among them was Sister Gerard Ryan of the Mercy Sisters of New York, who served in North Carolina and died "as a result of hardship." When Sister Coletta O'Connor of the Baltimore Sisters of Mercy died in Douglas Hospital in Washington, D.C., she was buried with the military honors of a major.[21]

By the end of the war Catholic bishops recognized the positive impact that the nursing sisters had on creating a positive view of Catholicism among the general American public.[22] After the war, Mary Livermore of the Chicago Sanitary Commission, and an advocate of women's suffrage, wrote about her impressions of the Roman Catholic sisters and their work. "I can never forget my experience during the War of the Rebellion," she recalled. "Never did I meet these Catholic sisters in hospitals, on transports, or hospital steamers, without observing their devotion, faithfulness, and unobtrusiveness. They gave themselves no airs of superiority or holiness, shirked no duty, sought no easy place, bred no mischiefs. Sick and wounded men watched for their entrance into the wards at morning, and looked a regretful farewell when they departed at night."[23]

Irish lay women also found work with the army. While the army supplied the men with everything from tents, rations, and military equipment to their transportation, it did not do their laundry. Soldiers had to look elsewhere for clean clothes, and many Irish women gladly stepped up as washerwomen for the troops.

For immigrant working-class women, following the military offered not only an opportunity to be with loved ones or demonstrate their political allegiances but also an escape from loneliness and poverty. In both the North and the South, states allotted six domestic positions in military units for wives who could not subsist without their husbands. Since company captains appointed them, it was fairly easy for women who followed a husband, brother, or son to be recommended by the men in their unit, since many units were made up of neighbors and friends. The military also preferred women to be related to one of the soldiers or have a letter testifying to their good character. If not accompanied by a male relative, gender norms of the time assumed that an unattached woman was a camp follower and prostitute. In fact, some laundresses did resort to selling sex to supplement their meager pay. If discovered, they were dismissed. Mothers and matronly women, however, were fondly remembered by the men.[24]

The life of a laundress was hard. It required a lot of heavy equipment that constantly needed to be moved, in addition to hauling water, and the cleaning process took days from start to finish. These women were paid directly by soldiers, not by the army. While laundresses were not technically part of the armed forces, they were expected to submit to military discipline. Not all complied. When her son joined the joined the 1st Minnesota Volunteer Infantry, Mrs. Hannah O'Neil became its laundress. She, however, had a hard time adjusting to the regimentation of military life. After burning a corner of her tent, Captain Charles P. Adams refused to issue her another, claiming it was her own fault. Mrs. O'Neil then proceeded to rip the entire shelter to shreds in order to get a replacement. Her aggressive response may have been driven by alcoholism, as it was rumored that she was fond of the bottle.[25]

Most laundresses were an appreciated part of camp life. Besides keeping the men clean, the demands of a nascent army in wartime offered Irish women other opportunities to serve. They mended uniforms and provided home remedies for soldiers suffering from a variety of ailments and camp diseases. Army surgeons were grateful for their assistance when dealing with the carnage of battle. Laundresses with the Army of the Potomac's Irish Brigade at Antietam cheered men on the battlefield. Their close proximity to the front lines led some to even join in the battle. One general claimed that they "tended to make the men more cheerful, honest and comfortable."[26]

One Irish woman gained fame for her role on the battlefield. She was Bridget Divers, fondly called "Irish biddy" and "Michigan Bridget." Divers left Ireland from County Londonderry during the Great Famine. She later joined the 1st Michigan Cavalry with her husband. She probably began work as a laundress, but as casualties mounted and medical staff were overwhelmed, she turned to nursing and eventually took to the field. While Divers was admired for her "'unsurpassed fortitude, enthusiasm, kindness, and courage,'" she also was highly regarded for her expertise on a horse and willingness to act as a substitute soldier when the need arose.[27]

Divers first appeared on the historical record in June 1862 at the battle at Fair Oaks, Virginia. Witnesses claimed Divers played a key role in rallying the Union troops when a Confederate assault began as the men were eating lunch. While most of the men rushed to take up arms, some panicked and refused orders to advance until Divers grabbed her soldier's cap and urged them on. One observer said that this was not the only time Divers' "enthusiasm and pluck cheered us up and sent us fo[r]ward with a hearty good will."[28]

Bridget Divers also had a remarkable memory. J.R. Miller, a field agent for the United States Christian Commission—an evangelical soldiers' aid organization—made a point of contacting her first when he needed information regarding the whereabouts of particular men. "Her whole soul was in her work. No day was too stormy or too cold for her. She encountered all obstacles, and battled successfully every discouragement in the prosecution of her duties." Divers also acted as an unofficial chaplain. According to Miller, she seemed "to take a very deep interest in the spiritual condition of the men, and to understand her work in this line even better than many chaplains, and certainly had more zeal than too many of them."[29]

In 1864 the 1st Michigan Calvary served under General Philip Sheridan during the Petersburg campaign in Virginia. That year, General Ulysses Grant excluded women from military operations. Divers then moved to Cavalry Corps Hospital at City Point, Virginia, operated by the U.S. Sanitary Commission. During that nine-month campaign to cut Confederate supply lines to the capital of Richmond, Divers went back and forth between the battlefield and the field hospital, tending to the wounded.[30]

An example of her dedication and endurance came at the close of the war at the Battle of Five Forks in April 1865. Divers got word that Captain George C. Whitney, commander of Company B of the First Michigan Cavalry, had been severely wounded. Another fellow nurse from Maine, Rebecca Usher, wrote to her sister of Divers' heroism. Although Divers had been without sleep for forty-eight hours, she set off to retrieve the fallen soldier. Usher said she "had just come in with the body of a Cpt ... bound to her horse & took him 15 miles on horse back & then came with him in the cars, procured a coffin & sent him home." The "Irish Biddy's" gallantry, Usher commented, was motivated by the self-sacrifice of the men she saw fight "the hardest battle they have had." Divers told her that "the ground was covered with the wounded & no one to take care of them."[31]

Another fellow nurse, Charlotte McKay, also spoke highly of "Michigan Bridget." She "has probably seen more of the danger and hardship than any other woman during the war," McKay wrote of Divers. "She had been riding with the cavalry all the time, going out with them on their cavalry raids—always ready to succor the wounded on the field—often getting men off who, but for her, would be left to die, and fearless of shell or bullet among the last to leave." McKay said Divers won the respect and protection of both officers and privates for her work and willingness to endure hardship: "She makes her home in the saddle or shelter tent; often sleeping in the open without a tent, and by her courage and devotion, 'winning golden opinions from all sorts of people.'"[32] Divers is believed to have gone to the western frontier with the 1st Michigan Cavalry in June 1865, after the war was over.[33]

Irish women were also among the estimated four hundred Civil War female soldiers who disguised themselves as men. One of these was Jennie Irene Hodgers, who was born in Clogherhead, County Louth, Ireland, in 1843. In 1862 Hodgers enlisted in the 95th Illinois Infantry, Company G, as Albert Cashier. This unit was attached to the Army of the Tennessee and fought in forty battles, including those at Vicksburg, Red River, and Guntown. At one time, Cashier was captured in battle but overpowered a guard and managed to escape. Cashier served until the end of the war, mustering out of the army on August 17, 1865. For the rest of her life, Cashier passed as a man, working as a farmhand. This deception had its benefits, as she collected veterans' benefits and could vote. Her female identity may have been known to some during her years of service, but it was not officially recorded until 1913, when Cashier, suffering from dementia in Watertown State Hospital for the Insane, was discovered by nurse who was bathing her. When she died in 1915, Cashier was buried in her Civil War uniform with her tombstone inscribed with a reference to the 95th Illinois Infantry.[34] Another Irish soldier in disguise was Elizabeth Finnan. She first joined the 81st Ohio Infantry as a laundress, but she eventually picked up a musket and also provided intelligence to the Union command at Lookout Mountain.[35]

Confederate Irish women likewise joined the war effort and rebel regiments, and working-class, slave, and immigrant women made up the majority of hospital workers in the South. The "Mother of the First Tennessee Regiment," Mrs. Betsy Sullivan, followed her husband John when he enlisted with Company K. In addition to working as a laundress, she nursed the sick and wounded. She marched with the regiment, just like the men, "on foot with her knapsack on her back through the mountains of West Virginia, slept on the frozen ground, under the cold skies, a blanket her only covering, her knapsack her pillow." After the Battle of Cheat Mountain in western Virginia in September 1861, Sullivan personally delivered the body of a dead soldier to a railway station to ship his remains home to his family. In 1862, after the Battle of Perryville, her husband was wounded and unable to leave field of battle. Betsy stayed and was captured by Union troops, and both became prisoners of war.[36]

Another Irish female soldier for the Confederacy was Rose Quinn Rooney, who served with the 15th Louisiana. For four years she sewed, cooked, nursed, and counseled the men under her care, and she also fought bravely at First Bull Run and at Gettysburg. The appreciation of the men of the 15th led to her appointment as matron of the Louisiana Soldiers' Home.[37]

At least one Irish American woman engaged in espionage. Certainly the most famous spy in the entire war was Rose O'Neal Greenhow. She was born on a Maryland plantation and, in 1835, married Dr. Robert Greenhow. For some years her husband worked in the State Department in Washington, D.C., where Rose became a socialite and gained access to important men. When the Civil War began, Rose was devoted to the South, and she turned her energies to defeating the Union through passing secret information to the Confederacy. Jefferson Davis gave her credit for the Confederate victory at the First Battle of Manassas (or Bull Run) in July 1861, thanks to the vital information she had provided on Union military movements. When this was discovered in 1862, she was imprisoned for five months. However, Greenhow continued to pass on messages in a variety of creative ways, particularly through her sewing and embroidery. Unable to stop her espionage activities, the Union exiled her to the Confederacy.[38]

In 1863 Rose sailed for Britain and France to persuade them to support the southern cause. After a year in Europe, Greenhow returned to the Confederacy on a British blockade runner, but the ship ran aground off the coast of North Carolina. The rowboat conveying Mrs. Greenhow to shore capsized, and the gold she had procured for the cause led to her death by drowning. Rose O'Neal Greenhow was given full military honors at her funeral at St. Thomas Catholic Church in Wilmington, North Carolina.[39]

The Democratic Party did not give Irish American women the same opportunities for public political participation that the reform-minded Republican Party offered. By 1863, however, Irish women had made their entry onto the political stage. In January of that year President Abraham Lincoln had issued the Emancipation Proclamation, which freed slaves in the rebellious states. The purpose of the war changed from saving the Union to abolishing slavery. In March, as casualties mounted and the demand for soldiers increased, Congress issued the Enrollment Act, which required all able-bodied men from the ages of twenty to forty-five, including immigrants who filed for citizenship, to be enrolled in quota rosters. Three hundred dollars, however, would allow prospective soldiers to buy their way out of the draft. This amount was beyond the reach of poor and working-class immigrants, thus making the conflict, in the eyes of immigrants and the working class, "a rich man's war and a poor man's fight."

That summer draft riots erupted in New York, Boston, and Pennsylvania, as well as across the Midwest, as enrollment officers made their lists and called out Irish names to report for duty. The prospect of certain destitution (to say nothing of losing a loved one) had special poignancy for many Irish women. The largest riot began in New York on July 13, and Irish ladies readily joined Irishmen and street-tough youths in nearly a week of mayhem. While a minority of rioters, the women cheered on their men, broke windows, and attacked and killed perceived opponents with everything from sticks and stones to saws, knives, and table legs. Their targets were the homes of Republicans and politicians enforcing the draft.[40]

Authorities had difficulty containing the violence, and before the unrest ended on July 16, it had turned into a race war. As African Americans became contraband of war and drifted northward, many Irish felt economically threatened by their presence and feared that freedom for blacks would spell greater economic hardship for themselves. Rioters proceeded to attack African Americans and burned a Colored Orphans Asylum to the ground. Irish women were among the rioting crowd that participated in this sordid event. Even more established Irish women, such Mrs. Charles Daley, who did not participate in the riot and even feared for her life and property, still sided with their kinsmen and hoped the riot would "give the Negroes a lesson." In the end, 120 lay dead and 2,000 were injured. Hundreds of women were among those arrested. After the riot, Irish women joined in repealing Republican authorities searching their neighborhoods for perpetrators to be punished.[41]

While Roman Catholic nuns were winning hearts and changing minds through their heroic service in the theater of war, the draft riots confirmed for Anglo-Protestant Americans their worst stereotypes of the Irish. George Templeton Strong, a lawyer and noted Civil War diarist, wrote of the New York rioters as follows: "Every brute in the drove was pure Celtic—hod-carrier or loafer" who sang "a genuine Celtic howl." He described "the fury of the low Irish women … young vixens and withered old hags."[42]

Despite the fact that they were a minority in the riot, many newspapers emphasized the role of women in a way that added to the stereotypes and distortions of the Irish in general as barbarians. In this view, Irish women did not "civilize" their men. "The sight of an Irish man or woman," wrote Elizabeth Gay to a victim of the riot, "became so odious to me, that I could not treat them with external decency." The cult of domesticity and true womanhood precluded any attempt to understand why these women took to the streets.[43]

The Boston riot started that same week, on July 14, when enrollment officers began delivering the sobering news to report to duty. The Boston Irish community had been founded during the Great Famine a little more than a dozen years before, and the Irish continued to suffer in poverty and squalid living conditions. While proud of their Union service, Irish units in Massachusetts suffered heavy casualties in 1862–1863, especially at the battles of Antietam and Fredericksburg. Attitudes of support for the war began to shift with the issuing of the Emancipation Proclamation and the Enrollment Act in early 1863. The riot began on Cooper's Street in the North End when an argument erupted between an Irish woman and David Howe, a conscription officer who arrived at her doorstep to serve draft notices. When she slapped him, the officer said he would have her arrested for obstructing the implementation of the law.[44]

When neighbors heard the woman's violent shouts, men and women descended on the draft marshal. Howe promptly fled the scene.[45] The riot then spread throughout the neighborhood when Irish laborers from the local gas company and a number of women and children took to the streets. One Irish woman held over her head a photograph of her son who had been killed in battle—a poignant reminder of what was at stake. As feelings intensified, women were reported to have thrown rotten apples, stones, and broken crockery at soldiers sent to calm the riot. They even held up their babies in their arms and dared the soldiers to fire on them. Some women beat and tramped upon one soldier. To squelch the disturbance, the First Battery Massachusetts Volunteer Heavy Artillery and police fired on the mob, killing between fourteen and twenty people, including some women. A reporter from the *Boston Herald* referred to them as "Amazonian women."[46]

Unlike New York, the Boston riot ended within a day. Local and state authorities, cognizant of the events in New York, had prepared themselves for a potential disturbance and moved quickly to defuse the tension. The Rev. James Healy, chancellor of the Boston diocese, also played a critical role in calling on priests to calm their parishioners. The editor of the city's Catholic newspaper, Patrick Donahoe, likewise called for an end to the lawlessness. Their words were heeded, and the crowds dispersed.[47]

Draft resistance had started the year before in Pennsylvania when the state issued its own Militia Act in July 1862. While Pennsylvania was only second to New York in fielding men for service, enthusiasm for enlistments sagged when soldiers were asked to enlist for three years. Nearly every county in the state experienced some resistance to conscription. Coal mining regions, largely settled by the Irish, had their share of unrest. The Irish were "undereducated, overworked, underpaid, and exploited, they saw no reason to leave their family and risk their lives to take up arms against southerners who had never bothered them," wrote historian Arnold Shankman. Like other poor, low-skilled Irish around the country, they feared economic competition from African Americans. In Tremont, Schuylkill County, one thousand Irish miners stopped a train carrying draft inductees to Harrisburg. Women and children threw hot water, stones, sticks, and other projectiles at enrollment officers. Violence, however, was limited, thanks to Bishop James Wood's call for obedience to the law. In 1863 the state faced more problems enforcing the draft, but there is no record of Irish women's participation.[48]

Across the Midwest, especially in Illinois, Wisconsin, and Indiana, Irish women supported their men in resisting enrollment officers and the draft. While usually a minority in these demonstrations, they resorted to the same physical assaults of authorities and participated in property damage.[49] Chicago had its share of draft opposition and some violence. Acts of resistance here, however, never escalated into a full-scale riot like in New York or Boston. A larger percentage of the working class in Chicago owned some property, however modest, and their strategy was to attack enrollment officers rather than waiting to hear their names called to report to duty. Irish women played a key role in the execution of this strategy in their attempt to stymy the draft.

Hardscrabble, as Chicago's Bridgeport neighborhood was originally called, was founded by Irish who worked on the Illinois & Michigan Canal, completed in 1848. Famine refugees joined them, as did subsequent waves of Irish immigrants. While Chicago boomed with the opening of the canal, the Irish took low-skilled, back-breaking work on the river docks and in grain silos, animal pens, and factories. Irish women ran boarding houses or worked as domestics. They resented the economic competition of African Americans and the change in war aims signaled by the Emancipation Proclamation.[50]

Resistance to the war effort actually began in the fall of 1862, when enrollment officers looking to fill state quotas made their way through Bridgeport. When one officer entered the grocery and boarding house of Mrs. Mulrooney and told her that he needed the names of her boarders, the *Chicago Tribune* reported that she "became oblivious. She couldn't remember the names of her boarders, and was mysteriously uncertain about their numbers. So rapidly did her memory fail her, that she soon forgot whether she had any boarders, and kept on forgetting at a rate which was rapidly tending towards a mental chaos."[51] The paper reported that her memory was restored when she was taken into police custody.

When draft marshals arrived at the doorstep of Mrs. Ellen McCafferty looking for Patrick, a night watchman for the McCormick Reaper Company, she "seized a bootjack and threatened to brain Mr. Lull on the spot, if he did not 'clear himself out of her house.'" The officer came back with a policeman. The *Chicago Tribune* wrote that as "they advanced toward the Amazon.... Mrs. McCafferty was ready for them ... armed with a large butcher knife with a blade something over a foot in length, which she brandished wildly in the air." Mrs. McCafferty was later arrested and held on one-thousand-dollar bail.[52]

The only recorded incident of anti-draft violence in Chicago took place on June 6, 1863, in the same area of the city that the *Tribune* described as "inhabited by a lawless, reckless class of the community, embracing the very lowers, most ignorant, depraved and besotted rabble that can be found in the city." When Mr. A.H. Carter, an enrollment officer, arrived to take names, the Irishmen refused to cooperate and threatened him. When Carter returned with other authorities, "a mob of three or four hundred infuriated Irish—men, women and children—gathered together, and howling like demons, commenced an onslaught upon the officers with bricks, stones, bottles and every missile they could find." All the officers suffered injuries.[53]

Southern women also participated in riots, although not ones related to the draft. In the spring of 1863, as economic conditions deteriorated and scarcity, inflation, and speculation ran rampant, "bread riots" spread throughout the South. The most violent occurred in Richmond. The city's population had swelled since the war began, and shortages were common. A local newspaper disparaged the participants as "prostitutes, professional thieves, Irish and Yankee hags, [and] gallow birds." While the rank-and-file protesters were more interested in food, when such was not forthcoming, order broke down and some turned to looting clothing and jewelry stores rather than the nearly empty bakeries. The riot was finally quelled when orders were given to fire on the mob and the women were arrested. A judge in Georgia who tried female rioters expressed the views of the age when he pronounced, "When women become rioters, they ceased to be women."[54]

While the Civil War brought Irish American women into street politics, it did not ultimately empower them as a group.[55] Their behavior not only challenged the law and support for war effort but also violated nineteenth-century gender norms. When male journalists called Irish women "Amazons," they signaled to middle-class Americans that they need not regard these women as worthy of respect, and some aid societies were reluctant to provide support for Irish women and their families.[56]

Yet, while some Irish women participated in opposing the war in the streets, there were always others who quietly did what they could to help those men who were in uniform. Many Irish women took up work in the textile industry in New England and supported the war effort by manufacturing cloth and sewing uniforms. In his memoirs of the war, Frank Moore wrote that Irish women were "no less praiseworthy and admirable." They contributed "the hearty good will, the vigorous sense, and the unwearied industry of the laboring class."[57] In her book *My Story of the War: A Woman's Narrative of Four Years of Service*, Mary Livermore of the Chicago Sanitary Commission wrote that the Irish women of southern Boston had sewed shirts for the Union Army at a rate of one thousand per day. "The zeal and devotion of the Irish no more flagged through the war than did that of the army in the field," she testified. "They rose to the height of emergency, and through all discouragements and reverses maintained a sympathetic unity between the soldiers and themselves, that gave the former a marvelous heroism."[58]

While the war ended in 1865, for Irish women who lost loved ones in the conflict, grief over their losses lived on for decades. Decoration Day memorials were an important ritual of mourning and remembrance. Finley Peter Dunne's fictional Bridgeport barkeep in Chicago, Mr. Dooley, noted the lingering pain of Irish women from the war into the 1890s. For a Memorial Day column in 1894, Mr. Dooley observed, "Th' sojers has thim that'll fire salutes over their graves an' la-ads to talk about thim, but there's none but the widdy f'r to break her hear-rt above the poor soul that died afther his hands had turn-rned to leather fr'm handlin's a pick."[59]

Like their male counterparts, Irish women's lives were disrupted by the Civil War. Hard work was not new to them, so the rigors associated with the war effort and even military life were just another feature of their hardscrabble lives. They were not always passive bystanders to the events around them, responding through avenues that were open to them as women, whether as nurses on the battlefield, laundresses who followed their men to war, soldiers, spies, or factory workers. At times their fury over the death and suffering of their husbands, fathers, sons, and brothers took the form of mob vengeance. For many, however, existing on a meager soldier's pay or a widow's pension was simply one more challenge to endure.

In the short term, the Civil War was not transformational for women in general or Irish women in particular. While postwar commentators sometimes acknowledged working-class women's contributions, they still harbored a suspicion that work compromised a woman's "respectability." The cult of domesticity was too powerful an ideology to allow American society to fully acknowledge the unconventional roles that some women played. The soldiers who witnessed the bravery and dedication of camp laundresses and nurses, however, did not forget. Veterans' reunions often extended invitations to these women as honored guests. The Grand Army of the Republic specifically honored Bridget Divers. But as the rosters of the men in the GAR dwindled through the years, public memory of these women also disappeared.

However, war often does lead to long-term social changes. The American Revolution inspired the ideal of republican motherhood. In an independent democratic republic, women were expected to educate their children to be virtuous citizens. This belief eventually opened up teaching as a profession for women in the nineteenth century. The Civil War likewise transformed nursing into a respectable occupation. Irish women flocked to both these fields by the end of the century, thereby carving out an avenue of freedom and independence for themselves.[60]

Notes

1. Sara M. Evans, *Born for Liberty: A History of Women in America* (New York: Free Press Paperbacks, 1997), 71–72.

2. In the past fifteen years or so, the historiography of women in the American Civil War has exploded. Some of the notable works are Jeanie Attie, *Patriotic Toil: Northern Women and the American Civil War* (Ithaca, NY: Cornell University Press, 1998); DeAnne Blanton and Lauren M. Cook, *They Fought Like Demons: Women Soldiers in the American Civil War* (Baton Rouge: Louisiana State University Press, 2002); Elizabeth D. Leonard, *All the Daring of the Soldier: Women of the Civil War Armies* (New York: W.W. Norton); Nina Silber, *Daughters of the Union: Northern Women Fight the Civil War* (Cambridge, MA: Harvard University Press, 2005); Judith Giesberg, *Army at Home: Women and the Civil War on the Northern Home Front* (Chapel Hill: University of North Carolina Press, 2009); James Marten, *Civil War America:*

Voices from the Home Front (Santa Barbara, CA: ABC-CLIO, 2003); and Richard Hall, *Women on the Civil War Battlefront* (Lawrence: University Press of Kansas, 2006).
    3. Evans, *Born for Liberty*, 114.
    4. Evans, *Born for Liberty*, 114.
    5. Sister Mary Denis Maher, "'To Do With Honor': The Roman Catholic Sister Nurse in the United States Civil War," Ph.D. diss., Case Western Reserve University, 1988, 2, 61, 78.
    6. Maher, "'To Do With Honor,'" 3, 86, 146–47.
    7. Maureen Fitzgerald, "Habits of Compassion: Irish American Nuns in New York City," in *Women's America: Refocusing the Past*, 8th ed., edited by Linda K. Kerber, Jane Sherron De Hart, Cornelia Hughes Dayton, and Just Tzu-Chun Wu (New York: Oxford University Press, 2016), 169–77. See also Carol K. Coburn and Martha Smith, *Spirited Lives: How Nuns Shaped Catholic Culture and American Life, 1836–1920* (Chapel Hill: University of North Carolina Press, 1999); Maher, "'To Do With Honor,'" 83–86.
    8. Maher, "'To Do With Honor,'" 143–44, 207.
    9. Archives of the Sisters of Charity of Cincinnati (ASCC), memoirs of Sr. Anthony O'Connell, n.p., as quoted in Maher, "'To Do With Honor,'" 149.
    10. Theodore J. Karamanski and Eileen M. McMahon, *Civil War Chicago: Eyewitness to History* (Athens: Ohio University Press, 2014), 68; Maher, "'To Do With Honor,'" 154.
    11. Karamanski and McMahon, *Civil War Chicago*, 69–70.
    12. Maher, "'To Do With Honor,'" 142–64.
    13. Maher, "'To Do With Honor,'" 151.
    14. Maher, "'To Do With Honor,'" 151, 219–20.
    15. Maher, "'To Do With Honor,'" 143–47, 164.
    16. Maher, "'To Do With Honor,'" 278–82.
    17. Evans, *Born for Freedom*, 87–89, 12–18.
    18. Maher, "'To Do With Honor,'" 221.
    19. Maher, "'To Do With Honor,'" 156, 192.
    20. Maher, "'To Do With Honor,'" 172–73.
    21. Maher, "'To Do With Honor,'" 253.
    22. Maher, "'To Do With Honor,'" 170.
    23. Mary Livermore, *What Shall We Tell Our Daughters? Superfluous Women and Other Lectures* (Boston: Lee and Shepard, 1883), 177–78.
    24. Vickie Wendel, "Washer Women," *Civil War Times Illustrated* 38, no. 4 (August 1999); Mary Elizabeth Massey, *Women in the Civil War* (Lincoln: University of Nebraska Press, 1966), 78–79.
    25. Wendel, "Washer Women."
    26. Wendel, "Washer Women."
    27. Frank Moore, *Women of the War: Their Heroism and Self-Sacrifice* (Hartford, CT: S. S. Scranton and Company, 1867), 109–10.
    28. C.E. McKay, *Stories of Hospital and Camp* (Philadelphia: Claxton, Remson, and Haffelfinger, 1876); Minnie Dubbs Millbrook, "Michigan Women Who Went to War," in *Michigan Women in the Civil War*, by Michigan Civil War Centennial Observation Commission (Lansing: n.p., 1963).
    29. Wendel, "Washer Women."
    30. Moore, *Women of the War*.
    31. Moore, *Women of the War*.
    32. McKay, *Stories of Hospital and Camp*.
    33. Millbrook, "Michigan Women Who Went to War."
    34. Amy Benck, "Albert D. J. Cashier: Woman Warrior, Insane Civil War Veteran, or Transman?" *OutHistory*, http://www.outhistory.org/exhibits/show/tgi-bios/albert-cashier, retrieved May 6, 2015.
    35. Wendel, "Washer Women"; Hall, *Women on the Civil War Battlefront*.
    36. Massey, *Women in the Civil War*, 78–79; Hall, *Women on the Civil War Battlefront*.
    37. Wendel, "Washer Women"; Hall, *Women on the Civil War Battlefront*.
    38. Rose O'Neal Greenhow Papers, News Clippings, Cs. October 1, 1864, Special Collections Library, Duke University, http://www.confederate-rose.org/GreenshowFunderal.

htm, accessed May 13, 2016; Ann Blackman, *Wild Rose: The True Story of a Civil War Spy* (New York: Random House Digital, 2006).

39. Rose O'Neal Greenhow Papers, News Clippings, Cs. October 1, 1864, Special Collections Library, Duke University, http://www.confederate-rose.org/GreenshowFunderal.htm, accessed May 13, 2016.
40. Silber, *Daughters of the Union*, 137–40.
41. Massey, *Women in the Civil War*, 173–74.
42. Allen Nevins and Milton Halsey Thomas, eds., *The Diary of George Templeton Strong*, abridged by Thomas J. Pressly (Seattle: University of Washington Press, 1988), 237–40.
43. Silber, *Daughters of the Union*, 159.
44. William F. Hanna, "The Boston Draft Riot," *Civil War History* 36, no. 3 (September 1990): 262–64.
45. Brett M. Palfreym, "The Boston Draft Riots," *New York Times*, July 16, 2013.
46. Hanna, "The Boston Draft Riot," 264–67.
47. Hanna, "The Boston Draft Riot," 264, 271.
48. Arnold Shankman, "Draft Resistance in Civil War Pennsylvania," *Pennsylvania Magazine of History and Biography* 101, no. 2 (April 1977): 190, 195, 197.
49. Robert E. Sterling, "Civil War Draft Resistance in the Middle West," Ph.D. diss., Northern Illinois University, 1974, 211.
50. Karamanski and McMahon, *Civil War Chicago*, 111–16.
51. *Chicago Tribune*, October 1, 1862.
52. *Chicago Tribune*, June 13, 1863.
53. *Chicago Tribune*, June 26, 1863.
54. Andrew F. Smith, *Starving the South: How the North Won the Civil War* (New York: St. Martin's Press, 2001), 59, 64.
55. Silber, *Daughters of the Union*, 137–40, 159.
56. Giesberg, *Army at Home*, 133–34.
57. Moore, *Women of the War*, iv–v.
58. Mary Livermore, *My Story of the War: A Woman's Narrative of Four Years of Service* (Hartford, CT: A.D. Worthington and Company, 1889), 111.
59. Charles Fanning, *Finley Peter Dunne and Mr. Dooley: The Chicago Years* (Lexington: University Press of Kentucky, 1978), 30–34.
60. Wendel, "Washer Women"; Massey, *Women in the Civil War*, 78.

BIBLIOGRAPHY

Benck, Amy. "Albert D.J. Cashier: Woman Warrior, Insane Civil War Veteran, or Transman?" *OutHistory.* http://www.outhistory.org/exhibits/show/tgi-bios/albert-cashier. Retrieved May 6, 2015.
Blackman, Ann. *Wild Rose: The True Story of a Civil War Spy.* New York: Random House Digital, 2006.
Evans, Sara M. *Born for Liberty: A History of Women in America.* New York: Free Press Paperbacks, 1997.
Fanning, Charles. *Finley Peter Dunne and Mr. Dooley: The Chicago Years.* Lexington: University Press of Kentucky, 1978.
Fitzgerald, Maureen. "Habits of Compassion: Irish American Nuns in New York City." In *Women's America: Refocusing the Past*, 8th ed., edited by Linda K. Kerber, Jane Sherron De Hart, Cornelia Hughes Dayton, and Just Tzu-Chun Wu. New York: Oxford University Press, 2016.
Giesberg, Judith. *Army at Home: Women and the Civil War on the Northern Home Front.* Chapel Hill: University of North Carolina Press, 2009.
Gleeson, David T. *The Green and the Gray: The Irish in the Confederate States of America.* Chapel Hill: University of North Carolina Press, 2013.
Hall, Richard H. *Women on the Civil War Battlefront.* Lawrence: University Press of Kansas, 2006.
Hanna, William F. "The Boston Draft Riot." *Civil War History* 36, no. 3 (September 1990).

Karamanski, Theodore J., and Eileen M. McMahon. *Civil War Chicago: Eyewitness to History.* Athens: Ohio University Press, 2014.
Livermore, Mary. *What Shall We Tell Our Daughters? Superfluous Women and Other Lectures.* Boston: Lee and Shepard, 1883.
Maher, Sister Mary Denis. *To Bind Up the Wounds: Catholic Sister Nurses in the U.S. Civil War.* Westport, CT: Greenwood Press, 1989.
_____. "'To Do With Honor': The Roman Catholic Sister Nurse in the United States Civil War." Ph.D. dissertation, Case Western Reserve University, 1988.
Massey, Mary Elizabeth. *Women in the Civil War.* Lincoln: University of Nebraska Press, 1966.
McKay, C.E. *Stories of Hospital and Camp.* Philadelphia: Claxton, Remson, and Haffelfinger, 1876.
Millbrook, Minnie Dubbs. "Michigan Women Who Went to War." In *Michigan Women in the Civil War*, by Michigan Civil War Centennial Observation Commission. Lansing: n.p., 1963.
Moore, Frank. *Women of the War: Their Heroism and Self-Sacrifice.* Hartford, CT: S.S. Scranton and Company, 1867.
Nevins, Allen, and Milton Halsey Thomas, eds. *The Diary of George Templeton Strong.* Abridged by Thomas J. Pressly. Seattle: University of Washington Press, 1988.
Rose O'Neal Greenhow Papers. News Clippings. Cs. October 1, 1864. Special Collections Library, Duke University. http://www.confederate-rose.org/GreenshowFunderal.htm.
Shankman, Arnold. "Draft Resistance in Civil War Pennsylvania." *Pennsylvania Magazine of History and Biography* 101, no. 2 (April 1977).
Silber, Nina. *Daughters of the Union: Northern Women Fight the Civil War.* Cambridge, MA: Harvard University Press, 2005.
Smith, Andrew F. *Starving the South: How the North Won the Civil War.* New York: St. Martin's Press, 2001.
Sterling, Robert E. "Civil War Draft Resistance in the Middle West." Ph.D. dissertation, Northern Illinois University, 1974.
Wendel, Vickie. "Washer Women." *Civil War Times Illustrated* 38, no. 4 (August 1999).

Judge Charles Daly and the New York Irish in the Era of the Civil War

AIDAN O'HARA

There are all the elements of a Horatio Alger story in the life of Charles Patrick Daly. The son of Irish immigrant parents recently arrived in New York, his mother died when he was three and his father remarried but died when Charles was twelve. He was left with a stepmother with whom he fought constantly, so he ran away to Georgia; after a few years as a cabin boy, he returned to take up an apprenticeship with a cabinetmaker. He devoured all the books in the trade union library and joined a local literary society, where a fellow member, a lawyer, was so impressed by the sixteen-year-old that he opened doors for him. Daly then studied law and, by the age of twenty-eight, was already a judge. He eventually became New York City's chief justice and entered high society, numbering among his friends the Astors, the Vanderbilts, and Andrew Carnegie, as well as Ulysses S. Grant, George McClellan, and Winfield Scott.

One of the more remarkable men of his day, Charles Daly's unusual powers of intellect and inquiry led him into many fields. He was a Shakespearean scholar and patron of the arts, a geographer and a historian. He lectured in law at Columbia University, wrote many learned volumes, and was much in demand as a speaker, with his sparkling "Irish wit" earning him great admiration. Daly was a champion of Irish rights and a lifelong member of the Friendly Sons of St. Patrick. During his tenure as president of the society (1860–1862), the Civil War broke out, and he was instrumental in organizing the "Fighting Irish" regiment, New York's famous 69th. In May 1861, when the unit was ready to go to the defense of Washington, Judge Daly presented its men with an American flag of silk, "made expressly for them by his wife." He was also a friend of the German community in New York and supported their efforts to raise regiments for the Union.[1]

As the first year of the war closed, Judge Daly gave the federal government the benefit of his learning in two famous cases: the first was that of the crew of a Confederate privateer captured in 1861 and sentenced to death for piracy, and the second that of the Union seizure of the Confederate envoys James Mason and John Slidell, known as the Trent Affair.[2]

Almost forgotten today, in his own time Daly was one of the best-known figures in New York City. He sat on the bench of the city's Court of Common Pleas for nearly forty years, serving as its chief judge for twenty-seven. His rise to eminence in the city's social, political, and intellectual circles was rapid. He was the sort of whom one might use the poet's words, "If you can talk with crowds and keep your virtue, or talk with Kings—nor lose the common touch." Daly fought for those who encountered bigotry and discrimination, and his fairness and keen judgments earned him the sobriquet "The Commoners' Judge."[3]

Daly's Early Years

Charles Patrick Daly was born on October 31, 1816, in a small hotel (where his father was manager) that stood on the east side of Broadway on the site later occupied by the Tribune Tower. His parents, Elizabeth and Michael Daly, natives of Omagh, County Tyrone, Ireland, had immigrated to America from Galway in 1814. Although twelve when his father died, Daly shared few memories of his early years, and documents reveal little about his parents or the first decade of his own life.

Michael Daly did manage to send his son to a private school for a short time, probably to Thomas Brady's Latin School in St. Peter's Parish. One schoolmate was James T. Brady, the teacher's son, later a celebrated New York lawyer and judge. John McCloskey, coadjutor bishop of New York from 1843 on (later made America's first cardinal in 1875), was a pupil at the school from 1817 to 1821 and may have overlapped with Daly. By the 1860s, all three men were leading "native" New Yorkers in an Irish community anxious for such a pedigree.

Shortly after Elizabeth's death in 1820, Michael Daly remarried. Charles lived briefly with his stepmother after his father died in 1829. One day he threw an inkstand at her during a quarrel and was locked in a closet as punishment. He broke it open and fled both house and city. Somehow the thirteen-year-old boy managed to travel all the way to Savannah, Georgia, where, in that city of only 8,000 souls, Charles apprenticed himself to a quillmaker. Under the harsh conditions of his term, the inevitable quarrel soon developed, and the quick-tempered apprentice struck his master. Young Charles then signed up as cabin boy with the next ship leaving port.

Daly was strangely reluctant to discuss his seafaring days, but he told of being shipwrecked off Holland, getting lost in Amsterdam, and being shanghaied by a Dutch captain. He spent two years at sea, returning to New York in 1832. The sixteen-year-old youth apprenticed himself to a cabinetmaker in the city, studying at night by using the Mechanic's and Tradesman's Society library.

Daly also joined a local literary society, where he so impressed the lawyer William Soule that the two became fast friends. Soule encouraged Daly to study law after ending his apprenticeship; not yet twenty, Daly then accepted a clerkship in Soule's law office. In 1839, with fewer than half the customary seven years of apprenticeship, he was considered ready for examination for the bar. On the motion of Soule's partner, before Chief Justice Samuel Nelson of the State Supreme Court, the seven-year requirement was waived and Daly was given his examination. He passed it easily. Though only twenty-two years old, Daly became junior partner in the firm of McElrath, Bloomfield and Daly.

Law, Politics and Marriage

Daly's two rather older partners willingly relinquished increasing amounts of work to the energetic young man. His letters between 1839 and 1841 reveal the growing role that he assumed in the firm. Further proof of his success was a request that he lend his aid "in an effort to revive the Law Association."[4]

In 1837, Daly joined the newly reorganized New York state militia, his lieutenancy in its 75th Regiment, 3rd Brigade and 3rd Division, attesting to his popularity. Unanimously elected as a member of the New York Cadets in 1838, Daly signed the roll at Captain Sayon's quarters and attended the regular drills. Multiple demands were proving burdensome, however, and Daly later handed in his resignation from the 75th Regiment. Only once did he regret this action—when the martial spirit moved him at the outbreak of the Civil War.[5]

Prominent New Yorkers saw Daly as man of many parts who combined political potential with financial and legal acumen. For a few years politics vied with law as his major concern. Later he was content to downgrade his political interests in favor of his legal career, except in the role of behind-the-scenes management. But in 1838 he had joined Tammany Hall (conveniently close to his office) and soon spoke at some of the meetings. Tammany had begun as a Jeffersonian political club and had grown during the Democratic years, especially when Martin Van Buren from upstate was president. The organization now sought to fuse a popular rights tradition with a more studied politics. Urban growth required countless services, but the rapid rise of business and finance created diverse pressures. Some, like the Locofoco Fernando Wood, wished to mobilize mistrust of rising wealth; others, like Daly, preferred to accommodate plain people without such confrontation; others sought to concentrate urban power as a balancing force in its own right. Tammany encouraged and ran voter turnout, facilitated city contracts and appointments, started schools, raised funds for debtors, and fitfully aided the needy. From the mid–1850s, as city became a Democratic "island" in an increasingly Republican state and nation, Tammany was a power in city and state politics (if never unchallenged), under variably corrupt bosses like Wood, William Magear Tweed and Richard Croker.[6]

The influence of each man was distinctive, as were their relations to both the city's elites and the vast Irish community. Fernando Wood gravitated to congressional politics after 1865 and remained there until 1881; William Tweed displaced Wood's power using Tammany localism, only to fall due to his extreme corruption in 1871; Croker rose through the revolt against Tweed and created a highly disciplined machine, before falling himself by stages in 1901. Daly's constant emphasis upon law could be seen as itself a riposte to their machine methods, just as his pro–Union stance was in part a response to the outlooks of Mayor Wood in 1860–1861, who was pro–South until war broke out, and then sought compromise.

Throughout his career, Charles Daly's advancement was swift and certain. Made a member of the Young Men's General Committee of Tammany under Wood, the Board of Aldermen subsequently appointed him an inspector of election for the Fourth Ward. On October 31, 1840, Charles Daly celebrated his twenty-fourth birthday. He was elected to the state legislature at Albany in January 1843. Meanwhile, he continued his work at his law practice. Yet his greatest interest remained judicial science. Even as a legislator, much of his time was spent devising improvements for the state's judicial system. Both judges and politicians directed legal and judicial matters to him.

Daly spent one year in the legislature, refusing a second term, as he was unsuited to the political climate. He turned instead to one of his interests, writing judicial histories, the first of which was a small volume on the Court of Common Pleas. These histories would earn him a reputation as the foremost historian of the New York courts; on the strength of this reputation, he was appointed judge of the Court of Common Pleas in 1844.[7] His handling of the Astor Street riot trial in autumn 1849 won praise for its coolness, sympathy and balance. His "firmness, and integrity ... at the recent trial of the rioters, has ... elicited the gratitude of all good citizens," claimed *The Era* of October 7, 1849.[8]

Daly's upright and fearless handling of cases on the bench eventually earned him the enmity of the Tweed ring. In 1871, as his term was about to expire, the Tweed politicians set out to defeat his renomination. At the same time, however, the *New York Times* published an exposé of Tweed and his followers' corrupt practices. As a result,

> The ring was broken up, and then happened what, up to that period, had never been known before. Judge Daly was nominated to succeed himself for a term of fourteen years, not only by all factions of the Democracy, but by the Republicans, and every vote cast in the City of New York for the judiciary that year was cast for Charles P. Daly.... During his long service on the bench Judge Daly rendered many important decisions and interpreted principles of law which have since become recognized as standard authority in this and other States.[9]

In 1856 Charles Daly married Maria Lydig, daughter of a leading merchant and a Lutheran. The Dalys became very active in New York society. Maria's family connections, as well her husband's rising eminence, admitted them to the highest social circles in the city. Mrs. Daly's *Diary of a Union Lady, 1861–1865* brings to life a portrait of a sorely divided society (as well as a President Lincoln as much hated as loved). The judge is the real hero of the diary, and the only person close to Mrs. Daly who escapes her caustic wit. "Her malicious and entertaining comments on New Yorkers high and low as well as national figures provide fodder for many points of view."[10]

American Civil War

In January 1861, Daly went to Washington, D.C., and met with the aging Winfield Scott, general in chief of the army, who was trying to organize plans for the defense of the city. In one of several meetings with William H. Seward, soon to be Lincoln's secretary of state, Judge Daly vainly tried to convince his acquaintance of the imminence of war. The two men had known each other since their days in the Albany legislature. Seward was reported as saying that there was no danger of war—that it would all be over in six weeks.

Although Daly remained a lifelong Democrat, he found himself in complete accord with the views that Lincoln enunciated in his inaugural address. He could not condone what his brother Democrats of the South were doing. And although Daly did not believe that Lincoln was a man of strong conviction or determination, the new president had at least set forth a policy that Daly believed to be right. However, northern antiwar sentiment sympathetic to the South had influence among many Democratic New Yorkers. Politicians such as Fernando Wood often played on this sentiment and on Irish prejudice against blacks. Daly was both an Irishman and a politician, but his loyalty to the Union compelled him to break with those who placed self-interest before the country.

The Civil War broke out on the morning of April 12, 1861, when Confederate forces fired on Fort Sumter. Suddenly there was a general call to arms, and among the New York regiments that promptly offered their services was the Irish 69th Infantry Regiment of the New York State Militia, later the first regiment of the Irish Brigade. The regiment's colonel was at this time under threat of court-martial. He was Michael Corcoran, a native of County Sligo, a close friend of the Dalys, and the most famous Irish soldier in America at the time. He had refused to turn out with his Irish regiment for a parade in honor of the visit of the Prince of Wales to New York in October 1860. This act made him the darling of the Irish, but Corcoran was placed under military arrest. With the outbreak of hostilities, however, his court-martial was set aside on April 20 by order of the commander of the state militia, Charles W. Sandford. Corcoran wasted no time in taking charge once again. Judge Daly helped recruit additional troops for the Irish 69th, and he and his fellow members of the Friendly Sons of St. Patrick contributed $1,500 to help equip and sustain the unit. The judge also headed a committee to provide similar support for the 75th Regiment. Within three days of the dismissal of charges against Corcoran, the 69th mustered more than 1,000 men and was ready to sail for the defense of Washington on April 23. A grand sendoff was provided.[11]

Foremost among those who marched down Broadway was Judge Daly, who carried a revolver in honor of the occasion. "I know he wished he were going with them," Maria observed in her diary. Colonel Corcoran accepted the flag with "the thanks of himself and the regiment, and desired Judge Daly to assure his estimable lady that her flag should never suffer the stain of dishonor while a man of the 69th remained alive to defend it."[12]

One of Corcoran's officers was Thomas Francis Meagher, the Young Irelander. He, too, was a favorite of the Dalys—at least for a time. Later, however, he came to be the villain of Maria's diary for what she described as his "double-faced" dealings when he replaced Corcoran as commander of the 69th after the latter was captured at the First Battle of Bull Run on July 21. The Dalys were also close to three famous Irish American lawyers, all of whom were Democrats, divided between factions of the party in the 1850s. James Shields, from County Tyrone, was a leading Douglas partisan. By contrast, the New York–born lawyer Charles O'Conor was an administration stalwart. Despite his harsher pro-slavery views, he did better in the long term than Shields (who lost major roles in Midwestern politics to rising anti-slavery sentiment). Of the next generation, the Young Irelander, Richard O'Gorman, also a lawyer with Tammany links, sought to model his life on those of Daly and O'Conor.[13]

Daly was also involved in generating German recruitment. He was the principal speaker at a ceremony honoring a new German unit—the First German Rifles.[14]

Later, Daly, again armed with a revolver, followed Michael Corcoran's soldiers to Camp Seward on Arlington Heights in Virginia and, with Richard O'Gorman, helped to guard the ramparts when there seemed a threat of attack.[15] The judge later reviewed the 69th with Baron von Gerolt and Secretary Seward.[16]

Several times in 1861, Maria expressed her fears that her husband might enlist as a soldier. On June 7 she wrote, "I am very thankful he has returned safely [from another visit to Washington], for I never feel he is safe out of my sight during this excitement. He is so impressionable." Fortunately, he resisted the temptation.[17]

First Battle of Bull Run, July 1861

In the untested enthusiasms after the attack on Fort Sumter, each side predicted the early destruction of its enemy. In the North people had quickly oversubscribed to Lincoln's requests for men, money and supplies. They were impatient for action. But the veteran General Scott was not anxious for a premature conflict that might well result in defeat for his still raw recruits. He eventually capitulated to pressure to from politicians, from elected and unseasoned commanders, and from General Irvin McDowell of the War Department. McDowell decided to advance upon the army of the Confederate General Pierre Beauregard, which was guarding the rail junction at Manassas in Virginia. According to the plan that Scott reluctantly submitted, McDowell's force of 36,000 men should overwhelm Beauregard's 22,000. This required the Irish-born General Robert Patterson's 14,350 men at Harper's Ferry to act promptly to prevent Joseph E. Johnston's 10,700 men from reinforcing Beauregard. But Patterson (believing he was facing a much larger force than his own) failed to engage, and Johnston's army moved on to join Beauregard on July 20. McDowell was unprepared the next day when fighting started at Bull Run. Initially the Union forces had some success, but in the afternoon the fresh troops of Colonel Thomas J. Jackson's Virginia Brigade stood fast against them (famously earning Jackson the nickname "Stonewall"). An orderly Union retreat soon turned into a rout.[18]

There were Irishmen on both sides of the battle that day, hailing from Corcoran's New York 69th for the North and, on the South's side, Richmond's Company C of the Montgomery Guards under John Dooley from Jackson's brigade, as well as Bob Wheat's Tigers of the 1st Louisiana Special Regiment. Colonel Corcoran and some of his men were captured, but his then subordinate, Thomas F. Meagher, made it back to Washington. Overall, the 69th New York Irish had acquitted itself well. Maria Daly reported that Union officers were still generally inexperienced and so led the men badly. But she noted that when the ensign who bore the green unit flag of his Zouave company was killed, Meagher had received it from their chaplain, Bernard O'Reilly; he then called to his men, "Remember Fontenoy!" and charged and carried the opposing battery.[19] Father O'Reilly gave Maria full details of the battle, and she was duly impressed: "He remained with Colonel Corcoran and was the last to leave the field. He was indefatigable in his attention to the wounded and dying ... [when Confederates searched the field for prisoners] he lay down upon the ground and feigned death until they passed." She adds that Colonel Corcoran, then a prisoner in Richmond, Virginia, refused to give his parole because that would prevent him from serving again during the war. She claims her husband "sent him a message telling him, if he wanted money, to draw on him."[20]

In November, Colonel Corcoran was informed that he would be hanged along with other high-ranking Yankee prisoners if the North carried out the sentence of death passed on members of the Confederate privateer, *Jefferson Davis*. When Daly heard this news from Corcoran in December, he went to Washington to convince the government to arrange for an exchange of prisoners that would free his friend. Lincoln held a special cabinet meeting to consider Daly's concerns.[21] At this cabinet meeting, to which he was invited, the judge pointed out the inadvisability of executing Confederate privateering crews and urged that they be given prisoner of war status. The authorities were persuaded to substitute Daly's plan, which he was told to send in letter form to Senator Ira Harris of New York. Harris served as an intermediary between the administration and the Radical Republicans of both the Senate and the press. On December 19, 1861, Mrs. Daly observed of her husband, "If he were in Washington he would be very useful, having such a just and impartial mind and the happy faculty of expressing himself clearly."[22]

Judge Daly pointed out that privateering "is a lawful means of warfare, except among those nations who by treaty stipulate that they will not, as between themselves, resort to it. Pirates are the general enemies of all mankind." His argument persuaded Horace Greeley, editor of the *New York Tribune*, who had originally wanted to hang all aboard southern privateers.[23] On February 3, 1862, it was reported that the government had resolved to "put privateerism on the level of prisoners of war," as the secretary of state might direct.[24]

Support for the Union

When a Union ship intercepted two Confederate agents on the high seas, an international conflict arose and Judge Daly's advice on the matter was solicited (and later circulated through various newspapers). The result was that the two agents were released and a U.S. apology followed.[25]

Charles Daly's great skills in actively supporting the Union were widely recognized. As a Union Democrat, he was an active supporter of the views of President Lincoln and spent considerable time advising him and the Union generals. As always, he was a welcome speaker at many events. For example, following one of Daly's orations, the Albany *Evening Journal*, on September 18, 1862, paid tribute to his defense of the Union cause.[26]

Daly's effective support induced Corcoran's revived Irish Legion to give itself the title of "Judge Daly Guard." Although offered inducements to accept public office or to enter politics, Corcoran said he simply wanted to go back to soldiering, and he immediately set about reassembling the Irish Legion. Several officers asked Judge Daly's approval for enrolling "The Judge Daly Guard" for the second regiment of the First Brigade of Corcoran's Irish Legion.[27]

At this point Thomas Francis Meagher decided to organize a separate Irish unit, the cornerstone of which would be the new 69th.[28] In this work, he had the support of Judge Daly, Archbishop Hughes and others prominent in New York City's Irish community.[29]

Daly was the main speaker on the occasion, and when presenting the colonel of the 69th with the unit's colors, he said:

> What is asked of an Irishman in this crisis? He is asked to preserve that Government which Montgomery died to create, and which those Irishmen who signed the Declaration of Independence, George Taylor, James Smith and Matthew Thornton, meant to transmit, with its manifold blessings, to every Irishman who should make this country the land of his adoption. To the Irish race it has been in every sense a country—a country where their native energy and stimulated industry has met with its appropriate reward; and where they have enjoyed an amount of political consequence, and exerted a degree of political influence not found in the land of their nativity."[30]

The judge then touched the usual chords of collective Irish memory regarding the Irish Brigades in Europe and their implication for Irish honor in America. Colonel Nugent responded in kind. Finally, the reporter for the *New York Times* wrote, "The band are chiming in, on their close, with ... the *Star Spangled Banner*, followed by a flash of *St Patrick's Day in the Morning*, a gleam of *Rory O'More*, and the whole blaze of *Vive l'America*."[31]

Contention arose as to who should command the emerging Irish Brigade. The Dalys were among those who favored Tyrone-born James Shields for the post. But Shields, an ex-judge from Illinois and former senator for Minnesota, believed that Lincoln had greater things in store for him, and he wisely stepped aside in favor of Meagher. "I know General Meagher well," he said, "and [I] hope to have the 'Irish Brigade,' with its gallant Brigadier, at some future day in my division."[32]

Following crop failures in Ireland beginning in 1861, Daly took the lead in promoting a relief campaign in New York, which resulted in $171,272 in cash along with large amounts of clothing and provisions. Contributions from merchants were supplemented by money donated by Irish soldiers and church parishioners.[33]

While her husband continued to work hard for the Union cause, Maria Lydig Daly had her own forceful ideas. Women on both sides had played a key role in fomenting division, so on June 11, 1862, she could write, "It is a pity that the abolition female saints and the Charleston female patriots could not meet in a fair fight and mutually annihilate each other." She also noted that her husband, then on a speaking tour, had been strongly advocating enlistment. One rising concern for many Irish people was the effect that black liberation would have on employment opportunities; Daly's view was that there would not be a black movement to the North in the wake of emancipation.[34]

It must be remembered that, in spite of the movement for emancipation, prejudice against blacks was widespread. Mrs. Daly was against slavery, but, in her diary, she stated her racial antipathy bluntly.[35] Charles Daly was conventional; he believed that compromises were needed for the solution of the slavery problem, and he had agreed with Lincoln that slavery should first be confined to those states where it already existed, with measures later taken to eradicate it gradually there. Wider thinking on matters of race in the mid-1800s among people who considered themselves enlightened is illustrated by what the renowned German scientist, Alexander von Humboldt,[36] once said to Judge Daly: "Even the lowest members of the human race are infinitely superior to animals. We may be greatly superior in every attribute to the Negro race, but the Negro stands on the same plane just as surely and firmly as we." The judge agreed.[37]

On his speaking tour, Charles Daly also addressed the argument that the South was only seeking the independence that many Irish people sought in rejecting British control. He forcefully rejected the analogy and went on to give his opinion of what the South was trying to achieve. As astutely as Jefferson Davis had bypassed the defense of slavery to portray states' rights as his primary motive, Daly, speaking for the Union, bypassed the offence of slavery to argue that what the Confederates now sought was not independence but separation, which he then interpreted as a drive for southern imperialism within the North.[38]

The Draft Crisis and After

In March 1863 Congress passed the first U.S. conscription act, enrolling all men between the ages of 20 and 45 for potential service on a quota basis to be administered by state governors. Secretary of State William Seward credited Charles Daly with being the first person to suggest conscription. According to the new act, family status was not a basis for exemption, but a man could exempt himself by paying a sum of $300 or providing a substitute. While Judge Daly was all for the draft, he was completely opposed to the $300 clause. The rich thought the law was fair, but the poor were outraged, and inevitably there was trouble. When the first call for three-year conscripts came in the summer of 1863, draft riots erupted in New York, Pennsylvania, Massachusetts, and the Midwest. New York City saw the worst of the devastation, with rioters attacking blacks, policemen and soldiers over five days in July.

Return casualties were far higher, given the balance of firepower. To the shame of Meagher, Nugent, Judge Daly, and every other respectable Irishman in New York, the surging lawless mob had been largely made up of fellow Hibernians.[39] As Iver Bernstein writes, "The awesome destruction of property and life stunned a generation of urban Americans well familiar with street violence."[40] It took much time and effort by Irish community leaders in America, and their influential friends, to counteract the negative effect of the riots. Even the Dalys felt the cold chill of alienation among their friends, but the judge's stature and personality eased this difficulty, as did the unambiguous support for the war effort from senior Irish officers like Nugent and Corcoran. The Dalys increased their aid to the war effort, and when Maria and her lady friends needed backing for their work with the U.S. Sanitary Commission,[41] the judge gave both time and money. He also spoke at rallies in support of soldiers and leaders, while Maria became president of the Women's Patriotic League, founded in 1863.[42]

On June 4, 1864, Lincoln was renominated for the presidency, and General George McClellan became the Democratic candidate. In early September, McClellan wrote to Judge Daly to say he would be in the city "very privately on Tuesday" and would be happy to see the judge at his home, begging him to say nothing about this visit. At the same time, Daly was invited to speak before the Central Democratic Club of Jersey City in support of Lincoln's reelection. While Daly opted for McClellan and was one of his electors, many close friends of the Dalys in New York supported Lincoln, who was comfortably reelected.[43]

Throughout the war, Judge Daly sat on the bench, and if most of his cases were routine, some were later cited for their keen, studied judgments. As Union victory neared and the northern Democrats sought to maintain their major roles in national life and New York's business world, the Dalys were caught up in a whirl of social engagements with leaders in the arts, society, theater, politics and military. This brought them into close contact with the historian George Bancroft; poet and newspaper editor William Cullen Bryant; the well-known champion of women's suffrage, Henry Ward Beecher; and leading merchant families, including the Astors and the Stewarts. On New Year's Day 1865, the Dalys held their annual open house and received more than one hundred visitors. Mrs. Daly had several comments to make in her diary regarding her guests. "I wish I were not given so much to dissecting character," she sighed, as she went on to describe one of them: "William Reid came in dressed in black velvet from head to foot, white cravat and diamond sleeve buttons. He looked well, but ridiculously; it's sort of shoddy."[44]

In March, Judge Daly chaired arrangements to celebrate Union victories, especially the taking of Georgia by General William Tecumseh Sherman. The resultant parade was reportedly six miles long. On March 26, 1865, Maria wrote in her diary, "Events seem hastening on to end this rebellion. Victories every day, and all our neutral friends are coming to shake hands with us on our success." On April 1, Daly's younger American Irish contemporary, General Philip Sheridan, achieved a decisive victory over the Confederates at Five Forks, going on the next day to cut off General Robert E. Lee's exhausted army. A week later Lee surrendered to General Grant at Appomattox.

Jurist, Man of Letters and Leading Citizen

After the Civil War, Judge Daly belonged to the reform element of the Democratic Party and sat in the State Constitutional Convention. He assisted his personal friends George McClellan, Samuel J. Tilden, and Winfield Scott Hancock in their unsuccessful bids for the presidency in the 1864, 1876, and 1880 elections. As a behind-the-scenes politician, Daly also vigorously supported Grover Cleveland in his three bids for the presidency. As a wit and orator, he acted as the unofficial host for the city of New York, welcoming dignitaries, dedicating monuments, presiding over public meetings, and leading movements for improvement and reform. He was central to the American Geographical Society from its infancy, serving as its president from 1864 to 1899. He drove to make the organization both commercial and popular, while also preserving its scientific interests. He invested in several expeditions, understanding that active heroism would prove more attractive to the public than quiet reports. Thus he knew well such great men as Henry Morton Stanley, Alexander Humboldt, Paul Du Chaillu, and Robert Peary. He funded Arctic missions: there are a Lake Daly and a Madam Daly Lake in Canada's far north, as well as a Cape Daly in northern Greenland.[45]

He wrote a major history of the Jews in America and supported Jewish causes, being praised by the *American Hebrew* for both actions and "for his unceasing indignation against anti–Semitism."[46] Other Irish spokesmen of the rising generation followed this example, such as Michael Davitt, John Boyle O'Reilly in Boston, and Humphrey Desmond in the Midwest. Daly's research and writing was constant, whether he engaged in diplomatic treatises or a history of drama or books on common law and juridical history.

Daly pursued a lifelong care for distressed Irish immigrants in America, headed charities for Irish relief, and variously supported the movement for Irish independence. This commitment was not diminished by the disappointment he felt on a major trip to the country in 1874 (a reaction then common to vigorous New Yorkers of Irish parentage on returning to Ireland).[47] With serious distress experienced again in Ireland in 1879–1880, New York papers published vivid accounts of the people's suffering. Among those Irish Americans in the city who offered their support and backing were members of the Fenian Brotherhood, such as jurist Richard O'Gorman and H.L. Hoguet, president of the Emigrant Industrial Savings Bank. Charles Daly was appointed chairman, O'Gorman secretary, and Hoguet treasurer of the Relief Committee, which sent an initial sum of $7,3650 to the Mansion House Committee in Dublin. As the crisis deepened, the committee published 40,000 copies of "An Address to the People of the United States," which appealed to the public for help.[48] People from all backgrounds across America contributed—even some neo-nativists, if one of the latter wished aid to go not to those he called "political Roman Catholic agitators" but to the relief committee of the Duchess of Marlborough instead.[49] By contrast, the *New York Daily Tribune* observed that "no sect or class among our fellow citizens ... has contributed more generously or with more hearty goodwill than the Hebrews," possibly due to Judge Daly's friendship with leaders of the city's Jewish community.[50]

As in the Irish appeals of the 1840s and 1860s, emphasis was placed on common language and religion, the huge role the Irish had played in building America, and the contributions of the Irish to the American wars of independence and self-preservation. But there was now a new note: at the drive's main Washington meeting, the Rev. Jeremiah Rankin declared that the audience had come less in their roles as Irishmen than as Americans, and more as Christians than as Irishmen or Americans.[51]

After Charles Daly's death on September 19, 1899, the *Jewish Encyclopedia* declared that "Judge Daly's profound scholarship, unquestioned integrity, brilliant conversational gifts, and commanding dignity combined to give him for many years a unique position in American life."[52]

Notes

1. Harold Earl Hammond, *A Commoner's Judge: The Life and Times of Charles Patrick Daly* (Boston: Christopher Publishing House, 1954), 130–31; Ronald H. Bayor and Timothy J. Meagher, eds., *The New York Irish* (Baltimore: Johns Hopkins University Press, 1996), 24.
2. Hammond, *Daly*, 13.
3. *American Hebrew* (New York), September 22, 1899, C.P. Daly obituary; A. Oakey Hall, *The Green Bag* (New York: 1894), "Judge Charles P. Daly"; *New York Tribune*, September 22, 1899; Hammond, *Daly*, 11–16.

4. Charles P. Daly Letters and Papers, New York Public Library (Manuscript Division); Hammond, *Daly*, 18–24.

5. Daly Papers, Daniel Robertson to Daly, February 1, 1841, and E. Ward to Daly, March 4, 1841; Hammond, *Daly*, 24–25.

6. Fernando Wood (1812–1881), W.M. Tweed (1823–1878), and Richard Croker (1841–1922). Unlike Wood and Tweed, who were native to Philadelphia, Croker, born in County Cork, came to the United States in 1846. Each of the three attempted to run changing cities, albeit in different contexts: see Jerome Mushkat, *Fernando Wood* (Kent, OH: Kent State University Press, 1990); Jerome Mushkat, *Tammany* (Syracuse, NY: Syracuse University Press, 1971); Chris McNickle, *To Be Mayor of New York* (New York: Columbia University Press, 1993); Lothrop Stoddard, *Master of Manhattan: The Life of Richard Croker* (New York: Longmans, Green, 1931).

7. Hammond, *Daly*, 26–29, 38.

8. Miklos Pinther in *Ubique* (American Geographical Society newsletter) 32, no. 2 (September 2003): 1–6.

9. *New York Times*, September 20, 1899.

10. Maria Lydig Daly, *Diary of a Union Lady, 1861–1865* (Lincoln: University of Nebraska Press, 2000), v, xiv–xxiv, 75; Hammond, *Daly*, 112–20.

11. *Third Annual Report of the Bureau of Military Statistics of the State of New York* (Albany: C. Wendell, 1866), https://dmna.ny.gov/historic/reghist/civil/annual_reports/3rd_Annual_Report_BMS_1866_p1_275.pdf.

12. Frank Boyle, *A Party of Mad Fellows: The Story of the Irish Regiments in the Army of the Potomac* (Dayton, OH: Morningside, 1996), 20–26; Phyllis Lane, "Colonel Michael Corcoran, Fighting Irishman," in P.S. Seagrave, ed., *The History of the Irish Brigade* (Fredericksburg, VA: Sergeant Kirkland's Museum and Historical Society, 1997), 13–23.

13. James Shields (1806–1879) had immigrated in 1827 and became a judge of the Illinois Supreme Court in 1843. A brigadier general in the Mexican War, he also served as a U.S. senator from Illinois (1849–1855) and then from Minnesota (1858–1859), each time as a Douglas Democrat. As a brigadier general of Union volunteers, from August 1861 onward he served in the western Virginia campaigns, and subsequently on the Rappahannock. Charles O'Conor (1804–1884) was a New York lawyer whose father, Thomas, was exiled after the 1798 rebellion. An administration Democrat in the 1850s, he fought cases to secure slaves to their owners temporarily in his state (1848, 1860). One of the northern Peace Democrats, he wished for negotiated peace with the South. He secured bail for Jefferson Davis in 1867 (who was ultimately not brought to trial). He also led the prosecution of the Tweed ring in 1871 and represented Samuel Tilden in the disputed election of 1876. Richard O'Gorman (1821–1895) fled Ireland in 1848. Prominent in New York Irish affairs, he was elected judge of the Superior Court in 1883.

14. *New York Times*, June 21, 1873.

15. *New York Times*, May 18, 1861; Maria Daly, *Diary*, 20.

16. Hammond, *Daly*, 146–47; Maria Daly, *Diary*, xxi–xxvi, 42, 15; *New York Times*, March 2, 1895.

17. Maria Daly, *Diary*, 19.

18. Robert Patterson (1792–1881) was another County Tyrone man, and the son of a United Irishman who fled after the 1798 insurrection. He was a noted soldier and businessman who saw service in the War of 1812 and the Mexican War. See Ella Lonn, *Foreigners in the Union Army and Navy* (Baton Rouge: Louisiana State University Press, 1951).

19. Maria Daly, *Diary*, 40–41. Father Bernard O'Reilly (1820–1907) was born in County Mayo, immigrated to Canada in 1836, and attended Laval University in Quebec. He entered the Society of Jesus and was attached to St. John's College, Fordham, New York. A close friend of the Dalys, Maria described O'Reilly as "unostentatious, refined, intellectual." He served as chaplain to the 69th and later Meagher's Irish Brigade. He later withdrew from the Jesuits and devoted himself to writing. He lived for years in Rome, where Pope Leo XIII appointed him a Protonotary Apostolic in 1887 and gave him special materials for his *Life of Leo XIII* (1887). Among the many other books he published were *Life of Pius IX* (1877), *Mirror of True Womanhood* (New York, 1876; and M.H. Gill, Dublin, 1927); *Key of Heaven* (1878); and *Life*

Part II: American Civil War

of John MacHale, Archbishop of Tuam (1890). See Maria Daly, *Diary*, xxxii–xxxiii; *The Catholic Encyclopedia*, vol. XI (New York, 1911).

20. Maria Daly, *Diary*, 45–46.
21. Hammond, *Daly*, 143–49, 153–54; Bayor and Meagher, *The New York Irish*, 196, 198, 202, 207; Seagrave, *The History of the Irish Brigade*, 24.
22. Maria Daly, *Diary*, 85; *Dictionary of American Biography*, vol. V (1930), article on Charles Patrick Daly.
23. *New York Daily Tribune*, April 20, 1861.
24. Hammond, *Daly*, 156.
25. Daly Papers, H. Barney to Daly, December 16, 1861; Hammond, *Daly*, 153–58.
26. Pinther in *Ubique* (September 2003), 4.
27. Boyle, *Party of Mad Fellows*, 168–74; Hammond, *Daly*, 165–66.
28. Robert Nugent was from Kilkeel, County Down, and was formerly lieutenant colonel of the 69th Militia. On his return from Bull Run, he and Meagher decided to form an Irish Brigade: see Boyle, *Party of Mad Fellows*, 54–79; William F. Fox, ed., *Final Report on the Battlefield of Gettysburg*, vol. 2 (Albany: J.B. Lyon, 1900).
29. *New York Times*, November 19, 1861.
30. Richard Montgomery (1736–1775), for whom many Irish militia units were named in America, was a revolutionary soldier who fell in the attack on Quebec. He was born at Convoy House, near Raphoe, County Donegal, and was the son of Thomas Montgomery, a member of the Irish parliament for Lifford (see http://www.revolutionarywararchives.org/biography-link/98-george-washingtons-generals-major-general-richard-montgomery).
31. *New York Times*, November 19, 1861.
32. D.P. Conyngham, *The Irish Brigade and Its Campaigns*, edited by L.F. Kohl (New York: Fordham University Press, 1994), 50, 68, 94; Michael Cavanagh, *Memoirs of General Thomas Francis Meagher* (Worcester, MA: Messenger Press, 1892), 428–30, quoted in Boyle, *Party of Mad Fellows*, 73. Meagher was commissioned as brigadier in February 1862, six months after Shields.
33. Merle Curti, *American Philanthropy Abroad* (New Brunswick, NJ: Rutgers University Press, 1988), 66–67; Hammond, *Daly*, 162; *New York Daily Tribune*, May 23 and 26, 1862.
34. West Farms, where this speech took place, was a rural village in the Bronx, then largely countryside. Several wealthy New York families owned large estates there, including the Lydigs, the Astors, the De Lanceys and the Morrises. It might be noted that the *New York Times* website gives the date of the West Farms speech, in its Wednesday, August 24, 1862, edition, as "Wednesday evening, the 26th inst.," although August 24 that year was a Sunday. If Mrs. Daly was correct in her information, then the meeting actually took place on Monday, August 18. See Maria Daly, *Diary*, 34, 165; http://query.nytimes.com/gst/abstract.html?res=9A06E2D91F3FEE34BC4C51DFBE668389679FDE).
35. Maria Daly, *Diary*, 43.
36. Humboldt wrote of Daly, "Few men have left upon me such an impression of high intelligence on subjects of universal interest, and in the judgment of apparently opposite directions of character among nations that inhabit the ever-narrowing Atlantic basin" (*New York Times*, September 20, 1899).
37. Hammond, *Daly*, 159–60.
38. Maria Daly, *Diary*, 165; *New York Times*, August 24, 1862. Later in this speech, Judge Daly referred to the threat of a state draft which Lincoln had first ordered, one that governors *might* use if volunteering proved insufficient. The city's Democratic elite knew well how divisive this option would be and sought to expand volunteering, as a sort of "popular sovereignty," which would enlist those who found the Union war effort fully acceptable, thus exempting state authorities from coercing the unwilling.
39. Boyle, *Party of Mad Fellows*, 310.
40. Iver Bernstein, *The New York City Draft Riots* (New York: Oxford University Press, 1990), 3.
41. As the war got under way, it was soon obvious that camp conditions were appalling and medical care totally inadequate. Women all over the North began to raise money and send volunteer workers to care for sick and dying soldiers, despite opposition from military

command. Organized at first in New York City, under Henry Bellows, in April 1861, Lincoln approved a federal version as the Sanitary Commission in June 1861. See *The Civil War Society's Encyclopedia of the Civil War* (New York: Wing Books, 1997), 307–9.

42. Maria Daly, *Diary*, 299–300.
43. Hammond, *Daly*, 183–86.
44. Maria Daly, *Diary*, 327–28.
45. Hammond, *Daly*, 281; Karen M. Morin, "Charles P. Daly's Gendered Geography, 1860–1890," *Annals of the Association of American Geographers* 98 (December 2008): 897–919.
46. *American Hebrew* (New York), September 22, 1899.
47. Mark K. Neville, "The Ireland of 1874: Journal of Charles P. Daly (1816–1899)," *Eire-Ireland* 14, no. 2 (1979): 44–51.
48. *New York Herald*, January 1, 7, and 31, 1880; *New York Daily Tribune*, January 18, 1880. See also Daly Papers: H.L. Hoguet, Emigrant Industrial Savings Bank, to Chas. Daly, February 12, 1880; Adolf Sanger (attorney to Daly) to Daly, February 18, 1880; Eugene B. Murtha to Daly, February 28, 1880.
49. Curti, *American Philanthropy Abroad*, 84.
50. *New York Daily Tribune*, February 25, 1880.
51. *Washington Evening Star*, January 21, 1880; *Washington Post*, January 21, 1880.
52. Stephen Fiske, *Off-hand Portraits of Prominent New Yorkers* (1884; reprint, New York: Arno Press, 1975), 83; *Jewish Encyclopedia*, http://jewishencyclopedia.com/articles/4858-daly-charles-p.

Bibliography

Bernstein, Iver. *The New York City Draft Riots.* New York: Oxford University Press, 1990.
Boyle, Frank. *A Party of Mad Fellows: The Story of the Irish Regiments in the Army of the Potomac.* Dayton, OH: Morningside, 1996.
Cavanagh, Michael. *Memoirs of General Thomas Francis Meagher.* Worcester, MA: Messenger Press, 1892.
Charles P. Daly Letters and Papers, New York Public Library (Manuscript Division).
The Civil War Society's Encyclopedia of the Civil War. New York: Wing Books, 1997.
Conyngham, D.P. *The Irish Brigade and Its Campaigns.* Edited by L.F. Kohl. New York: Fordham University Press, 1994.
Curti, Merle. *American Philanthropy Abroad.* New Brunswick, NJ: Rutgers University Press, 1988.
Daly, Maria Lydig. *Diary of a Union Lady, 1861–1865.* Lincoln: University of Nebraska Press, 2000.
Fiske, Stephen. *Off-hand Portraits of Prominent New Yorkers.* 1884; reprint, New York: Arno Press, 1975.
Fox, William F., ed. *Final Report on the Battlefield of Gettysburg.* Vol. 2. Albany: J.B. Lyon, 1900.
Hammond, Harold E. *A Commoner's Judge: The Life and Times of Charles Patrick Daly.* Boston: Christopher Publishing House, 1954.
Lonn, Ella. *Foreigners in the Union Army and Navy.* Baton Rouge: Louisiana State University Press, 1951.
Morin, Karen M. "Charles P. Daly's Gendered Geography, 1860–1890." *Annals of the Association of American Geographers* 98 (December 2008): 897–919.
Neville, Mark K. "The Ireland of 1874: Journal of Charles P. Daly (1819–1899)." *Eire-Ireland* 14, no. 2 (1979): 44–51.
Seagrave, P.S., ed. *The History of the Irish Brigade.* Fredericksburg, VA: Sergeant Kirkland's Museum and Historical Society, 1997.
Third Annual Report of the Bureau of Military Statistics of the State of New York. Albany: C. Wendell, 1866. https://dmna.ny.gov/historic/reghist/civil/annual_reports/3rd_Annual_Report_BMS_1866_p1_275.pdf.
Ubique (American Geographical Society newsletter) 32, no. 2 (September 2003).

Irish and African Americans in the Civil War Era

ANDRE FLECHE

In early April 1861, Thomas Francis Meagher, the Irish revolutionary hero of 1848 and founder of the Union's famous Irish Brigade, strode into Delmonico's in New York and bluntly proclaimed his position on the growing secession crisis. "In this controversy, my sympathies are entirely with the South!" he declared. He expounded upon his views in an argument with his Republican father-in-law, who referred to white southerners as "a set of rebels." "You cannot call eight millions of white freemen '*rebels*,'" Meagher maintained. "You may call them '*revolutionists*' if you will."[1]

Meagher's equation of Confederates with Irish nationalists specifically championed the white race's right to self-determination and pointedly ignored the claims of enslaved black southerners to freedom and liberty. When the attack on Fort Sumter and President Abraham Lincoln's subsequent call for volunteers forced Meagher to side with the Union, he justified his apparent change of heart by referring to the benefits a restored United States would bring to the cause of freedom for Ireland and liberty for citizens of European descent. "The Republic, that gave us asylum and ... is the mainstay of human freedom, the world over—is threatened with disruption. We could not hope to succeed in our effort to make Ireland a republic without the moral and material aid of the liberty-loving citizens of these United States," he wrote.[2]

The vision shared by many Irish Americans of the New World republic joining the struggle against despotism in Europe did not include concern for the rights of African Americans. Many of the Irish in Civil War America viewed racial difference in the United States as a problem that the existence of slavery helped mitigate. Ardent Irish nationalists feared that conflict between abolitionists and fire-eaters would weaken the United States, strengthen England, and threaten freedom for Ireland. The thousands of struggling immigrants who enlisted in the Union Army feared economic competition from freed black slaves. As members of the Democratic Party, both groups agreed that compromise and a speedy restoration of the "Union as it was" offered the best hope for the future of the Irish in both Europe and America.

Black Americans, however, seized the opportunity the war offered to lay claim to liberty, equality, and civil rights. In the eyes of the startled Irish, emancipation and the formation of the United States Colored Troops seemed to demonstrate that their goals of restored unity between white northerners and white southerners had given way to demands for black equality. The tension between a view of the war that advocated speedy white reconciliation and one that favored black liberation exploded in the New York City draft riots of 1863, during which Irish mobs targeted African Americans as a cause and symbol of the Lincoln administration's changing war policy. Although some Irish soldiers proved much more willing than historians have previously recognized to embrace emancipation in pursuit of Union victory, few abandoned their racist views or supported equal rights for the freedmen. Both African Americans and the Irish claimed to fight for liberty, human rights, and ethnic and racial acceptance, but Irish support for a melting-pot republic did not include commitment to racial equality.

Many of the Irish had long viewed abolitionist agitation, not southern insistence on states' rights and the expansion of slavery, as the greatest threat to the Union and the longevity of the nation. John Mitchel, revolutionary compatriot of Thomas Francis Meagher and later a supporter of the Confederacy, spoke for many of his countrymen when he labeled northerners "the aggressors" in the sectional conflicts of the 1850s. Attempts to halt the expansion of slavery westward by opposing the Kansas-Nebraska Act that would open territory to settlers set the principles of "centralization" against the "right of self-government" enjoyed by "the whites of Nebraska." Mitchel spoke of a "fraudulent freedom" that would "prevent the extension of slavery by restricting the natural growth of the States." Such misguided philanthropists, Mitchel believed, "love Uncle Tom more than Uncle Sam."[3]

Thousands of Irish immigrants shared Mitchel's views and flocked to the Democratic Party, which promised to preserve national greatness and unity by compromising on the political questions surrounding slavery and leaving blacks in bondage. Such a solution perfectly suited poor laborers and longshoremen who competed with blacks for jobs on the docks of New York and in cities throughout the North. Democratic politicians promised to keep African Americans enslaved, in the South, and out of politics. Republicans, by contrast, threatened to disrupt the racial and political status quo by agitating the slavery issue. When southern secession threatened to permanently divide the model American republic, the Irish blamed blacks and abolitionists for the nation's misfortune.[4]

Despite their misgivings, more than 140,000 Irishmen fought to suppress the rebellion. Irish recruits joined the Union Army for both practical and idealistic reasons. Nationalists such as Thomas Francis Meagher and Michael Corcoran wished to preserve the American republic that they believed served as an example and inspiration for downtrodden Ireland. Others hoped to secure acceptance in the United States by combating widespread anti-Catholicism and nativism. Many immigrant laborers sought little more than a steady paycheck. Few of the Irish, however, joined out of abolitionist principles or concern for the rights of enslaved black southerners. Captain D.P. Conyngham, historian of the Irish Brigade, stated the case bluntly: "The Irish soldier did not ask whether the colored race were better off as bondsmen or freedmen; he was not going to fight for an abstract idea. He felt that the safety and welfare of his adopted country and its glorious Constitution were imperiled; he, therefore, willingly threw himself into the breach to sustain the flag that sheltered him."[5]

As long as speedy reunion remained the Lincoln administration's primary goal, Irish soldiers could happily serve the federal government. In doing so, they hoped to gain assimilation into the American mainstream and strike a blow for Ireland's freedom by reuniting England's most powerful rival. Thomas Francis Meagher called preservation of the republic a "duty of us Irish citizens, who aspire to establish a similar form of government in our native land." Meagher, Michael Corcoran, and other committed Irish nationalists even believed that brief service in the U.S. Army would prepare Irish militia members for a coming war with Great Britain over freedom for Ireland. Conyngham hoped that "many a patriotic young Irishman" would "learn the use of arms and the science of war" and one day turn them "to practical use in his own country."[6]

The realities of war and the evolving policies of the Lincoln administration dashed such naive hopes. White northerners and white southerners would not quickly reconcile to lead the Celts in battle against the despotic Anglo-Saxons, nor would African Americans remain passive observers at the periphery of the war. Confederate muskets at the battles of Antietam and Fredericksburg devastated the Union's famous Irish Brigade, which included the 69th Regiment of New York, a prewar militia unit that had entertained hopes of fighting in Ireland. The mounting casualties shook resolve on the home front and opened Republicans to charges of needlessly wasting Irish lives in an idealistic crusade to aid the slaves. The Conscription Act of 1863 seemed to confirm that Lincoln planned to continue to fight the war with poor immigrant cannon fodder. Most alarmingly, the Irish military disasters during the autumn of 1862 coincided with Lincoln's preliminary Emancipation Proclamation, which threatened to transform the war for reunion into a struggle for black freedom.[7]

African Americans cared little for the opposition of their comrades-in-arms. They seized the opportunity to fight for their freedom and civil rights by enlisting in numbers greater than the Irish. Jacob Demus, an enlisted man in the Union's famous 54th Massachusetts Infantry Regiment, bluntly explained in a letter to his sister Mary Jane why many black men fought: "This [war] shall not end till the Colord [sic] people get their rights it goes very hard for the White people to think of it But by gods will and power they will have their rights." Robert Hamilton, editor of New York's *Anglo-African*, agreed, asking, "What better field to claim our rights than the field of battle?"[8]

Irish anger and frustration at African Americans' willingness to assert their equality in an apparently successful effort to shift Union war aims erupted in the New York City draft riots of July 1863. The Conscription Act passed that March made all male citizens between the ages of twenty and forty-five eligible for induction into the military. A clause allowing drafted men to avoid service by hiring a substitute or paying a $300 commutation fee alienated poor northerners and fueled charges of a "rich man's war and a poor man's fight." When government enrollment officers arrived in New York to hold the first draft lotteries, crowds of laborers, many of them Irish, gathered to prevent the selection of the first draftees. Mobs sacked and destroyed army recruiting centers, Republican Party offices, and the property of prominent men and merchants aligned with the Lincoln administration.[9]

Black New Yorkers bore the brunt of the mob's fury. The Irish masses blamed African Americans for causing the war and resented their demands for freedom and equality. Emancipation and the presence of blacks in uniform only prolonged the war, made reconciliation between northern and southern whites more difficult, and led to more Irish deaths. On July 13, a group of rioters invaded an asylum for black orphans and burned it to the ground. Scores of the city's African Americans shared the fate of William Jones, whom a group of protesters lynched and burned in the street. A crowd that gathered in front of the Republican-leaning *New York Tribune* articulated the motivations of the mob: "Down with the *Tribune*! Down with the old white coat what thinks a naygar as good as an Irishman!" they shouted.[10]

Not all Irish soldiers shared the views of their riotous countrymen. Some veterans supported harsh measures such as conscription and emancipation out of their overwhelming commitment to victory. Irish Brigade member Peter Welsh believed that "no conscription could be fairer than the one which is about to be enforced" and denounced the riots as "disgraceful." He believed the draft would "do more to end the war than the win[n]ing of a great victory" by showing the Confederacy "that we have the determination and the power to prosecute the war." Welsh felt "sorry that the Irish men of New York took so large a part" in the riots, but argued the perpetrators "should be hung like dogs they are agents of jef davis [sic]."[11]

Some Irish soldiers joined denunciation of antiwar rioters with support for the enlistment of black soldiers. Peter Welsh admitted, "the feeling against nigars [sic] is intensely strong in this army," and reported that "they are looked upon as the principal cause of this war," especially "in the Irish regiments." Still, he proved willing to see them serve as soldiers. "I see by late papers that the governor of Massachusets [sic] has been autheured to raise nigar regiments I hope he may succeed," he wrote to his wife. D.P. Conyngham, who had clearly stated that the Irish did not fight out of a concern for slaves, gave black troops credit for "carrying the first line by assault" during the Battle of the Crater.[12]

Most surprisingly, some Irish unionist commentators proved equally amenable to emancipation if it meant victory over the Confederates and unity for the nation. "If slavery is in the way of a proper administration of the laws and the integrity and perpetuety [sic] of this nation then i say away with both slaves and slavery," wrote Peter Welsh. Father William Corby, a chaplain with the Irish Brigade, reminded his men in a general absolution sermon during the Mine Run campaign that Confederates and their sympathizers sought "to maintain in perpetual slavery 4,000,000 human beings." Iron Brigade sergeant James P. Sullivan attributed secession to southern whites' desire that "slaves shall do all the labor." After the war, he authored a poem in which he prayed that God would not "prolong" slavery and asked that "the black man" share "freedom."[13]

Even the most enlightened of these committed Union soldiers failed to abandon the racism shared by most Irish and American whites during the nineteenth century, however. Peter Welsh qualified his support for emancipation with the hope that black slaves and abolitionists alike would be "swept from the land" after the war. He believed the Union would succeed in spite of, not because of, the policies of "nigar worshippers." Father Corby found it humorous to recount stories about "darkey" servants. James P. Sullivan joined him with anecdotes about a camp follower he called "Nigger Jack" and a black cook named William who dropped his kettles and ran in terror at the first sound of Confederate guns. If military service could change Irish attitudes toward slavery, emancipation, and black enlistment, it seems to have had little effect on their racial views.[14]

African Americans and the Irish alike hoped to gain acceptance into the American mainstream and claimed to fight for liberty, equality, and freedom. For the Irish, however, their black Unionist counterparts had no place in the reunited American republic they envisioned. In their view, whites alone would enjoy the full economic and political benefits of a restored United States, and the country would be just as well off with blacks in bondage. Divisions over slavery and race in America only weakened the nation and made it less likely that Irish freedom in Europe could be achieved with the aid of the New World. Even veterans who became convinced that the destruction of slavery offered the best way to defeat the Confederacy failed to modify their racial views. Assimilation into a racist American culture proved more important to the Irish than pushing the boundaries of racial acceptance by offering citizenship and equality to the freedmen.

NOTES

1. Michael Cavanagh, *Memoirs of General Thomas Francis Meagher* (Worcester, MA: Messenger Press, 1892), 367, 368.

2. Ibid., 369.

3. "Nebraska and Kansas," *The Citizen* 1, no. 9 (March 4, 1854): 136; "Saving the Union," *The Citizen* 1, no. 21 (May 27, 1854): 328.

4. For a discussion of the Democratic Party and its positions during the 1850s and 1860s, see Jean Baker, *Affairs of Party: The Political Culture of Northern Democrats in the Mid-Nineteenth Century* (New York: Fordham University Press, 1983), and Joel Silbey, *A Respectable Minority: The Democratic Party in the Civil War Era* (New York: W.W. Norton, 1977).

5. D.P. Conyngham, *The Irish Brigade and Its Campaigns* (Boston: Patrick Donahoe, 1869), 5–6. For an excellent discussion of Irish motivations, see Randall M. Miller, "Catholic Religion, Irish Ethnicity, and the Civil War," in *Religion and the American Civil War*, edited by Randall M. Miller, Harry S. Stout, and Charles R. Wilson (New York: Oxford University Press, 1998), 261–96. For a treatment of how nationalists and other factions in Ireland viewed the American republic, the Civil War, and its consequences for Ireland and the Irish, see Joseph M. Hernon, *Celts, Catholics, and Copperheads: Ireland Views the American Civil War* (Columbus: Ohio State University Press, 1968).

6. Cavanagh, *Meagher*, 369; Conyngham, *Irish Brigade*. For Irish enlistment numbers, see Miller, "Catholic Religion," 265; William L. Burton, *Melting Pot Soldiers: The Union's Ethnic Regiments* (Ames: Iowa State University Press, 1988); and Ella Lonn, *Foreigners in the Union Army and Navy* (Baton Rouge: Louisiana State University Press, 1951).

7. For a discussion of the effect of Antietam, Fredericksburg, emancipation, and conscription on Irish morale, see Craig A. Warren, "'Oh, God, What a Pity!' The Irish Brigade at Fredericksburg and the Creation of Myth," *Civil War History* 47, no. 3 (2001): 193–221.

8. Jacob Demus to Mary Jane Demus, May 13, 1864, letters of the Demus and Christy Family, *Valley of the Shadow: Two Communities in the American Civil War*, Virginia Center for Digital History, University of Virginia, http://valley.lib.virginia.edu/VoS/personalpapers/collections/franklin/demus.html. Hamilton quoted in Donald Yacovone, ed., *Voice of Thunder: The Civil War Letters of George Stephens* (Urbana: University of Illinois Press, 1997), 19. Almost 200,000 African Americans served in the Union armed forces. For an overview, see John David Smith, "Let Us All Be Grateful That We Have Colored Troops That Will Fight," in *Black Soldiers in Blue: African American Troops in the Civil War Era*, edited by John David Smith (Chapel Hill: University of North Carolina Press, 2002), 1–77. Thus more African Americans served in the Union forces than did Irishmen (estimated at a minimum of 140,000).

9. For an account of the riot and its causes, see Adrian Cook, *The Armies of the Streets: The New York City Draft Riots of 1863* (Lexington: University Press of Kentucky, 1974), and Iver Bernstein, *The New York City Draft Riots: Their Significance for American Politics and Society in the Age of the Civil War* (New York: Oxford University Press, 1990).

10. Cook, *Armies of the Streets*, 77–78, 82, 88. See also Bernstein, *New York City Draft Riots*, 21, 27.

11. Peter Welsh, *Irish Green and Union Blue: The Civil War Letters of Peter Welsh, Color Sergeant, 28th Regiment Massachusetts Volunteers*, edited by Lawrence Frederick Kohl and Margaret Cossé Richard (New York: Fordham University Press, 1986), 110, 113, 114, 115.

12. Welsh, *Irish Green and Union Blue*, 62; Conyngham, *Irish Brigade*, 469.

13. Welsh, *Irish Green and Union Blue*, 66; William Corby, *Memoirs of Chaplain Life:*

Three Years with the Irish Brigade in the Army of the Potomac, edited by Lawrence Frederick Kohl (1894; reprint, New York: Fordham University Press, 1992), 321; James P. Sullivan, *An Irishman in the Iron Brigade: The Civil War Memoirs of James P. Sullivan, Sergt., Company K, 10th Wisconsin Volunteers*, edited by William J.K. Beaudot and Lance J. Herdegen (New York: Fordham University Press, 1993), 13.

14. Welsh, *Irish Green and Union Blue*, 70; Corby, *Memoirs of Chaplain Life*, 83; Sullivan, *Irishman in Iron Brigade*, 39–41. See also Christian G. Samito, *Becoming American Under Fire: Irish Americans, African Americans, and the Politics of Citizenship during the Civil War Era* (Ithaca, NY: Cornell University Press, 2009).

BIBLIOGRAPHY

Baker, Jean. *Affairs of Party: The Political Culture of Northern Democrats in the Mid-Nineteenth Century*. New York: Fordham University Press, 1983.
Bernstein, Iver. *The New York City Draft Riots: Their Significance for American Politics and Society in the Age of the Civil War*. New York: Oxford University Press, 1990.
Burton, William L. *Melting Pot Soldiers: The Union's Ethnic Regiments*. Ames: Iowa State University Press, 1988.
Cavanagh, Michael. *Memoirs of General Thomas Francis Meagher*. Worcester, MA: Messenger Press, 1892.
Conyngham, David P. *The Irish Brigade and Its Campaigns*. Boston: Patrick Donahoe, 1869.
Cook, Adrian. *The Armies of the Streets: The New York City Draft Riots of 1863*. Lexington: University Press of Kentucky, 1974.
Corby, William. *Memoirs of Chaplain Life: Three Years with the Irish Brigade in the Army of the Potomac*. Edited by Lawrence Frederick Kohl. 1894; reprint, New York: Fordham University Press, 1992.
Hernon, Joseph M. *Celts, Catholics, and Copperheads: Ireland Views the American Civil War*. Columbus: Ohio State University Press, 1968.
Lonn, Ella. *Foreigners in the Union Army and Navy*. Baton Rouge: Louisiana State University Press, 1951.
Miller, Randall M. "Catholic Religion, Irish Ethnicity, and the Civil War." In *Religion and the American Civil War*, edited by Randall M. Miller, Harry S. Stout and Charles R. Wilson. New York: Oxford University Press, 1998.
"Nebraska and Kansas." *The Citizen* 1, no. 9 (March 4, 1854).
Samito, Christopher G. *Becoming American Under Fire: Irish Americans, African Americans, and the Politics of Citizenship during the Civil War Era*. Ithaca, NY: Cornell University Press, 2009.
"Saving the Union." *The Citizen* 1, no. 21 (May 27, 1854).
Silbey, Joel. *A Respectable Minority: The Democratic Party in the Civil War Era*. New York: W.W. Norton, 1977.
Smith, John David. "Let Us All Be Grateful That We Have Colored Troops That Will Fight." In *Black Soldiers in Blue: African American Troops in the Civil War Era*, edited by John David Smith. Chapel Hill: University of North Carolina Press, 2002.
Sullivan, James P. *An Irishman in the Iron Brigade: The Civil War Memoirs of James P. Sullivan, Sergt., Company K, 10th Wisconsin Volunteers*. Edited by William J.K. Beaudot and Lance J. Herdegen. New York: Fordham University Press, 1993.
Valley of the Shadow: Two Communities in the American Civil War. Virginia Center for Digital History, University of Virginia. http://valley.lib.virginia.edu/.
Warren, Craig A. "'Oh, God, What a Pity!' The Irish Brigade at Fredericksburg and the Creation of Myth." *Civil War History* 47, no. 3 (2001): 193–221.
Welsh, Peter. *Irish Green and Union Blue: The Civil War Letters of Peter Welsh, Color Sergeant, 28th Regiment, Massachusetts Volunteers*. Edited by Lawrence F. Kohl and Margaret Cossé Richard. New York: Fordham University Press, 1986.
Yacovone, Donald, ed. *Voice of Thunder: The Civil War Letters of George Stephens*. Urbana: University of Illinois Press, 1997.

Christopher Byrne, Civil War Soldier, Writes Home

RUTH-ANN HARRIS

Christopher Byrne, who enlisted in Company H of the 10th Regiment of the Minnesota Infantry in August 1862, was born in Greaghlone, County Monaghan, on November 1, 1833. The family had been tenants on the Shirley Estate for many generations, and it is in the estate records that Christopher's story first emerges. In 1863 he wrote to his brother, Patrick, a celebrated nineteenth-century harper, describing the American Civil War. The letter arrived after Patrick's death in Drogheda in April of that year, and it was preserved by Mr. Shirley, the executor of Patrick's estate.[1] Fortunately, another letter from their sister, Catherine Byrne Deutsch, then living in Ohio, was also preserved.[2] In his letter Christopher describes his brother as "the last of the Legitimate race of Irish Minstrels.... I was very glad to have a Brother worthy of such a complimentary tribute [having read in a New York newspaper of a concert his brother gave in the city of Derry] but at the same time sorry to think that the minstrels which gave the land of my Birth such notoriety would Terminate in you."[3]

Mr. Shirley drew up a genealogy[4] in order to determine bequests to the various members of the family, and it is from this document that we learn that Patrick was the oldest son of Mary Fitzpatrick and Thomas Byrne of Greaghlone, parish of Magheracloone, County Monaghan.[5] From a memoir Christopher wrote in 1898 for a compilation of distinguished early settlers of South Dakota, it appears that he was the son of Thomas Byrne's third wife, Agnes Connolly.[6] Most of the offspring from the third marriage apparently immigrated to England and America, and their names do not appear in the will. In the memoir Christopher says that by the 1890s his sisters Alice, Catherine and Anne, as well as his brother James, lived in Norwalk, Ohio; his sisters Ellen, Mary, and Margaret lived in New York City, and his sister Elizabeth lived in Taberg, Oneida County, New York State.[7] Thirty-six years earlier, when his letter to Patrick was written, Mary had been living in England.

Despite the fact that in his memoir Christopher says he was "given but limited advantages for education," his letter reflects a very literate and knowledgeable young man with excellent penmanship, well aware of current events and not afraid to comment on them. In his memoir he says that he left for America, at the age of eighteen, in November 1852. Arriving in January 1853, he went to Taberg to live with his sister Elizabeth, where he worked in a tannery. Later that year he moved to Norwalk, Ohio, where he lived for about a year with his brother James and sister Catherine (it was this sister who wrote to Patrick in January 1862). Christopher worked in a machine shop until 1854, when he moved to Clayton County, Iowa, on the western border with Wisconsin, where he was employed as a farm laborer. Later that year he moved north to Faribault, Rice County, Minnesota, eighty miles southwest of Minneapolis. The 1860 U.S. Census reports his age as 22—actually he was 27 and was working as a farm laborer for an E.P. Mills, who had moved west with his family from Vermont.[8] At this time Christopher qualified for a preemption claim of 160 acres, valued at $300. In his letter he describes his location: "I am here in Minesota as much as sixteen hundred miles into the Interior of America. I may say on the confines of civilization and on the frontier of Barbarism."[9]

On August 20, 1862, Christopher enlisted for three years in Company H of the 10th Regiment of the Minnesota Infantry, at Fort Snelling, Minnesota, for a bounty of $27. Apparently he believed that he would be drafted and decided to volunteer. He wrote:

> The draft was coming. People did not want to Volunteer. Martial Law was proclaimed all over the State. It was not until then that I saw despotism exist in its fullest extent—the people of this country not knowing the amount of Freedom the[y] possessed, no sooner was there Freedom checked by Martial law than they all became excited and a panic took place. A few day(s) previous to the day the draft was to come off, and sooner than have it said that they were drafted, the[y] rushed fourth and volunteered, every state in the Union with the exception of two or three furnishing there Quota, so that six hundred Thousand was mustered in to the United States Service.

At the time of Christopher's letter to his brother, he was stationed in Vernon Center, Blue Earth County, Minnesota, fighting Indians 200 miles west. His letter says that 7,000 soldiers were stationed along the frontier, and his memoir says that Indians had killed 1,000 inhabitants of Minnesota. He wrote:

> The Indians which were out on the Plains all winter has returned and committed some Depradations on the settler[s]. The[y] killed seven or eight persons but had no

chance to commit any more outrages as the soldiers are stationed all along the frontier to Check the Execution of their Barbarous designs. The Company that I belong to had an attack with the Indians about ten days ago. The Indians came at night and drove in our Picket yard but they were not in sufficient numbers to give much fight. The[y] returned and hid themselves in the woods.

Christopher did not have a high opinion of the war. Despite proudly calling himself "a Jacksonian Democrat" in the 1898 memoir, he did not as yet consider himself an American in the 1863 letter. This gave him the freedom to describe the war in the following terms:

> Feeling that you look on the unholy war as I may call it that distracts this country with intense interest, I will endeavor before I finish my letter to give you a brief synopsis of what was the cause and as near as I can Judge what will be the result. I know you never like to Interfere in Politick and that you advised me to that effect also, which I find was a very Judicious advice but in a time like this when a rebellion is raging which for Magnitude has no parallel on record I hope you will not consider it untimely for me who has a good opportunity of knowing how the war is conducted and for what end it is waged to give also my opinion of it. I know my opinion on such a subject is not worth much but a foreigner living in this country will be more apt to give an Impartial account of what is going on if he is not interested himself than a native born. In the first-place I must state that I am a soldier in the so-called Union Army, not from a conviction of Being fighting in a Just-cause but the excitement of the time and the misrule of the administration has forced me and thousands like me into it who never sympathized with the war. True I was not Drafted. I went voluntary but the country got into such a wild state of excitement that a young man would be looked on as a traitor if he did not go.[10]

A history of the Tenth Minnesota Regiment states that it was organized in August 1862 and originally commanded by Colonel James H. Baker of Mankato, Minnesota.[11] The regiment was stationed at frontier posts until June 1863. Christopher Byrne's memoir says that after crossing the Cheyenne River, the troops saw their first Indians at Big Mound (now Crystal Springs, North Dakota). The unit engaged with the Indians from July 24 to July 31, 1863. His memoir reports, "The brunt of the conflict was borne by the Tenth Regiment, with Colonel Baker in front, where the Indian assault was most gallantly met and broken."[12]

Joseph R. Brown, chief of scouts, estimated that there were four to five thousand Indians. The unit pursued the Indians to the Missouri River (now Bismarck, North Dakota), where they established Camp Slaughter after a march of 585 miles. Byrne says that while at Camp Pope on the Redwood River with General Sibley's expedition against the Indians, the regiment was ordered to Memphis, Tennessee, under the command of General A.J. Smith. Later moved to St. Louis, Missouri, in October 1863, the regiment did provost duty there until it was sent to Columbus, Kentucky, in April 1864 and thence to Memphis, Tennessee, in June 1864, where the soldiers were assigned to the

Sixteenth Army Corps. Byrne's army records say he was promoted from private to sergeant on December 17, 1863.

On July 13, 1864, the regiment attempted to cut the railroad at the Battle of Tupelo in Mississippi, where it was attacked by 6,000 Confederate soldiers under "the redoubtable" General Forrest.[13] The regiment next participated in the Oxford expedition, a raid "after General Sterling Price,"[14] where many of the men were disabled after an arduous march before they returned to St. Louis, Missouri.[15] Byrne's application for an army disability pension probably dates from this episode. Ordered to Nashville, Tennessee, the brigade burst through enemy lines with great losses, but the rebels lost more, he says, and the regiment captured many prisoners. Byrne says that the "Tenth won immortal fame in this fight" and later took part in the pursuit of Hood's forces. It participated in skirmishes at Cape Girardeau, then traveled by boat to Jefferson City, then to the Kansas line, and then to St. Louis.

The regiment also fought in the battles of Nashville, Tennessee, on December 15 and 16, 1864.[16] In February 1865 the soldiers were ordered to Dauphin's Island at the mouth of Mobile Bay, near New Orleans, Louisiana. Traveling up the Fish River to Spanish Fort in April 1865, they took part in the capture of rebel troops. After the fall of Mobile, they marched to Meridian, Mississippi, where they were ordered to march to Vicksburg in June when the war came to an end. Embarking for St. Paul, Minnesota, in August, Christopher Byrne was discharged from the army at Fort Snelling on August 19, 1865.

On September 18, 1865, a month after Byrne's discharge from the army, he married Catherine Byrne in Faribault, Minnesota, whom he probably met while living with his sister and brother in Ohio. In his memoir he states that she was the daughter of James and Katharine Clark Byrne of Kingscourt, parish of Enniskeen, County Cavan. The 1870 U.S. Census states that she was born in 1835.[17] Orphaned before the age of three, she was raised by her grandparents. Byrne's memoir says that Catherine immigrated with her brother in 1852 to Norwalk, Ohio. Her brother died while serving as a Union soldier.[18]

The 1870 U.S. Census for Faribault, Minnesota, reports Christopher Byrne as a butcher, 37 years of age, with real estate valued at $1,000 and property worth $300. While single, Catherine would have qualified for the homestead preemption claim of 160 acres, which would have been a desirable dowry. The couple lost no time in starting a family. After five years of marriage they had three children: Thomas P., born July 15, 1866; James, born October 25, 1867; and Agnes E., born July 13, 1869. The memoir says that while living in Faribault, Byrne dealt extensively in buying and shipping stock to Chicago, Duluth and the northwest, having shipped the first cattle on the Northern Pacific to provision the Northern Pacific Construction Company. While resident in Faribault he also served as the deputy sheriff of Rice County at the time when the notorious Younger brothers were captured. In 1879 he moved further west to Pipestone, Minnesota, near Fountain Prairie. The 1880 U.S. Census reported him as a farmer with a homestead and a tree claim, as well as a completed family of three more children: Edward C., born July 14, 1871; Christopher F., born November 17, 1876; and Mary C., born May 24, 1878.

In 1881 Byrne moved to Volga, Brookings County, South Dakota, just across the border from Minnesota, where he reports that he had a meat market and dealt in stock, buying a 160-acre farm.[19] In 1891 he made a trip to Idaho, where he purchased an eighty-acre tract of land. The money may have been provided by an army pension of $10 a month, for which he became eligible through an act of June 27, 1890, when the U.S. government established pensions for all persons who had served more than ninety days in "the late civil war." The pension was augmented by Byrne's successful application for a disability pension. His military record indicates that he had suffered sunstroke with nervous prostration in June 1864 while marching from Meridian to Vicksburg, Mississippi. At the time of his death he was receiving $20 every month. Byrne died on November 26, 1918.[20]

Catherine Byrne died on August 17, 1897, at the age of sixty-two. Sometime between the time of the 1898 memoir and 1916, Christopher relocated to Kendrick, Idaho. Then in his eighties, he moved in with his daughter, Agnes, at 428 50th Street, Lewiston, Nez Perce County, Idaho. More than two years later, in a letter received by the War Pensions Department on January 21, 1919, Agnes wrote to inform them that his pension should be suspended.

NOTES

1. Public Records Office of Northern Ireland (PRONI), D3531/G/6, Christopher Byrne to his brother, Patrick Byrne, March 21, 1863, and May 1, 1863. The Shirley Papers are in the care of the Public Records Office of Northern Ireland. I am indebted to the deputy keeper of the records and to the depositor, J.E. Shirley, for permission to quote from them. The estate is in the barony of Farney, which consists of the parishes of Donaglunoyne, Magheross, Magheracloone, Killanny, and Inishkeen.

2. PRONI, D353 1/G/5, Catherine Byrne Deutsch to her brother, Patrick Byrne. In her letter from Norwalk, Huron County, Ohio, dated January 1862, Catherine was responding to a letter of October 20, 1861, and enclosed photograph of Patrick portrayed with his harp. Responding with news of each family member, she wrote, "You asked where Christopher is. We have not heard from him for three years, but some one said that his address was at Shrelsville [Shieldsville?], Rice County, Minnesota, U.S.A." She also wrote that she had married a Peter Deutsch, "a man from Germany 7 years ago."

3. PRONI, D3531/G/6.

4. *Ibid.*

5. The children from Thomas Byrne's first marriage were Patrick and Alice Byrne Ward. Thomas' second wife was Anne McEneneny, and their children were Anne Byrne Freeman and Ellen Byrne Lamb.

6. *Memorial and biographical record: an illustrated compendium of biography containing a compendium of local biography, including biographical sketches of prominent old settlers and representative citizens of South Dakota* (Chicago: G.A. Ogle & Co., 1898), 447–50 (subsequently referred to as "*Memoir*"). I am indebted to Ann Heymann for bringing this memoir to my attention.

168   Part II: American Civil War

7. PRONI, D3531/G/5. Catherine Byrne's letter says of her brother James, "James fainted on top of a waggon load and fell to the frozen ground last Saturday which hurt his head. He is quite sick yet but is better than he was and we think he will gel well. His family is well. He has four children, Mary 12 years old, Thomas 9 years, Catherine 7 years, James 4 years. He is as sober a man as you could wish to see. He is worth $300. I mean 300 pounds. He will write as soon as he gets well." James worked on a farm and did "a good deal of droving." Elizabeth was married to a Phillip Finegan, who appears to have been from Carrickmacross; a niece was married to a James Finigan in Ireland and received a bequest of five pounds in Patrick Byrne's will.

8. U.S. Census, 1860, Faribault, Rice County, Minnesota, p. 466. E.P. Mills, born in Vermont, was then 33 years of age. His wife, Statia, was 28 and had been born in New York State. Their children were John, age six, and Harvey, age three, both born in Minnesota. Also included in their household was a Catherine Ryan, age 30, listed as a domestic.

9. PRONI, D3531/G/6.
10. Ibid.
11. See United States Army, Tenth Regiment Infantry, http://www.geocities.ws/Heartland/Estates/5418/10reg.html (subsequently called "Regimental History"). I wish to acknowledge the assistance of Keith Sanger in locating some of the ancillary records on Byrne.
12. Memoir.
13. Ibid.
14. PRONI, D3531/G/6. The text is placed in quotes because it is not clear which side Price led.
15. Memoir.
16. Regimental History.
17. U.S. Census, 1870 (Catherine's occupation was reported as "keeping house").
18. Catherine's brother may have been the Patrick Byrne listed as a sergeant in the Tenth Regiment.
19. There is a Katherine Byrne listed on a 1897 map of a plot of land in Volga Township, South Dakota, suggesting that Christopher's wife may have been holding the land in her own name.
20. National Archives, Civil War pension files, Christopher Byrne, 1918–1919. U.S. National Archives.

BIBLIOGRAPHY

Memorial and biographical record: an illustrated compendium of biography containing a compendium of local biography, including biographical sketches of prominent old settlers and representative citizens of South Dakota. Chicago: G.A. Ogle & Co., 1898.
National Archives. Civil War pension files, Christopher Byrne, 1918–1919.
Public Records Office of Northern Ireland, D3531/G/5 and D3531/G/6.
U.S. Census, 1860 and 1870.
United States Army, Tenth Regiment Infantry. http://www.geocities.ws/Heartland/Estates/5418/10reg.html.

Bishop Patrick Lynch of Charleston and the Confederacy

DAVID HEISSER

Patrick Neison Lynch was the Catholic bishop of Charleston, South Carolina, from 1857 to 1882, throughout both the Civil War and Reconstruction, and he was himself a slaveholder. He was a leading American churchman in his time and an ardent southern patriot. He was also a diplomatic emissary of the Confederate States to the Holy See in 1864.[1]

Bishop Lynch was born in 1817 in Clones, County Monaghan, in Ireland. His father, Conlaw Peter Lynch, was descended from the Lynches of Galway. His mother, Eleanor MacMahon Neison Lynch, came from a family long established in Monaghan, which reputedly did not favor her marriage to Conlaw. This disapproval probably prompted them to immigrate to America, where they settled in the town of Cheraw, South Carolina, on the Pee Dee River, close to the North Carolina border and about 150 miles from Charleston. Conlaw Lynch became a successful builder and saw mill owner. He was responsible for several buildings that still stand in Cheraw, including St. Peter's Catholic Church. The Lynches of Cheraw became wealthy and prominent, and they were the leading Catholic family of the district. Patrick was the second child and oldest son of a dozen children in all. Three of his sisters also took up religious life, two as Ursulines and one as a Carmelite.

In 1820 Pius VII established the Diocese of Charleston, to serve both Carolinas and Georgia, and appointed the legendary John England from County Cork as its first bishop. In the nature of things, Bishop England became a friend of the Lynches, staying with them when in the area and celebrating Mass in their home. He took an interest in Patrick, a bright and devout boy, who became his protégé.

Patrick was schooled in the Catholic boys' academy and later in the seminary in Charleston. Then Bishop England sent him to Rome to attend the Urban College, also called the Urbaniana. This seminary was run by the Sacred Congregation for the Propagation of the Faith, which had final administrative oversight for the Catholic Church in the United States until 1908. Bishop England placed Patrick under the guidance and protection of his friend, Dr. Paul Cullen, then rector of the Irish College in Rome, later archbishop of Armagh and, eventually, cardinal archbishop of Dublin.

In 1840 Patrick Lynch was ordained a priest, received his doctorate, and returned to America. Charleston was to be his home for the rest of his life. Bishop England made Lynch his secretary and a trusted assistant. After England's death in 1842, Lynch served as the right hand of the next bishop, Ignatius Aloysius Reynolds. He administered and taught at the Catholic boys' academy and edited *The United States Catholic Miscellany* (founded by Bishop England in 1822). Lynch was also in charge of overseeing the funding and construction of a cathedral dedicated to St. John and St. Finbar, designed by the Irish-born architect Patrick Charles Keely, who designed other such churches, including the cathedrals of Boston, and Brooklyn.

From time to time Father Lynch engaged in public polemical debate with leading Protestant clerics. Lynch was a man of learning and scholarship and a prolific writer. If his first love was the Catholic Church, perhaps a close second was his passion for science, especially the nascent branch of geology. He earned the respect of professional geologists for his contributions to that discipline. In his manner he was kindly and soft-spoken, dignified yet unpretentious, while also notoriously absentminded and careless of his frayed cuffs and worn socks. He often exasperated his correspondents by his tardy and all-too-infrequent replies to their letters. After Bishop Reynolds died in 1855, Lynch was named administrator of the diocese, and then he was appointed to the see in 1857. He was consecrated in 1858.

The Diocese of Charleston was truly mission territory. When Lynch was bishop, it comprised North Carolina and South Carolina. Although Georgia was separated from the diocese in 1850, it still had a total land area of more than 85,000 square miles. The total population was 1,697,000 in 1860; of these, the bishop estimated in 1864 that only 20,000 were Catholics, half of whom lived in and around Charleston, which then had a population of 40,000. During the war, to serve his flock, the bishop had the help of fifteen priests and around three dozen sisters.[2]

Bishop Lynch was always fiercely proud of his Celtic heritage. During the famine he helped, with others, to raise about $20,000 that South Carolina sent for to aid those affected by the natural disaster. He was later a vocal proponent of home rule and active in Charleston's benevolent Hibernian Society. He was solicitous of the needs of his immigrant faithful, many of them Irish, and often served as a communications link with their kin in the old country. He likewise founded a savings association for immigrants under the protection of the church.

When the war came, Bishop Lynch was a forthright supporter of secession. The years of his childhood, youth and early priesthood had seen the expansion of cotton and slavery into the Carolinas' sand hills and the Piedmont, with attendant prosperity. When Fort Sumter fell to the Confederates in April 1861, Lynch ordered a *Te Deum* sung in his cathedral. There were two communities of sisters in the diocese, consisting largely of Irish-born and Irish American women. The Ursulines had a convent and girls' academy in Columbia, the state capital. Bishop Lynch's sister Ellen, whose religious name was Mother Baptista, was the superior there. The Sisters of Our Lady of Mercy, founded by Bishop England, had their motherhouse, school and orphanage in Charleston. Both communities made regimental flags for South Carolina's Irish volunteer units, each showing the Irish harp.

In August 1861, Bishop Lynch defended the southern cause in a famous press debate with his friend, the Irish-born Archbishop John Hughes of New York. The Yankees, wrote Lynch, "taking up anti-slavery, making it a religious dogma, and carrying it into politics, ... have broken up the Union.... The separation of the Southern States is *un fait accompli*. The Federal Government has no power to reverse it. Sooner or later it must be recognized. Why preface the recognition by a war equally needless and bloody?"[3]

During the conflict Bishop Lynch, as well as his clergy and religious, worked tirelessly, assisting families impoverished by the war. He helped coordinate overall civic relief in the Charleston area. The local religious sisters and the bishop earned great reputations for kindness toward sick and wounded servicemen and northern prisoners of war, regardless of creed or race. In 1863 black Union soldiers of the famous Massachusetts 54th Infantry Regiment were taken prisoner near Charleston. A total of some two dozen black men (including other captured Negro soldiers and sailors) were locked up in the Charleston jail. Under Confederate law, all these men might have been executed or enslaved. This led to controversy. Bishop Lynch intervened on the side of treating the Negroes in a manner equal to that of white prisoners. After lengthy legal proceedings, this was done. While the treatment given all northern prisoners was lamentable, most Negro servicemen seem to have survived the war.

The war years brought great devastation to the Diocese of Charleston. In December 1861, the worst fire in Charleston's history destroyed Catholic institutions and homes, along with much of the city. The flames consumed the cathedral and the episcopal residence and library, leaving the bishop without even his mitre. In August 1863 the great siege of Charleston began, which brought 18 months of bombardment, destroying more homes and institutions.

The city was then entirely situated on a narrow peninsula between two rivers, and its southernmost neighborhoods were much damaged by the continuous shelling.

The bishop spoke of the war's sufferings in a pastoral letter of November 1863:

> Who shall count the thousands and tens of thousands already slain on the battlefield, or who died of disease in a camp or in the hospital, or who have returned home maimed or decrepit for life? Who shall tell of the aged parents, whose mourning for the untimely death of the sons God gave them, is intensified by the helplessness in which they must now linger on ... deprived of the support on which their old age fondly hoped to lean?[4]

The following spring, in March 1864, Bishop Lynch accepted an appointment by President Jefferson Davis as commissioner of the Confederate States of America to the States of the Church, or, in other words, the South's diplomatic emissary to the Vatican. The original commission, signed by Davis and Secretary of State Judah P. Benjamin, is preserved in the Diocesan Archives. The purpose of Lynch's mission, as described in his instructions from Benjamin, was to try to obtain diplomatic recognition from the Holy See. Failing in that goal, Lynch was to mold opinions of European leaders in favor of the South. In Patrick Lynch the Confederate government had chosen a respected leader of the Catholic Church in America, yet a man educated in Rome, fluent in Italian and knowledgeable of French. Lynch also knew Alessandro Barnabo, cardinal-prefect of the Propaganda, an influential advisor to Pope Pius IX.[5]

In mid–April 1864 Lynch ran the naval blockade out of Wilmington, North Carolina, and sailed abroad. From Hamilton, Bermuda, he wrote to his sister, Mother Baptista, that he had been able to sleep on a sofa next to cotton bales in the hold of his ship, the *Minnie*. From Bermuda he sailed to Halifax, Nova Scotia, and from there to Cobh (then called Queenstown) in Ireland, where he arrived on May 8.

He shortly wrote back to the government in Richmond that he had investigated the increasing immigration from Ireland, seeking ways to stop (or at least curb) it. He canvassed bishops and clergy about this situation, toured country districts to see and talk to the people themselves, and sought to judge the conditions and motives of the outflow. He sent his analysis back to a regime anxious about this issue: "I found the clergy, to a man, opposed to what they characterize as an insane frenzy ... the torrent is, for the present, too strong even for them." He added that they did at least "warn the emigrants of the dangers and snares they will encounter on their arrival." He also met other Confederate agents in Ireland, one of whom, Father John Bannon, had anticipated his work, contacts and inquiries; Lynch took Bannon with as his personal chaplain when he left Ireland.[6]

Lynch and Bannon went together to England and France. In London,

Lynch dined with Cardinal Wiseman, met with several members of Parliament and conferred with Confederate agents operating there. In Paris, in early June, he called on the apostolic nuncio, Cardinal Flavio Chigi-Albani, who helped to arrange an audience with the foreign minister, Edouard Drouyn de Lhuys. To Drouyn the bishop expounded the Confederacy's case. Shortly afterward, Drouyn arranged for an audience with Emperor Napoleon III. According to Lynch, after reviewing the military situation, the emperor "enquired about the demeanor of the negroes, which I said had never been more quiet and submissive; that the tumult of war seemed to have oppressed them with awe.... [The emperor] said he hoped there would soon be some decisive battle so that England and France might at once recognize the South." Lynch also met with Confederate agents in France, and with several French bishops and other clergy, explaining conditions in the South. To Benjamin, he wrote:

> If we could smooth down their prejudices on the subject of Slavery, our task would be easy. Our gallant fighting—the highest glory of a people in French eyes—has put Slavery, for the present, into the background. But I apprehend it will reassert its importance, whenever French Sympathy passes into action ... [so that] much more remains to be done ... if we would disabuse the French mind even partially of its deep prejudice against Slavery.[7]

Finally, on June 26, Bishop Lynch arrived in Rome. He declined an offer to stay at the new North American College (though he had helped to establish it), as he did not wish to sharpen tensions between northern and southern seminarians. Instead, he took lodgings in the city, where he was to acquire a reputation for hospitality over the next few months—perhaps his real reason for not staying at the college. He met with the papal secretary of state, Cardinal Giacomo Antonelli. When Lynch explained the diplomatic purpose of his visit, Antonelli was polite but entirely noncommittal. Antonelli impressed the bishop with his grasp of the international situation and of what factors might lead England and France to favor southern independence. Then, on July 4, Lynch was received by Pius IX.

The pope seems to have liked Lynch. In his report to Benjamin (which perhaps never reached Richmond during the war), Lynch wrote, "[The pope] went on to speak of the future, when terms of peace will have to be settled between these two nations. He added most emphatically] "it is clear you are two nations." In this relation he added:

> when some foreign power will perhaps have to be called in as umpire, when, perhaps, by a miracle, for it would be a miracle if the North should consent, that I might be called in as umpire, I wish it to be understood before hand that I could not say any thing directed to confirm and strengthen slavery. I hold that Christianity has benefited society as to the position of woman and as to the position of the Slave. The first has been elevated and made equal to man. The condition of the Slave has likewise

improved, until in the course of time it [slavery] ceased to exist. As to your slaves, I see clearly that it would be absurd to attempt as it were to cut the Gordian Knot, by an act of Emancipation, but still something might be done looking to an improvement in their position or state, and to a gradual preparation for their freedom at a future opportune time. I have already said this much to several Americans from the South and they seemed to agree with me. On this point, I did not deem it opportune to offer any reply.[8]

It soon became clear that the Holy See was not going to grant diplomatic recognition to the Confederacy. The Vatican would not give the appearance of supporting the institution of slavery. Cardinal Antonelli advised Pius against reasonably good diplomatic relations with the South, the more so as the Confederacy's precarious military situation gave no sign of its potential victory. So Lynch was officially received only as a prelate making his regular *ad limina* visit to the Holy Father, not as the diplomatic envoy of a government.

Lynch then turned his hand to public relations work and proceeded to draft a long pamphlet on the subject of slavery. This was intended as a kind of propaganda salvo aimed at the single most difficult issue faced by the Confederacy. During the months since the outbreak of war, Confederate agents had sought to turn European opinion in the South's favor. Much propaganda had been published in Europe itself with that object. Efforts had been made to present slavery as a benign institution, but without any noticeable success. Lynch decided to try his own hand. In his work on the pamphlet, the bishop benefited from the assistance of certain Vatican officials, including Monsignor Francesco Nardi, one of the judges of the Rota (or supreme court of the Papal States), and Monsignor Ferdinando Mansi, a member of the College of Consultors in the Congregation responsible for the Index, suggestive of the gravity with which any defense of slavery was now regarded in Rome. Lynch published his work anonymously in three editions.[9]

In late 1864 the pamphlet came out in Rome as *Lettera sulla schiaviiu domestica degli Stati Confederati di America* (Letter on Domestic Slavery in the Confederate States of America); in January 1865 it appeared in Mainz, Germany, as *Die Sclaverei in den Sudstaaten Nord-Amerika* (Slavery in the Southern States of North America); and finally there was a Paris edition in February 1865, titled *L'Esclavage dans les Etats Confederes* (Slavery in the Confederate States). No edition was published in the United Kingdom, perhaps because the war ended too soon, and also because Lynch had not been assigned responsibility for promoting the Confederate cause there. Fortunately, the Diocese of Charleston preserved four English-language drafts, of which this writer has now published an annotated text.[10] Bishop Lynch chose to identify himself only as an anonymous missionary who had labored in the American South for a quarter-century. However, the author's identity was an open secret, and the Confederate newspaper in London, *The Index*, published his name.

Before considering the pamphlet's argument, we must examine Bishop Lynch's own experience of slavery. He had been brought up in a slave-owning family. Human bondage was a central pillar of the Old South. Fully assimilated immigrants, like the Lynches, had come to consider it part of the natural order of society, as did other wealthy South Carolina families. In their letters before and during the war, the Lynches wrote of their concern for the health and needs of their slaves, especially the children. They would also occasionally discuss selling slaves in order to meet financial obligations, apparently without moral qualms. Southern upland patricians—and the Lynches were members of that class—were not in the least troubled by or ashamed of the institution. Indeed, it was to protect slavery that South Carolina and the other southern states seceded. In 1861 Bishop Lynch had written to the archbishop of Baltimore that the legitimacy of slaveholding had never been called into question in the South. Furthermore, Catholics were full participants in the institution. Charleston was one of the most important centers of the domestic slave trade, and Thomas Ryan, a prominent Irish-born layman, was one of the city's leading slave merchants and auctioneers. Across the South (notably in Maryland, Louisiana and Kentucky) many laypeople, and indeed Catholic clergy, were slaveholders, as were Charleston's first two bishops, John England and Ignatius Reynolds.

Bishop Lynch was himself a slave owner of real importance. Prior to secession he had paid taxes on ten slaves in Charleston. In 1861, before the outbreak of war, he purchased about 85 people through Thomas Ryan from the estate of William McKenna, a wealthy Catholic layman. McKenna had originally come from Ulster and had settled in Lancaster, South Carolina, just fifty miles from Cheraw. One assumes that the Lynches had known him. The bishop put the McKenna Negroes to work on plantations and at other sites around South Carolina; one of them worked for the Ursulines in Columbia. Much information survives about these African Americans: their names, ages, family groupings, occupations, and details about health, religious practices, and marital and extramarital relations. The sources also indicate that a principal motive in acquiring them was the protection of black Catholic families, for most of these slaves were baptized Catholics or had children who were such. In acquiring and then managing these slaves, Bishop Lynch received generous help from a number of his family members and Catholic friends.[11]

The question arises: Whose slaves were they? There were nearly 100 of them. Were these persons the bishop's personal property, or the property of the diocese, or a combination of the two? In both North and South Carolina, most diocesan property was held in the name of the bishop or ordinary, as required by prewar provincial councils. These sought to vest such properties in the name of the bishop, and to secure their orderly transfer to his successor. Bishops of course also had private, personal property. In 1884, after Bishop

Lynch's death, the third Plenary Council of Baltimore decreed that a bishop must keep lists distinguishing personal and diocesan property. Such lists may have existed before the war, but no extant document specifies whose property these slaves were. Circumstantial evidence on the disposition of William McKenna's estate suggests that Lynch acquired the slaves as part of a legacy to the church. These slaves are usually referred to in surviving documents as the bishop's people. In 1862 Lynch further acquired a woman and her two children from one of his debtors in Lancaster as surety for payment of a loan to another Irish native. On its repayment in 1864, the three slaves were returned to him. In 1863 Lynch purchased a woman named Flora in Charleston, but his motive for doing so is unknown. On two occasions during the war he also sold on troublesome slaves, but with their families, so as to keep these intact.

Regardless of who was the true owner of the slaves, Patrick Lynch as a diocesan bishop or as an individual property owner, it was Bishop Lynch the man who controlled their destinies during the war years. The sources portray him as a benign slaveholder for his day, attentive to his people's health and well-being and supportive of their marriages and families. He intervened when he felt it necessary to protect slaves' marriages and curb what he considered any immoral behavior. By the lights of the time and place, Patrick Lynch appears to have been a "good master." Indeed, one may well ask what would have happened to these people if the bishop had not acquired them. Yet his decency as a slave owner may also have blinded him to the institution's essential inhumanity and its harshness in others' hands.

Against this background, the bishop set out to describe the institution in his great southern pro-slavery treatise. It was the longest and most detailed exposition of the topic by a Confederate bishop. Lynch said at the outset that he intended to avoid "philosophical" discussion, instead giving a scientifically accurate description of slavery as it actually existed in the South. Hence much of his thinking was conventional to his place and time. Yet his credentials to speak with some scientific objectivity from within that outlook were sufficient. He usually preferred to write using such language. His target audience was the educated and largely secularized European elites and opinion makers. He had gained some renown for his own scientific studies in geology, as well as for his work on the evidence of miracles and on the trial of Galileo. At the time of his death in 1882, he was working on an article seeking to reconcile the Pentateuch with mid–nineteenth-century science.

The bishop chose not to defend slavery on scriptural or theological grounds. In 1864, even as he wrote, the Holy Office investigated a pastoral letter of Bishop Auguste M. Martin of Natchitoches, Louisiana, in which Martin cited the "Curse of Ham" and other scriptural passages in support of slavery. Possibly some Vatican official warned Lynch against using a similar approach.

Slave importation had been banned by the United States since 1808, and the Confederacy did not seek its revival. In his treatise Bishop Lynch deplored the old transatlantic slave trade, which had been condemned by Pope Gregory XVI in 1839, while he was in Rome. Lynch focused instead on what he called domestic slavery—that is, the retention in bondage of the descendants of people brought to America from Africa in the past. Lynch argued that this slavery was licit and in no way forbidden by the church. He declared,

> It is honorable to our century that the [international slave] traffic has been suppressed. Still one may believe, that it was no injury—perhaps on the contrary a benefit—to these captive negroes themselves that they were not left [in Africa] to be slain on some funeral pile, at some savage debauch, or in some demoniacal heathenish rite; but on the contrary were transferred, even though roughly, to a Christian land, where, if slaves, they might live in peace and security, and, if forced to earn their bread in the sweat of their brow, they might at least obtain a knowledge of the true God, and might save their souls.

And the institution, as he described and defined it, was benign and paternalistic:

> a system or state of mutual claims and obligations between the owner and the slave, whereby the [slave] is bound to give to the [owner] the produce of his reasonable life long labor under the owner's direction; and the owner is bound in return to give to the slave a reasonable support, according to his condition, from infancy to death. This idea was pithily expressed by the negroes themselves, when they said of their owner, "We belong to him, and he belongs to us."

Slaveholders, in Lynch's view, had an inescapable moral obligation to promote and protect slave marriages and families, despite the fact that no southern state recognized the legal validity of slave marriages.[12] Here, the bishop took a stand in opposition to southern laws and asserted the higher authority of divine law, as did many other southern clergymen of various denominations. By contrast, Lynch defended flogging as the usual punishment for slaves' transgressions. "Flagellation," he wrote, "is used for slaves as for children, because it pains without inflicting injury, and punishes without incapacitating for work." He also upheld state prohibitions on teaching blacks to read and write. This was necessary, he said, in order to prevent their being enticed into rebellion by abolitionist propaganda. Dread of the atrocities occasioned by the Haitian slave rebellion from the 1790s was especially strong among the whites of Charleston, where many French refugees from Saint-Domingue had settled and whose descendants were prominent in the Catholic community, as indeed they are today.

Some of Bishop Lynch's remarks about the character of African Americans would be quite unacceptable today—notably his comments on blacks' religious practices, laziness, wastefulness. Negroes, he wrote, "are, as a race, very prone to excesses, and unless restrained, plunge madly into the lowest depths of licentiousness." As Lynch described it, the plantation system worked to restrain immoral behavior:

> The work of the negro is light; his food is abundant; his condition is one of comfort, his necessities in sickness and old age are all provided for. It is felt to be the duty, and the well understood interest, and among his equals it is the pride of the owner, that his negroes are healthy, well ordered, and happy. And all the owners labor to secure this condition.

Lynch did not believe that those of African descent were ready to cope on their own in the modern world. He held that any sudden emancipation would result in social upheaval and race war: "Where the negroes would for a time obtain the upper hand, the atrocities of San Domingo would be reenacted; where the infuriated whites, from superior numbers and superior intelligence, would conquer, no mercy would be shown. The contest would cease only from exhaustion, to be renewed until the Negroes approached extinction."

But Lynch held out the hope that, if emancipation were to come, the Catholic Church could play an essential role in educating and guiding the freedmen. (His postwar actions later showed him to be sincere in this view.) He suggested that his church might establish special communities, under the governance of wise and holy priests, where freedmen would be educated and taught the ways of civilization, as had been done so well in the eighteenth century on the Franciscan missions of California and the Jesuit missions of Paraguay. In concluding, the bishop noted, "In the south, the question of Emancipation is not an abstract philosophical thesis [but] intimately connected with every interest, and the whole frame work of Society.... [T]he slaves of the Confederate States may ask to be left in their present state of quiet and content, awaiting the future which God only knows; and not be doomed at once to ruin, if not speedy extermination." Only the conditional "may" suggests Lynch's possible realization that blacks did not share South Carolina's then public outlook.

Bishop Lynch's pamphlet caused somewhat of a stir in Europe. In England and on the Continent it was praised in various publications, including an influential one in Rome edited by Jesuits. At Mainz the seminary rector, Dr. Christoph Moufang, gave a public address to a local Catholic society praising Bishop Lynch and his ideas and recommending that people read the pamphlet. Moufang was a famous Ultramontanist and later a leader of the Catholic Centre Party in Germany. However, Lynch's work also drew eloquent condemnation from French liberal Catholics, especially Charles de Montalembert.

The pamphlet appeared too late in the war to affect its outcome. Ironically, even as the German and French editions were at press, a Confederate emissary named Duncan Kenner arrived in London on a secret mission to offer full emancipation of all slaves in return for diplomatic recognition by

Britain and France. Kenner's mission failed, of course, and there is no evidence that Lynch was aware of its purpose.

On Christmas 1864 Lynch wrote to Cardinal Barnabo from Paris that he felt he had done what he could for his country. He said he had sent his resignation to Richmond and was planning to sail for America before the end of January 1865. There is no evidence that any such letter reached Richmond, and in fact Lynch did not return to Charleston for nearly another year. The speed of the Confederacy's collapse in the spring of 1865 caught him by surprise and left him high and dry in Europe, without a salary, essentially the guest of the Vatican. It took months for him to obtain a pardon from President Andrew Johnson. He was, after all, a high-ranking Confederate government official who had consciously worked against the interests of the United States. Lynch was compelled to swear an oath of allegiance to the United States at the American embassy in Paris before being allowed to sail home. When he finally arrived in Charleston toward Christmas 1865, he found his cathedral and his diocese in ruins. General William T. Sherman's army had marched through both Carolinas, bringing great devastation. Lynch wrote to Father John Bannon, "[I]n due course of time I got to Charleston to sit like Marius amid ruins architectural and ecclesiastical, and nerve myself for the work of 'Reconstruction.' But the sinews of war are as wanting to me as ever they were to Lee and to Johnson." in other words, there was no money. The bishop estimated the losses of the diocese at more than $300,000, excluding the savings of the immigrants lost during the war. Lynch would spend the rest of his life trying to rebuild. For many years he traveled around the United States begging assistance for his diocese.

Lynch did recognize the importance of an apostolate to African Americans. In fact, he attempted—albeit unsuccessfully—to found a church-run community for freedmen on one of the Sea Islands along the South Carolina coast. And he undertook other, more successful ventures to benefit black people. Lynch also tried to encourage Irish immigration to his diocese to help rebuild its society and economy. As a good friend of John Francis Maguire, mayor of Cork and member of Parliament, Lynch helped Maguire with the writing of his book, *The Irish in America*, published in 1868. To this he contributed an open letter, dated Charleston, February 23, 1867, extolling the attractions of South Carolina for the Irish immigrant. He described South Carolina as "probably, the most Irish of any states of the Union. While its inhabitants have always had the impetuous character of the Irish race, nowhere has there been a more earnest sympathy for the struggles of Irishmen at home; nowhere will the Irish immigrant be received with greater welcome, or be more generously supported in all his rights."[13]

Patrick Lynch died in Charleston in 1882. His tomb is in the crypt of the postwar Cathedral of St. John the Baptist, built to match the prewar design by P.C. Keely and constructed on the same site. Bishop Lynch is still much admired by South Carolina Catholics. He is remembered for founding the first African American parish and revered for his southern patriotism. A Charleston Catholic layman said to me recently, "We admire him so for standing up for our southern way of life." In the altar of the Lady Chapel of the present cathedral, there is a lovely marble statue of the Blessed Mother, which Bishop Lynch purchased from a Roman sculptor named Ferdinand Pettich in 1865. It did not arrive in Charleston until 1867, but some cathedral parishioners still lovingly refer to it as "Our Lady of the Confederacy." I rather doubt that Lynch ever called it that, but the statue seems a fitting monument to the man and his efforts on behalf of the southern cause.

NOTES

1. This chapter is based upon the Lynch Papers in the Archives of the Diocese of Charleston. There is no full biography of Lynch despite a concise summary by Michael McNally in the *American National Biography* (1999), 14:169–70. See further Henry Francis Wolfe, "The Life and Times of Patrick Neison Lynch (1817–1882)," unpublished MA thesis, Mount St. Mary's University, Emmitsburg, Maryland, 1928, ms. copy in the diocesan archives, Charleston; Paul J. Schmidt, *Patrick N. Lynch, Bishop of Charleston, South Carolina, Commissioner of the Confederate States of America to the States of the Church (1864–1865)* (Rome: Gregorian University, 1967); and Richard C. Madden, *Catholics in South Carolina: A Record* (Lanham, MD: University Press of America, 1985).

2. For the Irish component of these assistants, see Dee Dee Joyce, "White, Worker, Irish, and Confederate: Irish Workers' Constructed Identity in Late Antebellum Charleston, South Carolina," unpublished Ph.D. diss., Binghamton University, State University of New York, 2002.

3. John Tracy Ellis, ed., *Documents of American Catholic History* (Milwaukee: Bruce, 1956), 359, 364.

4. Patrick N. Lynch, "Pastoral Prayers for Peace," November 26, 1863, Diocese of Charleston, South Carolina, Archives, 29Y7.

5. Willard J. Wight, "Bishop Patrick N. Lynch, Confederate Propagandist," unpublished paper presented at the forty-fourth annual meeting of the American Catholic Historical Association, Washington, D.C., December 1963; Leo Francis Stock, "Catholic Participation in the Diplomacy of the Southern Confederacy," *Catholic Historical Review* 16 (1930): 1–18; David J. Alvarez, "The Papacy in the Diplomacy of the American Civil War," *Catholic Historical Review* 69 (1983): 227–48; Schmidt, *Lynch*; David T. Gleeson, *The Green and the Gray: The Irish in the Confederate States of America* (Chapel Hill: University of North Carolina Press, 2013), 180–82.

6. "Reports of Bishop Lynch of Charleston, South Carolina, Commissioner of the Confederate States to the Holy See," *American Catholic Historical Researches* 22 (1905): 252–54; Gleeson, *Green and Gray*, 183–85.

7. "Reports of Bishop Lynch," 258.

8. Lynch to Judah P. Benjamin, July 5, 1864, Diocese of Charleston, South Carolina, Archives, copy in Lynch's hand. Also discussed in Schmidt, *Lynch*, 22.

9. See more fully David C.R. Heisser, "Bishop Lynch's Civil War Pamphlet on Slavery," *Catholic Historical Review* 84 (1998): 681–96; Schmidt, *Lynch*.

10. Patrick N. Lynch, "A Few Words on the Domestic Slavery in the Confederate States of America," edited and annotated by David C.R. Heisser, Part I, *Avery Review* 2, no. 1 (1999): 64–103; Part II, *Avery Review* 3, no. 1 (2000): 93–123. All quotations from the pamphlet in the present chapter are from this source.

11. For a fuller treatment of what follows, see David C.R. Heisser, "Bishop Lynch's People: Slaveholding by a South Carolina Prelate," *South Carolina Historical Magazine* 102, no. 3 (2001): 238–62.

12. This was the case even in a state like Louisiana, where owners commonly allowed religious ceremonies: see Ann Patton Malone, *Sweet Chariot: Slave Family and Household Structure in Nineteenth-Century Louisiana* (Chapel Hill: University of North Carolina Press, 1992), 224–25.

13. John Francis Maguire, *The Irish in America* (New York: D. & J. Sadlier, 1868), 627–28.

BIBLIOGRAPHY

Alvarez, David J. "The Papacy in the Diplomacy of the American Civil War." *Catholic Historical Review* 69 (1983): 227–48.

Ellis, John Tracy, ed. *Documents of American Catholic History*. Milwaukee: Bruce, 1956.

Gleeson, David T. *The Green and the Gray: The Irish in the Confederate States of America*. Chapel Hill: University of North Carolina, 2013.

Heisser, David C.R. "Bishop Lynch's Civil War Pamphlet on Slavery." *Catholic Historical Review* 84 (1998): 681–96.

_____. "Bishop Lynch's People: Slaveholding by a South Carolina Prelate." *South Carolina Historical Magazine* 102, no. 3 (2001): 238–62.

Joyce, Dee Dee. "White, Worker, Irish and Confederate: Irish Workers' Constructed Identity in Late Antebellum Charleston, South Carolina." Ph.D. dissertation, Binghamton University, State University of New York, 2002.

Lynch, Patrick N. "A Few Words on the Domestic Slavery in the Confederate States of America, Part I." Edited and annotated by David Heisser. *Avery Review* 2, no. 1 (1999): 64–103.

_____. "A Few Words on the Domestic Slavery in the Confederate States of America, Part II." Edited and annotated by David Heisser. *Avery Review* 3, no. 1 (2000): 93–123.

_____. "Pastoral Prayers for Peace." November 26, 1863. Diocese of Charleston, South Carolina, Archives, 29Y7.

Madden, Richard C. *Catholics in South Carolina: A Record*. Lanham, MD: University Press of America, 1985.

Maguire, John F. *The Irish in America*. New York: D. & J. Sadlier, 1868.

Malone, Ann Patton. *Sweet Chariot: Slave Family and Household Structure in Nineteenth-Century Louisiana*. Chapel Hill: University of North Carolina Press, 1992.

Patrick N. Lynch Papers, Diocese of Charleston, South Carolina, Archives.

"Reports of Bishop Lynch of Charleston, South Carolina, Commissioner of the Confederate States to the Holy See." *American Catholic Historical Researches* 22 (1905).

Schmidt, Paul J. *Patrick N. Lynch, Bishop of Charleston, South Carolina, Commissioner of the Confederate States of America to the States of the Church (1864–1865)*. Rome: Gregorian University, 1967.

Stock, Leo Francis. "Catholic Participation in the Diplomacy of the Southern Confederacy." *Catholic Historical Review* 16 (1930): 1–18.

Wight, Willard J. "Bishop Patrick N. Lynch, Confederate Propagandist." Unpublished paper presented at the forty-fourth annual meeting of the American Catholic Historical Association. Washington, D.C., December 1963.

John Mitchel and the Confederacy

KELLY O'GRADY

> You, that Mitchel's prayer have heard,
> "Send war in our time, O Lord"
> Know that when all words are said
> And a man is fighting mad,
> Something drops from eyes long blind.
> He completes his partial mind,
> For an instant, stands at ease,
> Laughs aloud, his heart at peace.
> Even the wisest man grows tense
> With some sort of violence
> Before he can accomplish fate.
> Know his work or choose his mate.
> —"Under Ben Bulben," W.B. Yeats

In his 1854 masterwork, *Jail Journal,* firebrand Irish nationalist John Mitchel (1815–1875) prayed fervently for an armed struggle to free Ireland. "Give us war in our time, Oh Lord," the Newryman wrote, in anger over the famine and in frustration over seeming Irish acceptance of British misrule in his homeland.[1] Mitchel ultimately found a holy war for independence in his time, but it exploded in America, not in Ireland. Mitchel's war was the American Civil War, where, to the surprise of some, he took up the Confederate cudgel.

Why did this bright star in the Irish nationalist constellation orbit the American rebellion in the constitutional struggle that ended slavery? In contemporary Irish thought, the parallels between the Confederacy and Ireland were striking. Mitchel and other Irish leaders saw the South as a surrogate

Ireland; both countries were traditional, agricultural, even quixotic societies striving for independence from a powerful, progressive, industrial, and hegemonic neighbor.[2] Parallel political philosophies between the Confederate nation and Ireland can be traced back to the beloved Irish nationalist Thomas Davis, who passionately enumerated the politics of a free Ireland: self-determination, local control of government, decentralization of the economy, and trade and monetary policies that favored the agricultural over the industrial sector.[3] The republican views of Thomas Davis, who died suddenly in 1845, dovetailed with the political ideals of southern nationalists like Confederate president Jefferson Davis. John Mitchel's southern allegiance provided the link between the two notables named Davis.

Mitchel, a former colleague of Thomas Davis when both wrote for the *Nation* newspaper in Dublin in the 1840s, began his southern nationalist experience in America when he took up the life of a backcountry farmer in 1854. The year before, Mitchel had escaped from exile in Tasmania. In 1848, Mitchel had been sentenced to transportation after an unjust conviction for treason by a packed British jury. His southern journey ended in Knoxville, Tennessee, after a brief stint as a newspaperman with fellow Irish nationalist and exile Thomas F. Meagher in New York. When Mitchel's classic work, *Jail Journal*, was published, the biting critique of English injustice was hailed as the *Odyssey* of Irish woes, the Bible of Irish nationalism.[4] An Irish rebel of later times, Padraic Pearse, one of the 1916 Easter Rising leaders, called *Jail Journal* "the last of the four gospels of the new testament of Irish nationality, the last and the fieriest and the most sublime."[5]

At the dawn of the American Civil War, Mitchel's credentials as a strident Irish nationalist were well established. The conflict—really a war of rebellion, and not a civil war—gave voice to the southern nationalism he had adopted in his relatively short tenure in America. By 1862 Mitchel turned his sharp rhetorical skills to the service of the South as a newspaper editor in Richmond, the capital of the Confederate nation. While writing lead editorials for the *Richmond Enquirer*, an organ for the Confederate government under Jefferson Davis, Mitchel attacked Abraham Lincoln and the Republican Party, questioned the competence of Union military leaders, and painted the North and its Puritan Brahmins as an extension of the Cromwellian tradition that had repressed Ireland in the seventeenth century.[6] By 1864, Mitchel was editor of another hardline southern nationalist journal: the *Richmond Examiner*. In a letter to his family he described what his mission had become in the last year of the war: "I point out diligently and conscientiously what is the condition of a nation which suffers itself to be conquered ... such as we have experienced in Ireland, and endeavor to keep our good Confederate people up to the fighting point."[7]

Many southerners understood the connection between the experience of Ireland under the crown and the South under the boot heel of the federal government in America. Private Azariah Bostwick of the 31st Georgia Infantry reflected what many southern soldiers believed would result from Union victory when he wrote, "We will be to the North what Ireland is to England, a slave of the darkest kind."[8] Likewise, southern politicians lent sympathetic ears to Irish issues; in some cases this support was longstanding and heartfelt. Mitchel noted one instance of this mutual understanding in his writings about Virginia's Henry Wise. As U.S. minister to Brazil in the 1840s, Wise, later governor of Virginia and a Confederate general, "was surprised to see unloaded at Rio [an] abundance of the best quality of packed beef from Ireland."[9] Wise of course knew about the Irish famine and saw the duplicity and haplessness of a British policy that allowed famine in the same province that exported world-quality beef. Perhaps this international background gave Wise a sympathetic perspective on the plight of immigrant Irish Catholics in America. In 1856 Wise was elected to the Old Dominion's governorship with the help of Irish Catholic votes after he spoke out against his Whig opponents, who, while courting the Know Nothing vote, had called for the disenfranchisement of naturalized citizens. "With all my head and all my heart and all my might, I protest this secret organization ... [which is seeking] to proscribe Roman Catholics and naturalized citizens [from voting]," Wise proclaimed in a popular stump speech.[10] The 1856 election in Virginia set a precedent in the South, where pro-immigrant, anti–Know Nothing candidates swept statewide elections.[11]

These results demonstrate that the South by and large accepted Irish Catholics as political allies. No doubt this was in part due to the public support given to southern, and later Confederate, leaders by the Irish bishops and priests of the Catholic Church in the South. Bishop John McGill of Richmond, an Irish immigrant, blessed pike-carrying Irish Confederate troops in Richmond's cathedral, Saint Peter's Church, in 1861. His sympathies in the war were "entirely with the Confederacy and he strongly urged his people to fight for their beloved Southland."[12] Another Irishman, Father John Teeling, became chaplain of the 1st Virginia Regiment, and from the pulpit of Saint Peter's he appealed to the faithful "to stand firm in the assertion of their rights."[13] Perhaps no churchman was more strident as a southern partisan than Father Matthew O'Keefe, a native of Waterford, Ireland, who petitioned Bishop McGill for permission to join the Confederate infantry. Denied this opportunity, he served as a chaplain for the Virginia Brigade led by William Mahone, a man who later served as Virginia's governor.[14]

At a time when Catholics in the North were ridiculed, oppressed and even murdered for their beliefs, Roman Catholicism met more than tolerant accommodation in the South and indeed enjoyed a measure of political inclusion in the metropolitan areas, where Catholic adherents could sway an election. Even Thomas Meagher, who would lead the Union's famed Irish Brigade, noted before the war that there were no "convent-burners, no addlepated ranters, no Know-Nothings" in the South.[15] As war beckoned, southern leaders knew they could count on Irish support in their attempts to establish an independent nation. The editors of Virginia's *Alexandria Gazette* wrote in 1861, "Virginia was the first state to hurl aside the tide of Know-Nothingism and maintain the rights of Irishmen. They now gratefully lay down their lives, if necessary, to protect and vindicate her rights."[16]

In the spring of 1861, the Irish of the South celebrated Saint Patrick's Day and secession with equal gusto. Irish troops, taking up the southern sword, helped bombard Fort Sumter and capture Castle Pinckney from federal forces in Charleston Harbor that April. The Montgomery Guard of the 1st Virginia Infantry, led by Mitchel's friend, Captain John Dooley of Limerick, helped clear the way for a Confederate victory at Bull Run that summer. The "Old First," as it was called, traced its ancestry to the French and Indian War, when the unit had been commanded by George Washington. As a Confederate regiment, Washington's former command was held by another Mitchel acquaintance, Patrick Theodore Moore, a native of Galway. Moore was a leading citizen of Richmond, a businessman who had been active in Catholic circles and in the local militia before the war. In the conflict's first battle, his distinctive Irish brogue carried an unusual order across the Bull Run battlefield: "Faugh a Ballaugh and Charge!" Though a traditional Irish war call in Europe, this was the first Gaelic battle cry of the American Civil War.[17] Moore's Irish troops moved forward carrying a green flag and with brass harps on their army-issue black "Jeff Davis" hats, which also sported feathers tipped in green.

The following spring, Irish troops from Virginia and Louisiana constituted 10 percent of Thomas J. "Stonewall" Jackson's Army of the Valley during the renowned Shenandoah Valley campaign.[18] Jackson's Irish soldiers proved themselves happy southern warriors and stout fighters in a campaign still studied and admired by military historians. General Richard Taylor, an aristocratic Virginian, the son of President Zachary Taylor, commanded these Irish troops, whom he called "steady as clocks and chirpy as crickets."[19] In camp the night before the Battle of Port Republic, fought June 9, 1862, Taylor told his Irishmen that they would meet and match the Yankee hordes commanded by celebrated Irish Union General James Shields the next day. In response, Taylor "received loud assurances from half a hundred Tipperary throats: 'You may bet your life on that, sor. We are the boys to see it out,'" an Irish Confederate told him. "As argyles to the tartan, my heart has warmed to an Irishman since that night," Taylor wrote.[20] The men were true to their word: the Irish troops of Taylor's brigade were instrumental in carrying the field at Port Republic.

Other native officers also favorably noted the Irish in the ranks. In the celebrated Stonewall Brigade, Captain George R. Bedinger of the 33rd Virginia Infantry wrote of the Hibernians in his charge: "I am very much pleased with the conduct of my Irishmen. They are enthusiastic and brave and at the same time obedient. I think they are fond of me, at least they are very attentive to my comfort."[21] These Irishmen were the Emerald Guards, a company comprising mainly Irish laborers working on the Manassas Gap railroad before war broke out.

John Mitchel, more than any other Irish leader, understood the depth of support that the South's Irish bishops, Richmond's Irish businessmen, and Virginia's Irish rail workers gave to the new Confederate nation. Indeed, ensconced in Richmond by 1862, part of the milieu of rebel power, he realized the import of that time in history not just for the Confederacy, perhaps not even merely for Ireland, but also for independence movements throughout the world. He believed that consistency of purpose meant that the Irish in the American war must side with the rebels, not the power of the central government. Mitchel wrote of the inherent contradictions in the allegiance of the Irish in the northern states with the powers of the Union—powers that seemingly were their enemies in every way before the war:

> As for the Northern Irish, who seem to have got themselves persuaded that the enfranchisement of Ireland is somehow to result from the subjugation of the South, and that repeal of one union in Europe depends on the enforcement of another union in America, our friends here do not well understand the process of reasoning which leads to that conclusion, nor do I.[22]

Indeed, the Irish in America sometimes were confused as to what side they should take. Irishmen in Charleston organized a Confederate unit that they named the Meagher Guard after the darling of the Irish in America, Thomas Meagher, but had to change the name when they realized that Meagher went with the Union. Likewise, Irish units in the North named themselves after John Mitchel until they were informed that Mitchel staunchly supported the Confederacy.[23] Many Southern Irish could not fathom why any Irishman would support the Union. One man, Sergeant D.H. Hamilton of the 1st Texas Infantry, reasoned that the Yankee Irish Brigade was a in fact British army unit helping the North. He remarked that the Irish Brigade was so well equipped by Britain that even the lice its men carried could be found stamped "R.I.B. (Royal Irish Brigade) in gilt letters on ... [their backs]."[24] John Edward Dooley, the son of Mitchel's friend John Dooley, voiced similar thoughts after he was wounded and captured in what is remembered as Pickett's Charge at the Battle of Gettysburg. When Dooley, later a captain in the 1st Virginia and a seminarian at Georgetown College, realized that his Union guard had fought against Britain in the Young Ireland Uprising in 1848, he berated the Yankee for what he saw as his inconsistency of allegiance:

I began questioning him and asking him how it was possible for him who had in '48 fought ... for the same cause for which we were contending, how could he consistently turn his back on his principles and for the pitiful hire of a few dollars do all in his power to crush a brave people asserting their right of self-government ... what, we asked, would Mr. Mitchel think of him?[25]

Dooley, the aspiring Jesuit priest, so riddled the man with guilt that he was moved to tears. There is no evidence that Mitchel ever passed judgment on the Yankee guard, but the Irish nationalist might have seen Dooley's argument as proof that the Confederate rebellion, in terms of the numbers of Irish combatants involved, the unity of purpose between Irish and southern independence movements, and the commitment to a similar (if not single) political philosophy, was the largest "Irish" uprising in history.

"Give us war in our time, Oh Lord." What powerful, desperate and even rash words these seem in retrospect. But impetuous militancy was the essence of John Mitchel. In the end, the Almighty answered the Irish supplicant's prayer for war. This proved to be a tragic wish granted for the fire-eating nationalist. Mitchel lost two sons in the fight for southern independence. Captain John C. Mitchel, an engineer by training, died while commanding Fort Sumter, South Carolina—the landmark citadel in Charleston Harbor where the war began. His dying words, "I die willingly for South Carolina, but oh! That it had been for Ireland!" echoed the lyrical final farewell of the seventeenth-century cavalry general Patrick Sarsfield, another Irish exile who died in the service of a foreign land.[26] Seventeen-year-old Willie Mitchel died bearing the colors of the 1st Virginia Regiment in Gettysburg's Pickett's Charge. John Mitchel, ever defiant, said of his youngest son Willie's death, "He could not have fallen in nobler company, nor as I think, in a better cause."[27] A third son, James, suffered serious wounds in battle while serving as a Confederate staff officer in 1862. The so-called High Tide of the Confederacy rose with blood from Erin's shore.

Aside from these heartbreaking losses, Mitchel himself paid dearly for his Confederate allegiance. After the war, the Irish leader, though a noncombatant, was arrested and imprisoned by order of Union General-in-Chief Ulysses S. Grant. Mitchel was held at Fortress Monroe in a casemate cell next to his Confederate chieftain, Jefferson Davis. For four months, Mitchel suffered the same fate as the Confederate high command, unsure whether he would be tried for treason and perhaps hanged out of political expedience or revenge. Authorities released Mitchel in October 1865, and he returned to Ireland after periods in New York and Paris. In 1875, still revered in his homeland, the former Confederate won election to the British Parliament, though apparently he vowed never to actually set foot in the oppressor's legislature. The ensuing debate over Mitchel's legal standing as a Member of Parliament might have led to another fight for Hibernian self-determination. But the

Irish patriot died suddenly that year, and thus began his final journey into relative obscurity and often-personal disfavor among some modern Irish historians.

Mitchel's untimely death revived his Confederate allegiances as Virginia and the South erupted in expressions of sympathy for his family. Jefferson Davis remembered the Irish nationalist as a stalwart southern defender. Davis eulogized his friend as follows: "Together we struggled for states' rights, for the supremacy of the Constitution, for community independence, and, after defeat, were imprisoned together.... Mourn for him and regret his death as a loss to mankind."[28] Later generations of southerners would remember the Mitchel family's contributions to what was called by the early twentieth century "The Lost Cause." A memorial was built to Captain John C. Mitchel in Charleston's Magnolia Cemetery, commemorating the young Irish engineer's death while defending Fort Sumter.[29] And in Virginia, the Virginia Press Association erected a monument plaque on the prison cell casemate where Mitchel had been held with Jefferson Davis. It reads:

> In memory of John Mitchel
> Fearless and courageous Southern journalist
> Staunch supporter of the Confederacy
> Editor-in-Chief, Richmond Enquirer
> Associate Editor, Richmond Examiner
> 1862–1865 Who was confined in this casemate No. 6
> from June 17, 1865, to October 29, 1865
> A defiant and unrelenting opponent of oppression,
> An indefatigable and uncompromising proponent of the Southern cause,
> A martyr to the effectiveness and influence of the printed word.[30]

John Mitchel is often seen today by Irish scholars as the antihero of Hibernian history. In modern thought, his Confederate allegiance, often simplified as a pro-slavery crusade, has put him on the wrong side of history.[31] But his Confederate fight was more than an American interlude in a lifetime of Irish agitation. Mitchel's southern strategy can be seen as his defining moment. Taking the side of the South in America's struggle was consistent with every Irish uprising that had gone before. Mitchel was simply remaining constant in his opposition to heavy-handed central authority; the Irishman was a rebel on two continents.

"Give us war in our time." While Mitchel had wanted a war of rebellion in Ireland, the Civil War was the war he got. More than a symbolic showdown over slavery, it was a struggle between Celt and Anglo-Saxon, between feudalism and modernism, between conservative and liberal, or, as Irish historian Louis J. Walsh wrote in 1934, between two distinct ways of life. Walsh saw the conflict as "a struggle between two civilizations—the one static, agricultural, content to live on the land of its fathers and refusing to sacrifice its fundamental way of life, based on the land, for a temporary increase of wealth; the other dynamic, eager for wealth at any price and at any cost, and always seeking expansion." Mitchel, Walsh believed, saw in the northern states yet another example of the Anglo-Saxon society that he had fought against in Ireland, and so there was no doubt that he would take the southern side in the war.[32]

As the South went down to crushing defeat in 1865, so, too, did many of the hopes of nineteenth-century Irish nationalism. The outcome of America's civil war affected Ireland in ways that have never been properly explored. D.P. Crook has written that the chief aim of the United Kingdom during this period was to protect its Atlantic sea trade, not to weaken the American nation or form an alliance with the Confederacy, as is conventionally thought.[33] British leaders realized that the Union had built a world-class navy to strangle the Confederacy, as well as a modern merchant fleet to supply the Yankee armies that crushed the rebellion. The United States became a world power because of the Civil War, and the British government, recognizing this fact, and still eager for Atlantic trade, sought stronger alliances with the United States for the first time since the American Revolution. This new direction in U.S.-British relations worked to the detriment of the Irish independence movement. The United States cooperated with British authorities to abort a Fenian incursion into Canada, which culminated in the Battle of Ridgeway, Ontario, on June 2, 1867. In the same period, the British encouraged the United States in its effort to thwart French aspirations in Mexico.[34] Thus the war's aftermath affected a broad range of social and political realms. Union victory not only strengthened U.S.-British military and mercantile ties, but, in the social sphere, abolition, victorious in America and a powerful social movement in England, brought together liberal and progressive U.S. and British social engineers.

In domestic politics, one consequence of Reconstruction and the ending of southern dominance of the central government was the effective disfranchisement of the Democratic Party at the national level in the North as well as in the South for almost twenty years. While the Republican Party held absolute control over the (mostly) Democratic South during Reconstruction, the Irish Democratic voting blocs in the North found themselves part of an inconsequential voting minority. Out of the desperation of disenfranchisement, and in frustration over the ingratitude shown to the Irish who had fought and died for the Union, Irish nationalism in America turned away from the model of republican unity across traditions exemplified by the United Irishmen and Young Ireland. In that model's place, Irish nationalist sentiment, especially in America, turned to the fractious, feckless, radical exclusivity of the Irish Republican Brotherhood—popularly known as Fenianism.[35]

How different the world of Irish nationalism would have been if through southern independence there had arisen a strong Democratic Party in the North—a viable, pro-immigrant alternative to the Republican Party that would have failed in its effort to restore the Union. The Irish in the North could only have gained power if the Democratic Party in the North had remained strong at the national level after the war. In consequence of this outcome, the central government would not have evolved into the Anglophile entity that it became under subsequent Republican regimes. In the new southern nation, Irish nationalism would have found an American ally with cultural and political affinities. Irish republicans could have seen the newly independent Confederacy as a model of successful rebellion as well as a hopeful symbol that independence was possible. A victorious southern nation would have enjoyed the support of leading Irish nationalists in the states and in Ireland during its national struggle, and those nationalists could have looked to this American ally as a source of manpower and other resources to aid Ireland's struggle for independence. And in all of this, John Mitchel, it can be imagined, would have been a well-placed leader of both movements—Confederate independence and Irish freedom. None of this, of course, came to pass due to the defeat of the Irish uprising that was the Confederacy.[36]

Southern defeat may well have lengthened the Irish journey to eventual independence. John Mitchel, the leading Irish nationalist of his time, took his stand in Dixie and was vanquished by what he called the evil power that was Anglo-Saxon civilization. The two best examples of that evil, he believed, were Great Britain and the American North.

NOTES

1. John Mitchel, *Jail Journal* (Poole, England: Woodstock Books, 1996), 315.
2. Joseph M. Hernon, *Celts, Catholics, and Copperheads: Ireland Views the American Civil War* (Columbus: Ohio State University Press, 1968), 8; Kelly J. O'Grady, *Clear the Confederate Way: The Irish in the Army of Northern Virginia* (Mason City, IA: Savas, 2000), 309n99.
3. Arthur Griffith, *Thomas Davis: The Thinker and Teacher: The Essence of His Writings in Prose and Poetry* (Dublin: M.H. Gill & Son, 1914), 4.
4. Brendan O'Cathaoir, *John Mitchel* (Dublin: Clodhanna Teoranta, 1978), 5.
5. Ibid.
6. John Mitchel, editorials in the *Richmond Daily Enquirer*, October 1, December 11, 16, 20 and 27, 1862.
7. William Dillon, *Life of John Mitchel* (London: K. Paul, Trench & Co., 1888), 199.
8. Gregory C. White, *This Most Bloody & Cruel Drama: A History of the 31st Georgia Volunteer Infantry* (Baltimore: Butternut and Blue, 1997), 167. For a general study of Irish involvement, see Sean M. O'Brien, *Irish Americans in the Confederate Army* (Jefferson, NC: McFarland, 2007).
9. John Mitchel, *The Last Conquest of Ireland (Perhaps)* (Dublin, 1861; reprint, London: Burns, Gates & Washbourne, n.d.), 8.
10. James Henry Bailey II, *A History of the Diocese of Richmond* (Richmond: Whittet & Shepperson, 1956), 115. The Know Nothing movement was a secretive nativist political organization.
11. Ibid., 118.
12. Ibid., 148.
13. Ibid., 144.

14. "Chaplain Matthew O'Keefe of 'Mahone's Brigade,'" *Southern Historical Society Papers* 25 (1897): 176.
15. Paul Jones, *The Irish Brigade* (Washington, D.C.: Robert B. Luce, 1969), 14.
16. Lowell Reidenbaugh, *33rd Virginia Infantry* (Lynchburg, VA: H.E. Howard, 1987), 2; E.D. Sloan Jr., ed., *Memoirs and 1865 Journal of Samuel Wragg Ferguson, 1834–1917, Brigadier General, Confederate States Army* (Greenville, SC: Private Printing, 1998), 4–9; and Francis Potts, "Diary Kept by Francis Potts, a Private in Company C, 1st Regiment Virginia Volunteers July 14, 1861–September 21, 1861," Virginia State Library Archives.
17. O'Grady, *Clear the Confederate Way*, 60.
18. Richard Taylor, *Destruction and Reconstruction: Personal Experiences of the Late War* (New York: D. Appleton, 1879), 68.
19. *Ibid.*
20. Taylor, *Destruction and*, 76.
21. George R. Bedinger, unpublished letter, Fredericksburg & Spotsylvania National Military Park manuscript collection, vol. 30.
22. Hernon, *Celts, Catholics, and Copperheads*, 93.
23. O'Grady, *Clear the Confederate Way*, 309n98.
24. D.H. Hamilton, *History of Company M, First Texas Volunteer Infantry* (Waco, TX: W.M. Morrison, 1962), 40.
25. Joseph T. Durkin, ed., *John Dooley, Confederate Soldier: His War Journal* (Ithaca, NY: Georgetown University Press, 1945), 115.
26. Claudine Rhett, "Sketch of John C. Mitchel, of Ireland, Killed While in Command of Fort Sumter," *Southern Historical Society Papers* 10 (1882): 272.
27. Dillon, *Life of John Mitchel*, 180.
28. *Ibid.*, 302.
29. Rhett, "Sketch of John C. Mitchel," 272.
30. From Virginia Press Association monument on Casemate No. 6 at Fortress Monroe, Old Point Comfort, Virginia.
31. Mitchel, *Last Conquest*, 80–81. Mitchel confronted the slavery issue head on and did not mince his words about the political, social and economic aspects of the peculiar institution. In *Jail Journal* he noted the condition of the slaves he saw in Brazil and acknowledged that they had every right to overthrow their masters. However, he clung to the widely held belief that in general American slavery was a much better state than African slavery—a point of view that, if it can't be forgiven or condoned by modern historians, should at least be understood in its contemporary context. Like Meagher and many leaders of the Catholic Church, Mitchel believed that Americans should concentrate their attentions on regulating the treatment of slaves and bettering their living conditions, not simply on complete abolition. Perhaps most important for the Irish issues of the day, Mitchel believed that slavery was a red herring. He was especially disgusted with Daniel O'Connell's anti-slavery initiatives in Ireland, believing the issue distracted Irish attention from more pressing problems at home. Mitchel wrote that O'Connell "poured forth his fiery floods of eloquence in denunciation, not of the British Government, but *of American Slavery*, with which he had nothing on earth to do." Mitchel also battled with "The Liberator's" son, John O'Connell, over the slavery issue. In 1845, Mitchel took particular umbrage when the younger O'Connell returned donations for the Repeal Association because they had been raised by the Irish in a southern state. O'Connell believed the money tainted by the existence of slavery in the state. Mitchel came to believe that the slavery issue was used by the British government, with the O'Connells as their Irish dupes, to drive a wedge between Irish revolutionaries and Irish American supporters, many of whom were southerners.
32. Louis J. Walsh, *John Mitchel* (Dublin: Talbot Press, 1934), 86–87.
33. D.P. Crook, *Diplomacy during the American Civil War* (New York: John Wiley & Sons, 1975), 11. Crook wrote that British non-intervention was the key to Civil War diplomacy (185).
34. *Ibid.*, 180.
35. The once mighty Democratic Party did not send a president to the White House again until 1884. That year, Grover Cleveland, the governor of New York, won the election.

Irish Catholic votes figured prominently in Cleveland's political career in New York as well as in the national election. At this time, the Democratic Party was labeled by a Republican wag as the party of "rum, Romanism and rebellion," a phrase that perfectly identified the Irish (at least in the South): staunch Democrats, devout Catholics, loyal Confederates, and not unlikely to partake of election day cheer!

36. The Fenians did not enjoy the support of Young Ireland leaders, especially Mitchel. They were opposed by the Catholic Church in Ireland and, as the forerunner of Arthur Griffith's Sinn Fein party, began the road to a republican philosophy that not only alienated a majority of the Irish population but also confronted rather than co-opted British Ireland.

BIBLIOGRAPHY

Bailey, James Henry, II. *A History of the Diocese of Richmond*. Richmond: Whittet & Shepperson, 1956.
"Chaplain Matthew O'Keefe of 'Mahone's Brigade.'" *Southern Historical Society Papers* 25 (1897).
Crook, D.P. *Diplomacy during the American Civil War*. New York: John Wiley & Sons, 1975.
Dillon, William. *Life of John Mitchel*. London: K. Paul, Trench & Co., 1888.
Durkin, Joseph T., ed. *John Dooley, Confederate Soldier: His War Journal*. Ithaca, NY: Georgetown University Press, 1945.
Griffith, Arthur. *Thomas Davis: The Thinker and Teacher: The Essence of His Writings in Prose and Poetry*. Dublin: M.H. Gill & Son, 1914.
Hamilton, D.H. *History of Company M, First Texas Volunteer Infantry*. Waco, TX: W.M. Morrison, 1962.
Hernon, Joseph M. *Celts, Catholics, and Copperheads: Ireland Views the American Civil War*. Columbus: Ohio State University Press, 1968.
Jones, Paul. *The Irish Brigade*. Washington, D.C.: Robert B. Luce, 1969.
Mitchel, John. *Jail Journal*. Poole, England: Woodstock Books, 1996.
_____. *The Last Conquest of Ireland (Perhaps)*. Dublin, 1861; reprint, London: Burns, Gates & Washbourne, n.d.
O'Cathaoir, Brendan. *John Mitchel*. Dublin: Clodhanna Teoranta, 1978.
O'Grady, Kelly J. *Clear the Confederate Way: The Irish in the Army of Northern Virginia*. Mason City, IA: Savas, 2000.
Potts, Francis. "Diary Kept by Francis Potts, a Private in Company C, 1st Regiment Virginia Volunteers July 14, 1861–September 21, 1861." Virginia State Library Archives.
Reidenbaugh, Lowell. *33rd Virginia Infantry*. Lynchburg, VA: H.E. Howard, 1987.
Rhett, Claudine. "Sketch of John C. Mitchel, of Ireland, Killed While in Command of Fort Sumter." *Southern Historical Society Papers* 10 (1882).
Richmond Daily Enquirer, 1862.
Sloan, E.D., Jr., ed. *Memoirs and 1865 Journal of Samuel Wragg Ferguson, 1834–1917, Brigadier General, Confederate States Army*. Greenville, SC: Private Printing, 1998.
Taylor, Richard. *Destruction and Reconstruction: Personal Experiences of the Late War*. New York: D. Appleton, 1879.
Walsh, Louis J. *John Mitchel*. Dublin: Talbot Press, 1934.
White, Gregory C. *This Most Bloody & Cruel Drama: A History of the 31st Georgia Volunteer Infantry*. Baltimore: Butternut and Blue, 1997.

Patrick Cleburne, Irish Confederate General

MAURIEL P. JOSLYN

For centuries the Irish have distinguished themselves as soldiers in the ranks of the great armies of the world. The "Wild Geese" are legendary in the annals of France and Spain, while British military men long recognized the fighting qualities and physical stamina of rural Irish lads as the backbone of their fighting force. Ireland wasn't called the "nursery of the British army" for no reason.[1]

Perhaps the least studied soldiers of Erin are the Irish immigrants in the armies of the American Civil War, when the blood of Ireland's sons was spilled fighting each other on opposite sides. The cause for both groups was the same: freedom. However, the conception of that cause differed. While most of the Irish in the Union and Confederate armies remained in the rank and file, a few attained officer status, something less common in other armies. There is one participant in that war whose distinction stands high above his countrymen, either blue or gray, for he still holds the honor of being the highest-ranking Irish-born soldier in American military history. That soldier is Major-General Patrick Ronayne Cleburne of the Confederate army. Why had he so earnestly embraced the cause of the American South?

Patrick Cleburne was born at Bride Park Cottage, near Ovens, County Cork, Ireland, on March 16, 1823. His father, Dr. Joseph Cleburne, was surgeon to the small community and the British army barracks at nearby Ballincollig. His mother, Mary Anne Ronayne, came from old Irish stock at Great Island, where her father owned a large estate. Patrick, known as Ronayne to his family, was the second son and third child. By the standards of his society, Dr. Cleburne occupied a privileged position in the parish. Protestants were the ruling class, and Dr. Cleburne hailed from an old Anglo-Irish family from Tipperary. As a rural physician, he treated the local poor as well, most of whom were Catholic. Consequently, he exhibited more tolerance than many of his peers. He supported Catholic emancipation in 1829 and frequently offered his services out of humanity, asking no money in return. No doubt this example influenced his son Patrick.[2]

Tragedy entered Patrick's life at an early age. When he was eighteen months old, his mother died. Two years later, Dr. Cleburne married Isabella Stewart, a young neighbor and the children's tutor. She became very close to Patrick, and for his whole life he considered her his mother. The family recovered from its grief, and soon three half-siblings were born. Patrick's exposure to things military came at an early age, as he often accompanied his father when Dr. Cleburne attended soldiers at the Ballincollig Barracks.

Thus the first eight years of his life passed at Bride Park, a blissful and seemingly carefree existence for a young boy. But Dr. Cleburne's practice and growing family necessitated a move. In 1836, he relinquished the lease on Bride Park and leased the 205-acre Grange Farm, about a mile up the road. Here he would combine the lifestyle of a gentleman farmer with his medical practice. It was a social move as well as an economic one, for Grange was the largest manor house in the parish.[3]

While many Protestants continued to send their sons to England for an education, Dr. Cleburne decided his boys would receive theirs in Ireland. He made it clear that Patrick was expected to follow in his footsteps and pursue medicine. "This settled purpose probably defeated the object," noted a cousin, "for [Patrick] never applied himself to the medical books ... nor showed any diligence in his studies." Early schooling came with a tutor. When the family moved to Grange, Patrick was twelve. He attended the newly founded boarding school at Green Fields, run by the Rev. Thomas W. Spedding, curate at Athnowen, the family church, and military chaplain at the Ballincollig Barracks. Founded as "an establishment for a limited number of young gentlemen," where "the closest attention would be paid to health, morals and personal deportment," the school numbered about fifty students. There was no indication of interest in the military from Patrick Cleburne during these early years, although Spedding promised to prepare young men for entrance to the various universities and to naval and military colleges, and drill was part of the curriculum. English influence dominated education in Ireland, and Patrick, like other Irish boys, learned his country's history from English perspectives. The year that Patrick entered Spedding's school, his older brother William began his career at Trinity College in Dublin, in the field of engineering.[4]

Life dealt the Cleburne family a severe blow on November 27, 1843, when Dr. Joseph Cleburne died at age 51, after contracting typhus fever from a patient. His father's death came when Patrick was fifteen, the age in a boy's life when paternal influence is perhaps the most important for becoming a young man. Not only was Patrick deprived of this role model, but he also would be sent away to strangers to learn a profession for which he had little passion. A naturally shy and introspective lad, these two events had a profound effect upon his personality and emotional development. But decisions rested on the shoulders of his young stepmother, now widowed with seven children. William had to leave his third year of engineering at Trinity, and Patrick departed the Reverend Spedding's school for an apprenticeship in Mallow with Dr. Thomas Justice. This apprenticeship would fulfill obligations for the requirements to apply to Apothecaries Hall in Dublin. Patrick arrived in Mallow in autumn 1844. The Justices had no children, and life in Mallow was much different from the quiet estate existence at Grange. Patrick applied himself to his duties, accompanying Dr. Justice at the dispensary and infirmary or on his duties as surgeon to the North Cork Rifles, a militia whose past record of deeds made bad memories for many local Irish who had suffered at their hands.

In the year 1845, the course of events steered Ireland down the road to tragedy. In June, the potato blight hit Europe. It spread rapidly, appearing in Ireland by September, just in time to affect the harvest. Landowners in Cork discovered one-fifth of the crop ruined. And another upheaval was brewing, as Mallow became a battleground for political movements. Daniel O'Connell, so instrumental in gaining Catholic emancipation, held "monster meetings" to raise awareness for another cause: the repeal of the Act of Union—a movement to give Ireland more autonomy from England. He delivered the "Mallow Defiance" to a crowd of 300,000. Supporters marched in the streets shouting for repeal. The Young Ireland movement gained strength through the efforts of a Mallow attorney, Thomas Davis, whose influence on the political climate peaked while Patrick lived there. The movement for the fledgling idea of Irish home rule was given additional strength by the writings of Davis, a Protestant and son of a British army officer. Calling themselves *Confederates*, the leaders organized nationwide support for rebellion.[5]

While there is no evidence that Patrick Cleburne as a young man of seventeen actively supported Young Ireland, he could not ignore its presence. Cultural awareness made him question what he identified closest with—his Irishness or his more English upbringing? Discussions about why Ireland should remain a submissive colony of England instead of making its own laws suggested that separation from Britain was inevitable. Whatever Cleburne's feelings on the issue at this time in his youth, he evidently filed them away for future reference, for history shows that they came into play in America.

In February 1846, Patrick traveled to Dublin and Apothecaries Hall to take his entrance exam. What followed devastated him: he failed the exam, leaving him with seemingly no alternative but to return home as a disappointment. His sense of honor, knowing what his family expected from him, left him humiliated. He wandered the streets of Dublin in despair until, "without notifying anyone of his intentions," he decided to lose his disgrace in the ranks of the British army.[6]

On February 27, 1846, an awkward young man appeared at the barracks on Ship Street in Dublin and lied about his age, enlisting in the 41st Regiment of Foot for life. The regiment's motto seemed fitting: "Death Before Shame." Patrick concealed his identity, listing himself as a laborer, and made the conscious decision to go by his given name of Patrick instead of Ronayne. The army asked no questions. He became Private Patrick Cleburne, No. 2242, one of 173 Irishmen in the regiment of 912 men and officers. The regiment's orders were ship out to India, and this suited Patrick. No doubt he was horrified to learn that on March 19 the regiment would leave, not for India, but for Mullingar, barely 60 miles away.[7]

As the famine years from 1846 to 1850 paralleled young Patrick's military service, his army experience provided a window on the tragic events then rocking Ireland. Serving tours of duty throughout the country, he witnessed a devastated homeland with hundreds of thousands dying and displaced. No social class went unaffected. His own family's financial status declined as the country's economic fabric unraveled. In a land encompassed by death, enduring a lifestyle crushing his creativeness and sensitivity, and growing increasingly desperate with no foreseeable escape, the urge to leave became a driving force. His Ireland became "a hopeless case ... the elements of decay and destruction deeply seated in the heart of the body social [and] politic ... to stay would only be to witness a lingering dissolution."[8]

Cleburne became Corporal Patrick Cleburne on July 1, 1849, and was immensely proud of this achievement, a measure of his devotion to duty. Stationed on Spike Island in Cork Harbor, he obtained a pass to visit his family, and for the first time since he had left for Dublin more than three years earlier, he returned to Grange. It was a time of reconciliation, and, on seeing the strained financial and physical circumstances of his family, Patrick supported his stepmother's suggestion that they leave Ireland. She was in arrears with rent, and William had no means of turning the situation around. Patrick spent time pondering the decision, weighing the choice against his own future prospects. The continually worsening situation in Ireland had no end in sight. At least a million people had died, and another million had emigrated. Private soldiers in the 41st Foot were deserting at any opportunity.

Cleburne consulted with his captain, Robert Pratt, about the possibility of gaining more rank and a future in the British army. But captain was the highest position he could ever hope to achieve. One bought rank in the British army, and the cost of a captain's commission (£1,800) exceeded his means. On reaching 21 years of age, Patrick received some property held in trust for him by the Ronayne family, but it was not nearly enough to purchase a commission.

He said of his choices in disgust, "I should at best in my old age hold the commission of a petty officer, detested by inferiors and looked down on by superiors." Thus, Cleburne chose to utilize the reinstated option of purchasing a discharge from the army and bought his way out for £20. On September 22, 1849, he left the British army, receiving a copy of his discharge papers to prove that he had not deserted. At the bottom of the page, in a space provided for comments by superiors, were these words: "A good soldier." He would carry this paper on his person for the rest of his life.[9]

As Cleburne boarded the *Bridgetown* at Cobh Harbor on November 5, along with two brothers and a sister, bound for the United States, he carried with him the perception that Ireland had been destroyed by English laws, taxation and the attitude of the Irish as inferior. Ten years later this same perception would apply to the relationship between his new home, the American South, and the U.S. federal government. Substitute the Confederacy for Ireland in the equation, and you have Patrick Cleburne's motivation to risk his life for an adopted cause of independence.

A confident Patrick Cleburne arrived in the small Mississippi River town of Helena, Arkansas, in the summer of 1850. If he had felt closer to his English heritage in Cork, once he reached America, his Irishness reasserted itself. He felt much more like an Irishman than an American, and his Cork accent certainly set him apart. There were new foods, new social expectations, a different climate, and a rough frontier lifestyle. Fortunately, he had chosen to settle in the South, where a strong Scots-Irish/Celtic makeup found him readily acceptable, while his countrymen to the North suffered from discrimination similar to what they had experienced under English rule.

In Helena, Cleburne began a decade of establishing himself, first in a life that included a drugstore partnership, and later in a law practice. He became a leading citizen of the town and grew to love his new country. "I have some really kind and disinterested friends here," he wrote to his stepmother in 1853, "and on the whole I like the place and the people very much." Still, he retained an air of distance: "The life I have led, constantly mingling with strange people and making few attachments, has been well calculated to blunt the feelings, and harden the heart."[10]

Cleburne became known in Helena as a very modest, quiet gentleman. He lived simply, never owning a house or many personal belongings, and though he lived in a slave-owning society, he never owned a slave. His Irish background provided political sway with the Irish laborers and workers in town for the Democratic Party during the election of 1860. His poetic nature also found an outlet in the woods along the riverbank, and he penned some lines when an encounter moved him. Cleburne earned the reputation of being a very focused person. When he decided to do something, he studied it thoroughly to achieve the best results, avoiding rash decisions or impulsive opinions.

Everything he said and did was carefully weighed. This personality adapted well to an officer role, and he was voted captain of a militia company formed in 1860 in response to the growing threat of disunion. This rifle company became known as the Yell Rifles. When war clouds gathered in 1861, and Arkansas seceded, the Yell Rifles became part of the 1st Arkansas Volunteer Infantry, and Patrick Cleburne was elected colonel of the regiment.

His reputation as a strict disciplinarian gained him the respect of his command. Much of his attitude likely came from his British army experiences. However, while that service had taught him many valuable lessons, such as drilling and musketry exercises, it had also taught him that oppression and a rigid class system did little for an army's morale. Enlisting as a militia private, he rose to the rank of major general within eighteen months. While he commanded the Confederate troops at his disposal, one thing he forbade was any humiliating punishment of private soldiers. He once cashiered a lieutenant for having a soldier bucked and gagged, a common practice in both Union and Confederate armies for punishment. Cleburne instead preferred to withhold privileges, such as passes to town or leave to go home. Above all, his commitment to duty marked his command. He wrote to his brother Robert in 1861, "Life is a small matter to me, when duty presents itself." He also wrote that southern independence was crucial: "As to my own position, I hope to see the Union preserved by granting to the South the full measure of her constitutional rights. If this cannot be done, I hope to see all the Southern states united in a new confederation and that we can effect a peaceable separation." That he saw a parallel between the Irish quest for the repeal of the Act of Union and the southern attempt at essentially the same thing is obvious.[11]

A brief synopsis of Cleburne's Confederate army service shows his commitment to duty. At Shiloh on April 6, 1862, his first major battle and first time in command of a brigade, Cleburne distinguished himself by advancing his unit farther than any other Confederate brigade on the field. He received orders to halt with victory in sight. Four months later, at Richmond, Kentucky, he led a division for the first time. His careful deployment of his troops and critical decisions resulted in victory, though he had to retire to the rear when a piece of shrapnel tore through his cheek. The wound caused him to lose some teeth and took him out of action for six weeks.

Cleburne was promoted to major general in November and fought with his division at Murfreesboro, Tennessee, on New Year's Day 1863. Again he proved his capability as a commander and won his part of the field. However, the costly success was lost when General Braxton Bragg failed to follow up, instead opting to retreat. This act elicited criticism from Cleburne and other generals, who sensed that Bragg's constant indecisiveness was bleeding the morale from the army. The following months witnessed a slow decline in the troops' faith in Bragg, and also in themselves. Shortages in supplies and war materiel likewise plagued the South. Lives lost in battle were irreplaceable. The South's population of eight million was no match for the North's twenty-two million. After Confederate defeats at Missionary Ridge and Lookout Mountain in November 1863, Bragg ordered a desperate retreat into Georgia, hotly pursued by victorious Union troops under the command of Major General William T. Sherman.

The last hope of the Confederates lay with Patrick Cleburne's division, fighting a rearguard action and making a stand at Ringgold Gap, Georgia. It was Cleburne's shining moment, a brilliant military action reminiscent of Wellington's Peninsula tactics. The five-hour engagement saved Bragg's army, and Cleburne fell back in fighting order toward Dalton.

The army rested and licked its wounds through Christmas 1863, stationed around Dalton. This respite gave Cleburne time for thought, along with the opportunity to present an idea he had been contemplating for some time. It is possible that this idea brought his career to an abrupt end. For months he had pondered the difficulty of the South's shortage of manpower and came up with a controversial solution. He penned a lengthy manuscript titled "Proposal to Make Soldiers of Slaves and Guarantee Freedom to All Loyal Negroes." It was dated January 2, 1864, and began by reiterating the poor physical and intellectual condition of the Confederate Army of Tennessee after months of military reverses and bad command. The downward spiral of his army's effectiveness gave Cleburne cause for concern that the ultimate goal of southern independence would be lost.

What this proposal says about Cleburne as an Irishman is insightful. His ideas of freedom were more political than inalienable, and he believed in making every sacrifice "to place independence above every question of property." Cleburne's personal view of slavery had always been acceptance mingled with the tolerance of one who comes into an existing institution, even though he chose not to profit by it. But as the war ground on, and the Emancipation Proclamation of 1863 changed the war motives in the North from saving the Union to abolishing slavery, Cleburne realized that the South must respond if it ever expected to achieve independence. In 1863 he began to canvass planters and his military subordinates regarding the future of the South's efforts and how to win the war.[12]

Cleburne presented his proposal to a gathering of Confederate high command that included General Joseph Johnston, newly appointed to replace the incompetent Bragg. The Irish present and the Confederate future were both on Cleburne's mind when he predicted what defeat would spawn: "If this state continues much longer we must be subjugated. Every man should endeavor to understand the meaning of subjugation before it is too late. It means that the history of this heroic struggle will be written by the enemy;

that our youth will be trained by Northern school teachers; will learn from Northern school books their version of the war; will be impressed by all the influences of history and education to regard our gallant dead as traitors."[13] He specifically warned about the "influences of education." As an Irish schoolboy who had learned his country's history from English schoolbooks, he could confidently predict the consequences.

He then proceeded to detail a possible method for preventing this outcome. He cited three problems working against the South: (1) numerical inferiority in the army, (2) a single source of supply for the South (i.e., white males for soldiers), and (3) slavery, once a chief source of strength now becoming a chief source of weakness. He then pointed out the North's three sources of manpower as (1) a larger "motley" population, (2) slaves pressed into Union service in occupied areas of the South, and (3) European support from those whose "hearts are fired into a crusade against us by fictitious pictures of the atrocities of slavery."[14]

Cleburne considered slavery "a continued embarrassment." He felt certain that once it was removed as an issue, it would cause "a complete change of front in our favor of the sympathies of the world." He emphasized that ending slavery was "the most powerful and honestly entertained plan in [the North's] war platform. Knock this away and what is left? A bloody ambition for more territory, a pretended veneration for the Union, and poisonous selfish interests." Cleburne also noted that the Confederate Constitution had made a provision for just such an idea as he was promoting: the constitution "has reserved to their respective governments [citing states' rights] the power to free slaves for meritorious services to the state."[15]

His impassioned speech ended with a simple warning of what the failure to put independence above all else could mean. Perhaps remembering O'Connell's comparison to the Irish as slaves to the English, Cleburne said, "As between the loss of independence and the loss of slavery, we assume that every patriot will freely give up ... the Negro slave rather than be a slave himself." He reminded his audience of what Union sources constantly exclaimed: "It is said slavery is all we are fighting for.... Even if this were true, which we deny, slavery is not all our enemies are fighting for. It is merely the pretense to establish sectional superiority and a more centralized form of government, and to deprive us of our rights and liberties." Fitting words to come from an Irishman who had witnessed years of British government policy at work, and its unwavering belief that the Irish were inferior.[16]

Cleburne's plea ended on a pragmatic note: "Negroes will require much training; training will require time, and there is danger that this concession to common sense may come too late." Thirteen signatures of regimental officers in Cleburne's division accompanied his own as endorsement of the document. Among the signers were two Irish officers.[17]

The consequences of his proposal were personally devastating for Cleburne. Though accepted by the majority of those he canvassed, a handful of his professional enemies wielded the deathblow to its implementation. It would be another year before President Jefferson Davis committed to enlisting slaves in the Confederate armies—a year too late for significant gains on either the battlefront or the political front.

Patrick Cleburne served faithfully throughout the Atlanta campaign from May through August 1864. He led his division on the march into Tennessee that autumn. Outside his headquarters in Gadsden, Alabama, his soldiers serenaded their leader with loud hurrahs and brass bands. He came out on the balcony in response, and the audience cried out for a speech. He obliged them and likened their cause to that of Ireland, ending with the vow, "If this cause that is so dear to my heart is doomed to fail, I pray heaven may let me fall with it, while my face is toward the enemy and my arm battling for that which I know to be right."[18]

Cleburne led his division into battle at Franklin, Tennessee, on a bright autumn evening on November 30, 1864. He fell during the breakthrough on the Union breastworks, going in at the head of his favorite Irish regiment, the 5th Confederate. His death was reported in lengthy obituaries in the Dublin *Nation* and Cork *Examiner*.[19] After the war, Cleburne was revered by Irish groups in both the North and the South, but particularly in the South. Many literary societies, militia halls and even Fenian groups were named in honor of his bravery. In 1890 a monument was erected at his grave and adorned with many Irish symbols, including the rising sun.

Patrick Cleburne embodied the spirit of his countrymen, and indeed, as Robert E. Lee declared, he "shone like a meteor on a clouded sky" for the South. He died a beloved hero leading his men on the field of battle, many of whom were fellow immigrants from the Emerald Isle, men who had fled famine and oppression to fight for freedom in America.[20]

NOTES

1. Gerard Hayes-McCoy, *Irish Battles* (London: Longmans, 1969); Thomas Bartlett and Keith Jeffery, *A Military History of Ireland* (Cambridge: Cambridge University Press, 1996).

2. John O'Hart, *Irish Pedigrees: The Origin and Stem of the Irish Nation*, vol. 2 (New York: Murphy & McCarthy, 1915), 108–10.

3. Mauriel Phillips Joslyn, ed., *A Meteor Shining Brightly: Essays on Maj. Gen. Patrick R. Cleburne* (Milledgeville, GA: Terrell House, 1998), 1–2, 25.

4. Joslyn, ed., *Meteor*; Martina Cleary and Olive O'Driscoll, "Spedding's School and Hospital," *Times Past, Journal of the Ballincollig Community School* 2 (1985): 5.

5. Joslyn, *Meteor*, 8–9.

6. Letter, Calhoun Benham to Peter Alexander, December 21, 1863.

7. Patrick R. Cleburne, Service Record, 41st Foot, British Army, Public Records Office, London, WO 12/5446; Joslyn, *Meteor*, 11–12.

8. Letter to Isabella Cleburne, October 26, 1853, Patrick R. Cleburne Papers, David Mullins Library, University of Arkansas at Fayetteville.

9. Joslyn, *Meteor*, 22–23; Cleburne, Service Record.

10. Letter to Isabella Cleburne, October 26, 1853.
11. Letter to Robert Cleburne, January 1861, Cleburne Papers, David Mullins Library.
12. Joslyn, *Meteor*, 121–39.
13. Patrick R. Cleburne, "Proposal to Make Soldiers of Slaves and Guarantee Freedom to All Loyal Negroes—Address by P.R. Cleburne, January 2, 1864," reprinted in Joslyn, *Meteor*, 170–77.
14. *Ibid.*, 171.
15. *Ibid.*, 173, 175.
16. *Ibid.*, 173, 176.
17. *Ibid.*, 176–77. The two officers were Colonel John F. Murray, 5th Confederate Infantry, and Brigadier General John H. Kelly, cavalry division commander.
18. Edward W. Smith Sr., excerpt provided to author by Scott McKay.
19. *Nation*, December 13, 1864; *Examiner*, January 1865.
20. According to George W. Pepper, after the war Robert E. Lee described Cleburne as having "shone like a meteor on a clouded sky." See Pepper, *Under Three Flags* (Cincinnati, OH: Curts & Jennings, 1899), 332–33.

BIBLIOGRAPHY

Bartlett, Thomas, and Keith Jeffery. *A Military History of Ireland*. Cambridge: Cambridge University Press, 1996.
Cleary, Martina, and Olive O'Driscoll. "Spedding's School and Hospital." *Times Past, Journal of the Ballincollig Community School* 2 (1985).
Cleburne, Patrick R. Service Record, 41st Foot, British Army. Public Records Office, London, WO 12/5446.
Hayes-McCoy, Gerard. *Irish Battles*. London: Longmans, 1969.
Joslyn, Mauriel Phillips, ed. *A Meteor Shinning Brightly: Essays on Maj. Gen. Patrick R. Cleburne*. Milledgeville, GA: Terrell House, 1998.
O'Hart, John. *Irish Pedigrees: The Origin and Stem of the Irish Nation*. Vol. 2. New York: Murphy & McCarthy, 1915.
Patrick R. Cleburne Papers, David Mullins Library, University of Arkansas at Fayetteville.
Pepper, George W. *Under Three Flags*. Cincinnati, OH: Curts & Jennings, 1899.

Dick Dowling, Texas Irishman

ANN CARAWAY IVINS

On September 8, 1863, a tiny force of skilled Irish artillerymen at Sabine Pass, Texas, halted a massive federal invasion of Texas. The battle of Sabine Pass was one of the most astonishing military victories in the War between the States. It is said that the federal commander was "the first U.S. general to lose a fleet in a contest with land batteries alone."[1] With Confederate forces outnumbered by more than ten to one, their victory was deemed "more remarkable than the battle of Thermopylae" by Jefferson Davis, president of the Confederate States of America. Commanding the Irish Davis Guard at Sabine Pass was twenty-six-year-old Lieutenant Dick Dowling of the Confederate army.

The second of Pat and Bridget Quaker Dowling's eight children, Richard William Dowling was born in Knockballyvishteal, now called Knock (Milltown), County Galway. He was baptized in the Parish of Dunmore on January 14, 1837.[2] Living on a ninety-three-acre farm in Knock, at a time when less than 10 percent of all holdings in County Galway were more than fifteen acres,[3] it appears that, at least for a time, the Dowling family was comparatively comfortable. The famine years, however, took their toll. The family eventually left the farm, sending Dick and his oldest sister Honora to live with friends in New Orleans in July 1846. Dick was only nine years old and his sister ten when they were separated from their family. Pat and Bridget Dowling remained in Ireland with their other children for several years, finally reduced to living in the Tuam Workhouse by 1850.[4]

Sometime in the early 1850s, the Dowling family was reunited in New Orleans, the "Queen of the South." America's fourth largest city in 1846, New Orleans had a multinational population of more than 100,000; approximately 20 percent of these residents were Irish.[5] Sadly, soon after their arrival, Pat

203

and Bridget Dowling died in the horrible yellow fever epidemic of 1853, which claimed almost 9,000 lives in New Orleans. Dick Dowling was orphaned at age sixteen.

By 1856 at least, Dowling was earning a living as a bartender. The 1857 *New Orleans City Directory* lists "R.W. Dowling, barkeeper, Continental Coffeehouse." The Continental Coffeehouse (a pub) was well located near the waterfront and the busy Customs House in the French Quarter. However, by 1856, anti-foreign sentiment had manifested in local New Orleans elections, and the Irish were targets of great discrimination. Dowling decided to move on, and, in 1857, he settled in Houston, Texas, a town just about as old as he was. Houston had been founded in 1836, shortly after Texas had won independence from Mexico. By 1857, it had a population of 4,000; railroads had just entered the city, and business was booming, primarily in the cotton trade.

Dick Dowling quickly established himself in his new home, opening his own bar (The Shades) in October 1857 and marrying pretty Elizabeth Anne Odium the next month. She was the daughter of an early Irish Catholic settler, a veteran of the war against Mexico. In 1858 Dowling began purchasing land in and around Houston, eventually amassing significant holdings. He helped organize Houston's first gaslight company and installed the first commercial and residential gas lighting in the city. He was a founding member of the Houston Hook and Ladder Company No. 1 fire department, and he also joined the Houston Light Artillery, a local militia outfit. He acquired a half interest in a steamboat, as well as a partial interest in a liquor import business, and participated in the organization of the first streetcar company in Houston. In 1860 Dowling opened the famous Bank of Bacchus, a bar popular with the Irish dockworkers and railroad workers of Houston and Galveston.

When the United States began to splinter, and talk of war became familiar conversation at the Bank of Bacchus, Irishmen immediately formed militia companies consisting of their fellow countrymen. Chief among the contentious issues in the South was "states' rights"—in effect, "home rule," a familiar cause to the Irish. The North was perceived as a "foreign" aggressor. "The Civil War was not fought to liberate the slaves, but on the question of the Union—the South passionately upholding their right to preserve their own way of life in the face of Northern demands."[6]

Irish immigrants in the South became southerners, with little or no affiliation with the culture of the industrialized North, more than a thousand miles away from Texas. Lack of shared communication and transportation systems ensured that sectional differences were sharply distinguished. It was almost 2,000 miles from Houston and Boston, and as late as 1860, Houston was just being linked by telegraph line to Galveston, only fifty miles away. The railroad from Houston extended no farther east than 90 miles—not quite to the Texas-Louisiana border.

In September 1860 Dowling joined a predominantly Irish militia group, the Davis Guard, commanded by his wife's uncle, Captain Frederick H. Odium. Dowling was elected first lieutenant and treasurer of the company. On March 23, 1861, Texas officially ratified the Constitution of the Confederate States of America, and on August 13, 1861, the Davis Guard, 2nd Regiment Texas Infantry, was mustered into the service of the Confederacy. On November 1, 1861, the Davis Guard was officially named "Company F, Cook's (1) Regiment, Texas Heavy Artillery, CSA."[7] The first muster roll for the company lists a total of ninety-three men: four officers and eighty-nine enlisted soldiers, all from Houston and Galveston; all except two were Irish. These enlisted men were mature—their average age was twenty-nine.

For the first two years of the War between the States, Dowling and the Davis Guard were stationed at various points around Texas, training under artillery expert Colonel Joseph J. Cook and earning a reputation as the finest artillerymen on the Gulf Coast. In late 1862 Major General John Bankhead Magruder (known as "Prince John" for his dapper attire and love of lavish parties) assumed command of the Department of Texas, New Mexico and Arizona in the Trans-Mississippi District of the Confederate States. In the first great military action planned by Magruder in his new capacity, Dowling and the Davis Guard participated in the Confederate victory of the recapture of Galveston Island (fifty miles from Houston) on January 1, 1863.

On January 21, 1863, the soldiers of the Davis Guard distinguished themselves in action aboard one of two "cotton-clads" (paddlewheel steamers armored with cotton bales), capturing two federal blockading vessels off the coast of Sabine Pass, Texas. During the exciting five-hour, thirty-mile pursuit of the federal blockaders, Dick Dowling manned a sixty-four-pound rifled gun that the Davis Guard had named "Annie," in honor of Dowling's wife. Dowling was ordered to commence firing at a range of two-and-a-half miles, which he did with great effect, "striking the sloop repeatedly, and exploding one shell on the enemy's deck."[8] The *Galveston Weekly News* reported a week after the battle that, without the loss of a man or a gun, the victors had "added to the Confederate navy two excellent vessels, 11 heavy guns and stores of the most valuable character.... The gun ('Annie') was managed by Capt. Odium and his Davis Guards ... who are said to have fired with the most remarkable accuracy.... Not a man was scratched on our side."[9]

During the first two years of the war, Texas was comparatively untouched by federal attack, as it was geographically far removed from the heart of the Confederate states. Its chief importance to the Confederacy had been in terms of providing men and provisions from its abundant natural resources; profits from its huge cotton trade likewise helped finance the war effort. By the summer of 1863, federal forces had won major victories in southern areas, but a new challenge to the Union emerged in Mexico with Napoleon III's invasion of that country. U.S. President Abraham Lincoln turned his attention to Texas, deciding that an invasion of that state was necessary, principally to forestall a possible threat from Napoleon III's puppet ruler Maximilian and his French troops in Mexico.

Federal General Nathaniel P. Banks, former governor of Massachusetts and commanding general of the Department of the Gulf, was ordered to select an invasion site in Texas. In Massachusetts politics, Banks had a record as an anti–Irish Know Nothing; many immigrants there had wrongly believed his conversion to the Republicans indicated the coming of a strong nativist taint into the new, anti-slavery party of Lincoln. Banks had long considered Sabine Pass a likely entry point from which troops could be moved via railroad into Houston, and then Galveston, the state's leading city. Success at penetrating Sabine Pass with a combined naval/army attack would enable federal control of the vital points of Texas within a week. This was indeed a more intelligent scheme than the one preferred by his superiors, which required Banks to invade up the marshy and disease-ridden Red River Valley. But it was not to be.[10]

Sabine Pass is a narrow strait, six miles long, connecting the Sabine Lake with the Gulf of Mexico at the southeastern corner of Texas. It lies about 100 land miles east of Houston and 270 land miles west of New Orleans In 1863 Sabine Pass was divided into two channels by a shallow, mile-long oyster reef. Cotton, lumber, and other civilian and military provisions, including gunpowder, routinely streamed through Sabine Pass on blockade runners. As a lifeline for the Confederacy, it became vital earlier that summer when the fall of Vicksburg on July 4, and that of Port Hudson five days later, brought federal control of the Mississippi River all the way to New Orleans.[11]

During the summer of 1863, the Davis Guard was stationed at the hot, muggy, mosquito-infested Sabine Pass while a fortification was being constructed under the supervision of Major Julius Kellersberger. Fort Griffin, an earthwork structure reinforced by timber and railroad iron, was built on high ground at the point of exit from the oyster reef channels in Sabine Pass. It provided an irregular, sawtooth front for maximum protection for the garrison, described by Major Kellersberger as "forty Irishmen under a most energetic lieutenant (Dick Dowling)."[12] The fort was triangular in shape, about 100 yards long on the north and west walls, and about 150 yards long on the sawtooth front. The sloping outer walls were 16 feet high. The fort's casemates dropped five feet below the level of the ramparts, allowing room only for a man's head to see above them and for the gun barrels to project seaward through the embrasures. According to the plan, the fortress had spaces for six bombproofs and magazines, of which only four were to be completed. They were each eight feet high, eight feet wide and 30 feet long, built into the sawtooth front of the fort beneath the guns. The guns were reworked pieces: two 32-pounder smoothbores, two 24-pounder smoothbores and two 32-pounder brass howitzers.[13]

By September 1863, with Fort Griffin not quite complete, the fort's construction engineers had precisely calculated where incoming ships would lie in range of the fort's cannons and drove a pole into the Sabine Pass channel as a firing marker. The pole was also meant to be a reminder of the advantageous position the enemy would have should they pass the fort and aim their fire toward the rear, at the unfinished (and most vulnerable) part of the fort. The men of the Davis Guard repeatedly practiced firing at the pole, and they well knew the limits of their firing range.[14]

On September 4, 1863, a force of more than 5,000 infantry and five batteries of artillery sailed from New Orleans under the command of Major General William B. Franklin, the top graduate of the U.S. Military Academy Class of 1843 and a career military officer. Franklin had three brigadier generals to assist in the operation, which involved four gunboats and twenty-three transport ships.

In consultation with Lieutenant Frederick Crocker, commander of the expedition's naval forces, General Franklin planned a surprise attack at Sabine Pass for the morning of September 7. The simple plan called for gunboats to proceed up the channel and begin shelling the Confederate fortification while infantrymen, artillery and cavalry from the transport ships would land on a beach below the fort.

Franklin's plan for surprise attack was sound; the execution, however, was bungled through miscommunication and misjudgment. The Union soldiers knew that there was a fort at Sabine Pass, but they did not know the Confederates' position and number. The element of surprise was foiled when the alert Davis Guard saw the signal lights of some of General Franklin's fleet anchored off Sabine Pass at 2 a.m. on September 7. The Federals were awaiting the remainder of the expedition, including Lieutenant Crocker on the USS *Clifton*, who had actually sailed past the entrance to the channel in the dark night of September 6; Crocker did not rejoin the fleet until the next day. At about 11 a.m. on September 7, nine transport ships from Franklin's fleet steamed into the Sabine Pass channel, assuming that Lieutenant Crocker's gunboats and other transports had begun the attack as scheduled at dawn. With no sign of Crocker's forces in the channel, however, the transports recrossed the bar under the watchful eye of Dowling and his men.

On the evening of September 7, Captain Odium in the town of Sabine Pass received a message from General Magruder in Houston: "It would be a useless sacrifice to offer battle, with almost certainty of defeat." Odium relayed Magruder's message to Lieutenant Dowling at the fort about a mile from town. Dowling consulted with his men; they unanimously elected to remain and fight the enemy.[15]

At 6:30 a.m., Tuesday, September 8, the gunboat *Clifton* began firing on Fort Griffin. In his official report of the battle, Dick Dowling said that twenty-six shells were aimed at the fort, "most of which passed a little over or fell short; all, however, in excellent range, one shell being landed on the works and another striking the south angle of the fort, without doing any material damage." The six cannons at Fort Griffin remained silent even as a reconnaissance team approached, searching the marshy banks of the river for a place hard enough to land the federal infantry. The *Uncle Ben*, a Confederate cotton-clad steamer equipped only with two 12-pound guns, appeared out of Sabine Lake just north of Fort Griffin. Not alarmed by the sight of the *Uncle Ben*, the Federals continued their inspection of the pass and concluded that troops could only be landed several hundred yards below Fort Griffin, where the bank was hard and the water deep enough to accommodate the steamers. The disadvantage of this site was that it was within range of the Confederates' cannons, but Lieutenant Crocker assessed the position of the guns pointed at the Texas side of the channel and determined that with four gunboats on both sides of the channel at once, the forces of Fort Griffin and the *Uncle Ben* combined could not contain them.[16]

Lieutenant Crocker finalized his plan of attack; the gunboats *Sachem* and *Arizona* would draw the fire of the enemy to the Louisiana channel, while the *Clifton*, the best armored ship with the heaviest guns, would bombard the fort from the Texas side. The gunboat *Granite City*, also in the Texas channel, would protect the landing of troops from the transport *General Banks*, whose sharpshooters would then make a land assault against the Confederates.

While the Davis Guard silently waited at Fort Griffin, Captain Odium was doing his best to raise reinforcements for his company, although it is estimated that no more than 300 Confederates were within fifty miles of Sabine Pass at this time. Odium had contacted Acting Volunteer Major Leon Smith in Beaumont, who wired Houston headquarters as well all local forces on the morning of September 8 that the enemy was at hand. Major Smith sent troops across Sabine Lake by steamer from Beaumont and Orange, Texas, but decided that he and Captain W.S. Good of the ordnance department would head for the pass on horseback, the quickest means of getting there. Captain Odium assigned Lieutenant Nicholas H. Smith, Corps of Engineers, to assist Lieutenant Dowling at the fort. Lieutenant Smith knew the fort well, having served under Major Kellersberger in its construction. In addition, Confederate Calvary Assistant Surgeon George H. Bailey left his post at the hospital in Sabine Pass to join the fight. The job of manning the six cannons required 90–100 men under optimum conditions. This task now had to be managed by the force at hand: a total of 41 Davis Guard members along with Lieutenant Smith and Dr. Bailey.[17]

According to the *New York Times*, the attack on Fort Griffin was commenced by the *Clifton*, which carried nine heavy guns, two of which were 9-inch pivots, one at the bow and the other at the stern:

> Captain Crocker opened fire at a distance of about two miles from his bow pivot, and after an experimental shot or two, acquired the range, pouring in upon the enemy a continuous steam of fire, the bursting shells knocking huge holes in their works, and throwing the debris up in enormous quantities. The reports of the huge monster was absolutely deafening, and the ground fairly shook from the concussion.
> The *Sachem*, Capt. Johnson commanding, in the meantime took up a position where she could pour a raking cross-fire, and also opened with her broadside of rifled pieces, which were served with equal precision and effect.
> About the same time the powerful battery of the Arizona, Capt. Tibbetts, from a position at the stern of the *Sachem*, also opened upon the enemy with screaming shell and hissing round shot, every one of which could be plainly seen plowing up the interior of the fort and crashing through the breastworks.
> This continued for some time before the enemy replied, the ships gradually nearing the fort and increasing the rapidity of their fire, until they were within point-blank range, and the *Sachem* had nearly passed by the works—on the right hand side of the oyster reefs fronting them—when the enemy suddenly opened a terrific fire from his entire battery.[18]

At 3:40 p.m. on Tuesday, September 8, 1863, Dick Dowling fired the first Confederate round of the Battle of Sabine Pass.[19] The men of Fort Griffin shot an incredible 137 rounds without stopping to swab their guns. Their cannons became so hot that two gunners burned their thumbs to the bone; the largest guns remained untouchable for 24 hours after the battle.[20]

During the initial rounds of firing, one of the brass mountain howitzers slipped off its platform and was out of action. Dowling himself manned one of the remaining five cannons, a 32-pounder. Private Michael McKernan, a crack shot, manned one of the 24-pounders. In the midst of bombardment, Dr. J.G.D. Murray, a civilian from the Sabine City Hospital, rushed into the fort to assist with the casualties he assumed would be there. Instead of dead and wounded, he found his fellow medical practitioner, Dr. George Bailey, commanding two howitzers, dispensing "Magruder pills" (as the cannonballs were called). Dr. Murray was quickly followed into Fort Griffin by Captain Odium, Major Smith and Captain Good, the latter two having just arrived from Beaumont.

When, as the *New York Times* reported, "everything appeared most favorable, and the fortunes of war seemed about to assign the meed of victory to the gallant little [Union] vessels, the *Sachem* unfortunately grounded.... This was speedily taken advantage of by [the Confederates], and a perfect storm of shot and shell fell upon, over, and around her, making the water hiss and foam like a boiling cauldron."[21]

Private McKernan fired the shot that crashed through the iron plating and woodwork of the *Sachem*'s hull and into its steam drum and "opened the boiler horribly and sent floods of boiling water and steam over our men," according to the communications officer of the ship.[22] As his men "were becoming exhausted by the rapidity of their fire," Dowling asked the visitors to secure reinforcements; Dr. Murray and Captain Good left to do so, followed by Major Smith and Captain Odium, who shouted one piece of advice through the cannons' roar: aim for the wheelhouses and drive the gunboats into the mud.[23]

In the meantime, the USS *Clifton* was pulverizing Fort Griffin. The Davis Guard rushed to lower one of the 24-pounders, which was too high to aim at Crocker's ship. Quickly they dug out the earth from underneath the cannon to drop its muzzle. The *Clifton* charged for Fort Griffin at full steam, "keeping up a hot fire all the time from her pivot guns, and as she neared the works, loading with double charges of grape, sweeping the parapet at every discharge." Then the Confederates landed a shot that carried away the *Clifton*'s tiller rope. As Captain Odium had predicted, the unmanageable ship swerved into the channel's bank and came to a halt only 300 yards from the earthwork walls of the fort. Crocker and his men continued their fire as the *Clifton*'s signalman desperately flagged the trailing *Granite City* and *General Banks* for assistance. Soon another crack shot from the fort pierced the *Clifton*'s boiler; boiling water and steam sprayed its decks with grisly results.[24]

Lieutenant Crocker kept up the fight, unaware that his executive officer had raised the white flag. But with his crewmen jumping ship and no apparent help at hand from the *Granite City* or *General Banks*, Crocker finally capitulated. The disabled *Sachem* followed suit. The *Arizona* was uselessly stuck in the mud in the Louisiana channel. The captain of the *Granite City* reversed course and ran straight out of the pass. Major General Franklin gave orders for the rest of the fleet to follow suit. The Federals were shocked and confused. In only forty-five minutes, the Battle of Sabine Pass was over.[25]

In Dick Dowling's September 9, 1863, official report of the battle, he wrote, "All my men behaved like heroes; not a man flinched from his post. Our motto was 'Victory or death.' We captured with 47 men two gunboats, mounting thirteen guns of the heaviest caliber, and about 350 prisoners." There were no Confederate casualties.[26]

The day after the battle, General Orders No. 154, Headquarters District of Texas, New Mexico, and Arizona, was issued to J.B. Magruder:

> The major-general commanding has the satisfaction of announcing to the army a brilliant victory won by the little garrison of Sabine Pass against the fleet of the enemy.... The result of the engagement had with the enemy's fleet on the coast of Texas proves that true pluck and resolution are qualified which make up for disparity of metal and numbers, and that no position defended with determination can be carried by the enemy's gunboats alone. Should any of the forts on the coast or the forces on land be attacked, the troops need but remember the success of their comrades at Sabine, emulate their courage and skill, and victory will be the result.[27]

Magruder visited Fort Griffin four days after the battle to hail the soldiers of the Davis Guard as "the greatest heroes that history recorded."[28] Further accolades were heaped upon the Davis Guard, highlighted on February 8, 1864, when President Jefferson Davis signed the resolution of the Confederate Congress, thanking Captain Frederick Odium, Lieutenant Richard Dowling, and the men of the Davis Guard "for their daring, gallant, and successful defense of Sabine Pass ... and preventing the invasion of Texas, [which] constitutes ... one of the most brilliant and heroic achievements in the history of this war, and entitles the Davis Guards to the gratitude and admiration of their country."[29]

Although Union forces did manage to capture other Texas ports by the end of 1863, no genuine invasion of the state was even attempted for rest of the Civil War. Texans were spared the devastating consequences that federal occupation brought to the people and economies of neighboring Louisiana and other Confederate states. The Battle of Sabine Pass had affected the Union as well. According to historian T.R. Fehrenbach, "The outcome of Sabine Pass raised a great outcry about the efficiency of the Navy in the North; coming with Bragg's victory at Chicamauga, it gave the Union a severe psychological shock. U.S. credit declined abroad; the dollar lost 5 percent of its value against gold."[30]

The Battle of Sabine Pass was enormously significant, not only for military and political reasons but also for its impact on the status of the entire southern Irish community. As word spread throughout the South of the heroics of the men at Sabine Pass, the word "brave" became associated with "Irish," a trend popularized by Major General Magruder in his General Orders No. 156 of September 13, 1863, commending "the brave 'Irish Texans' of the Davis Guards." The Irish had saved Texas for the Confederacy!

At home in Houston, Dick Dowling's parish priest instigated a movement to have special medals made for the men of the Davis Guard. Each was fashioned from a smoothed-down Mexican silver dollar, or eight *real* piece, with "Sabine Pass, Sept. 8th, 1863" inscribed on one side and "DG" (Davis Guard) above a Maltese cross on the other. The medals were suspended from green ribbons in honor of the Guards' ancestry. Although the Confederate Congress authorized the issuance of a Confederate medal of honor in 1862, none were struck. The Sabine Pass medal was one of the few privately awarded badges of honor bestowed during the war and was highly prized. A Sabine Pass medal was forwarded to President Jefferson Davis, and it is said that he carried it with him among his treasured possessions until it was stolen from him during his imprisonment after the war.[31]

Capitalizing on the immense popularity of the South's new hero, the Confederacy assigned Dick Dowling to recruiting duty for the army in March 1864. However, the glory of the victory at Sabine Pass could only momentarily turn Texans' attention from the realization that the South was losing the war. On April 9, 1865, the South's revered General Robert E. Lee formally surrendered to General Ulysses S. Grant at Appomattox Courthouse in Virginia. On June 21, 1865, Major Richard Dowling left the service of the Confederacy.[32]

After the war Dick Dowling reopened his Bank of Bacchus in Houston and returned to civilian life with characteristic vigor. By the end of 1865, Fenian Circles were organizing in Texas; most likely because of his fame and demonstrated leadership as a war hero, Dowling was appointed head of the Fenian movement in the state. With his uncle-in-law, Captain Frederick Odium, a co-commander at Sabine Pass, he set up the Davis Circle of the organization. In 1866, among his many entrepreneurial activities, Dowling and two other Irishmen formed a partnership considered to be the first exploration oil company in Texas, a most prescient endeavor.[33] Dick Dowling was truly an Irish Texan!

In 1867, the scourge of the Gulf Coast, yellow fever, surfaced in Houston. Among its casualties was thirty-year-old Dick Dowling. The hero of Sabine Pass died on September 23, 1867, and was buried in St. Vincent's Cemetery in Houston.

Most of Dowling's children predeceased him, but a surviving son, called Felix Sabine Dowling (after the victory), would later become a religious lay brother, surely the only one named after a Civil War battle and Confederate success.

NOTES

1. Richard V. Francaviglia, *From Sail to Steam* (Austin: University of Texas Press, 1998), 206, quoting *Handbook of Texas*, vol. 2 (1952), 525. See also Edward T. Gotham, *Sabine Pass: The Confederacy's Thermopylae* (Austin: University of Texas Press, 2004). A general treatment of the Irish in Texas is provided by Sean O'Brien, *Irish Americans in the Confederate Army* (Jefferson, NC: McFarland, 2007), 200–209.

2. Baptismal Records, Parish of Dunmore, Diocese of Tuam Archives. Also found in Galway Family History Centre, Galway. For a fuller account of the background, see Ann Caraway Ivins, "Dick Dowling: Galway's Hero of Confederate Texas," *Journal of the Galway Archaeological and Historical Society* 57 (2005): 113–38.

3. T.W. Moody et al., eds., *A New History of Ireland, Vol. IX (A Companion to Irish History, Part II)* (Oxford: Clarendon Press, 1984), 67.

4. Baptismal Records, Parish of Dunmore; Galway Family History Centre, Galway.

5. Benjamin Moore Norman, *Norman's New Orleans and Environs* (1845; Baton Rouge: Louisiana State University Press, 1976), xxv.

6. Charles Dickson, "Notes," *Irish Sword: Journal of Military History Society of Ireland* 3, no. 13 (Winter 1958): 283.

7. Notes, Box 502, Record Group 109, War Department, Rebel Archives, National Archives, Washington, D.C.

8. Major Oscar M. Watkins, "Off Sabine Pass, January 23, 1863," *Official Records of the Union and Confederate Navies in the War of the Rebellion*, series I, vol. 19, 565.

9. *Galveston Weekly News*, January 28, 1863.

10. Frank X. Tolbert, *Dick Dowling at Sabine Pass* (New York: McGraw-Hill, 1962), 9.

11. W.T. Block, "Sabine Pass and Galveston Were Successful Blockade-Running Ports," *Beaumont* (Texas) *Enterprise*, February 5, 1984.

12. Getulius Kellersberger, *Memoirs of an Engineer in the Confederate Army in Texas*, trans. Helen S. Sundstrom (1896; Austin, Texas, 1957), 30.
13. W.T. Block, "Myths of Sabine Pass Fort Griffin Exploded: Shrine of Irish Confederate Heroes," *East Texas Historical Journal* (October 9, 1971): 137; see also *Port Arthur News*, January 24, 1971.
14. Kellersberger, *Memoirs of an Engineer*, 30.
15. Tolbert, *Dowling at Sabine Pass*, 89; Ernest Jones, "The Battle of Sabine Pass," *Blue & Gray Magazine* (August–September 1986): 21.
16. Ibid.
17. Jones, "Battle of Sabine Pass," 20.
18. *New York Times*, September 12, 1863. It inaccurately reported the existence of two forts, the first "a powerful earthwork of great length, mounted with six heavy guns, and garrisoned by a large number of men ... a second work of similar character, mounting from three to five heavy guns." It also reported the presence of three large cotton-clad river steamers, armed with one or more guns, and a schooner armed with one bow gun, probably of very large caliber.
19. *Official Records of the Union and Confederate Armies in the War of the Rebellion*, series I, vol. 26, part 1, 311–12, contains Lieutenant Dick Dowling's report of the battle of Sabine Pass dated September 9, 1863 (hereafter Dowling, *Official Report*). Dowling gives 3:40 p.m. as the time at which the federal ships came within firing range of Fort Griffin's guns, implying that the battle began only then.
20. *Houston Daily Post*, March 17, 1905.
21. *New York Times*, September 12, 1863.
22. Lieutenant Henry C. Dane, *New York Herald* interview, as reported by Tolbert, *Dowling at Sabine Pass*, 122.
23. Dowling, *Official Report*.
24. *New York Times*, September 12, 1863.
25. P.D. O'Donnell, "Dick Dowling," *Glimpses of Tuam since the Famine* (Tuam, County Galway, Ireland, 1997), 51.
26. Dowling, *Official Report*. Dowling reports a total of 47 men in the fort at the time of the battle; I believe this number includes 41 Davis Guard members, including Dowling, as well as Dr. Bailey and Lieutenant Smith, who actively participated in the battle, and the four visitors to the fort during the battle (Captain Odium, Dr. Murray, Major Smith and Captain Good).
27. *Official Records of the Union and Confederate Armies in the War of the Rebellion*, series I, vol. 26, part 1, 306–7: General Orders No. 154, Headquarters District of Texas, New Mexico and Arizona.
28. Andrew Forest Muir, "Dick Dowling and the Battle of Sabine Pass," *Civil War History* 4, no. 4 (1958): 421.
29. *Official Records of the Union and Confederate Armies in the War of the Rebellion*, series I, vol. 26, part 1, 312.
30. T.R. Fehrenbach, *Lone Star: A History of Texas and the Texans* (New York: Macmillan, 1968), 370.
31. Gregg S. Clemmer, *Valor in Gray* (Staunton, VA: Hearthside, 1996), xv, 435, 436.
32. The Rebel Archives in the U.S. National Archives do not contain evidence of Dowling's parole as a major, but this was not uncommon for end-of-war promotions in the Confederacy.
33. R.W. Dowling to T.J. Kelly, August 25, 1866, Fenian Brotherhood Collection, American Catholic History Research Center, Catholic University of America, Washington, D.C.

BIBLIOGRAPHY

Block, W.T. "Myths of Sabine Pass Fort Griffin Exploded: Shrine of Irish Confederate Heroes." *East Texas Historical Journal* (October 9, 1971).
_____. "Sabine Pass and Galveston Were Successful Blockade-Running Ports." *Beaumont* (Texas) *Enterprise*, February 5, 1984.

Part II: American Civil War

Clemmer, Gregg S. *Valor in Gray.* Staunton, VA: Hearthside, 1996.
Dickson, Charles. "Notes." *Irish Sword: Journal of Military History Society of Ireland* 3, no. 13 (Winter 1958).
Dowling, Richard W. Baptismal records, Parish of Dunmore, Diocese of Tuam Archives, Ireland.
Fehrenbach, T.R. *Lone Star: A History of Texas and Texans.* New York: Macmillan, 1968.
Fenian Brotherhood Collection, American Catholic History Research Center, Catholic University of America, Washington, D.C.
Francaviglia, Richard V. *From Sail to Steam.* Austin: University of Texas Press, 1998.
Galveston Weekly News, January 28, 1863.
Galway Family History Centre, Galway, Ireland.
Gotham, Edward T. *Sabine Pass: The Confederacy's Thermopylae.* Austin: University of Texas Press, 2004.
Houston Daily Post, March 17, 1905.
Ivins, Ann Caraway. "Dick Dowling: Galway's Hero of Confederate Texas." *Journal of the Galway Archaeological and Historical Society* 57 (2005): 113–38.
Jones, Ernest. "The Battle of Sabine Pass." *Blue & Gray Magazine* (August–September 1986).
Kellersberger, Getulius. *Memoirs of an Engineer in the Confederate Army in Texas.* Translated by Helen S. Sundstrom. 1896; Austin, Texas, 1957.
Moody, T.W., et al., eds. *A New History of Ireland, Vol. IX (A Companion to Irish History, Part II).* Oxford: Clarendon Press, 1984.
Muir, Andrew F. "Dick Dowling and the Battle of Sabine Pass." *Civil War History* 4, no. 4 (1958).
New York Times, September 12, 1863.
Norman, Benjamin Moore. *Norman's New Orleans and Environs.* 1845; Baton Rouge: Louisiana State University Press, 1976.
O'Donnell, P.D. "Dick Dowling." *Glimpses of Tuam since the Famine.* Tuam, County Galway, Ireland, 1997.
Official Records of the Union and Confederate Armies in the War of the Rebellion. Series I, vol. 26, part 1.
Official Records of the Union and Confederate Navies in the War of the Rebellion. Series I, vol. 19.
Record Group 109, War Department. Rebel Archives, National Archives, Washington, D.C.
Tolbert, Frank X. *Dick Dowling at Sabine Pass.* New York: McGraw-Hill, 1962.

Mahan and Son: Master Purveyors of U.S. Policy for Over a Century

DESMOND TRAVERS

Irish Americans are usually granted the part of significant fighters in America's nineteenth-century wars, and sometimes commanders allowed to demonstrate real competence, even if rarely achieving distinction. It is less well known, however, that a few played major roles in the development of the country's military strategies and geopolitical doctrine. Almost entirely unknown is that one family, that of Dennis Hart Mahan and his son Alfred Thayer Mahan, played significant roles in both. Recent world reorientations since 1990–1991, and especially since 2001, have drawn sustained attention back to such matters.

The post–Cold War world, rather than bringing about an "end to history," has highlighted threats and concerns that were marginalized during the rivalry of the great power blocs at that time. The September 11 outrage and its aftermath have, if anything, brought not one but several of these threats into the spotlight. These may be combined into two concerns: the rise of global terrorism and the "clash of civilizations" that gave rise to that terrorism. The United States appears to be moving in two seemingly opposite directions in achieving its aims: the need for security hegemonies abroad and greater internal vigilance within its own frontiers. Some commentators have seen the Bush (II) administration's "axis of evil" as a result of this mind-set. The United States has returned to the old verities in coming forward with a new millennium theory of international relations: it is, in essence, a theory of power.

This theory harkens back to the writings of Niccolo Machiavelli, who was one of the first to explore the nature of power.[1] One of the modern advocates of strength, John Mearsheimer, has argued that achieving dominant power is a nation's best means of ensuring its own survival.² Any other approach has been dismissed as utopianism.³

Those writers who have looked back into American history to find power continuities, and perhaps lessons from them, invariably arrive at one starting point: the military philosophy of "the father of American power," Admiral Alfred Thayer Mahan. While Mahan's studies rested largely on the utility and application of maritime power, the effects of its application merit an examination of his thoughts within the present climate. Moreover, the realism and professionalism of his mind-set (although not its naval and global applications) were derived partly from the influence of his father, Dennis Hart Mahan, a long-time instructor at West Point. This chapter shall outline their lives (largely forgotten), and then examine Admiral Mahan's teachings, before looking at what his father had previously taught in military science.

Dennis Hart Mahan and his son, Alfred Thayer, were the son and grandson, respectively, of John and Mary Mahan, a carpenter and his wife, immigrants from County Clare, Ireland. The surname is almost certainly a derivative of the Clare name Mahon or Mac Mahon (from the Gaelic *Maihun*); it is a strong surname there, having its origins in a high king of Ireland of that name dating back to 1119 A.D. This early example of immigration is unusual, and one can only speculate as to its cause, since local records for that period are unhelpful. The Rebellion of 1798 did not unduly affect life in County Clare. There was, however, some unrest as a consequence of the Act of Union in 1800, with many trades and skills being destroyed. It is significant that Clare was always "vexatious," especially when threatened in its agrarian and other livelihoods. Some of the most common illegal agrarian movements of that period, such as the "Terry Alts" and "Lady Clare's Boys," had their origins in this county. (Interestingly, some re-emerged later in the United States.) Also significant is the fact that many men among those arraigned for membership in the United Irishmen in 1799 in North Clare were tradesmen, including carpenters.

John Mahan and his wife set sail for a new life in America in 1800/1801. Immigrant patterns from that time indicate that they would have arrived at Chesapeake Bay (or the Delaware ports). John was a journeyman carpenter, and they moved to New York briefly, where Dennis Hart Mahan was born on April 2, 1802. John later took up employment in the Naval Yard at Norfolk, Virginia, where young Dennis received his early formation. From these modest beginnings developed two intellects of a world-class standard. The Mahans' achievements put them at the forefront of the diaspora Irish in a range of disciplines not then commonly identified with this group. Both father and son likewise became seminal personages in the development of U.S. military thought.⁴

Toward the end of the nineteenth century, the overwhelming justification that imperialists offered for American expansion overseas was the quest for American security. Here the influence of Alfred Thayer Mahan was central. A sailor-scholar, Mahan served his time during the Civil War as an officer of the U.S. Navy. His duties required him to be part of the Union's maritime blockade of the Confederate States. After the war he returned to more academic duties as an instructor in the navy's academy at Annapolis. There he began to study the naval profession. Mahan's fame rested on his thesis that the United States should go beyond having a navy that was largely employed to defend its shores and create an offensive naval force that would extend American influence overseas. He wanted a new American policy ensuring that "no foreign state should acquire a base within three thousand miles of San Francisco."[5]

Mahan's magnum opus was *The Influence of Sea Power upon History, 1660–1783*. In it he argued that Britain's rise during the eighteenth century was due to "her government's use of the tremendous weapon of her sea power," and, as Britain's strength lay almost exclusively in commerce, the country's goals "were secured by [its] powerful navy; and so long as this breastplate was borne, unpierced, over the heart of the great organism, over the British Isles themselves, Great Britain was—not invulnerable—but invincible. She could be hurt indeed, but she could not be slain."[6]

The Influence of Sea Power was read widely abroad. Mahan was feted in England, having honors conferred on him at both Oxford and Cambridge Universities. Kaiser Wilhelm II was an admirer of Mahan and ordered that a copy of his book be placed on board all German ships. Mahan's theories on maritime power are credited with leading to the rise of modern naval power in Japan and France, in addition to inspiring the reinforcement of the naval capacity of traditional maritime powers, especially that of Britain, which saw in his works a timely *raison d'être* for its soon-to-be-rejuvenated naval resources.

Mahan's purpose was also to argue for the improvement of the service to which he was so attached: the U.S. Navy. Although in the early 1880s the country's navy ranked behind that of Argentina and Chile, by 1898, nine years after Mahan's work was published, the United States was the world's strongest sea power after Britain and Germany. By the First World War, it had expanded by a factor of ten, and later, by the Second World War, by a factor of twenty. Admiral Mahan's personal friendship with Theodore Roosevelt shaped the first phases of naval development, and Franklin Roosevelt's service as assistant naval secretary in World War I helped carry the lessons forward.

Mahan was somewhat religious, and certainly an Anglophile, as was common in the United States at that time. (The writings of Josiah Strong, William G. Sumner, and Henry and Brooks Adams were then fashionable, linking the "Manifest Destiny" theories of Mahan's youth with Social Darwinism: the notion of collective competition for group advantage. They taught that the United States was chosen by God or history, or both, for a special destiny and that its capitalism and Anglo-Saxon ethnicity would prevail, as it had done before.) Mahan was often accused of being an imperialist, though he was not at all interested in the acquisition of territories (and certainly not the burdens that such acquisitions would demand). His aim was strategic. In sum, he was eager to get enough bases and coal stations in the Caribbean and the Pacific for the United States to be able to control the Western Hemisphere and to have unimpeded access to Asia.

Mahan is said to be one of only two of the United States' grand strategists on the world stage—a rare distinction, it must be said.[7] He nevertheless suffered from bad press from time to time. Indeed, subsequent editions of the series "Makers of Modern Strategy" seem to have relegated him to a much lower status.[8] Of the various biographies of Mahan, it would seem that almost half have been critical or qualifying in their acknowledgment of his teachings, if not his achievements.[9]

Now, however, Mahan's message has come into vogue again. It is frequently cited, if only to provide historical precedents or used for the purposes of comparison between varying power sources as a determinant of national power or dusted down to add a corpus of arguments in favor of present U.S. foreign policies. His enduring place as a military thinker arises from his profound influence on American policies, and indeed elsewhere at that time, and the effects of those policies. It has been said that if one wishes to discourse on maritime matters, one must invariably return to Mahan.

His second most enduring influence is a less technocratic one: the matter of command in wartime. On this subject, he is at one with Carl von Clausewitz (1780–1831), who remained untranslated before 1873 in English and began to influence American thinking only starting in the 1890s. Even before this time, and moving on from the more mechanistic aspects of sea power, Admiral Mahan had come to realize that in the uncertainties of conflict, command was all, requiring moral as well as intellectual qualities. Like his father, Professor Dennis Hart Mahan, he rejected the notion that the central nature of command in war could be encompassed by a system of rules.[10]

One senses that Mahan would look with approval on the technological vigor of U.S. forces in recent times. He would also, like his father, have had more than a passing interest in the human dimensions of the employment of such resources and how commanders respond to the challenges of the modern battlefield. He may, of course, go out of fashion again, but in one respect Mahan will remain pertinent, and that is in the area of questions he forces us to answer from time to time. Such questions are "the meaning of national interest; the *moral* dimensions of military force; the *responsibilities* [my italics] as well as the opportunities of world power; the use of [force] as an instrument of national policy."[11]

When one considers the duality of U.S. security concerns, it is also necessary to examine the teachings of Professor Dennis Hart Mahan, father of Alfred Thayer Mahan. Dennis Hart Mahan, a professor at West Point from 1831 to 1871, was the leading proponent of his day regarding the theory and practice of war fighting insofar as the fledgling U.S. power was likely to need it. He performed so ably during his first year as a cadet at West Point that he was offered an assistant professorship and remained on the teaching staff until his death in 1871. As a commissioned officer, and suffering from a "pulmonary disease" that was to plague him all of his life, in 1826 he sought a leave of absence in a climate that would alleviate his condition and traveled to Europe. There he acquainted himself with current teaching on the employment of military forces, with special emphasis on engineering and field fortifications. He also acquainted himself with the canal systems of both France and Britain. Repeated applications to extend his stay were no doubt granted, as this most able soldier continued to send important information home. He also attended the premier school of military engineering, the Ecole Polytechnique at Metz, which marked the culmination of his stay in Europe.[12]

Having spent four years in France studying the Jominian theory of the application of military resources, Mahan returned to West Point to take up an assistant professorship of engineering position in 1830. It must be pointed out here that the engineering arm of the army was considered the elite corps and West Point itself was one of the repositories of the profession of engineering in the United States at that time. Such emphasis was no doubt the product of the influences emanating from Europe and from "Jeffersonian technicism." The prevailing belief of most Americans in the early 1800s was that the sole enemy of the United States was Great Britain, and therefore fortifications and the coastal defense arrangement must be the country's primary security concern. On day-to-day matters, the small army of less than twenty thousand soldiers was engaged in maintaining order in the territories, with little time for or interest in professional development. In such circumstances, Mahan came to be the very embodiment of the profession of arms in the United States. He "gained the reputation of being a foremost military thinker of his time, or, indeed of any time."[13]

Professor Mahan wrote extensively on military engineering, field fortifications, civil engineering and industrial drawing. In the case of military subjects, he wrote, first, to inform his cadet charges and the officers of the army and, second, to propagate the message of the importance of a professional army and the need to uphold the source of such professionalism—West Point. The work for which he is most well known, *An Elementary Treatise on Advanced-Guard, Out-Post, and Detachment Service of Troops* (or *Outposts*, as it came to be known), was in every officer's knapsack during the Civil War (purloined copies, it was said, in the case of Confederate officers).

The Civil War was the first "modern war." It involved the movement of large formations over vast distances, with a consequent demand on communications and logistics. Mahan's detractors would argue that his theories, which were seemingly centered on the primacy of defense and on fortifications, were outmoded by this maneuver war.[14] However, the theories that informed his own were those of Baron Henri Jomini (1779–1864), which were, in essence, the systematization of the Napoleonic application of warfare, if using conventional eighteenth-century categorizations. He analyzed offensive as well as defensive operations. Jomini had begun to publish during the time of Napoleon and continued to do so for forty years. With his contemporary Clausewitz's work unavailable to English speakers, no other real analysis of war was extant at that time, and none (so far as this writer is aware) arose as a consequence of the American war. The connection with the ideas of the son, Admiral Alfred Mahan, would prove direct, since the latter (after his Civil War service) applied Jomini's ideas, such as theater dominance and command through clear lines of operations, concentration, and "turning movements," to the high seas. Like Jomini himself, the admiral built up his ideas empirically from the study of warfare—in his case, naval warfare from the 1670s to the 1820s. To be sure, Jomini shrank from a general theory of war (such as Clausewitz's total, and political, war); this scruple moderated the American war and was in accord with the country's culture and Dennis Hart Mahan's outlook. By contrast, Alfred Thayer Mahan would move to more political and world-dominant notions of war, but, as applied at sea, these portended less destruction than his German contemporary Hans Delbruck's land versions.[15]

Dennis Hart Mahan's long tenure at West Point meant that he taught practically every significant higher-level commander on either side of the Civil War, Robert E. Lee excepted. (Lee was superintendent during a period when Mahan was on the faculty.) "Of the sixty important battles of the Civil War, West Point graduates commanded on both sides in fifty-five, and on one side in the other five." In their work on this subject, Colonels Ernest Dupuy and Trevor Dupuy go on to assert that "Dennis Hart Mahan was the War College of the United States and his influence is discernable in each of the great generals of the Civil War." The colonels cite eighteen circumstances in the Civil War in which Mahan's fundamentals of combat would have been applied (or sometimes flaunted) by commanders who were aware of his teachings. Principal among these teachings was Mahan's dictum: "Celerity is the secret of success."[16]

Among these examples of the application of his teachings, three in particular merit reference, for they challenge the idea that Mahan was "fixated" on entrenchment and position warfare. These examples are Thomas "Stonewall" Jackson's Valley campaign of June 1862 against vastly superior forces, which showed that he "had been strongly influenced by Dennis Hart Mahan"; Robert E. Lee's two invasions northward, which were "in line with the elder Mahan's dictum: 'carrying the war into the heart of the assailants country ... is the surest way of making him share his burdens and foiling his plans'"; and George Meade's failure at Gettysburg "to reap the fruits of complete victory by swift unrelenting pursuit" ("A battle gained," wrote Mahan, "is always a fine thing; but ... [if we] simply force him to retreat without further loss than that on the battlefield ... the enemy will soon be able to rally his forces and offer a new battle").[17]

Dennis Hart Mahan's other influence during the Civil War came from making himself available as an adviser to the federal government. He was in regular contact with the secretary of war on such matters as the selection and appointment of officers for senior command. He was also an adviser to Sherman and a confidante of Abraham Lincoln. Lincoln, it is said, refused to accept his services as an officer (Mahan had to relinquish his commission on being awarded a professorship at West Point) on the grounds that he was too valuable to the Union effort to put at risk in combat.[18]

While records are unhelpful regarding Mahan's influence or worth on the latter score, it is significant that at the time of the formal recapture of Fort Sumter—scene of the first Confederate action—the War Department directed him to attend as a representative of the military academy: "This unusual and specific designation, in a way an affront to the Superintendent [of West Point] provides some indication of the stature enjoyed by the little professor.... It was a fitting recognition of the lifetime of service which this intense and dedicated soldier had given his country and students."[19]

The senior Mahan is now virtually forgotten, washed away in the post–Civil War America that had enough of war and the institution that spawned most of its leader protagonists, and also in the internal reshuffles that would marginalize engineering as an integral subject of West Point's curriculum. Aside from short articles and essays, no published biography or assessment of Dennis Hart Mahan's worth exists. As a protégée of Jomini, he stands as one who "never produced a theory of war ... *though he was the first great American military theorist*" (italics mine).[20] Overlooked in this somewhat contradictory and ungracious summation is the fact that Mahan very ably adapted Jomini's ideas to suit American circumstances. Moreover, these ideas gave rise to what may be the first (if not the sole) philosophy of combat based on the necessity of avoiding unnecessary loss of life. Mahan saw the American soldier as an important citizen with a vote who was commanded by a small cadre of professional officers, all of whom could not (and should not) be squandered in frontal assaults similar to the European model. He was singularly unencumbered by theories when the maneuvers that followed from them would not survive against the lethality of emerging U.S. weapons development.

Quite simply, no new theory of war was necessary at that time, and none emerged until his son developed one on an entirely different métier. That said, the senior Mahan's most well-known work, *Outposts*, still ranks as one of the foremost American contributions to the study of war.[21]

Both father and son's careers and worldviews were remarkably similar, and for this reason it is quite impossible, in this writer's estimation, to examine one without examining the other. (They had their differences, too, of course. Dennis Hart Mahan was an ardent Hibernophile, no doubt influenced by his immigrant parents, whereas Alfred would seem to have been more influenced by his Anglophile mother and uncle.)

Both Dennis Hart Mahan and Alfred Thayer Mahan, as young men, were seemingly unfit for their chosen profession (the elder due to ill health, and the younger in his father's estimation). Both moved into the more academic aspects of their careers at an early time. From there both were chosen for their exceptional abilities and encouraged in their teaching posts by seniors who saw their worth, often against opposition. Both, in order to perfect their teaching abilities, continued their studies to a point of exceptional competency and the attainment of national and international acclaim (Dennis Hart Mahan's work was taught in every school of military engineering of worth worldwide). Both were vehement defenders of their chosen arm or service, as well as the academy attached to that arm or service. They were, as a consequence, at times the sole defenders of these institutions against an administration that was traditionally antagonistic to the military. Both had a grand vision of an emerging United States, so much so that the tag "imperialist" has sometimes been applied to them (especially Alfred Thayer Mahan). Significantly, both men in later life moved from their essentially technical discipline to the "philosophic" when they came to appreciate the importance of command in battle.

Examined in this fashion, one can observe an intellectual continuum in which both father and son offer a seamless contribution to American security. (One can only surmise whether Alfred Thayer Mahan could have developed his theories if the events that his father had lived through and helped to shape were otherwise.) This contribution allowed the Mahans to endure as the leading influence of the day for almost a century. Looking further into the twentieth century, one sees that Alfred Mahan's theories on maritime power rather perversely contributed to the arms build-up that was a precursor of the First World War. Dennis Hart Mahan's theories, if applied, would have certainly avoided the stalemate of the Western Front. Indeed, tracts of his work *Outposts* are so logical and ordered that they could well be a tactics manual for a weapon that (in his time) had yet to be developed and that would ultimately end that stalemate when it emerged—the tank! The senior Mahan's writings are such that in reading them today, one is struck by the method used in their drafting. This method seems to have become the "manual of style" for subsequent U.S. Armed Forces operations texts even up to the present time. The Mahans, without doubt, constitute the United States' greatest military family. In view of present circumstances, their combined outputs and efforts deserve to be reviewed.

NOTES

1. Paul Kennedy, "The Modern Machiavelli," *New York Review of Books*, November 7, 2002, 52.
2. John J. Mearsheimer, *The Tragedy of Great Power Politics* (New York: Norton, 2001), xi.
3. Jonathan Haslam, *No Virtue Like Necessity: Realist Thought in International Relations Since Machiavelli* (New Haven, CT: Yale University Press, 2002).
4. M. de Lourdes Fahy, *Education in the Diocese of Kilmacduagh in the Nineteenth Century* (Ennis: Clare County Library, 1972); Andres Eriksson, "Crime and Popular Protest in Clare, 1815–1852," unpublished Ph.D. diss., Trinity College, Dublin, 1991; Tim Kelly, "Ennis in the Nineteenth Century," MA thesis, University College, Galway, 1971; FAS Project, *Crime and Punishment in Clare from the 15th to the 19th Century* (Ennis: Clasp Press, 1995).
5. Warren Zimmerman, *First Great Triumph: How Five Americans Made Their Country a World Power* (New York: Farrar, Straus and Giroux, 2002).
6. Alfred T. Mahan, *The Influence of Sea Power in History* (Boston: Little, Brown, 1918), 527.
7. Edward Mead Earle, ed., *Makers of Modern Strategy: Military Thought from Machiavelli to Hitler* (Princeton, NJ: Princeton University Press, 1971), ix.
8. Peter Paret, ed., *Makers of Modern Strategy: From Machiavelli to the Nuclear Age* (Princeton, NJ: Princeton University Press, 1986).
9. Ibid., 904–5.
10. Jon Tetsuro Sumida, *Inventing Grand Strategy and Teaching Command: The Classic Works of Alfred Thayer Mahan Reconsidered* (Baltimore: Johns Hopkins University Press, 1997), 110.
11. Phillip A. Crowl, "Alfred Thayer Mahan: The Naval Historian," in Paret, *Makers of Modern Strategy*, 477.
12. Thomas Everett Greiss, "Dennis Hart Mahan: West Point Professor and Advocate of Military Professionalism, 1830–1871," unpublished Ph.D. diss., Duke University, 1969, 120.
13. Ibid., 216.
14. Edward Hagerman, "From Jomini to Hart Mahan: The Evolution of Trench Warfare and the American Civil War," *Civil War History* 13 (1967): 197–220.
15. Mark Grimsley, "Modern War/Total War," in *The American Civil War: A Handbook of Literature and Research*, edited by Steven Woodworth (Westport, CT: Greenwood Press, 1996), 379–89; Mark Neeley, Jr., "Was the Civil War a Total War?" in *On the Road to Total War*, edited by Stig Forster and Jorg Nagler (Cambridge: Cambridge University Press, 1997), 29–51.
16. R. Ernest Dupuy and Trevor N. Dupuy, *Military Heritage of America* (New York: McGraw-Hill, 1956), 212, 241.
17. Ibid., 241, 252, 264, 270.
18. Greiss, "Dennis Hart Mahan," 336–38.
19. Ibid., 339.
20. Franklin D. Margiotta, ed., *Brassey's Encyclopedia of Military History and Biography* (Washington, D.C.: Brassey's, 1994), 969.
21. James L. Morrison Jr., *"The Best School in the World": West Point, 1833–1866* (Kent, OH: Kent State University Press, 1986), 49; Edward G. Hagerman, *The American Civil War and the Origins of Modern Warfare: Ideas, Organization, and Field Command* (Bloomington: Indiana University Press, 1988), 3–30.

Bibliography

Dupuy, R. Ernest, and Trevor N. Dupuy. *Military Heritage of America*. New York: McGraw-Hill, 1956.

Earle, Edward M., ed. *Makers of Modern Strategy: Military Thought from Machiavelli to Hitler*. Princeton, NJ: Princeton University Press, 1971.

Eriksson, Andres. "Crime and Popular Protest in Clare, 1815–1852." Unpublished Ph.D. dissertation, Trinity College, Dublin, 1991.

Fahy, M. de Lourdes. *Education in the Diocese of Kilmacduagh in the Nineteenth Century*. Ennis, Clare County Library, 1972.

FAS Project. *Crime and Punishment in Clare from the 15th to the 19th Century*. Ennis: Clasp Press, 1995.

Greiss, Thomas Everett. "Dennis Hart Mahan: West Point Professor and Advocate of Military Professionalism, 1830–1871." Unpublished Ph.D. dissertation, Duke University, 1969.

Grimsley, Mark. "Modern War/Total War." In *The American Civil War: A Handbook of Literature and Research*, edited by Steven Woodworth. Westport, CT: Greenwood Press, 1996.

Hagerman, Edward G. *The American Civil War and the Origins of Modern Warfare: Ideas, Organization and Field Command*. Bloomington: Indiana University Press, 1988.

———. "From Jomini to Hart Mahan: The Evolution of Trench Warfare and the American Civil War." *Civil War History* 13 (1967): 197–220.

Haslam, Jonathan. *No Virtue Like Necessity: Realist Thought in International Relations Since Machiavelli*. New Haven, CT: Yale University Press, 2002.

Kelly, Tim. "Ennis in the Nineteenth Century." MA thesis, University College, Galway, 1971.

Kennedy, Paul. "The Modern Machiavelli." *New York Review of Books*, November 7, 2002.

Mahan, Alfred T. *The Influence of Sea Power in History*. Boston: Little, Brown, 1918.

Margiotta, Franklin D., ed. *Brassey's Encyclopedia of Military History and Biography*. Washington, D.C.: Brassey's, 1994.

Mearsheimer, John J. *The Tragedy of Great Power Politics*. New York: Norton, 2001.

Morrison, James L., Jr. *"The Best School in the World": West Point, 1833–1866*. Kent, OH: Kent State University Press, 1986.

Neeley, Mark, Jr. "Was the Civil War a Total War?" In *On the Road to Total War*, edited by Stig Forster and Jorg Nagler. Cambridge: Cambridge University Press, 1997.

Paret, Peter, ed. *Makers of Modern Strategy: From Machiavelli to the Nuclear Age*. Princeton, NJ: Princeton University Press, 1986.

Sumida, Jon Tetsuro. *Inventing Grand Strategy and Teaching Command: The Classic Works of Alfred Thayer Mahan Reconsidered*. Baltimore: Johns Hopkins University Press, 1997.

Zimmerman, Warren. *First Great Triumph: How Five Americans Made Their Country a World Power*. New York: Farrar, Straus and Giroux, 2002.

Twice in the Gap of Danger

FRANK BOYLE

In the American Civil War of 1861–1865, the U.S. government raised more than two thousand regiments of soldiers to fight the nation's battles and subdue the Confederacy. The infantry or cavalry regiment was the crucial unit of organization, usually made up of about one thousand men when first formed. The regiment was to the army as the family is to the city—that is, the regiment was a kind of cell, a vibrant part of the whole, but self-sufficient. Its casualties, for instance, were intelligible, like a loss in a family, whereas the greater mortuary figures of a city (or of the army at large) leave no personal impression on the mind. The fortunes and duties of the Civil War were distributed somewhat unevenly. Some soldiers served far from the scenes of carnage and never heard a shot fired in anger. Others were constantly in the maelstrom of battle and suffered heavily. But only one regiment was in the gap of danger twice: the 69th Pennsylvania Veteran Volunteer Infantry, formed in 1861 from Philadelphia militia companies, most of them Irish immigrants who had come to the United States as a result of the Irish famine of the 1840s and 1850s.

The founder of Philadelphia, Quaker William Penn, had hoped that his city would be a "Green Countrie Towne" where all men would live as brothers. However, the Irish famine victims found from the start that no one wanted to be brothers with them, or even distant cousins. The sign "No Irish Need Apply" was everywhere in those days, directed at the poor who lived in the dilapidated shacks of Southwark, Kensington, the Devil's Pocket, and Moyamensing. They served as the muscle for their economic betters, hiring out for two or three dollars a week when they could get it.

In 1861, when Lincoln called for 75,000 volunteers to stare down the new Confederacy, the militias of the various states stepped forward in the mounting war hysteria to do their duty. In Philadelphia the Irish militia companies formed the 2nd Regiment of the 2nd Brigade of the 1st Division of the city's military establishment, and Colonel Patrick Conroy, who was universally disliked by the higher command structure, commanded them. So the services of the regiment were refused until a replacement for Conroy was found. This worthy turned out to be one Joshua T. Owen, a lawyer (born in Wales) with some background in politics. So the Philadelphia Irish went off to war under a man they hardly knew. Somewhat later they found themselves with three other regiments in what was unofficially called the "Philadelphia Brigade." In a somewhat roundabout fashion, they had become Philadelphians.

In the Union Army the "compartmentalization" of the Irish continued as it had in civilian life. Anti-Irish feelings were prevalent throughout the Army of the Potomac. In order for the Irish to contribute to the war effort, it was probably better to serve in "Irish" regiments or separate companies in "American" regiments. That "state within a state" arrangement reduced friction on the common soldier level, but it did not preclude difficulties at the command level.[1]

It is most ironic that in two very important battles—those of Glendale, Virginia (June 30, 1862), and Gettysburg (July 2–3, 1863)—the 69th would win immortal fame. In both battles the 69th stood at the spot where the outcome was decided. Twice the regiment faced the peerless Army of Northern Virginia commanded by General Robert E. Lee, and on both occasions the soldiers held their position and beat off the foe. The historian of the South, Douglas Southall Freeman,[2] and the wartime Confederate officer who came forth as the Army of Northern Virginia's soundest analyst, E. Porter Alexander, both agree that Glendale was Lee's best chance for a victory of annihilation over General George McClellan's Army of the Potomac. That was Lee's intention when he sent his troops, previously successful at Gaines's Mill, eastward to attack the retreating federal army.[3] Victory here, on the outskirts of Richmond, would have left the Army of the Potomac divided and without a supply base. In 1862, a collapse of this nature in the eastern theater would have left Washington defenseless and the seaboard cities open to invasion, putting the war into a new phase. Whether the Union would have endured under these circumstances is a very interesting question.

On June 1, 1862, Lee assumed command of his army with a very difficult task before him. McClellan's army was on the outskirts of Richmond, the industrial and political heart of the Confederacy. Should the Unionists occupy the city, the war might be as good as over. In the next thirty days, however, Lee wrought almost a miracle. He managed to fortify Richmond and reorganize his army. Then he began a series of battles that pushed the Union soldiers back twenty miles. It was a bravura performance. But Lee wanted to accomplish even more. He aimed at not only the defeat of the Unionists but also their surrender and capture! That this mammoth feat did not occur was not the fault of Lee. He was ill served by some of his subordinates, and he ran into hard-fighting soldiers in blue uniforms. His grand plan failed, but it was a very close-run event.

Lee began by severing the Union supply line and capturing the supply base at White House at the head of the York River. This forced the Unionists to march to the James River, where the U.S. Navy could supply its ailing comrades. As this march took place, Lee had a great chance to attack this host, and he grasped it at once. In his report of the Seven Days, Lee wrote, "Under ordinary circumstances the Federal Army should have been destroyed." However, due to Confederate mismanagement and much valiant fighting by the Army of the Potomac, this objective was not achieved. It was a near-miss. When thousands of men engage in battle over a wide area, it is folly to say that victory or defeat depended on the actions of any single regiment or battery. Yet, in such situations, often the actions of a few help to turn the tide, even when it seems an overwhelming one.[4]

On June 29, 1862, the Army of the Potomac wound its way through thick woods and desolate swamps on narrow roads, marching for the James River. The Fifth Corps, which had been heavily engaged at Gaines's Mill, led the way, followed by the Fourth Corps amid 2,000 supply wagons and 2,500 head of cattle. The Second, Third and Sixth Corps formed a protective shield for this exodus. If Lee had burst through this thin layer, McClellan would have been in deep trouble. Lee surveyed his map and saw a crossroads hamlet called Glendale, where the blue columns could be attacked with advantage. The ensuing battle has a number of names: Glendale (of course), Frayser's Farm, Nelson's Farm, Charles City Crossroads, and Turkey Bend. The fighting stretched all around these place names. The Confederates brought elements of James Longstreet's and A.P. Hill's divisions against the angle formed by the Long Bridge Road with the Quaker Road. A Confederate breakthrough here would split the Army of the Potomac; its supply element would be compromised, and the ammunition supply placed in great danger.[5]

The Union forces that were to fend off the attack included one very tired and battle-worn division: the Pennsylvania Reserve Corps, which had fought well at Mechanicsville and Gaines's Mill, sustaining heavy losses. Perhaps it was too much to expect that these soldiers could endure a third day of heavy combat. In any case, they were placed in the line at the critical angle of the Long Bridge Road and the Quaker Road. Meade's brigade was north of the Long Bridge Road, Seymour's brigade south of it and Simmons' brigade in reserve, backing the others up.

Not everything turned out as Lee had planned. Some of his columns did not hurry down the wooded roads to the Glendale position, where they were intended to go. Most disappointing to Lee was the lack of initiative of Stonewall Jackson, who failed to pressure the Union rearguard through a strong movement across the White Oak Swamp bridge. The morning hours of June 30 passed, and there were no artillery blasts heralding Confederate attacks on the strung-out federal lines. Finally, only the two divisions led by Longstreet and Hill attacked at the crux of the angle. This effort fell on the Pennsylvania Reserve Corps, which offered only token resistance, and the Confederates made good headway into the Union center.[6]

As the brigades commanded by Wilcox (Alabamians), Jemkins (South Carolinians) and Kemper (Virginians) approached the position held by the Pennsylvanians, the keyed-up southerners raised their fearsome yell and plunged forward. The Unionists were dislodged from a strong point on their left flank, and Brigadier Seymour reported that they put up "weak resistance … and lost us a very strong point." Suddenly his men turned and ran. The Union commander on their left flank, Joseph Hooker, looked to his right and saw "the whole of McCall's division was completely routed and many of the fugitives rushed down the road on which my right was resting … broke through my lines from one end to the other.… Following closely on the footsteps of these demoralized people were the broken masses of the enemy."[7]

According to Hooker, at this time Major General Edwin Sumner of the Second Corps "voluntarily tendered me the services of a regiment that was posted in an open field on my extreme right … the 69th Pennsylvania Volunteers under Colonel Joshua Owen." The Irish from Philadelphia leveled their muskets and exchanged volleys with Kemper's Virginians, stopping them in their tracks. Then the Irish fixed bayonets and charged, with the setting sun glinting off their steel. Joe Hooker had problems as an army commander later on in the war, but no one could ever say that he was not a good judge of fighting men. He rode over to where the 69th had departed from and demanded of Joshua Owen, "Colonel, where is your regiment?" "On that hill," returned Owen, proudly pointing to where his men were drawn up in the form of an arc adorning the crest of the hill. "Nobly done! Well done!" said Hooker as he rode away.[8]

Hooker did not forget these men when he wrote his report of the battle some weeks later:

> After great loss the enemy gave way and were instantly followed with great gallantry by Grover, at the head of the 1st Massachusetts while the 69th Pennsylvania, heroically led by Owen, advanced in the open field on their flank with almost reckless daring. As Colonel Owen has rendered me no report of the operations of his regiment I can only express my high appreciation of his services and my acknowledgment to his chief for having tendered me so gallant a regiment.[9]

The Philadelphia Brigade was commanded by an old regular army officer, Brigadier William Burns (West Point, 1847), who had seen much service and was regarded as an unbending martinet. But he also gave fulsome praise to the 69th in his report:

> Another heavy attack broke McCall's center and sent the fugitives shamefully through our ranks. Our line was advanced and Colonel Owen, 69th Pennsylvania Volunteers, unsupported, pursued the victorious rebels back over the ground through which they were passing and crowned the crest of the hill where McCall had lost his artillery. Gallant 69th! The line followed this noble example and McCall's position was held and the enemy discomfited.[10]

There are several items of note here. First, of course, there are the deeds of the 69th at the point of contact where the deepest penetration of the Union position occurred at the critical moment of the battle. Second, Glendale was the key battle of the East for Lee, as attested by Freeman and Alexander. Never afterward would Lee have such manpower at his disposal on ground of his choosing. If things had gone his way, the Army of the Potomac would have been cut in two with a real ammunition problem and no supply base from which to operate. Third, there is the testimony of Hooker, extolling a regiment that was not under his command. Very few Union (or Confederate) commanders ever spoke well of other troops. Fourth, an old regular, Burns, waxed almost lyrical about a volunteer regiment! Fifth, the 69th met in battle Kemper's brigade of the Army of Northern Virginia. Almost a year to the day later, these two groups would meet again on the hillside just south of Gettysburg.

By the summer of 1863, the 69th had seen the terrible shambles of Antietam, the awful day at Fredericksburg, and the wasted opportunity of Chancellorsville. In 1863 the strength of the regiment had declined to 344. A new commander, Dennis O'Kane, a bearded ex–tavern owner who had been born in County Derry, had succeeded Joshua Owen as colonel. Now, in a warm and humid June, the Army of the Potomac was on the march, heading north out of Virginia into Maryland. After his miracle at Chancellorsville, Lee was about to invade the North for the second time.[11]

On June 28, 1863, the Philadelphia Brigade got a new commander: Brigadier General Alexander S. Webb, a West Point graduate of the class of 1855 and, so far in this war, an artillery staff officer. It is evident from his first actions after taking command that he had been told to "ride" the brigade, which, as a veteran unit on a lengthy campaign, was not as spit and polish as it might have been. Said Webb, "Officers were to wear their insignia of rank" (even if it made them better targets for sharpshooters). There also would be a more stringent policy regarding straggling while on the march, and so on. The grimy soldiers probably wrote Webb off as a bandbox soldier and one more torment in their lives. They had just finished an exhausting march on the preceding day, in which thirty-three miles had been covered in 100-degree, dust-choking heat.[12]

The column moved out of Frederick, Maryland, and sometime later found the Taneytown road. As the soldiers neared Gettysburg, they began to encounter heavily laden ambulances carrying the wounded from the first day's fighting. Terrible combat had taken place north and west of the town, and the First and Eleventh Corps of their army had been shattered. The Second Corps made camp about four miles from the town and settled down for a merciful night's rest. The men were awakened at 3 a.m. for breakfast and roll call; there were only thirteen stragglers in the entire brigade, and the new commander, Webb, gave an inspirational speech about fighting on the soil of their own state. The soldiers then moved off, and at 6:30 in the morning the 69th was posted on the downward slope of a gentle ridge, known locally as Granite Ridge, although most historians have called it Cemetery Ridge. They faced west along a low stone wall directly in front of a grove of trees that came down almost to the wall. The rest of the brigade members, the 71st, 72nd, and 106th, were on the reverse slope of the ridge. Directly in front of the 69th was a country road that ran from their left to their right, the Emmitsburg Road, about 250 feet in front of them. Between the stone wall and the road was pastureland. There were fences along both sides of the road.

The action on July 2 did not start until well into the afternoon, when Lee's right-hand man, James Longstreet, began an offensive with his corps against Union troops that had been placed out in front of the Union main line. These were the men of the Union Third Corps, commanded by a "political" general, Daniel Sickles. After much hard fighting, the soldiers were driven back past the position of the Union Second Corps. From their stone wall, the 69th could see the onslaught coming their way, notably a brigade of Georgia troops led by General A.R. Wright. After driving back two Second Corps regiments (15th Massachusetts and 42nd New York) that had advanced past the Emmitsburg Road, and the Georgians engulfed Brown's Battery, which had been sent out to support the other regiments. Now the Confederates headed for the 69th. The Philadelphia Brigade skirmishers put up a good fight and were finally driven in. Wright's men came on with singular determination, but after a number of volleys they were stopped well short of the stone wall. To their left the Georgians had penetrated Harrow's brigade before being turned back. As the warm darkness of a July twilight spread over the field, Union and Confederate soldiers alike drew long breaths and sank down to the earth, exhausted, glad to have survived.[13]

The dreadful sound of the wounded lying out in front of the men of the 69th was a kind of lullaby they did not need. They had suffered 11 killed and 17 wounded in the firefight with Wright's Georgians, including their second-in-command, Lieutenant Colonel Martin Tschudy, who refused evacuation. A full moon shone down on the medical personnel of both sides as they plied their grisly trade. The light also helped the men of the 69th who went over the stone wall and scoured the field for the rifles of the fallen Georgians.

These were cleaned, loaded, and placed along the wall. The next day, they would prove very useful indeed.[14]

The sun of July 3, 1863, rose on a day that would live forever in American history. On Seminary Ridge the Confederate artillery was lined up, ready to lay down the most stupendous fire the North American continent would ever see or hear. After a night march up from Cashtown, the division of General George Pickett was in place, fresh and unblooded. Lee's attack orders were that after his artillery had neutralized the Union artillery on Cemetery Ridge, Pickett's men, plus a division and a half from A.P. Hill's corps under James Pettigrew, would move out from Seminary Ridge, cross the rolling terrain and destroy the Union infantry. The point of attack for Pickett was the same clump of trees behind the 69th: the Philadelphia Irish were the bull's eye in the target. Two entire divisions, or what was left of them after the Union artillery had carried out its retaliatory fire, would assault the 69th at the center of the Union line.[15]

Colonel Dennis O'Kane had arranged his ten companies along the low stone wall: Company G on the left flank, followed by K, B, and E; Company C was the color company with the two faded and shot-torn banners, then companies H, D, F, A, and I on the right flank. The men tried to get as much shade as they could by the wall. Then, at about one o'clock, a single Confederate gun fired as a signal, and the tempest burst forth.

All the batteries were covered with smoke, through which the flashes were incessant, while the air was filled with shells whose sharp explosions, along with the hurtling of their fragments, formed a running accompaniment to the guns.

In Company I, one Anthony McDermott, usually a company clerk, but on the day of battle an infantryman (by his own choice), crouched as close as he could get to the stones of the wall. Fervently he wished for it to be over, for never had the Confederates mounted so many guns to bear on one position.

> The air is filled with the whirring, shrieking, hissing sound of the solid shot and the bursting shell. All throw themselves flat upon the ground behind the low stonewall; nearly one hundred and fifty guns belch forth messengers of destruction, sometimes in volleys, again in irregular, but continuous sounds, traveling through the air above us or striking the ground in front of us and ricocheting over us.[16]

The enemy fire was particularly noticeable among the Union batteries on the flanks of the 69th, where Brown's Rhode Island Battery B and Alonzo Cushing's 4th U.S. Battery A stood. Guns were dismounted, horses disemboweled, and finally, worst of all, two limber boxes were exploded in Cushing's battery, completely destroying some of the gunners. After a while, Cushing, through great leadership, got his men pulled together and fired back. The commander of the Union Second Corps, Winfield Hancock, had the idea that his infantry would be somewhat reassured if they could see and hear answering artillery from their side. However, artillerymen hated this "firing for effect" because it lowered their ammunition supply. Brown's battery was so badly used up that it had to be replaced. A Sixth Corps battery, Cowan's 1st New York Independent, came through a rain of shot and shell and took a position behind and to the left of the 69th. Just as it arrived, the Confederate fire slackened.[17]

The Union infantrymen knew that their time had come. All along the stone wall men raised their heads from the ground and looked at each other, and then, almost fearfully, gazed across the distance to Seminary Ridge. The first sight of the Confederate infantry was a relief to Anthony McDermott:

> From the dread of being plowed into shreds or torn to fragments by the solid shot and bursting shell that had filled the air just a few moments before. While the enemy was advancing across the plain toward us, Colonel O'Kane, commanding the regiment, ordered the men to reserve their fire until they could distinguish the whites of their eyes; he also reminded the command of their being upon the soil of their own State, concluding his remarks with the words, "And let your work this day be for victory or to the death!"[18]

There is something almost pathetic in O'Kane's words. Considering the low esteem in which many of the men of the 69th had been held by the nativists and the general anti–Irish attitude prevalent in the army, this encouragement certainly carried a bittersweet note. However, the regimental flag had the arms of both Pennsylvania and Ireland emblazoned on it. This day was the time to fight for both sides of the flag. The new brigade commander, Alexander Webb, walked up and down the companies, telling them, "If you do as well today as you did yesterday, I will be satisfied."[19]

The first Confederate infantry troops to come in sight of the 69th were those of Pettigrew's division, a panorama of butternut figures coming out of the trees on Seminary Ridge. It looked as though the trees were becoming men, men who formed block-hard units, took their intervals and moved forward with long, swinging strides. "Here they come! Here comes the infantry!" The mutter ran along the Union line, and the bluecoats stood in wonder at the sight of these men who were coming to kill them, to break the Union and bring a Confederate peace. The line of soldiers covered the entire front of the Second Corps.

To the 69th, it seemed as though the newcomers were walking in the footsteps of Wright's Georgians. At the wall the men were calm, watching with rapt attention. Alonzo Cushing, the battery commander, stood on the right flank of Company I, directing the fire of one of his guns, which had been run down to the wall. He had been hit twice, but he still kept up his directions to the gunners. The skirmishers of the Philadelphia Brigade, under a very hard soldier from the 106th, Captain James Lynch, had gone across the Emmitsburg Road earlier, and now they opened fire on the graybacks, shooting and falling back, trying to take the sting out of the Confederates. Lynch recorded, "I cannot refrain from crediting the skirmish line composed of details from the 69th, 72d, and 106th with holding its ground with a tenacity which caused some onlookers to blame its officers for needlessly sacrificing men's lives." They but carried out the instructions of General Webb to their commander, Capt. James C. Lynch, in contesting every inch of ground and holding on to the Emmitsburg road as long as possible. One of these skirmishers was Lieut. Charles McAnally of Company D of the 69th. When the skirmishers finally made a run for it and joined with their fellows behind the wall, he was met by his good friend, Sgt. James Hand, with a canteen of water. "Why," asked Hand, "did you delay so long out there?." The old 69th, he went on, "was waiting for them." All along the ridge, the Union soldiers thumbed back the hammers of their rifles. The Virginia brigades of James Kemper (old friends of the 69th from Glendale) moved from the left of the position to the right as they came over the Emmitsburg fences and breasted the slope. The 69th fired a solid sheet of flame and reached for the scavenged weapons of yesterday. That would make about 800–900 rounds fired at a range of 50 to 75 yards in less time than it takes to tell about it. Still the Graybacks came on. Lt. McAnally says "hand to hand they charged on us twice and we repulsed them. Grimly the fight went on, the 69th kneeling down to reload, then to spring up and fire into the smoke clouds." The Virginians mirror-imaged the Irish, similarly employed. No one took any backward steps and minutes went by. At least twice the Graybacks fought hand to hand over the wall. Robert Whittick with the color guard in the middle of the regimental line grasped Sgt. Andrew B. Willingham of the 53rd Virginia and pulled him over the wall and subdued him. "Then the Confederates appeared to drift to the right of the 69th and suddenly came over the wall in a howling mob."[20]

There had been four companies of the 71st Pennsylvania on the right flank of the 69th, manfully doing their duty, when an unexpected force from Pettigrew's division appeared on their flank and poured in devastating fire. Many soldiers of the 71st fell, and the rest turned and ran up the slope, leaving a sizeable hole at the angle of the wall. Some of the Confederates came over in small bunches while others stayed on the western side of the wall and fired up the slope, where the reserve regiment of the Philadelphia Brigade stood, outlined against the ridgeline. Up there was Brigadier Webb, struggling to make the 72nd charge down to the wall and fill up the hole. He had quite a tussle with the color bearer and lost out when the latter was hit with a variety of bullets. The 72nd, also known as the Fire Zouaves, stood stubbornly and fired downhill, but they did not move forward to meet the Confederate host and close the gap in the Union line.

Through the smoke billows some of the 69th saw a Confederate officer running along the line of the enemy, gesticulating with his sword. He had seen the open space vacated by the 71st. A torrent of Confederates rose up and, with unearthly yells, followed him. There was a large boulder at the angle of the wall, and they used it as a gangplank to come over the wall. Down in the middle of the 69th, Corporal Joseph McKeever of Company F heard the keening of the rebel yell and turned to look at the breakthrough. Years later, he remembered, "We thought we were all gone."[21]

But O'Kane, Tschudy, and Webb thought differently. Webb had been trying to bring up the 72nd Pennsylvania, but he gave up the task and ran down to the 69th, still engaged grimly at the wall. By dint of much shouting and shoulder grabbing, he managed to get Companies A and I to come away from the wall and face to their right, where the Confederate wave posed a real threat. Anthony McDermott was on the extreme right flank of Company I and remembered falling back "in some kind of order" up the slope. Webb stayed with these tough men as they adjusted to their new target. Company F, the next one in from A, lost its captain, George Thompson, at that very instant and, without a leader to provide direction, stayed at the wall. This opened up a sizeable gap, and a wave of graybacks ran through it and overwhelmed Company F from behind. This fantastic feat brought the Confederates to Company D, known in their militia days as the Montgomery Guards, and captained by the redoubtable Patrick Tinen. Somehow Tinen got his right section turned around to meet the fresh onslaught. A terrible hand-to-hand combat took place, with both sides fighting like souls in torment. Before the gap was sealed, some Confederates penetrated into the clump of trees that Longstreet had selected as the focal point of his assault. The crux of the battle was reached. The 69th was fighting for its life.

A huge corporal in Company D, Hugh Bradley, led his comrades into the breach with clubbed muskets and hoarse shouts. Somehow, they closed off the gap. Then the focus of action shifted to where a single Confederate officer was making his way across the terrible web of fire on foot. He was up the slope a little way from the wall, moving ponderously, for he was not a young man. Suddenly, he was struck down, pressing his hand to his midsection as he fell. Anthony McDermott was not fifteen paces away from him, and, looking to his right, he saw Alexander Webb, who had left the right flank of the 69th to attempt to bring the 72nd down again. Excitedly, McDermott ran to Webb and pointed to the downed Confederate officer, who later proved to be Brigadier General Lewis Armistead. All of a sudden, there appeared to be less firing and noise. Not many Confederates had penetrated past the wall, although some were still engaged in the clump of trees with the 19th Massachusetts and 42nd New York, sent over from Harrow's brigade. The fighting dwindled down all at once, and then it was over.

The 19th Massachusetts men were amazed at the exploits of the 69th Pennsylvania. Their adjutant, Captain William Hill, said:

The fighting, of course, ceased as soon as these men threw down their arms and came in. Then there appeared to be a lull in the battle and our men went down to about the angle where the 69th were, at all events, only, I suppose, to see the 69th.... Here was no fighting at this point after the enemy came in. The few who retired to get back across the field were not followed up and there was no fire, except an occasional shot. There was no organized fire, I mean, the men who went down there immediately after seemed to be prompted more by a sense of curiosity than through any need of their presence there.... The 69th appeared to be fighting on their own hook.[22]

It is strange that even in in the greatest battles, the mechanics of the decisive action may be in the hands of a comparatively small number of soldiers. Here was one undersized regiment, reinforced by two others of like size, disputing the key position with what was left of three brigades. There were, of course, many Irish soldiers in the 19th Massachusetts and the 42nd New York. In his report Colonel Arthur Deveraux of the 19th spoke of "the steady courage of New England and the fiery valor of Ireland" as helping to overthrow the Confederate thrust.

Many Confederate writers and historians have wished to crown Pickett's valiant division with the glory of having broken the Union line beyond repair. Major Charles Payton of the 19th Virginia of Garnett's brigade, in his report written on July 9, while the experience was fresh in his mind, offered the best witness of how the 69th kept the wall:

> His strongest and last line was instantly gained. The Confederate battleflag waved over his defenses, and the fighting over the wall became hand-to-hand, and of the most desperate character; but more than half having already fallen, our line was found too weak to rout the enemy. We hoped for support on our left (which had started simultaneously with ourselves) but hoped in vain. Yet a small remnant remained in desperate struggle.[23]

If anyone can tell a true tale of the events in front of the stone wall, it is Major Payton, for he was there, and it is clear that the Virginians did not drive the 69th from the position that had been entrusted to them. There was tremendous fighting over the wall, attested to by both sides, but a handful of tough Irish from Philadelphia refused to give way even in the face of foemen as valiant as themselves.

The 69th would learn in the days to come that Alexander Webb, although a brave and capable commander, did not really like Irish soldiers. A month after the battle he wrote to Governor Andrew Curtin of Pennsylvania concerning the applications of three men (including Lieutenant Charles McAnally) to be commissioned officers: "I would especially call the attention of your Excellency to the fact it is impossible to govern 'Irish regiments' when their officers do not keep command of them."[24]

The great charge was over. Again, as at Glendale, the 69th Pennsylvania

Volunteers had occupied the gap of danger. Twice they stood steadfast. They had, indeed, fought for both sides of their flag. One of the champions of the 69th was Lieutenant McAnally, of whom Alexander Webb had spoken so harshly in his letter to Governor Curtin. McAnally wrote to the wife of his close friend, Sergeant James Hand, who was killed in the battle. He summed up the spirit of the regiment in one sentence: "We were determined that as long as a man lived he would stand to be killed, too, rather than have it said that we left on the battlefield in Pennsylvania the laurels that we so dearly won in Strange States."[25]

McAnally would later receive the Medal of Honor for capturing a Confederate flag at the battle of Spotsylvania in May 1864. In the spring of that year, the 69th reenlisted and served until the end of the war—the only regiment of the Philadelphia Brigade to do so. Then the men in shabby blue uniforms went back to Moyamensing, Kensington, Southwark, and the Devil's Pocket to eke out the hard existence common to the nineteenth-century poor.[26] The nativist society took no notice of them and did not celebrate their achievements. However, in their hearts and in the hearts of their descendants, the memory would remain forever green. An obelisk stands at the stone wall at Gettysburg with the Harp of Ireland on it, and ten stone company markers are connected by an unbroken chain, emblematic of the unbroken determination of the Philadelphia Irish.[27] Gallant Sixty-ninth!

Notes

1. Michael H. Kane, "The Irish Lineage of the 69th Pennsylvania Volunteers," *Irish Sword: Journal of Military History Society of Ireland* 18, no. 72 (Winter 1991): 184–98.
2. Douglas S. Freeman, *Robert E. Lee: A Biography*, 4 vols. (New York: C. Scribner's Sons, 1934), 2:179ff.
3. E. Porter Alexander, *Fighting for the Confederacy* (Chapel Hill: University of North Carolina Press, 1989), 110.
4. Ibid., 106.
5. National Archives, *Official Records of the War of the Rebellion*, series 1, vol. 11, part 2, p. 390.
6. Ibid., 402.
7. Ibid., 111.
8. *Philadelphia Public Ledger*, July 8, 1862.
9. *Official Records*, series 1, vol. 11, part 2, p. 111.
10. Ibid., 92.
11. Joseph Ward, *History of the 106th Pennsylvania Volunteers* (Philadelphia: Faries & Rodgers, 1883), 178–79.
12. Henry T. Hunt, "The Third Day at Gettysburg," *Battles and Leaders of the Civil War*, 3 vols. (New York: Century Company, 1894), 3:372–73.
13. A.W. McDermott, *A Brief History of the 69th Regiment, Pennsylvania Veteran Volunteers* (Philadelphia: D.J. Gallagher, 1889), 30–31.
14. Ibid., 31.
15. Supreme Court of Pennsylvania, May Term 1891, #20, Middle District Appeal of the Gettysburg Battlefield Memorial Association, from the Decree of the Court of Common Pleas of Adams County (hereafter cited as "*Trial*"), testimony of Joseph McKeever, 256–71.
16. McDermott, *A Brief History of the 69th*, 29–30.

17. *Trial*, testimony of Robert Whittick, 81.
18. *Trial*, testimony of Anthony W. McDermott, 222.
19. *Ibid.*, 231.
20. *Pennsylvania at Gettysburg*, Vol. 1 (Harrisburg: Pennsylvania Stationary Office, 1904), Dedication of 106th Pennsylvania Monument, 553.
21. National Archives, Washington, D.C., Pension File of Sergeant James Hand, *Letter of Lt. Charles McAnally to Mrs. Jane Hand*, July 5, 1863.
22. *Trial*, testimony of William Hill, 19th Massachusetts, 210.
23. National Archives, *Official Records*, series 1, vol. 27, part 2, pp. 385–87. "Brigadier General Alexander S. Webb to Governor Andrew Curtin," August 11, 1863, Alexander S. Webb Papers, 69th Pennsylvania File, Pennsylvania Archives, Harrisburg, Pennsylvania.
24. *Official Records*, series 1, vol. 27, part 2, p. 348.
25. "General Alexander S. Webb to his father," July 17, 1863, Webb Collection, Yale University Library, New Haven, Connecticut; National Archives, Pension File of Sergeant James Hand.
26. "General Alexander S. Webb to his father," July 17, 1863, Webb Collection, Yale University Library, New Haven, Connecticut.
27. National Archives, Pension File of Sergeant James Hand.

BIBLIOGRAPHY

Alexander, E. Porter. *Fighting for the Confederacy*. Chapel Hill: University of North Carolina Press, 1989.
Alexander S. Webb Papers, 69th Pennsylvania File, Pennsylvania Archives, Harrisburg, Pennsylvania.
Freeman, Douglas S. *Robert E. Lee: A Biography*. 4 vols. New York: C. Scribner's Sons, 1934.
Hunt, Henry T. "The Third Day at Gettysburg." *Battles and Leaders of the Civil War*. 3 vols. New York: Century Company, 1894.
Kane, Michael H. "The Irish Lineage of the 69th Pennsylvania Volunteers." *Irish Sword: Journal of Military History Society of Ireland* 18, no. 72 (Winter 1991): 184–98.
McDermott, A.W. *A Brief History of the 69th Regiment, Pennsylvania Veteran Volunteers*. Philadelphia: D.J. Gallagher, 1889.
National Archives. Civil War pension files. Washington, D.C., 1863.
_____. *Official Records of the War of the Rebellion*. Series 1, vol. 11, part 2; vol. 27, part 2.
Pennsylvania at Gettysburg. Vol. 1. Harrisburg: Pennsylvania Stationary Office, 1904.
Supreme Court of Pennsylvania. May Term 1891, #20: Middle District Appeal of the Gettysburg Battlefield Memorial Association. From the Decree of the Court of Common Pleas of Adams County, 1891.
Ward, Joseph. *History of the 106th Pennsylvania Volunteers*. Philadelphia: Faries & Rodgers, 1883.
Webb Collection, Yale University Library, New Haven, Connecticut.

The American Civil War, the Fenians and Ireland

OWEN MCGEE

While few terms have become better known in modern Irish history than "Fenian," in actual fact there have never been any Fenians in Ireland at all: the Fenian Brotherhood was an Irish American body that attracted international attention during the American Civil War by protesting against Britain's policy toward America and against its government of Ireland.[1] As a result, the terms "Fenian" (an Anglicized form of the ancient Irish term "Fianna") and "Fenianism" became synonymous with Irish opposition to British rule in the contemporary British political imagination. In turn, these terms became popularized in Ireland as well. Nevertheless, their usage was rather misleading, as the secret nationalist-revolutionary movement formed in Ireland during 1858 was only ever known as "the IRB"—an acronym that sometimes denoted "the Irish Revolutionary Brotherhood" but generally meant "the Irish Republican Brotherhood."

The origins of both the IRB and the Fenian Brotherhood were rooted partly in the Irish experience of the Europe-wide "February revolutions" of 1848. However, for various reasons (not least of which was geography), each developed a decidedly different character. Nominally, the Fenian Brotherhood was established in New York during 1859 solely to provide financial, and potentially even material, assistance to the IRB in Ireland, which had already been established in Dublin partly at the behest of the same post–1848 Irish political exiles in America who later formed the Fenian Brotherhood.[2] The history of the Fenian Brotherhood itself, however, came to be shaped by circumstances peculiar to America. For about a decade prior to its establishment, recent political exiles from Ireland had taken the lead in establishing semi-official, state militia forces among the Irish population in America with essentially three objects in view: (i) to overcome American "nativist" prejudice against the poor, mostly Catholic, recent famine immigrants from Ireland, (ii) to demonstrate the political devotion of all the Irish in America to their new homeland, and (iii) to acquire greater influence for themselves in American politics. The existence of these militia forces was generally frowned upon by the British consulates in the United States, because their leaders were often ex-rebels of 1848 who were fond of issuing anti–British propaganda.[3] Indeed, by the mid–1850s, the British consulates were already employing intelligence services to supervise their activities and, in some instances, even persuaded state courts (such as that in Ohio) to instigate legal proceedings against them for supposedly violating American neutrality laws.[4]

The situation changed significantly, however, with the outbreak of the American Civil War in April 1861. American politicians now began patronizing the volunteer movements to assist the Union's war effort. This gave the leaders of these units greater standing in American politics and helped to turn the Fenian Brotherhood into a vehicle for expressing American patriotism among the Irish American community rather than being merely a support organization for the IRB, which its founder and official leader, John O'Mahony, had originally intended. O'Mahony himself would join a Union brigade during the Civil War (thereby nominally acquiring the title of an army officer), but he took little or no direct part in the war effort and remained focused primarily on his goals as an Irish revolutionary.[5]

During the 1860s, aside from the question of planning for an Irish revolution, the Fenian Brotherhood set a pioneering and fairly practicable example by offering Irish American financial (or propagandist) support for political endeavors in Ireland. This chapter will assess separately the dual impact that American Fenians had on nineteenth-century Irish politics, focusing first on the Fenians' revolutionary planning before tackling the broader question of establishing trans-Atlantic Irish political communications.

A Soldier's Business: The Fenian Brotherhood, the IRB and Revolutionary Planning

Although the Fenians and the IRB were supposed to be closely linked, the political world of the IRB—shaped by a mid–Victorian environment of trade unions and reading rooms as well as political, literary and sporting clubs in the small cities and provincial towns of Ireland (all under the watchful eye of a military-police force and an essentially *ancien regime* administration at Dublin Castle)—was far distant from the freedom of life on the streets of New York, Philadelphia, or Chicago. Consequently, it would be very misleading to portray the IRB and the Fenian Brotherhood as one and the same movements.

The ambition of the founder of the IRB, James Stephens, was to create a secret revolutionary organization "with a discipline never before equaled by men not trained in open war" that would begin purchasing (with Irish American financial support) large quantities of firearms if an opportune moment for rebellion arose. In the meantime, the main priority was establishing powerful underground political networks in Ireland.[6] For most men who joined the IRB in its early years, the possibility of receiving financial support from America was evidently a source of great excitement. Between 1859 and 1864, IRB leaders such as Stephens, T.C. Luby, C.J. Kickham or John O'Leary went to the United States once or twice a year looking for this support, often at the behest of an impatient IRB "rank and file." By 1862, however, many IRB men (including Stephens himself) became disgruntled by the fact that the American support thus promised was not forthcoming. This situation occurred because of the unusual position in which John O'Mahony found himself after the American Civil War broke out in 1861.

Determined to keep the revolutionary plan of assisting the IRB alive, O'Mahony tried to maintain complete control over the resources and organization of the Fenians. This goal ultimately proved impossible to achieve once the movement grew and developed a different political focus. These problems were not understood by the IRB. Consequently, O'Mahony naturally became angry at Stephens' regular complaints about the Fenian movement's failure to provide material assistance to the IRB on demand. During 1863, against Stephens' wishes, O'Mahony decided it was necessary to keep the Fenian movement public and under the protection of American state law to prevent "the ultramontane plotters against human freedom" from having any opportunity to criticize them.[7] Furthermore, that November, partly to forestall a split in the Fenian movement (and partly to prevent the American Catholic hierarchy from extending against the Fenians the example of the Irish hierarchy's denunciation of the IRB), O'Mahony also felt it necessary to declare publicly that the Fenian movement was completely separate from any organization in Ireland. Meanwhile, a new secret constitution for the Fenian Brotherhood was introduced, which greatly concerned Stephens, as its tone suggested that henceforth the Fenians could theoretically claim the power to direct the IRB rather than the other way around.[8]

By this time, Stephens himself was facing "trouble in the ranks" because many IRB members disapproved of his decision to launch the *Irish People* (Dublin) to counter the influence of a seemingly reactionary press in Ireland. Furthermore, several figures, essentially following their own initiative, began recruiting Irish soldiers from the British army into the IRB due to their impatience to put the organization on some kind of military footing; the most successful of these agents was John Devoy, formerly a French soldier.[9] It seems clear, however, that Devoy and other IRB men, while making estimates of their following at this time, simply guessed at how much public support they could potentially receive from the public in the event of a rebellion; they did not compile actual statistics of the organization's sworn membership.[10] This determination to ascertain as quickly as possible all potential sources of support reflected the inexperience of the men involved, who failed to understand how time-consuming careful revolutionary planning needed to be.[11] Another illustration of this weakness of the IRB (albeit a far more excusable one) was its leaders' failure to understand the situation in America.

During their American visits of 1863–1864, at the request of the Fenians, IRB leaders such as Luby and Stephens performed "inspection tours" of Union troops under the command of Fenian officers. These demonstrations initially impressed the IRB leaders considerably, causing Stephens, for instance, to consider momentarily the possibility of a Fenian invasion of Ireland instead of simply building up the resources of the IRB. It took time before Stephens and Luby realized (to their great disappointment) that the vast majority of these Union troops were *not* members of the Fenian Brotherhood at all: only the officers were! Indeed, the membership of the Fenian Brotherhood across the entire United States may have been no more than 10,000 men,[12] and only those commanding officers who, like O'Mahony or indeed Stephens, had also been republican political exiles from Ireland during the late 1840s tended to share the revolutionaries' political preoccupations. The vast majority of the Fenians were simply soldiers who, quite naturally, had little interest in anything other than the American war they were fighting.

Between 1859 and 1863, the financial assistance of the Fenians to the IRB never exceeded £200 a year—only half the annual salary of the average Irish bank manager at that time, and even less than the amount a single priest managed to collect in Irish America within a few months during 1862 for poor relief in Ireland.[13] This reflected how little the Fenians and IRB were actually working together at this time. Wartime restrictions on American transportation probably contributed to this development as well. While the Fenians were able to send a few envoys to Ireland to assist the IRB prior to the outbreak of the Civil War, few or none were sent after the war broke out (although some accompanied the body of T.B. McManus back to Ireland for a major political funeral in November 1861).[14] Indeed, it seems that very few "returned Americans" of any kind arrived in Ireland at this time, with the notable exception of J.F.X. O'Brien, a former Young Irelander (and nominal member of the Fenians in New Orleans) who had served briefly as a medical assistant for a Confederate army unit up until the summer of 1862, before the collapse of his business prompted him to move to Cork, where he became a tea merchant and joined the IRB.[15] O'Brien also became a contributor to the *Irish People*, but the fact that most businesses in Ireland were unwilling to risk placing advertisements in the columns of this seditious journal meant that the paper failed to generate revenue for the IRB. As a result, although the IRB had succeeded in establishing some support networks across Ireland, and even among the Irish in Britain (a significant indication of how closely intertwined the lives of workers on both sides of the Irish Sea were at this time), as an organization it essentially remained in a stillborn condition, having yet to find means of consolidating its resources.

Stephens succeeded in collecting £1,700 for the IRB during his 1864 American tour, and he also assisted O'Mahony in establishing a more efficient system for managing the American movement. But it was not until early 1865, when it was clear that the American Civil War was coming to an end, that the prospect of extensive Fenian assistance to the IRB really arose.[16] Unfortunately, internal divisions within the American organization (combined with the fact that it had been heavily infiltrated by British Intelligence) had already effectively ensured that the chances of any successful trans-Atlantic revolutionary enterprise being launched were very low, if not nonexistent.

Although Dublin Castle began improving its policing services in Ireland during 1864, up until the arrival of some Fenians from America in early 1865 it had not paid much attention to, or even noticed the existence of, the IRB (although one informer was employed within the *Irish People* offices) due to a clear lack of any real security threat.[17] James Stephens and many IRB men felt that the Irish public was not yet sufficiently in favor of Irish nationalism to make the idea of an insurrection opportune, and indeed very few nationalists in Ireland at this time would have disagreed with this assumption. The Fenians' envoys from America evidently felt differently, however. Their arrival prompted Dublin Castle to suppress the *Irish People* and arrest its editors in September 1865, seizing much of the IRB's capital (possibly as much as £7,000) in the process.[18] Around the same time, the British consulates in America politically engineered the seizure of a large amount of Fenian funds (nominally meant for the IRB) from a New York bank.[19] Reputedly, the Fenians collected somewhere in the range of £30,000 for the IRB and actually sent this money to Ireland between 1865 and 1867,[20] although this seems very unlikely if one considers that, in total, the IRB was able to purchase only a few hundred firearms at this time (during the period 1869–1870, it fared much better in purchasing firearms despite the fact that it was then receiving no American financial support whatsoever).[21] Indeed, it seems self-evident that the IRB remained relatively starved of resources during the mid-1860s.

In September 1865, to coincide with Dublin Castle's movement against the *Irish People*, British Intelligence agents in America (most notably James McDermott, who had recently left Archbishop Cullen's Clonliffe College in Dublin[22]) worked to ensure that the Fenian movement would implode. Indeed, the Fenians split that October, causing O'Mahony to be deposed and a new Fenian Brotherhood (governed by a "senate") to be established. The

Fenian senate immediately ordered that all resources should be deployed *not* to Ireland, which O'Mahony had been calling for, but instead into organizing raids into Canada, which were led partly by some ex–American army officers (such as John O'Neill and Thomas W. Sweeny) and partly by British Intelligence agents, who were effectively acting as *agents provocateurs* (hoping to waste the Fenians' resources).[23] Meanwhile, the rump "O'Mahony wing" of the Fenians found a few men of sterling character (most notably Ricard O'Sullivan Burke and William Halpin) who were willing to go to Ireland to assist the IRB members to arm and drill themselves between 1865 and 1867, but others who offered their services and came to Ireland at this time, including F.F. Millen, J.J. Corydon, D.J. Buckley, Godfrey Massey and Rudolph Fitzpatrick, were simply adventurers who either were already in or soon entered the pay of British Intelligence.[24] Their arrival led to the arrest of many more IRB leaders, the suspension of habeas corpus in February 1866 and ultimately (after the Americans claimed a right to depose Stephens) a completely abortive, one-day attempt (March 6, 1867) at insurrection among many unarmed IRB followers in Dublin and Cork, leading to several more arrests. Corydon and Massey and others had told in advance all the plans for the rising to Dublin Castle.[25]

For many IRB leaders, and for the few Fenian soldiers who genuinely risked their lives in coming to Ireland, their arrest during the mid–1860s and lengthy imprisonment were seismic events in their lives that naturally figured prominently in their later recollections. Many of these recollections were also inclined to celebrate the one seeming success the rebels could claim during 1867—namely, the rescue of a leader from a prison van in Manchester that September (although this action soon led to three men involved being caught and executed on dubious evidence, the so-called "Manchester martyrs"). Such books of recollections were memoirs rather than histories, however, and the actual significance in Irish history of the 1867 "rising" was minimal.

The only real significance of the events of 1867 was that they occurred as a result of a three-year concerted effort by Dublin Castle to suppress the IRB, beginning in late 1865. Owing to the social tensions caused by the suspension of habeas corpus for much of 1866–1868, this campaign affected many Irish people adversely to some degree—a development that, in turn, ensured that the British government would need to introduce pacifying reforms after its security forces in Ireland had finished their manhunt for the revolutionaries.[26] Regardless of the number of arrests, however, it seems clear that Dublin Castle's efforts to suppress the IRB were far from successful: after 1869, the revolutionary group not only developed a more systematic means of propagating its organization and political beliefs but also managed to retain a very large membership, acquire more arms and make its presence felt to a greater degree at a popular political level.[27]

The principal significance of the Fenian movement of the 1860s clearly did not lie in John O'Mahony's dream of an Irish revolution, but instead in the Fenians' role in creating a new Irish American pressure group in U.S. politics at a time of Anglo-American tensions. This was evident in the thousands of Irish Americans who became involved in the Fenian movement without having any communications with the IRB or nationalists in Ireland, as well as the role that this Fenian impetus in American politics played in creating (by the early 1870s) some of the first post-famine Irish American congressmen of note, including men such as P.A. Collins, William Roberts and John F. Finerty, all of whom became well known through making the tensions in Anglo-American relations their principal political platform.[28]

The revolutionary dimension to the history of the Fenian Brotherhood was never very significant, and, indeed, the Fenian movement is really an aspect of American (or "Irish American") history rather than Irish history. A parallel of sorts could be said to exist between the role of the Fenians in Irish American history and the role of the IRB in Irish history, however, in that both movements became significant instruments of popular political mobilization in their respective countries. Furthermore, owing to developments in transportation and communications technology, the frequent movement of print material, money and men (though not of arms or soldiers) between Ireland and America became not only much more possible at this time but also far more natural. Indeed, the main impact that the Irish American "Fenian" world had on nineteenth-century Irish life essentially lay in its willingness to offer financial assistance to political movements in Ireland and, last but not necessarily least, in the influence of its press.

A Writer's Business: Fenian Propaganda and Irish Political Debate

The nineteenth century might well be described as a great age of journalists who believed they could create revolutions. For example, the European "revolutions" of 1848 were forecasted, imagined, partly enacted and then given postmortems by idealistic middle-class journalists (most notoriously Karl Marx) who—being exponents of political change and custodians of what they believed to be powerful and irresistible ideas—imagined themselves exaggeratedly to be instruments of revolution or soothsayers of "history." Relatively little political change was actually brought about in 1848, however, and what these revolutions really reflected, both culturally and politically, was the great detestation that many forward-looking (yet powerless and perhaps slightly naive) contemporaries felt for the whole *ancien regime* world of

Europe (a concept that some revolutionaries applied to church as well as state).[29]

Thanks to Dublin Castle, most of Ireland's "revolutionary journalists" in 1848 were banished to the United States, and, notwithstanding Americans' relative lack of interest in the European revolutions, it was as heroes of 1848 (not Irishmen) that T.B. McManus, Thomas Frances Meagher and John Mitchel were first celebrated by politically influential "nativist" Americans.[30] Soon, the predominant feature of the journalism of the Irish political exiles in America was a need to define a potential role for themselves, and all other Irish exiles, as American citizens. However, many continued to write on Irish affairs as well. Indeed, some American publications at this time exercised a fairly significant influence on opinion in Ireland itself, most notably John Mitchel's *Jail Journal* (1855)—a famous book that was published in conjunction with a much lesser-known, yet pioneering, history of Irish nationalism since the 1790s, written by John Savage.[31] Meanwhile, New York newspapers were imported into Ireland fairly frequently, such as Mitchel and Savage's *Irish Citizen* (1854–1856) and later John O'Mahony's *Phoenix* (1860–1865) and *Irish People* (1866–1872). Still later, Mitchel's revived *Irish Citizen* (1871–1873), Patrick Ford's *Irish World* (1873–1881) and John Devoy's *Irish Nation* (1881–1885) were imported. Owing to their rebellious tone, however, Dublin Castle greatly limited the circulation of these papers by seizing copies of them at Irish ports.[32]

Unlike Patrick Ford, writers like Mitchel, O'Mahony and Devoy not only could see Ireland within a broad international context but also knew little of life within Ireland themselves. Indeed, they continued to read (and reprint sections of) imported editions of Dublin and London newspapers. Some contemporary Irish writers who disliked American Fenian journalism dismissed it as rooted simply in emotional hatreds stemming from their experience of the famine,[33] but this was a simplification: much of Fenian journalism was characterized not by emotion but by reasoned argument, attempting to apply modern democratic (often American) notions of political liberty to assessments of Irish circumstances. Naturally, such writers were aware that the political and social freedoms enjoyed in America contrasted greatly with the reality of life in Ireland: a country ruled by a mostly alien aristocracy and standing army supported by a completely unaccountable administration at Dublin Castle. Where their understanding of the political situation in Ireland generally fell short was in their misconceptions about what it was possible to achieve or, indeed, how much public support one might win in Ireland: men of the "new world" very often had little patience with the slowness and conservatism of life in the "old world," including "Old Ireland" itself (as Ireland was invariably referred to by Irish Americans).[34]

As a result of these misunderstandings, many Irish American journalists developed an exaggerated belief in their own capacity to act as effective judges of all political developments within Ireland, even to the point of proposing initiatives to Irish politicians. Not surprisingly, this interference was never really appreciated within Ireland. For example, John Martin was frequently perplexed that Mitchel (his brother-in-law) wrote weekly columns in the *Irish Citizen* claiming that, from New York, he understood the political situation in Ireland better than Irish politicians in Dublin, while John Dillon, MP, would later write to Devoy, noting that—much though he admired Devoy's writings on Irish affairs in the *Irish Nation*—"it is utterly absurd for a man who has not been in Ireland for years to be so positive and final in his views as you are" in passing judgments upon the realities of Irish politics.[35] In later years, even Michael Davitt—who liked America and became a very popular figure within Irish America (he married an Irish American and dedicated his memoirs to the "Celtic peasantry" in America)[36]—sometimes lost his patience with Irish Americans' claims of understanding the political situation in Ireland, once complaining to a Chicago audience that it might seem "very easy to establish an Irish Republic three thousand miles away from Ireland," but "I assure you it is no easy task to do it in Old Ireland."[37]

Perhaps the most famous Fenian input into nineteenth-century Irish life was its role in reviving interest in revolutionary circles regarding the notion of establishing an Irish Republic. How far this idea permeated IRB opinion due to an American or European (principally French) or simply Irish influence is difficult to ascertain. However, this very question of republicanism does raise some illuminating paradoxes within the history of both Irish and Irish American nationalism at this time. For instance, Thomas Meagher (the creator of the Irish republican tricolor) and John Mitchel first managed to endear themselves to the American political community partly by calling for the destruction of the temporal rule of the pope in the name of international republican and "human" liberty. This "1848" viewpoint, which they continued to hold as members of the Fenian Brotherhood, was shared by John O'Mahony as well as (at least reputedly) James Stephens.[38] However, general Catholic opinion, whether in Ireland or America, was never likely to espouse or even tolerate such an idea. Indeed, the professed republicanism of many Irish Americans may have been rooted not so much in ideological considerations as in tactical political considerations. For example, John Savage, an exiled Dublin rebel of 1848 who served in Meagher's Irish Brigade and later became president of the "official wing" of the Fenian Brotherhood (1867–1871), was commissioned to write political literature for the U.S. Republican Party before and after the Civil War.[39] In the late 1860s, he also persuaded President Ulysses Grant to issue appeals for leniency toward all Irish American prisoners then in English jails (a fact that probably forced the British government to offer early release, albeit on the condition of expulsion from

Ireland, to those IRB leaders who had been convicted alongside the Fenians).[40] Reputedly, however, the main political motivation of Savage in endearing himself to the U.S. Republicans ever since the late 1850s was creating sufficient leverage to allow American Catholics to champion their desire for schools independent of state control without being subject to intense Republican Party criticism.[41] Meanwhile, although some of Savage's Fenian propaganda was reprinted fairly regularly in the *Irishman* (Dublin) up until 1871,[42] the example of the dwindling and failure of John O'Mahony's *Irish People* at this time certainly illustrated how little Catholic opinion in either Ireland or America was inclined to tolerate men who dared to preach republican political beliefs.

Roughly during the period 1869–1871, the British Home Office thought that the rise of republican enthusiasms in France would give a major boost to the IRB in Ireland, noting how Irish revolutionary circles had always exhibited "an anxiety to see France a republic" owing to their belief that "it would be impossible to inaugurate a republic in Ireland without a sister republic in France, or some other country near." Indeed, during the republican upheavals in France in the winter of 1870, the Home Office believed that "if France remains a republic after the war, it must exert an influence favorable to Irish Fenianism."[43] O'Mahony defended the cause of French republicanism in the *Irish People* during 1870–1871, even to the point of celebrating the excesses of the Paris Commune, which (eager to emulate the example of 1789–1793) had begun committing acts of violence against Catholic clergymen[44]; however, this created very strong public aversion when O'Mahony's journalism was read in Ireland. While writing for the IRB's journal during the mid–1860s, J.F.X. O'Brien (who was amnestied from prison in March 1869) had often criticized Catholic clergymen for taking too prominent a role in Irish politics, arguing (in line with the general IRB view) that it would be detrimental both for religion and for Irish politics if Catholic bishops and priests were not permanently excluded from political activity.[45] During the time of the Paris Commune, however, O'Brien (now officially the IRB leader in Cork and Munster) publicly disavowed any expression of Irish sympathy for its example. Indeed, after an ensuing controversy in Cork City (arising from clerical condemnations of a supposed republican infestation in the town),[46] he resigned completely from the IRB, even though he remained a friend of its nominal leader, C.J. Kickham.[47] Around the same time, the Dublin *Irishman*—which was often suspected by contemporaries of being an IRB journal (it never actually was)[48] because it republished Savage's Fenian propaganda—also responded to the Paris Commune controversy by emphatically denouncing "red republicanism."[49]

A major factor in the great decline of the Fenian Brotherhood after 1869, apart from internal splits and the waste of resources caused by the Canadian raids, was that the papacy modified its position in January 1870 to include an unequivocal condemnation of "the American or Irish society called Fenians," which was placed alongside "those sects called Freemasons, Carbonari, or any other kinds of sects which either openly or privately plot against the Church or legitimately constituted authorities."[50] The papal condemnation does not seem to have greatly affected the membership of the IRB in Ireland, which remained at roughly 40,000 men from 1868 to 1875.[51] However, it practically ensured that the senate wing of the Fenian Brotherhood would decide to disband during 1870, while the "official wing" also lost many members. For one reason or another, Savage resigned as leader in early 1871, despite the fact that this condemnation was requested by the Catholic hierarchy in Ireland rather than in America.[52]

Meanwhile, even if the IRB was willing to ignore church condemnations, its leaders were clever enough not to ignore the fact that, rightly or wrongly, the very phrases "republic" or "republicanism" had connotations to contemporaries throughout Europe (including Ireland) not only of sympathies for the entire intellectual freemasonry behind (and the terrific legacy of) the French Revolution but also of a ferocious anti–Catholicism that was almost Cromwellian in its intensity. Obviously, this was something that no Irish nationalist rebel with any intention of winning widespread and cross-denominational popular support within Ireland could ever be seen to espouse. For example, although never an outright republican (he believed there was little real difference between a republic and a liberal constitutional monarchy),[53] John O'Leary, an anticlerical IRB leader who was released from prison in 1871 on pain of expulsion from Ireland, was clearly aware of this reality.[54] Similarly, the absence of the "R word" in much of the IRB's nationalist propaganda issued to the Irish public was evidently intentional, as was perhaps best evidenced by the final contribution that IRB veterans of the 1860s made to nineteenth-century Irish life: namely, the IRB's role (with some Irish American support) in launching a 1798 Centenary Committee. At a time when the French Republic was closing many Catholic schools (it would soon expel the Jesuits from France as well), the IRB celebrated the example of Wolfe Tone, stressed the necessity of an Irish patriotism that could "embrace the three great sects" if Ireland was ever to be a nation, claiming that past "denunciations of 'French principles,' of 'revolution' and of 'secret societies'" had prevented this from happening,[55] but it refrained from using the contentious words "republic" or "republicanism," to which many Irish Catholics took such grave offense.[56] Indeed, it seems highly unlikely that the very self-consciously Catholic Irish patriots of the subsequent generation (most notably Eamon de Valera) would ever have decided to express their separatist resolve to the international community by championing the idea of an "Irish Republic" (something that relatively few of the 1916 rebels supported)[57] were it not for the tactical need of Ireland (along with all other small countries) to win the support of the American Republic during the inevitable restructuring of Europe that would follow the end of the First World War.

Apart from causing many defections, the papal condemnation prompted the official wing of the Fenian Brotherhood to become a mostly secret organization after 1871, and it continued to exist in this form for at least a decade afterward under the successive leaderships of John O'Mahony (1871–1873, 1876), T.C. Luby (1874–1875), James Stephens (1880) and finally Jeremiah O'Donovan Rossa (1877–1879, 1881–1885).[58] The last major Irish American fundraising venture in which members of the Fenian Brotherhood were in any way involved was in support of the semi-revolutionary Land League of 1879–1881. This agitation, however, served to revive some of the controversies of the previous decade. When IRB activists decorated Land League platforms with blue, white and red banners bearing the French republican motto of "liberty, equality, fraternity"; called for cheers for an Irish Republic; and claimed that all Irishmen should study the political example of "the Great Republic of the West" (citing the principles of political liberty embodied in the American Declaration of Independence in 1776 while justifying a demand for Irish independence), they were immediately denounced by a variety of Irish Catholic politicians and priests for making gestures "that smacked too much of Belleville and Montmartre for Catholic feeling to approve."[59]

By 1880, the Fenian Brotherhood had practically been replaced by other Irish American organizations. On one hand, the secret revolutionary dimension to its politics was all but taken over by the "Clan na Gael," a revolutionary movement that was first formed in New York during 1867 and affiliated with the IRB from 1876 onward. On the other hand, the principal public Irish American organization was now the Land League of America.[60] Curiously, this group was first practically governed by the Clan na Gael, although—repeating the exact same pattern of the Fenian Brotherhood during the 1860s—the Clan's energies would soon become totally dissipated because of its members' heavy involvement in American party politics combined with the effect of British Intelligence intrigues designed to create permanent dissension in its ranks.[61]

Excepting a nominal and very tenuous link with a tiny IRB faction up until roughly 1880, the Fenian Brotherhood had no connection with any Irish political organization after 1872.[62] Probably the most committed of all the ex-IRB rebels who joined the Fenian Brotherhood on arriving in New York during 1871 was John Devoy. Although Devoy transferred his allegiance to the Clan in 1874, on first arriving in America, he had met John Mitchel at a Fenian Brotherhood debate. On this occasion, Mitchel told him that, in retrospect, he believed the single greatest mistake made in Irish nationalist politics in recent times was when he and the Young Ireland party decided during

1846 to secede from Daniel O'Connell's Repeal Association in Dublin. This decision had deprived them of the leadership of the repeal movement that would have naturally fallen into their laps a year later, following O'Connell's death, and also created an unfortunate legacy of divisions and inadequate political leadership.[63] It is quite likely that this 1871 conversation with Mitchel was somewhere in the back of Devoy's mind when, seven years later, he made a fairly effective appeal from New York for nationalists within Ireland, both revolutionary and moderate, to embrace a "new departure" by finding a common political platform and, in turn, seeking the support of the Irish nationalist exiles in the United States. Whatever the case, Devoy's initiative (who secretly visited Ireland thereafter to meet Parnell, Davitt and the IRB to promote the idea) soon formed a basis for the launch of the Land League, the branches of which, perhaps even more so than the IRB's activities during the 1860s, were reportedly sustained by Irish American financial support.[64] Unfortunately, no financial statements or papers of the Land League have survived to indicate exactly how much this was the case.

Conclusion

The legacy of the American Civil War and the durability of the Fenian movement's appeal remained evident to some degree in Irish America right up until the 1890s. For example, the Fenian Brotherhood still existed at this time as a public U.S. Civil War veterans' association, at least within New York. It expressed its total opposition to all "secret" and "nihilistic" revolutionary conspiracies and, true to old traditions, formed the Fenian Volunteers among young Irishmen in New York as a militia force "who shall hold themselves ever in readiness to aid the United States in case of a war with a foreign power."[65] During 1895, some of these same Fenians attended a large convention held in Chicago, Illinois, designed to form a new Fenian Brotherhood-style pressure group in American politics (complete with its own affiliated militia) known as the Irish National Alliance. Although this turned out to be an essentially abortive affair, middle-aged delegates from almost every state, including some old ex–Union and ex–Confederate soldiers, turned up at its initial convention that September.[66] To great cheers, the chairman, John Finerty (a veteran of the Civil War, the Canadian Fenian raid of 1870 and the 1876 war against the Sioux Indians), expressed his desire to see a major deterioration in Anglo-American relations, his detestation for British imperialism and his belief in Ireland's right (according to the principles of freedom underpinning the American constitution) to complete independence as a republic. However, he concluded by saying (to equally great cheers) that his greatest wish was "to set the example to all my countrymen that I love America and, as the adopted son of America, I will never live in any government other than that of the Stars and Stripes!"[67]

This speech of Finerty's (who was also the editor of the Chicago *Citizen* and a member of the Ancient Order of Hibernians) might be said to have been a fitting epitaph for the Fenian movement. Even while expressing support for the idea of a "free Ireland," the patriotism of most members of the Fenian Brotherhood had always been primarily a matter of proving to their fellow Americans their worthiness as American citizens, notwithstanding their self-evident lack of identification with the prevailing white, Anglo-Saxon, Protestant political culture in America. By the mid–1880s, however, the old Fenian political culture of Irish Americans forming militias in an attempt to highlight the potentially great contribution they could make to American society had been largely replaced, or perhaps one might say "outgrown," by a less exaggerated and somewhat more confident brand of politics. Indeed, by the mid- to late 1880s, the most influential politicians in Irish America, as well as its most influential journalists (such as John Boyle O'Reilly of the Boston *Pilot* and Patrick Ford of the *Irish World*—both of whom now abandoned their initial radicalism), had become concerned primarily with acting as spokesmen for the Catholic community in America.[68] The "cause of Ireland" featured less prominently in their writings (and Irish nationalists ceased to import their papers), while collections for Irish political organizations among the general Irish American public became much less frequent, although collections for the Irish Party MPs in London were sustained with the help of some very wealthy Irish American businessmen, most notably Eugene Kelly, a millionaire who headed the Emigrant Savings Bank in New York.[69]

The British government's expulsion of talented Irish nationalists from Ireland during the late 1840s, the late 1860s and again in the early 1880s (following the suppression of the Land League) undoubtedly limited the potential of many Irish political organizations of the day. Among the growing Irish diaspora of the mid- to late nineteenth century, however, the example of revolutionary journalists like O'Mahony or Mitchel of remaining focused (more or less) on the goal of revolution in Ireland and resisting integration into their host societies was ultimately very exceptional. The path taken by Meagher, Savage, Finerty and countless others (including, albeit in a very different fashion, Thomas D'Arcy McGee in Canada) was effectively the norm. Similarly, ex–IRB political activists from the 1860s who became newspaper editors abroad after their release from prison (including J.P. McDonnell, who became a leading American labor activist during the 1870s[70]) tended to follow the same integrationist example. This usually occurred because their initial Irish nationalism (often rooted in their exposure to the nationalist writings of men like Thomas Davis or John Mitchel while still living in Ireland) was quite naturally dissipated by an ever-growing political or editorial responsibility to represent the viewpoints and concerns of the (often beleaguered) Catholic immigrant communities that surrounded them. For instance, the example of John Boyle O'Reilly as a Catholic journalist in Boston, Massachusetts, was repeated in this respect by other ex–IRB figures, such as John Denvir in Liverpool, James Mullin in Cardiff and John Flood in Sydney, Australia.[71]

The one great exception to this pattern would seem to be John Devoy, who was later described by Patrick Pearse as "the greatest of the Fenians." Devoy, after fifty-five years in New York, dedicated his memoirs not to comrades in America but instead to the memory of three generations of "my departed comrades in the IRB in Ireland."[72] Being a leader of the Clan na Gael, Devoy always remained in contact with and supportive of the IRB in Ireland, though he, too, had an intermittent career (of sorts) in American politics, first during the 1880s[73] and later (after launching a commercially successful newspaper, the *Gaelic American*) as a supporter of Daniel Cohalan, a prominent Irish American New York judge.[74]

The main reason for Devoy's generally exceptional example would seem to have been his rather unusual personality. An intellectual who felt a mixture of both contempt and patronizing sympathy for "the Irish peasant and his gross mental habits of exaggeration," he always maintained an acute and Victorian-like respect for personal privacy and consequently found it very difficult to identify with the openness of American society. That he never married compounded this outlook. Devoy, writing in a private diary, once reflected that the reason why he often felt "as little of an American today ... as on the day the English government sent me to these shores" (twenty-four years previously) was that he had never grown accustomed to listening every day to Americans with "rasping or buzz-saw voices that affect me like sandpaper" and who lived in what he considered a vulgar culture, where every man felt obliged to "live in public," "disclose family troubles to the first reporter who comes along" and "evidently thinks he is the greatest man you ever met" while "talking incessantly in a loud voice" about themselves or "their infallible plans for 'ketchin' a gurl,' pointing out the best places in N.Y., Boston, Philadelphia and Chicago for promenading with that end in view." Feeling a great sense of disgust for such people, a single day spent within earshot of an Irish, French or English tourist—people "much more to my liking," who "talk[ed] in a half jocular, half serious way about politics, war, poetry, Napoleon, Wellington, Moltke, Bazaine, Dreyfus, Victor Hugo etc."— seems to have caused Devoy to be struck by a tremendous sense of his own loneliness and cultural isolation, something that he evidently tried to overcome by devoting all his mental energies to focusing or writing upon Irish politics, the one world to which he felt he really belonged.[75]

However, even Devoy himself would eventually come to realize that America was his true home. Although a significant organizer of the 1916 rising, he found himself painfully dismissed as a tool of American politicians during Eamon de Valera's American tour of 1919–1920, and, notwithstanding the Irish Free State granting him a state reception during 1924, he resolved to return to New York after only a very brief stay in an independent Ireland to live out his final days under the proverbial Stars and Stripes. The magnetic pull of America had once again proved irresistible within the world of Fenian patriotism.

NOTES

1. The most detailed history of the American Fenian Brotherhood to date remains William D'Arcy, *The Fenian Movement in the United States, 1858-1886* (Washington, D.C.: Catholic University of America Press, 1947).

2. Among accounts by contemporaries, this aspect of the history of the formation of the IRB and Fenian Brotherhood, respectively, was covered best in Joseph Denieffe, *A Personal Narrative of the Irish Revolutionary Brotherhood* (1906; reprint, Shannon: Irish University Press, 1969). The best recent historical treatment is Marta Ramon, *A Provisional Dictator: James Stephens and the Fenian Movement* (Dublin: University College Dublin Press, 2007).

3. D'Arcy, *Fenian Movement*, 1–15.

4. *United States vs. W.G. Halpin, D. Reidy, E. Kenifeck, S. Lumsden et al.* (Columbia, 1856). The defendants were found not guilty.

5. Brendan O'Cathaoir, "John O'Mahony," *Capuchin Annual* (1977): 180–93.

6. Denieffe, *Personal Narrative*, 195; John O'Leary, *Recollections of Fenians and Fenianism*, 2 vols. (London: Downey, 1896), 2:46.

7. D'Arcy, *Fenian Movement*, 33–34.

8. Ibid., 33–37.

9. John Devoy, *Recollections of an Irish Rebel* (New York: Young, 1929), 128–51.

10. William O'Brien, *Irish Fireside Hours* (Dublin: M.H. Gill and Son, 1928), 107; Owen McGee, *The IRB* (Dublin: Four Courts Press, 2005), 34.

11. Ramon, *A Provisional Dictator*, 102.

12. D'Arcy, *Fenian Movement*, 40–42.

13. Ibid., 29.

14. L.R. Bisceglia, "The Fenian Funeral of Terence Bellew McManus," *Eire-Ireland* (Fall 1979): 45–64.

15. Pat McCarthy, "James Francis Xavier O'Brien (1828-1905): Dungarvan-born Fenian," *Decies* 54 (1998): 107–38.

16. Ramon, *A Provisional Dictator*, 165.

17. The best examination completed to date of RIC and DMP intelligence material during the early to mid-1860s can be found in Shin-ichi Takagami, "The Dublin Fenians," Ph.D. diss., Trinity College, Dublin, 1990.

18. This is the estimate given by John O'Leary in a letter published in *Freeman's Journal*, November 8, 1877.

19. Sean O Luing, *John Devoy* (Baile Átha Cliath: Clo Morainn, 1961), 130–32.

20. Ramon, *A Provisional Dictator*, 279, fn.20.

21. Takagami, "Dublin Fenians," 141.

22. For the activities of McDermott (nicknamed "Red Jim") at this time, see the index entries for him in D'Arcy, *Fenian Movement*.

23. For the context and history of the Canadian raids, see Brendan O'Cathaoir, "American Fenianism and Canada, 1865-71," *Irish Sword: Journal of Military History Society of Ireland* 8 (1967), and Hereward Senior, *The Last Invasion of Canada: The Fenian Raids, 1866-70* (Toronto: Dundurn Press, 1991). For the careers of British agents in these episodes, see D'Arcy, *Fenian Movement*, and Christy Campbell, *Fenian Fire* (London: HarperCollins, 2002).

24. For the career of these informers, see the index entries for them in D'Arcy, *Fenian Movement*.

254   Part II: American Civil War

25. The most detailed examination of the attempted rising to date is Shin-ichi Takagami, "The Fenian Rising in Dublin, March 1867," *Irish Historical Studies* 29 (1994): 340–62.
26. R.V. Comerford, *The Fenians in Context: Irish Politics and Society, 1848–82* (Dublin: Wolfhound Press, 1985), 152.
27. McGee, *IRB*, chapter 2.
28. W.S. Neidhardt, *The Fenians in North America* (University Park: Pennsylvania State University Press, 1975). Entries for Collins, Roberts and Finerty can be found in *Biographical Dictionary of the American Congress* (Washington, D.C.: United States Government Printing Office, 1961).
29. R.J.W. Evans and H.P. Von Strandmann, *The Revolutions in Europe, 1848–1849* (Oxford: Oxford University Press, 2000), is an excellent collection of essays on this theme.
30. L.R. Bisceglia, "The McManus Welcome, San Francisco, 1851," *Eire-Ireland* (Spring 1981): 6–20.
31. John Savage, *'98 and '48: The Revolutionary and Literary History of Ireland* (New York, 1856). During 1848, Savage was the editor of the *Irish Patriot* (Dublin), but this publication was quickly suppressed by Dublin Castle while he was also expelled from the Royal Irish Academy. Savage later wrote *Fenian Heroes and Martyrs* (1868).
32. Fenian Papers, National Library of Ireland, 8980R and CSORP 1877/6742.
33. A.M. Sullivan, *New Ireland* (London, 1877), 247.
34. On Irish American journalism at this time, see T.N. Brown, *Irish American Nationalism* (Philadelphia: J.B. Lippincott, 1966), and W.L. Joyce, *Editors and Ethnicity: A History of the Irish American Press, 1848–1883* (New York: Arno Press, 1976).
35. John Martin to John O'Leary, letter of January 4, 1874, John O'Leary Papers, National Library of Ireland (NLI), Ms 5926; John Dillon to John Devoy, letter of August 6, 1891, reproduced in W. O'Brien and D. Ryan, eds., *Devoy's Post Bag*, vol. 2 (Dublin: Fallon, 1953), 320.
36. Michael Davitt, *The Fall of Feudalism* (New York: Harper & Brothers, 1904), opening dedication.
37. Speech of Davitt at the 1886 Chicago Convention of the Irish National League of America, quoted in Michael Funchion, *Chicago's Irish Nationalists* (New York: Arno Press, 1976), 97–98.
38. W.F. Lyons, ed., *Brigadier-General Thomas Francis Meagher* (London: Oates & Washburn, 1869), 142–47; D'Arcy, *Fenian Movement*, 4, 33–34.
39. In the late 1850s, Savage owned and edited *The States* (Washington, D.C.), and then he wrote the Republican party publication "Our Leading Representative Men" for the 1860 U.S. presidential election and, in 1866, was chosen as the biographer of the (ex–Democratic) president, Andrew Johnson. See T. Kunitz and P. Haycraft, eds., *American Authors, 1600–1900* (New York: H.W. Wilson, 1938), 672.
40. *Dictionary of American Biography*, 8 (1935); *New York Times*, October 11, 1888 (obituary).
41. *Dictionary of American Biography*, 8 (1935). Savage was a lecturer at various American Catholic colleges during the 1870s. Although an often forgotten figure in Irish American history today, Savage was an award-winning playwright in the United States during the 1860s and was awarded an honorary doctorate by Fordham University, New York, in 1879 for his contributions to U.S. literature. He also wrote verse, mostly patriotic Irish and American ballads (several were used by the Union troops during the Civil War). See S.A. Allibone, *Critical Dictionary of English Literature*, vol. 2 (New York, 1870).
42. Savage initially wrote the "American letter" column in the *Irishman*, a job taken up after 1871 by Jeremiah O'Donovan (Rossa), an exiled IRB convict in New York.
43. Home Office Papers, British National Archives (Kew), H.O. 144/1538 (6), letter of Sir Robert Anderson, December 14, 1870.
44. For an analysis of O'Mahony's journalism at this time, see Brian Sayers, "'John O'Mahony, Revolutionary and Scholar," Ph.D. diss., National University of Ireland, Maynooth, 2005, chapter 9.
45. *Irish People* articles on this theme by O'Brien and other IRB men are reproduced copiously in O'Leary, *Recollections of Fenians and Fenianism*, and with extensive criticism in T.D. Sullivan, *Recollections of Troubled Times in Irish Politics* (Dublin: Sealy, Bryers & Walker, 1905).

46. This controversy is detailed in Sean Daly, *Ireland and the First International* (Cork: Tower Books, 1984), chapter 2.
47. Parts of O'Brien's unpublished recollections of his time in the IRB are reprinted in Pat McCarthy, "James Francis Xavier O'Brien."
48. Its proprietor, Richard Pigott, was never a member of the IRB, but he was willing to act as a general informant to the British on IRB affairs. Sir Robert Anderson Papers, British National Archives (Kew), HO 144/1538/8, letters of Richard Pigott, March–October 1872.
49. Comerford, *Fenians in Context*, 185–86.
50. *Acta Sanctae Sedis* (5th ed., Rome, 1872–1911), V (1911), 389, quoted (in translation from Latin) in D'Arcy, *Fenian Movement*, 329.
51. Fenian Papers, NLI, 7931R.
52. D'Arcy, *Fenian Movement*, 329–33.
53. *Gaelic American*, December 12, 1908 (biographical article on O'Leary by Devoy).
54. O'Leary seems to have deliberately expressed something of an aversion for republicanism during his 1871 interviews. See Marcus Bourke, *John O'Leary* (Tralee, Ireland: Anvil Books, 1967), 166.
55. Henry Dixon Papers, National Library of Ireland (NLI), Ms 35262(26), circulars of the 1798 Centenary Committee (quotations from circular of February 22, 1897).
56. The *New Ireland Review*, the journal of the Jesuits' University College in Dublin, published articles during 1898 by D.P. Moran and others claiming that republicanism was a concept that was and must remain completely alien to "the Irish mind." Moran's article on this theme was later republished as the concluding chapter in *The Philosophy of Irish Ireland* (Dublin: James Duffy, 1905).
57. G. Doherty and D. Keogh, eds., *1916: The Long Revolution* (Cork: Mercier Press, 2007), 7–8, 107, 117–20.
58. Lyons, *Brigadier-General Thomas Francis Meagher*, 142–47; D'Arcy, *Fenian Movement*, 4, 33–34, chapter 9.
59. McGee, *The IRB*, 75–77, 117; A.M. Sullivan, *New Ireland*, 2nd ed. (London, 1882), 440.
60. The only history of this movement written to date is a short entry in Michael Funchion, ed., *Irish American Voluntary Organizations* (Westport, CT: Greenwood Press, 1983), 189–93. See, however, John Devoy, *The Land of Eire* (New York: Patterson & Neilson, 1882).
61. The full history of the Clan has yet to be written, although John Devoy wrote an incomplete series, "The Story of Clan na Gael," in the *Gaelic American* (1923–1925). See also Funchion, *Irish American Voluntary Organizations*, 74–93.
62. McGee, *IRB*, 45, 83.
63. Devoy, *Recollections*, 9.
64. Comerford, *Fenians in Context*, 234; T.W. Moody, "The New Departure in Irish Politics, 1878–9," in *Essays in British and Irish History*, edited by H.A. Cronne, T.W. Moody and D.B. Quinn (London: F. Muller, 1949), 303–33.
65. *The Times* (London), October 24, 1890.
66. Biographies of all the delegates appear as an appendix in the souvenir journal: M.F. Fanning, ed., *The New Movement Convention which Gave Birth to the Irish National Alliance* (Chicago: M.F. Fanning, 1896).
67. Ibid., 97.
68. J.P. Rodechko, *Patrick Ford and His Search for America* (New York: Arno Press, 1976); F.G. McManamin, *The American Years of John Boyle O'Reilly* (New York: Arno Press, 1976). On this theme, see also Alec Sullivan, "The American Republic and the Irish National League of America," *American Catholic Quarterly Review* 9 (1884): 35–44.
69. Funchion, *Irish American Voluntary Organizations*, 204–6.
70. Cormac O'Grada, "Fenianism and Socialism: The Career of J.P. McDonnell," *Saothar* 1 (1975): 31–41; L.A. O'Donnell, "Joseph Patrick McDonnell (1847–1906): A Passion for Justice," *Eire-Ireland* 22, no. 4 (1987): 118–33.
71. John Denvir, *Life Story of an Old Rebel* (Dublin: Sealy, Bryers & Walker, 1910); James Mullin, *The Story of a Toiler's Life* (London: Maunsel & Roberts, 1921); Keith Amos, *The Fenians in Australia* (Kensington: University of New South Wales Press, 1988), 280–81.

72. Devoy, *Recollections*, opening dedication.
73. See, for example, John Devoy, *Cleveland and the True Story of the Great Irish Revolt of 1884 and Why We Oppose Him Today* (New York, 1892). Devoy had been a prominent member of the New York branch of the Land and National Leagues of America during the 1880s.
74. For this aspect of Devoy's later career, see Michael Doorley, *Irish American Diaspora Nationalism: The Friends of Irish Freedom* (Dublin: Four Courts Press, 2005).
75. John Devoy Papers, National Library of Ireland (NLI), Ms. 9820, diary, 71-74 (entries for February 7-11, 1895).

BIBLIOGRAPHY

Amos, Keith. *The Fenians in Australia*. Kensington: University of New South Wales Press, 1988.
Biographical Dictionary of the American Congress. Washington, D.C.: United States Government Printing Office, 1961.
Bisceglia, L.R. "The Fenian Funeral of Terence Bellew McManus." *Eire-Ireland* (Fall 1979): 45-64.
_____. "The McManus Welcome, San Francisco, 1851." *Eire-Ireland* (Spring 1981): 6-20.
Bourke, Marcus. *John O'Leary*. Tralee, Ireland: Anvil Books, 1967.
Campbell, Christy. *Fenian Fire*. London: HarperCollins, 2002.
Comerford, R.V. *The Fenians in Context: Irish Politics and Society, 1848-82*. Dublin: Wolfhound Press, 1985.
Daly, Sean. *Ireland and the First International*. Cork: Tower Books, 1984.
D'Arcy, William. *The Fenian Movement in the United States, 1858-1886*. Washington, D.C.: Catholic University of America Press, 1947.
Davitt, Michael. *The Fall of Feudalism in Ireland*. New York: Harper & Brothers, 1904.
Denieffe, Joseph. *A Personal Narrative of the Irish Revolutionary Brotherhood*. 1906; reprint, Shannon: Irish University Press, 1969.
Denvir, John. *Life Story of an Old Rebel*. Dublin: Sealy, Bryers & Walker, 1910.
Devoy, John. *Cleveland and the True Story of the Great Irish Revolt of 1884 and Why We Oppose Him Today*. New York, 1892.
_____. *The Land of Eire*. New York: Patterson & Neilson, 1882.
_____. *Recollections of an Irish Rebel*. New York: Young, 1929.
_____. "The Story of Clan na Gael." *Gaelic American* (1923-1925).
Doherty, G., and D. Keogh, eds. *1916: The Long Revolution*. Cork: Mercier Press, 2007.
Doorley, Michael. *Irish American Diaspora Nationalism: The Friends of Irish Freedom*. Dublin: Four Courts Press, 2005.
Fenian Papers, National Archives of Ireland.
Funchion, Michael. *Chicago's Irish Nationalists*. New York: Arno Press, 1976.
_____, ed. *Irish American Voluntary Organizations*. Westport, CT: Greenwood Press, 1983.
Henry Dixon Papers, National Library of Ireland.
Home Office Papers, British National Archives (Kew).
John Devoy Papers, National Library of Ireland.
John O'Leary Papers, National Library of Ireland.
Kunitz, T., and P. Haycraft, eds. *American Authors, 1600-1900*. New York: H.W. Wilson, 1938.
Lyons, W.F., ed. *Brigadier-General Thomas Francis Meagher*. London: Oates & Washburn, 1869.
McCarthy, Pat. "James Francis Xavier O'Brien (1828-1905): Dungarvan-born Fenian." *Decies* 54 (1998): 107-38.
McGee, Owen. *The Irish Republican Brotherhood*. Dublin: Four Courts Press, 2005.
McManamin, F.G. *The American Years of John Boyle O'Reilly*. New York: Arno Press, 1976.
Moody, T.W. "The New Departure in Irish Politics, 1878-9." In *Essays in British and Irish History*, edited by H.A. Cronne, T.W. Moody and D.B. Quinn, 303-33. London: F. Muller, 1949.
Mullin, James. *The Story of a Toiler's Life*. London: Maunsel & Roberts, 1921.

Neidhardt, W.S. *The Fenians in North America.* University Park: Pennsylvania State University Press, 1975.
O'Brien, W., and D. Ryan, eds. *Devoy's Post Bag.* Vol. 2. Dublin: Fallon, 1953.
O'Brien, William. *Irish Fireside Hours.* Dublin: M.H. Gill and Son, 1928.
O'Cathaoir, Brendan. "American Fenianism and Canada, 1865–71." *Irish Sword: Journal of Military History Society of Ireland* 8 (1967).
———. "John O'Mahony." *Capuchin Annual* (1977): 180–93.
O'Donnell, L.A. "Joseph Patrick McDonnell (1847–1906): A Passion for Justice." *Eire-Ireland* 22, no. 4 (1987): 118–33.
O'Grada, Cormac. "Fenianism and Socialism: The Career of J.P. McDonnell." *Saothar* 1 (1975): 31–41.
O'Leary, John. *Recollections of Fenians and Fenianism.* 2 vols. London: Downey, 1896.
O Luing, Sean. *John Devoy.* Baile Átha Cliath: Clo Morainn, 1961.
Ramon, Marta. *A Provisional Dictator: James Stephens and the Fenian Movement.* Dublin: University College Dublin Press, 2007.
Rodechko, J.P. *Patrick Ford and His Search for America.* New York: Arno Press, 1976.
Savage, John. *'98 and '48: The Revolutionary and Literary History of Ireland.* New York, 1856.
Sayers, Brian. "John O'Mahony, Revolutionary and Scholar." Ph.D. dissertation, National University of Ireland, Maynooth, 2005.
Senior, Hereward. *The Last Invasion of Canada: The Fenian Raids, 1866–70.* Toronto: Dundurn Press, 1991.
Sir Robert Anderson Papers, British National Archives (Kew).
Sullivan, A.M. *New Ireland.* London, 1877; 2nd edition, 1882.
Sullivan, Alec. "The American Republic and the Irish National League of America." *American Catholic Quarterly Review* 9 (1884): 35–44.
Sullivan, T.D. *Recollections of Troubled Times in Irish Politics.* Dublin: Sealy, Bryers & Walker, 1905.
Takagami, Shin-ichi. "The Dublin Fenians." Ph.D. dissertation, Trinity College, Dublin, 1990.
———. "The Fenian Rising in Dublin, March 1867." *Irish Historical Studies* 29 (1994): 340–62.

About the Contributors

Frank **Boyle** served in combat in the Army Air Force in World War II. He obtained a master's degree in chemistry from Saint Joseph's University and became a researcher with Sun Oil. He published a lively account of Irish units in the Union Army, "A Party of Mad Fellows."

Andre **Fleche** is the author of the award-winning book, *The Revolution of 1861*. With a Ph.D. from Syracuse University, he is an associate professor at Castleton College in Vermont and has contributed several articles on African American soldiers in the Union Army.

Ruth-Ann **Harris** earned a Ph.D. at Tufts University, with her dissertation resulting in a book on short-term Irish migration to Britain before the Great Famine. At Northeastern University she established an Irish studies program. She completed her academic career as an adjunct professor of Irish studies at Boston College.

The late David **Heisser** received his undergraduate degree at the College of Charleston, followed by a doctorate from the University of South Carolina. After serving as a history professor and librarian at several institutions, he concluded his career at the Citadel in Charleston. He died in 2007.

Michael F. **Hogan** has had a long career as head of humanities at American schools abroad, culminating with his appointment as professor of international relations at the Autonomous University of Guadalajara in Mexico. He is the author of the leading account of the St. Patrick's Battalion in the Mexican War.

The late Ann Caraway **Ivins** was a popular historian of Texas during the Civil War. She held a BA in anthropology from the University of Texas at Austin and an MBA from Our Lady of the Lake University in San Antonio. This essay was a prelude to further study of Richard Dowling, pioneer, businessman and solider. She died in 2004.

Mauriel P. **Joslyn** has studied a wide field of the Civil War period, including a comparative study of John Mitchel and Thomas Francis Meagher. She has also written about southern women and Confederate prisoners, in addition to editing and contributing to a biography of the Irish-born Confederate general Patrick Cleburne.

About the Contributors

D.R. O'Connor **Lysaght** is an accomplished critic of Irish and socialist developments. A graduate of both Trinity College, Dublin, and University College, Dublin, he has published widely on a variety of Irish social and political movements and is the editor of works of several early revolutionary socialists in Western Europe.

Lawrence J. **McCaffrey** is one of the outstanding historians of the Irish in the United States. A professor at the Catholic University of Chicago, he is the author of the seminal study of this major ethnic group. He has also produced a parallel survey of the political development of nineteenth-century Ireland.

Owen **McGee** is a Dublin-based independent scholar. He has degrees from University College, Dublin, in history and archives, and worked for several years as a researcher on the *Dictionary of Irish Biography*. He produced a major study of the Irish Republican Brotherhood and a biography of Arthur Griffith.

Eileen M. **McMahon** is coeditor of *Civil War Chicago* as well as the author of a study of an Irish parish undergoing racial change. A native of Chicago with a doctorate from Loyola University Chicago, she is a history professor at Lewis University in Romeoville, Illinois.

Arthur H. **Mitchell** has focused most of his historical work on the Irish in nineteenth-century America and early twentieth-century Ireland. With a doctorate from Trinity College, Dublin, he has also written histories of the Korean War and Hitler's Obersalzberg. He is a distinguished professor of history at the University of South Carolina Salkehatchie campus.

Kelly **O'Grady** was a staff member at the Fredericksburg Battlefield National Park for decades. Among his publications is a major study of the Irish presence in the Confederate Army of Northern Virginia (*Clear the Confederate Way!*) as well as a treatment of the Union siege of Charleston, South Carolina.

Aidan **O'Hara** has had an extensive career as a historian, journalist and broadcaster. His research has extended from Newfoundland to Ireland and beyond. His latest book, *Atlantic Gaels*, traces the links between Donegal and the Hebrides. With a renaissance capacity, he has also studied Irish folk music and traditional culture.

Phillip G. **Pattee** is a retired U.S. Navy submarine officer and associate professor of strategy and operations at the U.S. Army Command and Staff College in Kansas. He has a Ph.D. from Temple University in Philadelphia.

Desmond **Travers** served for forty years as a member of the Irish Army, reaching the rank of colonel. Since his retirement, he has acted as a consultant to several other military organizations and has pondered the fields of strategy and tactics.

Marion **Truslow** has served as chair of the Department of History and Social Sciences at Rabun Gap–Nacoochee School in northeast Georgia for many years. His interest in the New York Irish role in the Civil War was sparked while earning a Ph.D. at New York University.

Index

Adams, John Quincy 25
African Americans *see* Irish and African Americans
Alexander, E. Porter 226
American Academy of Arts and Sciences 98
Andrew, John 96, 98, 100–101
Antietam 116, 231
Armistead, Lewis A. 69, 234

Banks, Nathaniel 96, 206
Bannon, John 102, 172, 179
Barry, John 27
Benjamin, Judah 172
Bernstein, Iver 117, 150
Boston 96, 104
Bostwick, Azariah 184
Boyle, Frank 60
Bradley, Hugh 234
Bragg, Braxton 198–199
Brownson, Orestes 25, 100
Buena Vista battle 14, 28
Burke, Ricard O'Sullivan 243
Burns, William 228–229
Burton, William L. 78
Butler, Thaddeus 79
Byrne, Christopher 163–167
Byrnes, Richard 100, 105

Carter, A.H. 134
Casey, Peter 87
Cass, Thomas 99
Cassidy, Lewis 62, 70
Catholic Church 15–16, 28, 97, 107, 158, 247; Chicago 85; Fenians 248; institutions 40, 91, 101; Mexico 28–30; New York 40–41; Philadelphia 61; South 184
Chancellorsville battle 67
Chapultepec battle 20, 30
Charleston 170–171
Chicago 82, 90
Chicago Evening Journal 83
Chicago Evening Post 90
Chicago Times 86
Chicago Tribune 80, 82, 86–88, 134

Churubusco battle 14
Clanna Gael 249
Clark, Dennis 37
Cleburne, Patrick: army 198; black freedom 199–201; Civil War 198–201; military 198; in U.S. 197; youth 193–194
Cohalan, Daniel 252
Collins, Patrick A. 107–108
Comiskey, John 88
Confederate Army 85, 116, 185
Conyngham, David P. 43
Corby, William 61, 67, 160
Corcoran, Michael 145–147
Crocker, Lt. 208, 210
Crook, D.F. 189
Cullen, James B. 27
Curtin, Andrew G. 70, 235

Daley, Charles P.: Civil War 144–45; draft crisis 149; early years 149–142; 1864 election 150; Jews 151; judge 143; recruiter 144, 148
Daley, Maria Lydig 144, 145, 146, 147, 149, 151
Davis, Jefferson 188
Davis, Thomas 183, 251
Davitt, Michael 246
Demas, Jacob 159
Democratic Party 26, 115, 131, 144, 157, 189–190
Denvir, John (Liverpool) 252
DeValera, Emon 248, 253
Deveraux, Arthur 253
DeVoto, Bernard 14
Devoy, John: 240, 245–246, 249–250; and IRB 252–253
Divers, Briget 128–130
Dix, Dorothea 123–124, 126
Donahoe, Parick 26, 96
Dooley, John 146, 185, 187
Douglas, Stephan 80, 82–83, 96
Dowling, Dick: Houston 204; militia 204–205; New Orleans 203; Sabine Pass battle 205–211; youth 203

261

262 Index

Doyle, Don H. 45
Draft *see* United States military pensions
Duggan, James 79, 89
Dunne, Denis 85–86, 89–90
Dunne, Peter Finlay 86, 135–136

Emancipation Proclamation 87, 103–104
Emerson, Ralph Waldo 18
Ernst, Robert 38

Fanning, Charles 86
Fehrenbach, T.R. 211
Fenian Brotherhood 78–79, 82, 103, 107–108, 117; British response 242; Canada 189, 250; Clanna Gael 248; exiled journalists 244–246; IRB 238, 241–243; significance 250–251; split 242–243
Filene, Rachel 64
Finerty, John 250–251
Finn, Michael 52
Finn, Patrick 37, 52
Finnaw, Elizabeth 130
Fitzgerald, John F. 108
Fitzpatrick, John 27, 97–98, 101
Flood, John (Sydney) 252
Ford, John 245, 251
Foster, John G. 125
Franklin, William B. 207
Freeman, Douglas Southall 226

Gaines's Mill 226–227
Gallagher, Patrick 1, 100
Gallagher, Thomas 15
Garrison, William Lloyd 26
Gay, Elizabeth 132
Gettysburg battle 67–69, 70, 100, 226, 230
Gilmore, Patrick S. 106
Glendale battle 226–228
Gorman, John 46
Grand Army of the Republic 48
Grant, Ulysses S. 25, 70, 246
Greeley, Horace 44, 147
Greenhow, Rose O'Neal 131
Griffin, Martin 105
Griffin fort 206–207
Guadalupe Hidalgo treaty 20
Guiney, Patrick 99–100

Hamilton, Robert 159
Hancock, Winfield 68, 69
Hand, Jams 233, 236
Handlin, Oscar 40, 101
Hanley, Patrick T. 105
Harney, William 19–20, 30–31
Harper's Magazine 106
Harrison, Brian 43
Hart, Denis 18
Harvard University 97
Healy, James 104
Hill, A. P. 100–101
Hill, William 234–235

Hodgers, Jennie Irene 130
Hoey, John Cashel 101
Hooker, Joseph 228
Howe, David 132
Hughes, John 26, 28–29, 40–42, 44, 102; debate with Bishop Lynch 171

Ignatiev, Noel 70, 71
Irish American newspaper 107
Irish and African Americans 26, 81, 86, 114–115, 117–118, 132–134, 149, 156–159, 161
Irish and Irish Americans in Confederate military 101, 126–127, 130
Irish and Irish Americans in Union military 98, 100; in Army of Potomac 226; Irish People (New York) 109–110
Irish Brigade: 40–41, 46–48, 51, 53, 100–101, 105, 116, 148, 158; and black enlistment 160
Irish emigration 152
Irish famine 15, 32, 48
Irish Legion 82, 86–87
Irish People (Dublin) 107, 240–242, 237
Irish Republican Brotherhood 238–239, 248, 250
Irish women in religious organizations: 122–123, 125; in Confederacy 126–127; general involvement in war 121–122, 127–128; Sisters of Charity 125; Sisters of Mercy 83, 123, 124; Sisters of St. Francis 125

Jackson, Thomas 185, 220–221, 228
Johnston, Joseph 199

Kellersberger, Julius 206, 208
Kelly, Eugene 251
Kemp, James 69, 238
Kendall, George 31
Kennedy, Joseph P. 118
Kickham, Charles T. 240, 247
Knobel, Dale T. 18, 42–44
Know Nothings 33, 61, 64, 80, 98, 184

land league, Irish 250
Land League of America 249
Lee, Robert E. 87–88, 101, 226–227, 230
Leeds, William R. 70–71
Lincoln, Abraham 25, 44, 81, 87, 89, 96–97, 106, 158
Livermore, Mary 127, 135
Longstreet, James 101, 230
Luby, T.C. 240–241, 249
Lynch, James 232–234
Lynch, Patrick: bishop 170; Confederacy 172; to Ireland and Rome 172–173; Irish birth to U.S. 102, 169; postwar 179; secession 171; slave owner 175–176; slavery pamphlet 174, 176–178

Macnamara, Eugene 29
Magruder, J.D. 207, 210–211

Index 263

Maguire, John Francis 179
Mahan, Alfred Thayer: 216; author 217–216; naval duty 217
Mahan, Dennis Hart 216; early years 216; studies 219; professor 220–221
Mahone, William 184
Martin, John 246
Marx, Karl 244
Massachusetts Irish regiments 99–100, 108
McAnally, Charles 233, 235–236
McAuley, Joseph 123
McCafferty Ellen 134
McClellan, George 226
McDermott, Anthony 231–232
McDermott, James 242
McElroy 28–29
McGee, Thomas D'Arcy 251
McGill, John 184
McKeever, Joseph 234
McManes 70, 71
McManus, T. B. 241, 245
McMullin, John J. 79
McMullin, William 62–64
McPherson, James 45, 47
McReynolds, Andrew T. 28
McSorley, John 43
Mead, George G. 60, 68
Meade, George 60
Meagher, Thomas Francis 53, 98–99, 117, 146–147, 158, 184–185, 245
Mexico: 13; agreement 31; appeal to immigrants 30; invasion of 26–27, 115; opposition 27;
Milan, William 70
Miller, Kerby 50
Milne, Joseph S. 69
Mitchel, John: 116, 17, 182; journalist 183, 187, 190, 243, 246, 248
Mitchel, John C. 187–188
Mitchel, Willie 187
Mixcoac 19
Monholland, Mary Francis 124
Monteith, William 100
Moore, Frank 135
Moore, Theodore 185
Mulholland, St. Clair 60, 72
Mulligan, James A. 78–79, 83
Mulligan, Marion Nugent 82–84, 85
Mullin, James (Cardiff) 252
Mullin, priest 29
Mulrooney, Mrs. 134
Murray, J.G.D. 209–210
National Police Gazette 31

Native American Party 61, 62, 80
New Orleans 203
New York City: 37–38; and Boston 132–133; elsewhere 86, 131–132; opposition to war 134–135; riots 44–45, 87–88, 131–132
New York Herald 99
New York Times 84, 208–209

Odium, Lt. 207, 210–211
O'Brien, Hugh 97, 107
O'Brien, J.F.X. 241, 237
O'Brien, John Paul Jones 28
O'Connell, Anthony 124–126
O'Connell, Daniel 26, 81, 125, 250
O'Conner, Franci s 20
O'Connor, Colletta 127
O'Donovan Jeremiah Rossa 249
O'Gorman, Ricard 145–146
O'Hara, Timothy 104
O'Kane, Dennis 60, 68, 229, 231, 234
O'Keefe, Mathew 184
O'Leary, John 240, 248
O'Mahony, John 239, 249, 242
O'Meara, Timothy 87
O'Neil, Hannah 128
O'Reilly, Bernard 26, 147
O'Reilly, John Boyle 108, 251–252
Owen, Joshua T. 68, 226, 228

Parker, Theodore 27
Parnell, Charles S. 250
Payton, Charles 235
Pearse, Patrick 252
Pettigrew 233
Philadelphia: 28, 60; 1844 riots 61; at Gettysburg 60, 230–235; at Glendale 229; Peace Democrats 66, 73; Protestant opposition 16, 18, 73; 69th Infantry Regiment 60; War Democrats 70, 73
Pickett, George 101, 231, 235
Pilot 27, 29, 31, 96–97, 103–106
Pittsburgh 125
Polk, James K. 13, 24–25, 28
Poole, John F. 53
Price, Sterling 83
Purcell, Bishop 124

Quarter, William J. 85

Republic of Ireland 248
Republican Party 106, 115, 131, 158, 244
Rey, Anthony 28–29
Riley, John 14, 30–31
Ripley, R. S. 31
Rooney, Rose Quinn 130
Ryan, Gerard 127
Ryan, Thomas 175

Saint Patrick's Battalion 14–15, 18, 21, 30, 114; hangings 32
Santa Anna 13, 19, 30
Savage, John 245–247
Savannah: and Jasper Greens 27
Scanlan, Michael 79
Scott, Winfield 19–20, 30–32
Seidman, Rachel 65
Seward, William H. 103
Seymour, Horatio 44
Shankman Arnold 133

264 Index

Sheridan, Philip 105, 117–118
Shields, James 28, 145, 148
Sickles, Dan 67, 230
Sinnott, P. A. 107
Stanton, Edwin 25
Stephens, James 240–241, 248
Stewart, Owen 87
Stewart, Robert L. 67
Strong, George T. 132
Sullivan, Betsy 130
Sullivan, James P. 160

Tammany Hall 42–43
Taylor, Richard 185
Taylor, Zachary 13–14, 29–30, 32
Teeling, John 184
Thompson, George 234
Thoreau, Henry D. 24
Tinen, Patrick 234
Treanor, Bernard 99–100
Tschudy, Martin 230, 234
Tucker, Johm C. 97
Twentieth Massachusetts Regiment: "Faugh-a-Ballaghs" 100

The Union 29
Union Army 81–82

Union Institute for Savings 101
United States: relations with United Kingdom 103, 116, 147, 189, 247
United States military pensions: 38, 48, 53; bounties 47, 66, 103–104; draft laws 103–104; opposition 131–134, 149–150
U.S. Sanitary Commission 81, 122, 124–125

Vicksburg battle 126
Volunteers of Ireland 32

Walsh, Louis 188–189
Warren, Craig A. 66
Webb, Alexander 68–69, 70, 229, 233–234
Webb, Peter 100, 159, 160
Welles, George 99
Welsh, Peter 100, 159, 160
Western Irish Brigade (23rd Illinois Infantry Regiment) 78–84
Western Tablet 81
Wise, Henry 184
workers, occupations: New York city 39–40, 47; Philadelphia 62–66, 71–72

Yeats, William Butler 182

www.ingramcontent.com/pod-product-compliance
Ingram Content Group UK Ltd.
Pitfield, Milton Keynes, MK11 3LW, UK
UKHW041932140426
5217IPUK00014B/431